The CQ Shortwave Propagation Handbook-4th Edition

By
Carl Luetzelschwab, K9LA
Theodore J. Cohen, N4XX
George Jacobs, W3ASK
Robert B. Rose, K6GKU (SK)

CQ Communications, Inc.

Library of Congress Control Number: 2021931054

ISBN: 978-0-943016-62-7

Editor: Caryn Eve Murray, KD2GUT
Associate Publisher/Editorial: Richard Moseson, W2VU
Layout and Production: Elizabeth Ryan, Emily Leary and Dorothy Kehrwieder
Illustrations: Hal Keith, K&S Graphics
               Carl Luetzelschwab, K9LA

Cover Photo: NASA/SDO/AIA/HMI/Goddard Space Flight Center
This image combines images from two instruments on NASA's Solar Dynamics Observatory (SDO): the Helio-seismic and Magnetic Imager (HMI), which takes pictures in visible light that show sunspots and the Advanced Imaging Assembly (AIA), which took an image in the 304-angstrom wavelength showing the lower atmosphere of the sun, which is colorized in red.

Published by CQ Communications, Inc.
45 Dolphin Lane
Northport, New York 11768

Printed in the United States of America

Dedication

This book is dedicated to the radio amateur, the pioneer of shortwave radio, and to the generations of experimenters who came before them: Heinrich Hertz, Guglielmo Marconi, Arthur Kennelly, Oliver Heaviside and all those scientists and tinkerers who found themselves after the first World War in academic settings, the military and the world's research laboratories.

It also is dedicated to the new breed of experimenters who will "show the way" toward using shortwave radio ever more efficiently through the use of modern technology and a better understanding of how shortwave signals propagate. As amateur radio operators experiment once more on the original wavelengths used at the beginning of our hobby in the early 1900s, we thank them for helping us all gain a better grasp of the sun-earth relationship that is so criticial to life on earth – and to us as radio amateurs.

Preface to the Fourth Edition

Reader reception to the series of shortwave propagation handbooks published by CQ Communications, the first edition of which was published in 1979, has surpassed even our wildest expectations. These handbooks have found many friends in the telecommunications community, professional and amateur alike, and it is heartening to see them referenced in both the popular and professional literature. Now, as we are about to embark on yet another solar cycle—Cycle 25 since the Swiss Federal Observatory began keeping sunspot records in 1749—this seems like an auspicious time to release the next edition in our series: *The CQ Shortwave Propagation Handbook – 4th Edition.*

To be sure, any text dealing with solar and geomagnetic activity and the effects they have on shortwave propagation requires periodic updating. *The CQ Shortwave Propagation Handbook - 4th Edition,* is no exception. Given how much our knowledge of these phenomena has expanded over the last 25 years—that is, since the publication of the 3rd edition—it should surprise no one that the material presented here must, and indeed does, represent one of the most exhaustive updates and reviews to be found in the popular literature regarding how shortwave propagation is impacted by the sun.

That said, be assured we haven't ignored the workhorse aspects of dealing with day-to-day variations in shortwave propagation. We are especially proud of the fact that the techniques we introduced decades ago for use in preparing 27-day recurrence forecasts of ionospheric propagation conditions still are used by operators worldwide, and most, if not all, DX bulletins now include forecasts prepared using our method. The methodologies and tables that form the bases for the forecasts remain an important part of this book.

We also want to call our readers' attention to a significant change that has taken place in how solar scientists report solar activity. Specifically, the Royal Observatory in Belgium began reporting a new Version 2 (V2.0) sunspot number in July, 2015. Our new handbook provides tables of both the new and old (V1.0) numbers as well as directions for how to accommodate the new numbers when using the propagation forecasting tables we include here.

And what will happen during Cycle 25? Will it be a "high" or a "low" cycle? These are the questions on everyone's minds! Here, we devote an entire chapter to the new cycle's predictions, one of the most comprehensive summaries you'll find anywhere.

Given the phenomenal surge in the use of personal computers over the last 25 years, we would be remiss if we didn't devote significant attention to computerized propagation applications now available to high-frequency operators. If you've ever wondered about such programs as MINIMUF-3.5, VOACAP, VOACAP derivatives, W6ELProp, NON-VOACAP prediction programs, ray tracing programs such as Proplab Pro V3, and others, this volume presents some of the most detailed educational material you'll find on these applications.

We have enhanced other material as well. Here you'll find expanded material on uncommon propagation conditions, including sporadic-E in all its manifestations as well as on meteor propagation. And, where necessary, references to data sources and publications of interest to shortwave users have been updated. Finally, an index is included to render the text more usable.

So, even more than the first three editions, this new edition should be one of the most useful volumes available to the professional as well as the amateur communicator on the subject.

Acknowledgements

The update of this book involved efforts by a number of people and organizations around the world. Because of the explosion in the use of the Internet since the last edition of this book in 1995, I thank all of these people and organizations for providing their data for easy access by the public.

A big thank you to those who read my drafts of each chapter and offered excellent comments to improve the text: Theodore Cohen, N4XX, Caryn Eve Murray, KD2GUT; Rich Moseson, W2VU; and Dick Ross, K2MGA. Thanks also to Liz Ryan for her great efforts in putting together the page layouts. And thanks to all the other CQ Communications personnel who worked to get this book published.

In summary, thank you all!

Carl Luetzelschwab, K9LA
Fort Wayne, Indiana
December 2020

About the Authors

Carl Luetzelschwab, K9LA

Carl Luetzelschwab, K9LA, started his radio career as a shortwave listener in the late 1950s using a National NC-60 receiver. He was registered as a shortwave listener with *Popular Electronics* magazine as WPE9BQH. After discovering amateur radio through "SOS at Midnight," a book by Walker Tompkins, K6ATX, "The Short-Wave Mystery" in the Hardy Boys series and listening on the NC-60, he studied for his Novice license using the September 1960 issue of *Electronics Illustrated.* He took his Novice test in 8th grade from his social studies teacher, Alva Walters, W9MNO, and received his Novice license and call sign WN9AVT in October 1961.

He spent most of his Novice days on 40 meters because the NC-60 didn't have an RF stage, making 15-meter contacts few and far between. He received his General, with the call sign WA9AVT, in May 1962 and received his Extra in early 1976. When the FCC allowed Extras to choose 1x2 call signs, he selected K9LA in 1977.

In the mid-1960s Carl became active in the CW traffic nets on 80 meters. He continues to be active in the National Traffic System, as a regular check-in to CW traffic nets in his region and state, including service as a net control station, or NCS.

Carl enjoys solar topics and propagation issues, DXing (he's at the Top of the DXCC Honor Roll and needs four zones on 80 meters for *CQ*'s 5-Band Worked All Zones award). He also enjoys contesting and was the editor of the *National Contest Journal* from 2002-2007. Carl's other interests are modeling and experimenting with antennas and fixing/using vintage equipment.

Carl is a graduate of Purdue University (BSEE 1969, MSEE 1972), where his interest in propagation started. He worked for Motorola (in Schaumburg, Illinois and Fort Worth, Texas) and Magnavox (now Raytheon) in Fort Wayne, Indiana as an RF design engineer. He designed solid-state RF power amplifiers for both commercial and military applications. He retired in October 2013.

He and his wife, Vicky, AE9YL, reside in Fort Wayne, Indiana and enjoy traveling, which has included DXpeditions to Syria (YK9A in 2001), Market Reef in 2002 (OJ0/AE9YL and OJ0/K9LA) and numerous trips to the Cayman Islands (Carl is ZF2LA and Vicky is ZF2YL).

Carl is currently the ARRL Central Division Vice Director. He has received the Bill Orr W6SAI Technical Writing Award, the YASME Foundation Excellence Award and the Indiana Radio Club Council Technical Excellence Award. Carl also enjoys giving presentations and writing about solar topics, propagation issues, antenna topics, vintage equipment and other topics. He has been published in *CQ, QST* and other amateur radio publications.

Theodore J. "Ted" Cohen, N4XX

Theodore J. (Ted) Cohen, N4XX [ex W9VZL, W4UMF, NNN0XTV (Navy MARS)], holds three degrees in the physical sciences from the University of Wisconsin-Madison. He has been involved in communications and electronics for more than 68 years. First licensed as WN9VZL in 1952, he has held an Amateur Extra Class license since 1974. An avid DXer who has earned multiple phone and CW DXCC and WAZ awards (including some for 160 meters), Ted probably is best-known for his early (c. 1964) work [together with Copthorne Macdonald, WA2BCW/VY2CM (SK), and Don Miller, W9NTP (SK)] in slow-scan television (SSTV); for his pioneering efforts [together with Vic Clark, W4KFC (SK)] on technical and legislative approaches to solving the problem of radio frequency interference (RFI) to electronic home-entertainment equipment; and for his seminal work with George Jacobs, W3ASK, on the development of simplified techniques for the preparation of ionospheric propagation forecasts.

For these and other contributions to the radio art, Ted was inducted into the *CQ* Amateur Radio Hall of Fame in 2005. He previously received the American Radio Relay League's 1975 Technical Merit Award for his work on RFI. Ted is a Life Member of the League.

During his professional career, Ted has been a Senior Member of the Institute of Electrical and Electronics Engineers (IEEE), a Fellow of the Radio Club of America, and a Regional Vice-President At-Large for the Armed Forces Communications and Electronics Association (AFCEA). As a contractor, he assisted both the Navy and the Department of Defense with their preparations for the World Administrative Radio Conference of 1979.

From December, 1961, through early March, 1962, Ted participated in the 16th Chilean Expedition to the Antarctic, during which he operated from CE9AF on the North Antarctic Peninsula, CE9AS in the South Shetland Islands, CE9AY/mm from the Fleet Tug *Yelcho*, and CE9AW/mm from the Fleet Transport *Piloto Pardo*. The U.S. Board of Geographic Names in October, 1964, named the geographical feature Cohen Islands, located at 63° 18' S. latitude, 57° 53' W. longitude in the Cape Legoupil area, Antarctica, in his honor.

Finally, since 1973, Ted has published more than 450 papers, articles, columns, essays, and interviews, most of which can be found in *CQ* magazine, though some also have appeared in *QST, WorldRadio, 73, Ham Radio, SIGNAL*, and other communications and electronics publications, including those pertaining to shortwave listening and the Citizens Band.

George Jacobs, W3ASK

Born in 1924 on the same day the ionosphere was discovered, George Jacobs is a legend in the field of shortwave communications.

Amateur radio has been a part of George's life for almost as long as he can remember. First licensed in 1941, but exposed to amateur radio a decade earlier, George credits amateur radio with launching him into telecommunications professionally.

In a distinguished career that has spanned well over half a century, George has successfully combined innovative engineering talents, diplomacy, and a fierce belief in the free flow of information to forge the government-funded Voice of America, Radio Free Europe, and Radio Liberty into major voices of the Free World. Moving into private practice in 1980, he continued to develop shortwave broadcasting stations throughout the world.

Of his many contributions to amateur radio, George is most proud of his simplified propagation forecasts and predictions that appeared monthly in *CQ* magazine from March 1951 through December 2001 (his methods continue to be used today). He also is most proud of the pioneering role he played in the development and launching of the OSCAR and AMSAT radio amateur satellite projects.

Included in the honors bestowed upon George are the Air Medal for radar service during World War II, rank of Life Fellow in both the IEEE and the Radio Club of America, two U.S. Government awards for outstanding and superior achievements, a Commission from President Reagan, the Marconi Gold Medal Award for Engineering Achievement, and the Jack Poppele Award for excellence in engineering. He was inducted into the inaugural "class" of the CQ Amateur Radio Hall of Fame in 2001.

George is a Charter Life Member of the American Radio Relay League (ARRL). Academically he has an MSEE from the University of Maryland, and he is a Registered Professional Engineer. He has represented the United States at multiple major international telecommunication conferences dealing with the shortwave bands, including WARC-59, WARC-79, and WARC-92. George is a prolific writer, having authored hundreds of articles that have appeared in technical publications throughout the world.

Robert B. Rose, K6GKU (SK)

Amateur radio was the "great motivator" in Bob Rose's life. First licensed in 1954 at the age of 15, he spent most of his teenage years on "40 phone" as Cycle 19 climbed to its record peak. Because of his amateur radio background, Bob went on to get a BSEE in 1962 from California State Polytechnic College. Subsequently, he went to work for the Department of the Navy.

In the early 1970s, Bob managed the La Posta Astrogeophysical Observatory near San Diego, California. This facility was involved in a number of solar and ionospheric measurement programs. After the closing of the La Posta facility in 1976, Bob went on to a career in ionospheric experimental science and the development of HF signal assessment systems for advanced signals warfare analysis. He was the co-developer (with Dr. Paul Levine) of the MINIMUF HF MUF prediction model in 1975. This model, published in *QST* in 1982, is the backbone of many PC-based HF prediction programs.

Until his retirement from government service in January 1994, Bob was involved with a variety of experimental ionospheric measurement programs that led to the revision of many ionospheric theories. Bob regularly lectured at amateur radio clubs and conventions on solar-terrestrial relationships and what these relationships mean to amateur radio operators. He also was a regular guest lecturer at the Naval Postgraduate School in Monterey, California, where he taught courses on the art of HF radio.

K6GKU was active on the HF bands for more than 50 years, mostly on 10 meters. He enjoyed working with vintage receivers and transmitters, which radio amateurs often refer to as "boat anchors." Bob was also a prolific writer, with most of his papers and articles having been published in the technical literature. This edition and the previous edition of this shortwave propagation handbook are his only books. Bob became a Silent Key (passed away) in 2010.

Table of Contents

Chapter 1

The Principles of Ionospheric Propagation

The electromagnetic spectrum extends from nearly DC ("direct current," or no variation in frequency) to daylight . . . and beyond! A portion of it, as seen in Figure 1.01, is referred to as the "radio spectrum." It is in this region—from the extremely low frequency (ELF) band through the extremely high frequency (EHF) band that the majority of our communications—including cellular telephone, digital television, satellite communications, and the like—take place today.

Excluded from this conversation are optical communications involving the light spectrum. Actually, the band above EHF is called the terahertz or tremendously high frequency band and it extends from 300-3,000 GHz. Amateur operators may conduct operations here.

Importantly, within the radio spectrum, governments, including the U.S. government, have carved out allocations for the amateur, amateur satellite, and a number of personal radio services (including the citizens band radio service), as these services are formally known within the International Telecommunication Union (ITU) community.

Principles of Ionospheric Propagation

The *high-frequency*, or HF, portion of the radio spectrum lies between approximately 3 and 30 megahertz (MHz), or between 3,000 and 30,000 kilohertz (kHz). In the metric system, it is called the *shortwave* range, and, expressed in wavelengths, it lies between 100 and

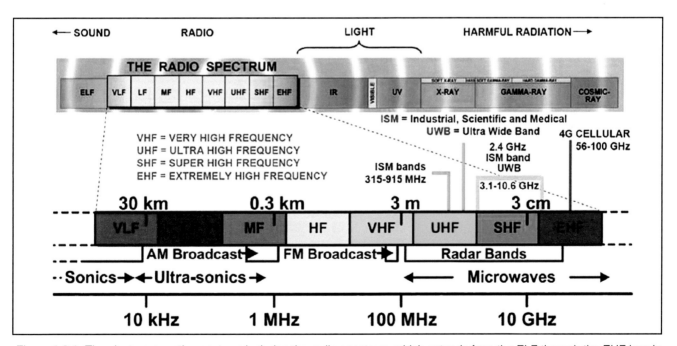

Figure 1.0.1. The electromagnetic spectrum includes the radio spectrum, which extends from the ELF through the EHF bands (courtesy Aktinovolia.net).

Figure 1.0.2 The Arvin 927 "Rhythm Queen" is a large, nine-tube wood console radio that was made in 1936 by Noblitt-Sparks Industries. It is easily recognized by its large round dial and green "cat's eye" tuning indicator at the top of the dial. Shown on the dial, at the appropriate frequencies, were the cities in which major international broadcasters were located (e.g., London, Berlin, and Moscow). Used with the permission of C. E. "Sonny" Clutter, also known as "Radiola Guy."

10 meters. This is the region where the majority of amateur, CB, and shortwave listener (SWL) activities are conducted (although amateur activities in the VHF and UHF portions of the spectrum are certainly giving HF operators a run for their money. We'll talk about propagation in these bands toward the end of this handbook).

In this book, the terms *high frequency* and *shortwave* will be used interchangeably, something not unknown to many old-timers, who undoubtedly got their start listening to the many international broadcast stations that dotted the dial on their parents' multiband console radios like the dial pictured in Figure 1.0.2.

Wavelength expressed in meters, and frequency expressed in kilohertz, are related by the following equation:

$$\text{Wavelength} = \frac{300,000}{\text{frequency}} \qquad \text{Equation 1}$$

Radio communication in the high-frequency range is possible because there exists in the Earth's upper atmosphere a region called the *ionosphere*, which reflects (actually it refracts, or bends) radio waves over long distances.

In this chapter we will review how the ionosphere was first detected, how it is formed and measured, how its structure varies with time of day and other factors, and how it makes possible long-distance radio communications. We also will discuss the role of the ionosphere in high-frequency communications from a practical point of view by examining the relationship among factors such as the maximum usable frequency (MUF), signal absorption, and optimum antenna design.

A High-Level View of Propagation from the Laws of Physics

Although we've only talked so far about the HF bands, this book covers propagation from the 2,200-meter band (135.7-137.8 kHz) through to our 6-meter band (50-54 MHz). That's a huge range, and it should be obvious that propagation at 136 kHz is quite different from propagation at 50 MHz.

But we have to remember that regardless of the frequency, all electromagnetic waves follow the same laws of physics. The results of these laws are refraction (bending), ionospheric absorption (loss) and polarization.

We can generalize these results this way:

1. The amount of refraction incurred by an electromagnetic wave through a given electron density is inversely proportional to the square of the frequency. In other words, the amount of bending is more as we move down in frequency. Thus the lower the frequency, the shorter the hops as the wave doesn't get as high into the ionosphere.

2. The amount of ionospheric absorption on 160 meters (MF) and in our HF/VHF bands incurred by an electromagnetic wave through a given electron density is also inversely proportional to the square of the frequency. In other words, the amount of loss in our MF and HF/VHF bands increases as we move down in frequency. But this trend does not apply on the LF bands – we'll look at this in more detail when later chapters in the book discuss propagation on 2,200 meters and 630 meters.

3. The polarization of an electromagnetic wave that is going through the ionosphere

on 50 MHz (and above) and in our HF bands is for all intents and purposes circular. On 1.8 MHz, polarization through the ionosphere can be anywhere from circular to linear (vertical or horizontal) depending on which way your RF is going with respect to the direction of the Earth's magnetic field and the orientation of the field. (We'll look at 2200 meters and 630 meters in more detail later.)

What also comes out of these laws of physics is our understanding that in general the higher bands (15 meters, 12 meters, 10 meters and 6 meters) are dependent on the MUF. Ionospheric absorption is low due to #2 above, and propagation depends on having enough ionization to refract the wave back to Earth.

Similarly, the lower bands (with wavelengths of 80 meters and longer) are in general dependent on ionospheric absorption. There's usually enough ionization to refract the wave back to Earth, so propagation depends on how much loss is incurred in the absorbing region.

The middle bands (60 meters through 17 meters) depend on both having enough ionization and having low enough ionospheric absorption.

In summary, a very general look at propagation as we go from VHF down to MF indicates that the hops become shorter, the loss due to absorption increases and polarization can be circular to linear. In later chapters we'll use ray tracing software to confirm these three laws of physics. Now let's get started with more details of propagation.

1.1   The Ionosphere

There exists in the Earth's upper atmosphere a region consisting of several electrified layers that are capable of bending (refracting) high-frequency radio waves and returning them to Earth at great distances.

The electrified characteristics of these layers, which are collectively referred to as the ionosphere, are subject to wide variations. This is so because the ionosphere is formed by various wavelengths of solar radiation – from EUV (extreme ultraviolet) at wavelengths of roughly 10 to 100 nm (nanometers) to soft X-rays at wavelengths from 1 to 10 nm and to hard X-rays at even shorter wavelengths from 0.1 to 1 nm.

The amount of radiation illuminating the ionosphere varies hourly, seasonally, and geographically, depending on the relationship between the sun and the Earth. In addition, year-to-year variations occur in the ionosphere's capability to refract radio waves over an approximate 11-year cycle [reference 1]. These changes result from the difference in the number of sunspots that occur on the face of the sun.

Sunspots are stormy areas on the solar surface that produce a considerable amount of EUV (the solar radiation source for the F2 region of the ionosphere). When the sun's surface is covered with a great number of spots, the ionosphere is electrically strong and shortwave radio communications are generally very good; when the number of sunspots diminishes, conditions become poorer. It should be noted that sunspots and 10.7 cm solar flux are but proxies for the true ionizing radiation for the F2 region – radiation at EUV wavelengths.

Because the ionosphere plays such a vital role in long-distance high-frequency communication, it is desirable at this point to go into greater detail about its characteristics as well as the factors that influence changes in its behavior. Once this has been accomplished, the reader will be better equipped to interpret the changes that take place, and to determine how they affect transmission and reception on the HF bands. Again, discussions of 2200 meters, 630 meters and 6 meters with respect to the ionosphere will be undertaken in later chapters.

Early Discoveries

In 1901 Guglielmo Marconi successfully completed one of the most historic experiments ever conducted – the transmission of a radio signal without wires across 2,000 miles of ocean.

Prior to Marconi's experiment, it had generally been believed that radio propagation was restricted to line of sight. However, a German physicist, Heinrich Hertz, demonstrated that while radio waves travel in straight lines, their direction of travel can be altered by interposing an electrically conducting obstacle in their path.

In 1902, a year after Marconi's initial success, two scientists, Arthur Kennelly in the United States and Oliver Heaviside in Great Britain, suggested in independent scientific papers around the same time that the Earth's upper atmosphere consists of an electrically conducting region [references 2, 3 and 4]. It was this region, they theorized, that acted as an obstacle and deflected Marconi's signals across the Atlantic Ocean. They reasoned that such a region was probably produced by solar radiation, but two decades were to pass before the existence of this region was verified.

Early radio experimenters knew little or nothing about the physics of propagation. The experimental sciences had not evolved, and so experimenters could only guess about the characteristics of a propagating signal. Early radio was primarily practiced at long waves – what we know today as the LF (low frequency) band and the MF (medium frequency – including AM broadcast) band. These bands are between 30 and 3,000 kHz. Here, the normal mode of propagation is by ground wave. At night, however, especially in winter, early experimenters noted that distant stations could be heard. They also noted that the higher frequencies in the MF bands demonstrated this phenomenon more often than the lower frequencies did. This is how early theories of "sky wave" or "skip" were formulated.

One early theory was that the "ether" in the Earth's atmosphere was modulated by the transmitted signal's waveform. This modulated wavefront propagated outward from the aerial in a manner similar to the way ripples propagate away from a point when a rock is thrown into a pond. In one early paper Dr. Lee de Forest stated:

"Radio is simply a cause and effect. The cause is the transmitter. It makes an electro-magnetic splash that sets up radio waves. These waves travel through space in all directions. The effect is the setting up of delicate currents in the aerial or loop. These delicate currents are detected and converted into audible sounds by means of the radio receiving set. Imagine a boy operating a paddle at one end of a pond of still water. Ripples are set up in the water. They travel farther and farther away from the paddle, getting weaker as they move along until they reach a piece of wood which bobs up and down as it rides the waves. Put a bell on the piece of wood, in order that it will ring with the action of the waves. This illustrates the mechanical parallel of radio communication [reference 5]."

The sought-after electrified region was discovered in 1924 by a British scientist, Edward Appleton. In 1925 he and his co-workers found conclusive evidence of its existence by measuring the angle of arrival of radio signals from a nearby transmitter. The angle of arrival was such that the signals could have arrived from only one direction – by reflection from an area in the Earth's atmosphere about 100 miles high. Kennelly and

Heaviside's visionary theory of 22 years earlier had been verified. For this pioneering work in the field of radio wave propagation, Edward Appleton was subsequently knighted by the British Empire.

In 1925, Gregory Breit and Merle Tuve, two American physicists, demonstrated the existence of a reflecting region high above the Earth's surface in an even more striking manner. By transmitting short bursts of radio energy straight up, they were able to detect, using suitable receiving and measurement equipment, the presence of an echo that had been reflected and returned to Earth. By determining the time that had elapsed between the transmission of the pulse and the echo, and by knowing that radio waves travel at the speed of light, they were able to deduce the height of the reflecting medium with considerable accuracy. Later, by varying the frequency of the transmitted pulses over a wide range, they discovered that above a certain "critical frequency," the reflecting region would no longer return signals to Earth. This was the first documented use of a vertical incidence ionospheric sounder.

Extensive studies using the Breit-Tuve technique, made at a large number of locations throughout the world, soon showed that the critical frequency varied hourly, seasonally, and geographically. This strongly implied that the reflecting layer was under solar influence.

Further evidence linking ionospheric behavior with the characteristics of solar radiation was obtained in 1927 when a sharp decrease in the critical frequency was observed during a total eclipse of the sun. Figure 1.1 shows graphically how the critical frequencies (the intensity of ionization) of the various ionospheric regions varied during the Aug. 21, 2017 solar eclipse across North America [reference 6].

It was concluded from the historic 1927 experiment that the primary solar agent responsible for forming the ionized layer (more appropriately called a region) was ultraviolet radiation, an amazingly accurate deduction, as the chemical constituency of the ionosphere was unknown at that time. As we know today, EUV is the primary photo-ionizing agent for what became known as the F region, which supports most long-range shortwave transmissions. This 1927 observation has been verified many times during subsequent solar eclipses (such as the Aug. 21, 2017 event in Figure 1.1).

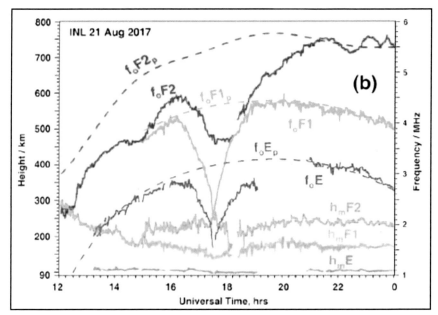

Figure 1.1 The Moon's shielding effect prevents solar radiation from reaching Earth's atmosphere during a solar eclipse. The dashed lines are critical frequencies for no eclipse and the solid lines are critical frequencies for the eclipse. Critical frequencies are discussed later in this chapter. The eclipse maximum was 1730 UTC at the Idaho National Labs ionosonde.

In the late 1920s, amateur experimenters started probing what was later to be known as the ionosphere. They noted that when a very short (200-microsecond) pulse was transmitted and the receiver output was recorded on an oscilloscope, they could see the ground-wave signal and a delayed signal that was reflected (more correctly, refracted) overhead. The duration of the delay was roughly equivalent to the height of the reflecting medium. This work further substantiated the existence of the Kennelly-Heaviside layer that was theorized 20 years earlier.

The Kennelly-Heaviside layer, or ionosphere, as it came to be known in the middle 1930s, is used to designate that electrically conducting region of the Earth's atmosphere that is responsible for the propagation of radio waves to great distances by means of multiple refractions, or reflections, between the conducting surface of the Earth and this layer. The ionosphere is not sharply defined: It extends to several hundred miles in altitude. Conductivity begins to be important at various heights above the earth, depending on the wavelength, but the conductivity at heights as low as 50 miles may be of importance in the case of low-frequency (long-wave) propagation. Subsequently, the term *ionosphere* has been introduced to describe this whole region. However, the ionosphere does have sub-regions-in which the conductivity varies more rapidly with altitude than in others. These are given special names according to their refracting properties for waves of different frequencies.

As early as 1930 Marconi theorized that "radio waves may travel long distances, even millions of miles, beyond the Earth's atmospheric layer." He did not see any reason why waves produced on Earth should not travel such a distance, since light and heat waves reach the Earth from the sun by penetrating the atmospheric layer.

Ionospheric Measurements

The rapid development of long-distance radio communication stimulated intensive investigation of the ionosphere throughout the 1930s. The need to solve newly developing communication problems required the establishment of more modem engineering techniques that would meet the demands for uninterrupted use of the ionosphere for reliable worldwide communication.

Equipped with pulse-sounding equipment, ionospheric measuring stations began to spring up in all areas of the world. Ionospheric sounding is similar to radar. A pulse is emitted upward and the time it takes to reflect back to the receiver is measured. This time can be translated to the height of the layer that reflects the signal back. The frequency is incremented upward and the procedure is repeated. This process continues until a frequency is reached where the pulse is not reflected (that is, it continues upward into space, where it may hit a second layer and reflect back). The frequency where the signal penetrated the first layer is called the critical frequency (f_o, where the subscript o refers to the ordinary wave – there is also a critical frequency called f_x for the extra-ordinary wave), and this frequency can be related to the maximum electron density (Nmax) of that particular layer by the expression:

$$Nmax = 1.24 \times 10^{10} \ (f_O)^2 \ \text{m}^{-3} \qquad \text{Equation 2}$$

where f_O is in MHz.

This procedure is repeated for each layer until a picture (called an ionogram) of the ionized medium and how it is structured is formed. Photo 1.A shows a typical vertical incidence sounder (VIS) ionogram. Note that *electron density* is the controlling factor in determining the refractive (reflective) properties of the ionosphere.

From a mere handful in the 1930s, to a peak of about 250 stations in the late 1980s, nearly 100 stations today are charting the ionosphere hourly throughout the world. In 1957, the International Geophysical Year, more than 250 stations collaborated in mapping the global ionosphere. At one point in the 1970s and 1980s, the former Soviet Union had a large, integrated ionosonde network that could literally map the overhead ionosphere over their entire country as well as neighboring countries. Modern ionosondes consist of both FM-CW swept frequency sounders, called "chirpers," and modern pulse sounders. Photo l.B shows a typical vertical-incident station (antennas not shown).

Formation of the Ionosphere

In 1927 the upper atmosphere was thought to consist mostly of helium, nitrogen, and argon. It was theorized that above 140 km, the atmosphere was entirely helium. We now know that the Earth's upper atmosphere is composed mainly of oxygen and nitrogen and their compounds, with small amounts of hydrogen, helium, and several other gases. This description was experimentally derived from rocket, high-altitude balloon, and satellite measurements in the latter part of the 20th century.

Gases, like all material, are composed of atoms made up of negatively charged electrons that are classically

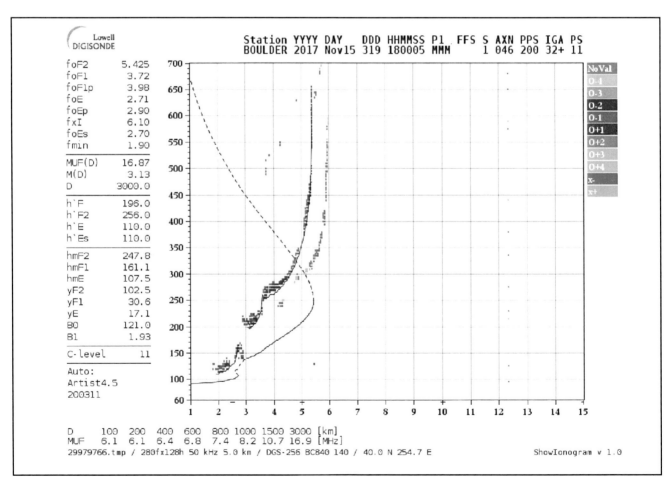

Photo 1.A An example of an ionogram produced by a modern vertical-incidence sounder. From the Lowell Global Ionospheric Radio Observatory website at http://giro.uml.edu/

Photo 1.B Digisonde-4D (circa 2008)
(http://giro.uml.edu/instrumentation.html)

portrayed as traveling in orbit about a positively charged center (or nucleus). Atoms, unless they are under the influence of energy forces, are in electrical equilibrium, with the negatively charged electrons counterbalancing an equal number of protons in the nucleus. A neutral atom exerts no electrical force outside its own structure. An atom remains neutral until subjected to external energy forces that are great enough to detach electrons from its structure, causing it to become unbalanced, or charged.

Data gathered from rocket and satellite probes of the ionosphere have confirmed earlier theories based on solar eclipses that extreme ultraviolet radiation from the sun is the principal agent responsible for the formation of ionization in the upper ionosphere. The great amount of energy associated with this radiation, sweeping through the upper atmosphere, causes electrons to become detached from the gas atoms present there. This leaves the originally neutral gas atoms unbalanced, with an excess of positive charge. Such unbalanced atoms are called ions, and the process by which they are formed is called ionization (see Figure 1.2).

If the ultraviolet energy is removed, the detached electrons can recombine with the positive ions to again form atoms in electrical equilibrium. This process is the opposite of ionization, and it is called *recombination*. Recombination takes place during the nighttime hours, when the ionosphere is shielded from the sun's direct radiation. The ionization process starts up again when direct sunlight (at ionizing wavelengths) strikes the ionosphere, which means that the daytime ionosphere starts forming immediately at sunrise.

Because it is a relatively slow process due to a low collision rate between electrons and positive ions, recombination at high ionospheric altitudes (which we'll later see is the F region), causes the electron density at high altitudes to decay at a slower rate after sunset as compared to the rapid rate of increase in electron density at high altitudes observed at sunrise. Recombination at low ionospheric altitudes (which we'll see later are the E and D regions) occurs much more quickly due to a high collision rate between the electrons and positive ions.

It is of interest to note that although ultraviolet radiation from the sun is considered the principal ionizing agent for the upper ionosphere, modern aeronomy (the science dealing with the chemistry of the ion-

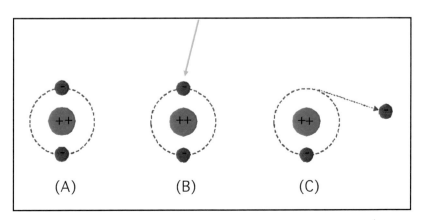

Figure 1.2 Diagram illustrating how ionization is produced by energy from solar radiation. At (A) is the neutral atom with equal plus and minus charge. At (B), solar radiation strikes an electron. At (C), the electron is "knocked off" the atom, leaving a positive ion and a negative electron.

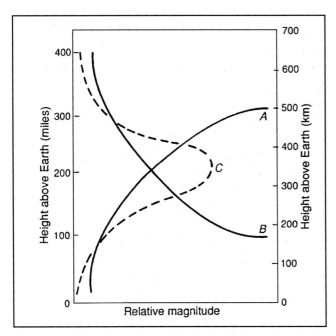

Figure 1.3 The formation of an ionized layer by single-frequency radiation. At (A), the intensity of the radiation increases with height. At (B), the density of neutral atoms decreases with height. At (C), the result is the variation of the amount of ionization with height.

osphere) shows that solar X-rays, certain spectral lines of hydrogen (such as the Lyman-alpha line), and cosmic rays also play a role in the formation of the lower ionosphere.

The Structure of the Ionosphere

As ultraviolet radiation sweeps into the Earth's atmosphere from above, it first produces ionization of the rarefied gases it encounters. As the radiation penetrates deeper into the atmosphere, it encounters greater densities of gases, and the amount of ionization increases. Penetrating further, it produces more and more ionization, but the radiation also is attenuated because it is giving up energy in the ionization process. Finally, the radiation penetrates to a level where its energy is completely dissipated and the ionization process stops. Thus, there is formed a region of maximum ionization, with intensity falling off above and below it. The details of the formation of an ionized region in the Earth's atmosphere are shown conceptually in Figure 1.3.

Solar radiation spans the entire electromagnetic spectrum from visible light to energetic (very short wavelength) particles. Because the gases comprising the upper atmosphere respond to different frequencies

in the solar radiation spectrum, there is a tendency for ionization to occur at several different levels. These layers are between approximately 30 and 250 miles (50 and 400 kilometers) above the Earth's surface.

While these ionized regions are usually referred to as "layers," they are not completely separated one from the other – that is why it is better to call them regions. Each region overlaps to some extent, forming a continuous but non-uniformly ionized area with at least four levels of peak intensity that, as we will see, are designated the D, E, F_1, and F_2 regions. Figure 1.4 shows typical electron density profiles and the relationship among the regions.

Important differences in the plots in Figure 1.4 include:

1) A winter day has the most F2 region electrons. This results in the highest MUFs, which is a major reason why the CQ WW DX contests in October and November are so popular.

2) A summer day has the most E region electrons. Unfortunately this may also block your RF from getting up to the higher F2 region for longer-distance propagation.

3) A summer day has the most D region electrons, which limits low-band propagation during the day. Note that there are still D region electrons during the night – there is still ionospheric absorption at night on the low bands.

4) The electron density valley above the E region peak is most pronounced during a winter night. This is where amateur radio operators believe ducting on 160 meters occurs to help make extremely long-distance QSOs. The valley is essentially non-existent during the day.

5) Note that the D region and the F1 region (around 150 km) are not usually peaks in the electron density. They are more of an inflection point in the electron density profile.

There's a significant difference between the summer and winter F2 region profiles. This is one of the so-called F2 region anomalies. Since the sun is lower in the sky during the winter, the radiation comes in at more of a grazing angle – not from overhead as in the summer. The measure of this angle is the *solar zenith angle*. When the sun is overhead, the solar zenith angle is 0 degrees. When the sun is on the horizon (at sunrise or at sunset), the solar zenith angle is 90 degrees.

Because of radiation coming in at more of a grazing angle, you would expect the F2 region to be less dense in winter than the summer. But what happens is the opposite, and it's mainly due to a change in the composition of the atmosphere over the seasons. In the northern hemisphere winter, there are many more oxygen atoms present than in summer. Oxygen atoms are important for electron production in the ionization process.

As the sunspot number (or 10.7 cm solar flux) increases, the peak electron densities in the F2 region increase. The results in Figure 1.4 are for a smoothed sunspot number of 20. At a smoothed sunspot number of 120 (an average solar cycle), the daytime winter and summer F2 region and E region electron densities roughly double. At the same smoothed sunspot number of 120, the daytime winter and summer E region electron densities increase by roughly 50%.

In the early days of radio, scientists operated with a lot of deduction and conjecture and without a lot of experimental evidence to back them up. Surprisingly, they were close to the truth at times. In 1920, S. Chapman and E.A. Milne, using certain assumptions, calculated the distribution of ionization that would result from the absorption of various types of radiation in the Earth's atmosphere [reference 7]. Their calculations showed that the ionization should start with a small value near the Earth and increase with height, reaching a maximum value somewhere in the upper atmosphere.

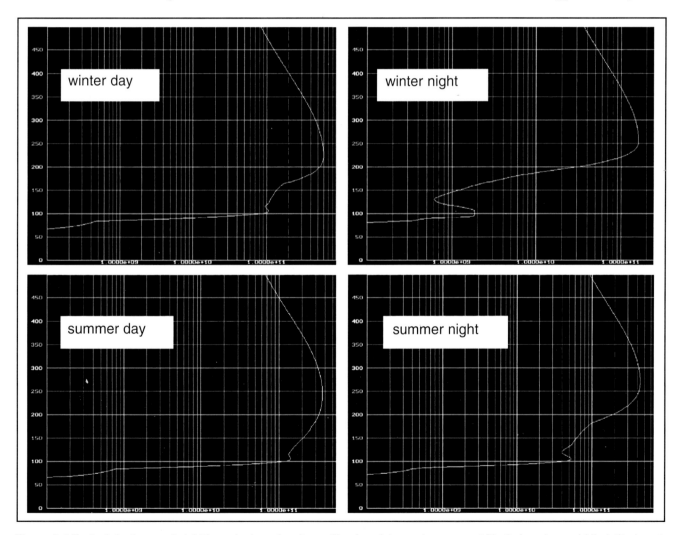

Figure 1.4 Typical daytime and nighttime electron density profiles for winter and summer at North American middle latitudes at a low sunspot number (from Proplab Pro V2 by Solar Terrestrial Dispatch)

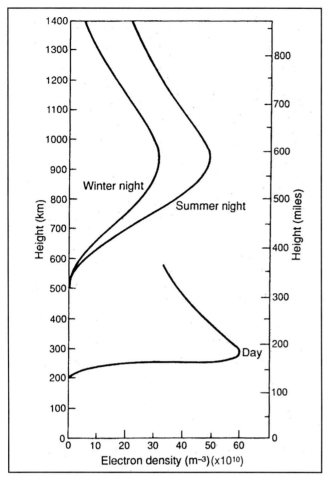

Figure 1.5 An early attempt to chart the distribution of ionization in the upper atmosphere.

Ionization should then decrease again to a small value at very great heights. This distribution is shown in Figure 1.5. It does a decent job of producing an electron density profile in the daytime, but significantly overestimates the heights during the night.

The allocation of the letters to designate the various regions of the ionosphere was the work of Sir Edward Appleton upon his discovery of the Kennelly–Heaviside layer in 1924. He allocated the letter "E" to this layer, using the symbol generally employed to designate an electric vector. In 1925, when he discovered another ionized region at a greater altitude, he used the term "F" to designate the electric vector reflected from it. This, as he has said, left several letters at the disposal of future workers for allocation to other layers they might discover, either above or below the layers identified by him. Sir Robert Watson-Watt, an early co-worker of Appleton and one of the original developers of radar,

gave the name *ionosphere* to the entire region, and it was adopted internationally.

The height and characteristics of these regions, or layers, change from day to night, and season to season. Several of these changes are illustrated in Figure 1.6. A brief description of each region follows.

The D Region

Even in the heyday of ionospheric experimentation in the late 1960s and into the 1970s, the D region remained somewhat of an enigma. This layer, which extends from 40 to 60 miles (65 to 95 kilometers) above the Earth's surface, was originally thought to exist only during the day while it was illuminated by the sun. However, its exact chemistry was difficult to determine, even using modern experimental probes. At these altitudes the pressure is large, producing a high electron collision frequency; as such, conventional study techniques cannot be used. Vertical sounding is not possible, because the collision frequency exceeds the critical frequency, and a signal return is never seen. Normal rocket experiments do not work well at these altitudes for several reasons. And satellites cannot function this low in altitude because of drag. The chemistry of the D layer is the least well-defined of all the ionospheric layers.

The D layer is ionized by three sources, depending on altitude. Between roughly 55 and 60 miles (90 and 95 kilometers) the primary source is solar X-rays at wavelengths from 0.1 to 1.0 nanometers (often called *hard* X-rays). At heights between roughly 50 and 55 miles (80 and 90 kilometers) the Lyman-alpha line of hydrogen (at 121.6 nanometers) is the controlling source (an interesting fact – there's an absorption window in the upper atmosphere that lets radiation at 121.6 nm get down to D region altitudes before ionizing atmospheric constituents). Between roughly 40 and 50 miles (65 and 80 kilometers) galactic cosmic rays have been shown to be a primary ionizing source. Enhancements in any of these sources (for example, a deep solar minimum lets in more galactic cosmic rays) cause an immediate increase in ionization of the D layer.

With respect to shortwave communications, the D layer is a gigantic attenuator, absorbing HF signals as they pass through it. Because attenuation varies as the inverse square of frequency, the higher the HF frequency used, the less the D layer absorbs the signal.

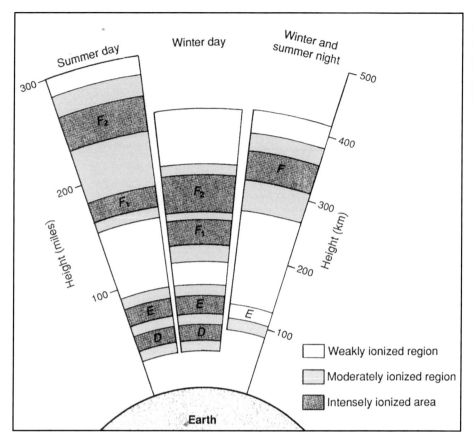

Figure 1.6 Daily and seasonal variations in the ionospheric regions (typical characteristics shown). Note that there is still residual ionization in the E region at night as in Figure 1.4 (and in the D region as in Figure 1.4, but not shown here).

□ Weakly ionized region

▨ Moderately ionized region

▩ Intensely ionized area

After sunset the layer quickly recombines, and lower frequencies "go sky wave." That is why at night at certain times of the year you will hear AM broadcast signals over very long distances by means of sky wave (ionospheric) propagation.

The E Region

The upper boundary of the D layer blends into another distinct region called the E layer, which occurs mainly during the daylight hours at heights between roughly 60 and 75 miles (95 to 120 kilometers). It is a thin layer, roughly 10 kilometers thick during the day, and it remains at a predictable height all day. There are many types of ionization mechanisms that appear to operate at this altitude depending on latitude, season, and level of solar activity. For now, this discussion will center on the simple mid-latitude E layer.

Traditionally, this layer has been typified as a simple Chapman-type layer, which is characterized by having only one type of gas, plane stratification, single wavelength ionizing radiation, and a constant-temperature atmosphere. The layer ionizes and recombines with the rise and fall of solar radiation. Theoretically, the E layer mostly disappears at night. During the day, photo–ionization is produced by X-rays at wavelengths from 1 to 10 nanometers (often called *soft* X-rays) and EUV in the 100-150 nanometer range.

Experiments in the early 1980s, during the peak of solar Cycle 21, demonstrated that contrary to popular belief, the E layer does not go away at night, but in fact has enough residual ionization to affect refraction and absorption at frequencies at and below 1.8 MHz. The 1980s was a decade in which experimental science raised more questions about ionospheric structure and mechanics than were answered. It also was during a five-year experiment measuring ionospheric variations between the peak and minimum of Cycle 21 that the correlation time of an ionospheric phenomenon was found to be two minutes. Put another way, it was observed that the value of any given ionospheric measurement will change after two minutes. This was an early indicator of turbulence in the ionosphere [reference 8].

Sporadic-E

In addition to the regular D, E, and F regions, there are ionized regions that occur sporadically in the ionosphere. Unlike the regular layers, these sporadic regions come and go irregularly, and there are several theories about what causes them. The height of these regions, or patches, is variable, but they occur most commonly at an altitude of roughly 65 miles (105 kilometers). Since this is about the same height as that of the regular E layer, the phenomenon is collectively called sporadic-E.

Sporadic-E has very definite geographical characteristics. Mid-latitude sporadic-E, which is most-frequently observed by the amateur radio community, occurs mainly in May, June, July, and August during daylight hours (peaking in late morning and early evening) and in December (peaking at night). It appears as a very intensely ionized thin region (ordinary wave critical frequency $f_oEs > 5$ MHz), several kilometers thick and generally of limited geographical extent. A sporadic-E cloud might be roughly 50 to 100 miles (80 to 160 kilometers) in diameter, and it may last only for a few hours before dissipating. Many sporadic-E clouds appear to drift with velocities as great as a few hundred miles per hour. In the Northern Hemisphere the drift is usually to the west.

Meteor deposition of longer-lifetime metallic ions at E-layer altitudes is believed to be the cause of mid-latitude sporadic-E ionization. Neutral winds and shearing forces, in conjunction with the Earth's magnetic field, compress these metallic ions into thin patches of high ionization. The fact that we can't predict sporadic-E, other than its general occurrence patterns, suggests that we may not fully understand the mechanism involved in this important 6-meter propagation mode.

In the equatorial regions, sporadic-E is a daytime phenomenon, thought to be caused by plasma instability in the equatorial electrojet. The high electron drift velocities found here create dense patches. Sporadic-E exists during 90% of the daylight hours around the geomagnetic equator.

In the auroral and polar cap regions there are several forms of sporadic-E, each with a different signal support capability. During daylight summer hours, the same type of sporadic-E that is seen at mid latitudes is observed in the auroral region. At night, a form of sporadic-E called auroral-E can be observed, centering on local midnight. Auroral-E is associated with disturbed magnetic activity when the K-index rises above 3 (see Chapter 5). Also, there are two forms of auroral-E, one associated with the eastward auroral electrojet (occurring prior to local midnight) and one associated with the westward electrojet (occurring after local midnight). Auroral-E is best described as random ionized "blobs" driven by the high-latitude electric current system that forms the electrojets. Average auroral-E events tend to last about 10 minutes, although some have been observed to last up to two hours and to produce signals of 20 to 30 dB above the receiver detection threshold [reference 9]

The F Regions

The F layers are the most important regions of the ionosphere insofar as long-distance shortwave radio communications are concerned. During the daylight hours there are two regions, the F1 layer and the F2 layer. The winter day F1 layer begins slightly above the upper boundary of the E layer at about 90 miles (145 kilometers), and it extends up to about 150 miles (240 kilometers). During the summer day, the F1 layer is found at somewhat higher altitudes (see Figure 1.6). The F2 layer, the height of which varies seasonally, ranges up to about 200 miles (320 kilometers) during the winter and close to 300 miles (480 kilometers) during the summer. Most shortwave communications are accomplished using the F2 layer. This layer is formed from EUV solar radiation at wavelengths of 10 to 100 nanometers. In fact, about 60% of the F2 region is formed by radiation between 26 and 34 nanometers.

The F1 layer, at least at solar minimum, also approximates a Chapman Layer. This means that it rises and falls with the rise and setting of the sun. By this process, the F1 layer should disappear at night; experimental evidence shows that it does. During the day, the F1 layer supports shortwave circuits of short to medium length. The F1 layer behaves much like the E layer. Maximum ionization occurs near noon at the midpoint of the path.

Unlike all of the other layers, the F2 layer exists throughout the day and night, and it almost always is capable of sustaining sky wave propagation at some HF frequency. This is the most ionized layer of all, and it is the most important to shortwave signal propagation. It is the behavior of this region that is most important in HF propagation prediction programs. See Chapter 6 for more information on computerized prediction programs.

During the nighttime hours the F2 layer height varies from approximately 150 to 250 miles (240 to

400 kilometers). Because the recombination rate of this region is relatively slow, the layer exists around the clock. Were it not for this fact, long-distance shortwave radio communication would be virtually impossible during the hours of darkness.

The intensity of ionization in the F2 region is in an almost continuous state of flux, with hourly, seasonal, geographical, and solar cyclical changes interacting in a somewhat complicated manner. Experiments between 1980 and 1985 indicated, for example, that instead of being characterized by a nice stable plasma (a plasma is a highly ionized gas), the F2 layer is in a constant state of motion [reference 8].

Above The F2 Region

Roughly 95% of the atomic and molecular elements that form the ionosphere are contained below an altitude of 1,000 kilometers. Topside (above the F2 region peak) sounder measurements from orbiting satellites indicate that the electron density above the F2 region peak decays exponentially. The electron density is of such a low value that if an electromagnetic wave does penetrate the F2 region peak, it is not affected by the topside ionosphere.

1.2   Regular Ionospheric Variations

Because the existence of the ionosphere depends on solar radiation, changes in the position of the Earth with respect to the sun (rotation and revolution), as well as changes in the patterns of solar radiation, will influence the variations in the ionosphere.

It's also important to note that electrons are charged particles, and thus the ionosphere is ordered about geomagnetic coordinates, not geographic coordinates.

The regular variations of the sun — that is, those which are relatively predictable and can be anticipated — fall into the following categories:

1. Diurnal (over 24 hours) and Day-To-Day
2. Seasonal
3. Geographical
4. Cyclical

Diurnal and Day-To-Day Variation

The diurnal variation, or the hour-to-hour changes in the various layers of the ionosphere, is caused by the rotation of the Earth on its axis. This rotation not only is responsible for variations in the amount of sunlight reaching the Earth, resulting in day and

night, but also for a corresponding variation in the intensity of ultraviolet radiation reaching the ionosphere at any point. During daylight hours, when ultraviolet radiation strikes the Earth's upper atmosphere, the ionosphere can become highly ionized with several stratified layers; during the hours of darkness very little radiation reaches the upper atmosphere on the side of the Earth away from the sun, and the ionosphere loses its electron density. For all intents and purposes, it becomes a single, relatively weak layer.

As already indicated, diurnal variations in the D, E, and F1 layers exhibit a regular pattern that principally is dependent on the sun's elevation (i.e., the solar zenith angle). Ionization in these layers increases from a very low level at sunrise, reaches a maximum at noon, and then the ionization decreases towards sunset. At night, for all practical purposes, these layers exhibit such a low electron density that they have no usefulness at shortwave frequencies.

Typical hour-to-hour changes in the critical frequency for the various layers are shown in Figure 1.7A. From this figure it can be seen that only the F2 layer's existence is not directly dependent on the sun's position as ionization exists before sunrise and after sunset.

Ionization in the F2 region, as shown by the increase in critical frequency, rises steeply at or just before sunrise. Maximum ionization is reached about the time that the sun has reached its zenith, its highest point in the sky (around local noon). Ionization then decreases, reaching low values during the nighttime hours. The lowest electron density is found just before sunrise, and the dip observed in the critical frequency is called the "pre-sunrise" depression.

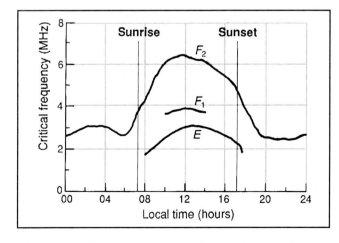

Figure 1.7A Typical hour-to-hour changes in the refraction capability of the ionospheric layers

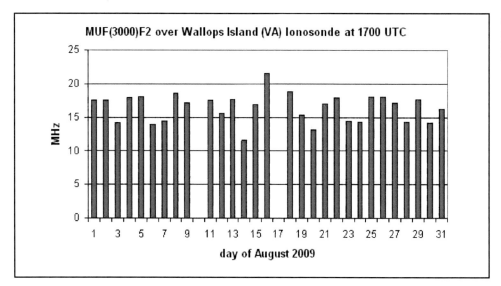

Figure 1.7B Variation of the F2 region MUF at the Wallops Island ionosonde throughout the month of August 2009.

The F2 layer is the most highly ionized of the regular layers, with the ability to support the propagation of higher shortwave frequencies. In addition, because of slow recombination rates, it can remain in existence for many hours after sunset. For these reasons, the F2 layer is of greater importance to long-distance shortwave radio communications than all of the other layers. Almost all DX openings take place by refraction from the F2 layer.

In addition to the hourly variation of the F2 region during a day, there is a significant variation day-to-day. This is shown in Figure 1.7B.

The MUF varied from a low of about 11 MHz to a high of 22 MHz at the same time of day over each day of the month. This is due to two other parameters besides solar radiation that ultimately determine the amount of ionization at any given location and time – geomagnetic field activity and events in the lower atmosphere coupling up to the ionosphere. This will be discussed in the chapter about propagation predictions.

Seasonal Variation

Because the position of any point on the Earth relative to the sun is constantly changing as the Earth orbits, the ionospheric properties also change.

Ionization in the E layer behaves regularly, being dependent almost entirely on the solar zenith angle. Ionization is much stronger in the summer because the sun is higher in the sky (lower solar zenith angle).

During all but the winter months, the F1 layer critical frequency varies in much the same manner as does the E layer, being dependent on the sun's solar zenith

angle. During the winter, however, the F1 layer usually merges with the F2 layer, and it cannot be separately identified, except in the equatorial regions.

The seasonal behavior of the F2 layer is complicated. During the winter in the Northern Hemisphere, the atmosphere has more atomic oxygen constituents, which are important for electron production. What is measured is the ratio of atomic oxygen to molecular nitrogen, and the O/N_2 ratio is higher in the Northern Hemisphere in the winter. Molecular nitrogen is conducive to electron loss. During the day, the winter ionosphere is more intense than in summer. But during the long hours of winter darkness, the ionosphere has more time to lose its electrical charge, and nighttime critical frequencies fall to lower values than in summer.

In the summer the O/N_2 ratio decreases from that observed in the winter. As a result, summer daytime F2 layer critical frequencies are lower than winter val-

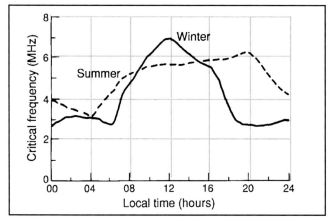

Figure 1.8 Typical seasonal variation in the F2 layer of the ionosphere.

ues. Because of the longer hours of daylight during the summer, recombination does not occur to the extent that it does in winter. As a result, nighttime F2 layer critical frequencies during the summer months are significantly higher than they are during the winter months.

The complex seasonal behavior of the F2 layer's critical frequency is shown in Figure 1.8.

Geographical Variation

The intensity of ionizing radiation that strikes the ionosphere varies with latitude, being considerably greater in the equatorial regions, where the sun is more directly overhead, than in the higher latitudes.

Critical frequencies for the E and F1 regions vary directly with the sun's elevation which is highest in equatorial regions and decreasing proportionately north and south of these latitudes.

F2 layer variations with latitude are more complex. In addition to variation due to solar radiation, the F2 region can vary due to winds at F2 region altitudes and traveling ionospheric disturbances, or TIDs, that are induced from atmospheric gravity waves that couple up from events below the ionosphere.

Although complex, the F2 layer critical frequency does follow a general pattern of being higher in equatorial regions and lower as one moves towards the polar regions. In Figure 1.9 the latitudinal variation in the F2 layer is shown by comparing critical frequency measurements made at three locations of different latitude. Not shown in Figure 1.9 is the double-humped characteristic of the F2 region along the geomagnetic equator at certain times of day. This will be discussed later.

Although not as complex as the latitude variation, F2 layer ionization also differs along meridians of longitude (at the same local time and along the same parallel of latitude). Much of this variation is believed to be due to the influence of the Earth's magnetic field. F2 layer critical frequencies are generally higher in the Asiatic region and Australasia than they are in Europe, Africa, or the Western Hemisphere.

Cyclical Variation

If diurnal and seasonal variations were the only influences affecting ionospheric behavior, the long-range pattern of critical frequencies would be easy and straightforward to establish, with seasonal values expected to repeat from year to year at the same geo-graphical location. Unfortunately, this is not the case. There also is a cyclical variation that is the most influential factor affecting the ionosphere. This variation depends on the level of sunspot activity, which is constantly changing throughout an approximately 11-year cycle. This solar cycle influence will be touched upon only lightly at this point, because sunspots, what they are, and how they influence the ionosphere and shortwave propagation, will be discussed at greater length in Chapter 2.

Figure 1.10 shows the variation in the F2 and E layer critical frequencies during the periods of maximum and minimum sunspot activity. It can be seen that the sunspot cycle exerts considerable influence on the level of ionization in the Earth's upper atmosphere. The greatest change throughout the entire solar cycle takes place in the F2 layer, with noontime

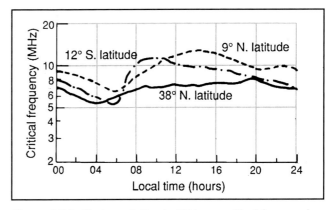

Figure 1.9 Latitude variation in F2 layer critical frequencies along 77° West longitude in June at the same local time.

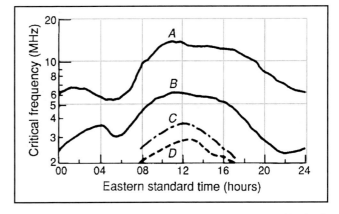

Figure 1.10 Comparison of diurnal variation in E layer (dashed curves) and F2 layer (solid curves) critical frequencies. Curves A and C were measured near Washington, D.C. during December 1957 when a sunspot number of 200 was recorded. The data in curves B and D were recorded during December 1964 when the sunspot number was 11.

critical frequencies approximately twice as high during the maximum of the cycle compared to the minimum of the cycle. The variation during the nighttime hours is about the same, with the midnight critical frequency being about two times greater during the peak of the cycle than at sunspot minimum.

The critical frequencies of both the E and F1 layers also show a close, linear correlation to the sunspot numbers, although the E layer variations between the extremes of the cycle are not as pronounced as they are in the F2 layer.

Up to this point we have discussed the electrical characteristics of the ionosphere in terms of the *critical frequency*. This is the highest frequency from which an echo is received when a pulse of radio energy is sent vertically into the ionosphere. Next we will show that frequencies used for communication between any two points (oblique propagation, as compared to vertical pulse transmission) bear a direct relationship to the critical frequency.

1.3 Optimizing High-Frequency Communications

A fairly wide range of shortwave frequencies when transmitted vertically, will be returned to Earth by the ionosphere. The highest frequency returned in this manner by each of the layers is called the "critical frequency" for that layer.

In the previous section we discussed the importance of the critical frequency in determining the physical characteristics of the ionosphere. Although the critical frequency is invaluable for this purpose, it is not useful for long-distance communication because vertically incident energy is returned to earth near the transmitter. To enable a signal to cover the great distances required in radio communication, the radio wave must leave the transmitting antenna at an angle such that the wave will enter the ionosphere obliquely, or at a slant.

The proper slant, or radiation angle, as well as the optimum frequency to use over a particular path, depends on many factors, including the height of the reflecting layer, the extent to which it is electrified, and the distance between the transmitting and receiving locations. There also is a direct relationship between the critical frequency at the point the wave enters the ionosphere and the optimum frequency for the path.

A knowledge of the relationships that exist among the critical frequency, layer height, radiation angle, path length, etc., are fundamental to understanding the principles of long-distance shortwave communication via the ionosphere.

This section explains, in a simplified manner, how some of these factors are related to each other, and how these relationships may be used to determine which specific frequency bands will be most useful over any given circuit, at any time of the day or night.

Trigonometric Relationships

To begin with, there is a simple trigonometric relationship that exists among the critical frequencies measured at vertical incidence, the height of the ionosphere at which refraction takes place, and the optimum radiation angle and frequency required for long-distance transmission. This relationship is expressed by the equation:

$$f = f_o / \sin a = f_o \csc a \qquad \text{Equation 3}$$

where: f is the equivalent signal frequency for oblique transmission;
f_o is the critical frequency; and
a is the radiation angle for oblique transmission.

The mathematics expressed in Equation 3 are shown pictorially in Figure 1.11.

It's important to note that the Earth and ionosphere are a spherical system, not a planar system as suggested by Figure 1.11. At very low radiation angles, Equation 3 would give an equivalent signal frequency f approaching infinity because *sin a* approaches zero (*csc a* approaches infinity). In a spherical system, a very low radiation angle results in the equivalent signal frequency being limited due to the wave encountering the ionosphere at a higher angle than suggested by Figure 1.11. A good rule of thumb to use at low radiation angles is *csc a* = 5 for the E region and *csc a* = 3 for the F2 region.

Using geometrical relationships shown in Figure 1.11, Equation 3 can be modified as follows to permit an even more direct solution for the optimum frequency required for long-distance transmission:

$$f = f_o \, SQRT(D^2/4h^2 + 1) \qquad \text{Equation 4}$$

where: f is the signal frequency that will give optimum long-distance transmission over a path length of D;

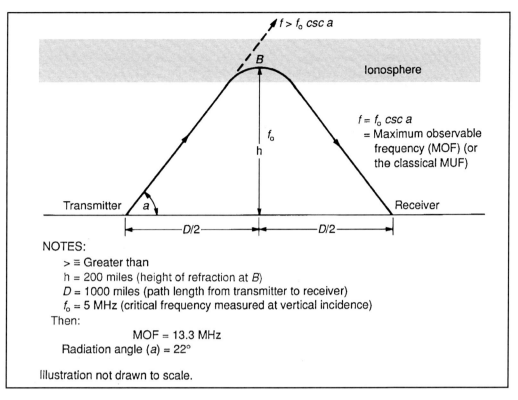

$f > f_o$ csc a

B

Ionosphere

$f = f_o$ csc a
= Maximum observable
frequency (MOF) (or
the classical MUF)

f_o
h

Transmitter /a\

Receiver

|← D/2 →|← D/2 →|

NOTES:
> ≡ Greater than
h = 200 miles (height of refraction at B)
D = 1000 miles (path length from transmitter to receiver)
f_o = 5 MHz (critical frequency measured at vertical incidence)
Then:
MOF = 13.3 MHz
Radiation angle (a) = 22°

Illustration not drawn to scale.

Figure 1.11 Illustrative example of MOF (MUF) calculations.

f_o is the critical frequency; and

h is the height at which ionospheric reflection takes place (D and h must be given in the same units, either miles or kilometers).

The significance of Equations 3 and 4 is that given the critical frequency and the height of the ionosphere, and knowing the distance between the transmitting and receiving locations, it is possible to determine the highest frequency that the ionosphere will support over this path. This frequency, f in Equations 3 and 4, is called the Maximum Observable Frequency (MOF) or the Classical Maximum Usable Frequency (MUF). This is the upper frequency limit at any given time and over any given path. This is **not** to be confused with the MUF values produced from prediction programs, which are monthly median values of the Classical MUF computed from monthly median ionospheric data taken over long periods of time (we will discuss these topics later in this chapter).

For a radio wave to be refracted between two distant points via the ionosphere, its frequency must be equal to, or less than, the Classical MUF. As the operating frequency is raised toward the Classical MUF, the signal will be received with increasing strength. When the frequency exceeds the Classical MUF, ionization at the point where the signal refracts off the ionosphere will not be strong enough to bend the wave back to earth at the receiving location, and it will continue on through into outer space. To ensure satisfactory communications between two distant points, the operating frequency should be as near to the Classical MUF as is possible.

Maximum Usable Frequency (MUF) Calculation

Because the Classical MUF is related directly to the critical frequency, its value is a function of the intensity of ionization in the Earth's upper atmosphere. For a given transmission path, the Classical MUF follows the same diurnal, seasonal, geographical, and cyclical variations as does the critical frequency. During periods of high solar activity Classical MUF values are approximately twice as high as they are during periods of low sunspot activity.

It should be noted at this point that the amount of power radiated does not enter into the determination of the Classical MUF. The ionosphere either has sufficient electron density to refract (or bend) the signal back to Earth or the signal escapes into space. It depends entirely on the frequency and the electron density. This situation applies to normal shortwave signal propagation and does not apply to the case of "scatter" reflections from the ionosphere (known as an above-the-MUF mode, which will be discussed in a later chapter) that may occur under certain conditions, or when powers on the order of hundreds of kilowatts are radiated. Under the last two conditions, radiated power will enter into the determination of the Classical MUF.

The Classical MUF is a very important quantity in radio communications, but it is extremely difficult to predict in the short term, meaning on a daily basis. However, relatively straightforward graphical methods and computer programs have been devised for predicting its *monthly median* value for transmission paths for any distance, without the necessity for resorting to tedious mathematics. Such a median value is what is usually referred to simply as the Maximum Usable Frequency (MUF).

Prior to the computer age, contour charts containing worldwide monthly median values of predicted critical frequencies for the F2 layer and monthly median values for the F2 region MUF for a 4,000-km path were published in *Ionospheric Predictions* published by the Institute of Telecommunication Sciences of the U.S. Department of Commerce. Appropriate graphs were also published for determining the MUF for any distance, using these values.

Using these charts involved a graphical method (also called the "manual method") and was quite tedious and not very flexible. But it was a great way to develop an excellent understanding of the propagation prediction process. These data on global critical frequencies as a function of time of day, season and sunspot number were the basis for the tables of ionospheric coefficients used in the first computerized HF propagation prediction programs.

Nowadays these contour charts are available in some propagation prediction programs, which will be discussed in Chapter 6. For example, Figure 1.12 shows an example of a global plot of the MUF over a 3,000-km path for 1700 UTC during October at a smoothed sunspot number of 120.

Other worldwide parameters are available: critical frequencies of the E layer, maximum height of the F2 region electron density, solar zenith angles and several others. Also note that the terminator is shown at the designated time and month.

Ionospheric Absorption

Up to now we have discussed the characteristics of the ionosphere as a refractor of radio waves. Ionization, however, not only causes a radio wave to bend, it causes energy to be absorbed as well. Ionospheric absorption is one of the main reasons the signal strength of a radio wave is reduced as it passes through parts of the ionosphere.

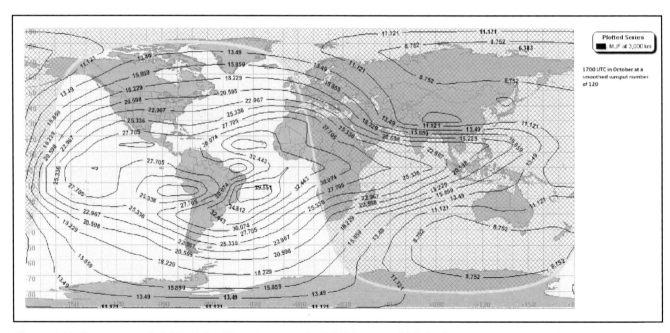

Figure 1.12 Contour map in MHz of the F2 region 3,000 km MUF for 1700 UTC in October at a smoothed sunspot number of 120. Maps are easily generated for any time, month and sunspot number. The map is from Proplab Pro V3 (Solar Terrestrial Dispatch).

As a radio wave passes through the D layer during the day or the lower E layer during the night, it imparts energy to the electrons in this electrified region. The electrons are set into motion by the transfer of energy, and thus convey the radio wave through the ionized region. While moving through the ionosphere, electrons vibrating in rhythm with the radio wave collide with neutral constituents (non-ionized atoms and molecules) and with positive ions also present in this region. As a result, the electrons lose some of the energy imparted to them by the radio wave. In effect, this lost energy is not propagated. The radio wave emerges with less energy than when it entered the ionosphere, resulting in decreased signal strength. Simply put, the D layer acts as an "RF sponge" at shortwave frequencies. Technically, there also are some minor losses in the F layer; however, they are negligible compared to the twin passage for each hop through the D layer.

Exactly how much energy is lost as the radio wave propagates through the D layer depends on the number of collisions per second between electrons and positive ion/neutral constituents. This quantity, in turn, depends on the radio wave's frequency as well as on the number of electrons and positive ions/neutrals present. As the wave frequency increases, the wavelength decreases, and the number of collisions also decreases. The higher the frequency, the less the absorption.

For HF, the amount of ionospheric absorption incurred varies inversely with the square of the signal frequency. If the signal frequency is doubled, the ionospheric absorption will decrease by a factor of four. For example, the absorption on 27 to 30 MHz (11-meter citizens band and the 10-meter amateur band) is one-fourth the intensity of the absorption found on 14 MHz (20-meter amateur band). When both bands are open (high enough MUF) at the same time, it will require considerably more power on 20 meters to equal the strength of the 10-meter transmission over the same path. This accounts for the strong signals often observed on the 10-meter band, even when relatively low power is used.

Because the Classical MUF is the highest frequency that can be used at any given time on a given circuit, and because ionospheric absorption decreases rapidly with the increase in frequency, this type of absorption is minimal near the Classical MUF.

Ionospheric absorption on HF signals depends upon the intensity of ionization in the D layer. This level of absorption varies throughout the day, with the season of the year, and geographically, being proportional to the solar zenith angle. The higher the sun is in the sky, the more absorption there is. Absorption is much more intense in equatorial regions, where the sun is more directly overhead, than in the temperate latitudes, and it generally is greater during the summer than in the winter. To reiterate, at night the absorption process moves up to the lower E region.

The best example of absorption can be found in the AM broadcast band. Typically, these medium-frequency signals propagate by surface waves (also known as ground waves). But during the winter, at night, these signals propagate via the ionosphere because the absorption has dropped drastically. This is the reason why AM signals are heard hundreds of miles away from their source during the winter nighttime hours.

As you might expect, the absorption of HF radio waves as they pass through the ionosphere varies throughout the solar cycle. During the years of low sunspot count, when ionization is at a minimum, ionospheric absorption also is at a minimum.

Signal-strength measurements made during previous sunspot cycles show that during the daylight hours, ionospheric absorption on a frequency of 20 MHz is approximately 25% less during periods of low solar activity than it is at the peak of a cycle. The difference at 10 MHz is close to 50%, and at 5 MHz it is 75%.

During the hours of darkness, when ionospheric absorption normally drops to very low values, there is a reduction of between 25% and 50% as the solar cycle declines from maximum to minimum activity, with the greatest reduction taking place in the lower frequency bands.

Lower absorption means stronger signals. Consequently, the signal strengths of radio waves refracted by the ionosphere during years of low solar activity are often noticeably stronger than during years of higher solar activity, particularly on the 40-, 80-, and 160-meter amateur bands and on the corresponding broadcast bands.

Lowest Usable Frequency

The Lowest Usable Frequency, or LUF, is the lowest frequency that can be used for satisfactory communications over a particular path at a particular time. The LUF is defined as the frequency at which the received signal strength is equal to the minimum signal strength required for satisfactory reception.

The strength of the received signal depends upon the power of the transmitter, the gain and directivity of the transmitting and receiving antennas, the path length, ground reflection losses if it's more than one hop and absorption losses.

In effect, the LUF is a signal-to-noise ratio (SNR) boundary. Further, the minimum level of signal intensity required for satisfactory reception depends upon the noise level at the receiving location and the type of modulation used. Atmospheric noise, or static, is generally the predominant type of noise that the signal must overcome – but local man-made noise may also be an issue. For satisfactory reception, a manual Morse (or CW) signal in a 500 Hz bandwidth requires an SNR of about 3 dB; a speech-quality single-sideband (SSB) signal with 3 kHz bandwidth requires an SNR of about 12 dB for 90% intelligibility.

At frequencies below the LUF, satisfactory reception will generally not be possible because the received signal will be lost in the prevailing noise. As the operating frequency is raised above the LUF, the signal-to-noise ratio improves. Optimal conditions occur near the Classical MUF, where both the signal-to-noise ratio and the propagation reliability are maximum.

Unlike the MUF, which is dependent entirely upon ionospheric characteristics, the LUF can be controlled to some degree by adjustments in the effective radiated power or by changes in the type of modulation used. As a general rule of thumb, the LUF can be lowered approximately 2 MHz for each tenfold increase in effective radiated power, and vice versa. Also, new digital signal processing (DSP) techniques and the new digital modes like FT8 have the capability to effectively "lower" the LUF. (More on the digital modes in a later chapter.) In reality, this technology allows us to see deeper (20-30 dB) into the noise through the use of coherent signal detection techniques.

Because ionospheric absorption increases as solar activity increases, the LUF for any particular circuit is expected to be somewhat higher during a period of peak solar activity than during a period of low sunspot activity.

Circuit Analysis Curves

Between the Classical MUF and the LUF there is a range of frequencies over which radio communications can be maintained on a particular circuit. The upper limit of the range (the Classical MUF) is determined by the ionization density at the point of refraction, while the lower limit (the LUF) is determined by ionospheric absorption along the path, by noise conditions at the receiving terminal and by any other losses, such as ground reflection losses in a multi-hop path. It is of great operational importance to know both of these limits as well as the intervening range of useful frequencies. Such data, plotted conveniently in graphical form, are often referred to as "circuit," or propagation, analysis curves.

On a real-time basis the highest frequency that will support propagation between any two points, as we noted earlier, is referred to as the Classical MUF. In Figure 1.13 the circuit analysis curve shows the "predicted median MUF" for the given month. This means that on 50% percent of the days the Classical MUF will be above this value and on 50% of the days the Classical MUF will fall below it. Frequencies lying between the median MUF and the LUF will support propagation on a greater percentage of the days. It should be noted that if the predicted (median) MUF is

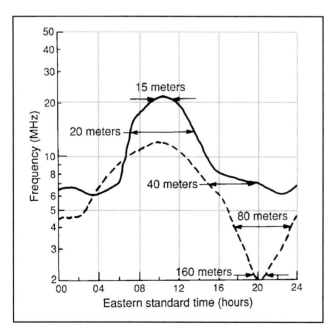

Figure 1.13 Circuit analysis curves, east coast U.S. to western Europe; low sunspot activity (SSN 10); winter season (December). Solid line is predicted median MUF; dashed line is LUF. LUF based on 250 Watts of CW effective radiated power.

multiplied by 0.85, the resulting frequency "should" support propagation on 90% of the days of the month, provided that it is above the LUF. This frequency is referred to as the Frequency of Optimum Traffic, or FOT. If the predicted (median) MUF is multiplied by 1.15, the resulting frequency should support propagation on 10% of the days of the month. This frequency is referred to as the Highest Possible Frequency, or HPF.

For example, using Figure 1.13, at 12 noon EST the predicted median MUF is seen to be 20 MHz, the FOT = 20 x 0.85, or 17 MHz; and the HPF = 20 x 1.15, or 23 MHz.

Figure 1.13, which is a typical circuit analysis curve, represents data for the circuit between the east coast of the U.S. and western Europe for a winter period of low solar activity (this is for December 1986). From this example it is possible to see at a glance what bands are expected to be open at any time of the day. For example, the 15-meter band should open approximately 50% of the days between 9 a.m. and noon EST, while 20 meters should be open 90% of the days between 8 a.m. and noon. The figure also shows that 40 meters should open a bit more than half the days of the month between 1500 and 2000 EST (3 and 8 p.m.). The circuit analysis shown in Figure 1.13 is based on an "effective radiated power" of 250 watts. Effective radiated power, or ERP, is defined as the power supplied to an antenna multiplied by the gain of the antenna in the given direction relative to gain of a dipole antenna at a height of one-half wavelength above the ground.

During times when the LUF exceeds the MUF, a "blackout" condition occurs, and it becomes very difficult, if not impossible, to maintain communications on the circuit. In Figure 1.13 a blackout condition is seen to occur between 4 and 7 a.m. Further, between 1300 and 1500 EST (1 and 3 p.m.) only a narrow band of frequencies around 10 MHz should support propagation on this path. Since there now is an amateur frequency allocation in this range, however, communications between the east coast of the U.S. and western Europe still should be possible in this time period.

It can be seen from Figure 1.13 that unless we are familiar with ionospheric conditions, the chances of maintaining effective radio communications are slim, especially during periods of sunspot minimum. Haphazard selection of the operating band easily can result in the signal either penetrating the ionosphere and being lost in space or being completely lost in the noise. On the other hand, proper band selection based on propagation analysis will result in refraction of the signal between transmitter and receiver with a minimum loss of energy.

The ability to maintain efficient long-distance short-wave communications depends to a great extent on the ability to predict far enough in advance what ionospheric conditions will be so that adequate operational plans can be made. Such long-range propagation studies are made possible because of the close relationship that is known to exist between monthly median ionospheric conditions and smoothed sunspot numbers. Figures 1.13 and 1.14 are examples of propagation analyses calculated for the path between the eastern U.S. and western Europe during the winter months of previous periods of low and high solar activity, respectively.

There are two methods by which the radio amateur can develop circuit analyses such as those shown in Figures 1.13 and 1.14. These methods are the "tabular" method and "computer modeling." To enable readers of this book to perform tabular circuit analyses, we have chosen paths to major points on all the world's continents from the three main geographical regions of North America (eastern, central, and west-

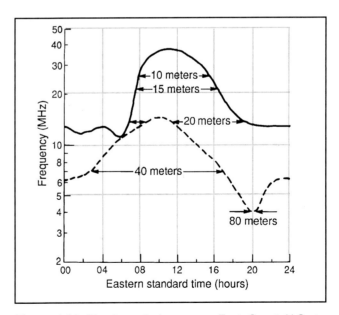

Figure 1.14 Circuit analysis curves, East Coast U.S. to western Europe; high sunspot activity (SSN 110); winter season (December). Solid line is predicted median MUF; dashed line is LUF. LUF based on 250 watts of CW effective radiated power.

ern) and have constructed circuit analysis curves similar to those shown in Figures 1.13 and 1.14. The results are presented in Chapter 4 in a simplified tabular format that permits reliable do-it-your-self forecasts to be made to just about any part of the world for any time during a solar cycle.

For readers who prefer using personal computers, Chapter 6 will discuss in some detail computerized methods for circuit analysis, what software is available, and how to interpret the results. It is important for the reader to remember one fundamental fact: no matter which method you use, the MUF values derived are **median** values. That is, 50% of the time the Classical MUF values observed each day will be higher than the median, and 50% of the time they will be lower. Unfortunately, it is extremely difficult to predict which days will be "better" and which days will be "worse."

A more detailed explanation of the complexities involved in constructing circuit analyses can be found in *Ionospheric Radio* [reference 10]. Detailed data for calculating LUF and field strengths appear in "Sky wave Field Strength at Frequencies between 2 and 30 MHz" [reference 11].

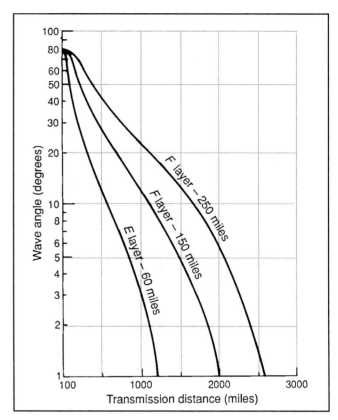

Figure 1.15 Relationship between optimum antenna wave angle and height of the E and F regions.

Optimum Radiation Angle

Figure 1.15 shows the optimal relationship between radiation angle, or the slant angle at which the radio wave must leave the earth, and distance for transmission via the ionosphere. Radiation angles (or wave angles, as they also are called) are shown for refraction from an average E-layer height of 60 miles, and for normal F-layer limits of 150 and 250 miles.

From Figure 1.15, assuming 1 degree as the minimum attainable wave angle, it can be seen that the geometry of sky wave propagation is such that one-hop reflection from the E layer is limited to approximately 1,200 miles (2,000 km), and one-hop F-layer propagation is limited to a maximum distance of between 2,000 and 2,600 miles (3,200 and 4,160 km). As we saw earlier, this depends on the frequency – these distances are typical for 28 MHz. Propagation beyond these distances is usually accomplished by means of multi-hop propagation, or successive refractions between the Earth and the ionosphere.

For the most efficient shortwave propagation, the radiation angle of the transmitting antenna and receiving antenna should be optimized according to the geometry of propagation. This is directly a function of the type and height of the antenna used. Figure 1.16 illustrates the radiation angles for a typical amateur three-element beam at various heights above the ground.

This type of antenna is called a "directive antenna" because it can focus energy into certain directions instead of radiating uniformly in all directions. It is the vertical radiation pattern that controls the distance of transmission. For distances less than the one-hop limit, the optimum wave angles can be determined directly from Figure 1.15. For multi-hop propagation, experience has shown that the lower the radiation angle, the more efficiently the wave is propagated.

The radiation angle of the antenna is determined primarily by its electrical height above ground. Figure 1.17 shows how the wave angle varies with the antenna height.

The higher the antenna, the lower the wave angle. But always remember that the ionosphere - not the antenna's height - determines the required elevation angle. Using the data in Figure 1.15, and for an F layer height of 250 miles, the coverage of the three-element beam is approximately 750 miles (1,200 km)

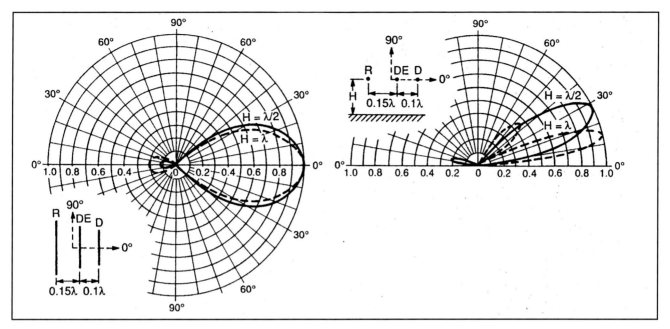

Figure 1.16 Horizontal (on the left) and vertical (on the right) polar diagrams of a three-element Yagi at a height of λ/2 (solid line) and 1λ (dashed line). The spacing of the elements is given in the figure.

when the beam is up one-half wavelength. When the antenna is raised to a full wavelength in height, one-hop coverage extends to 1,400 miles (2,240 km).

Here is an example that ties together the geometry of propagation, optimum radiation angles, and height of the antenna above ground. Suppose that shortwave communications must be conducted between two points 1,000 miles (1,600 km) apart. From Figure 1-15 for an F-layer height of 150 miles, the optimum wave angle is 13 degrees; for a height of 250 miles, it is 23 degrees. In practice, the antenna's design radiation angle is generally taken as the average value of the two limiting heights, which in this example would be 18 degrees.

From Figure 1.17, a wave angle of 18 degrees can be achieved with a horizontal antenna approximately 0.8 wavelength above ground. If the optimum band for this circuit is 20 meters, the antenna should be placed 16 meters, or 53.5 feet, above ground (1 meter = 3.28 feet).

Data concerning the design of antennas for use by radio amateurs can be found in *The ARRL Antenna Book* [reference 12]. Additionally, detailed analysis of antenna elevation patterns can be done using High Frequency Terrain Analysis, or HFTA, software. This software is available on the CD in recent editions of *The ARRL Antenna Book*. HFTA also allows terrain profiles to be built for your specific location in the

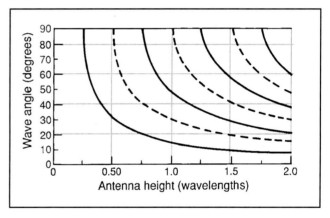

Figure 1.17 Antenna radiation angles for various horizontal antenna heights above ground. The solid lines are maxima and the dashed lines are nulls.

case of non-flat terrain, and diffraction calculations are done to simulate the true antenna elevation pattern. The antenna systems of many big contest stations have been designed using HFTA software.

In summary, to optimize shortwave communications over a particular path, use only those amateur bands that lie between the predicted median MUF and the LUF, and make sure your transmitting antenna is designed for the optimum radiation angle.

1.4   Disturbances to Propagation

This section in this book's previous edition (*The NEW Shortwave Propagation Handbook*, 1995) was written around the belief that was stated in the right-hand column on page 1-20 of that edition – that "solar flares provide events that have the most profound impact on the Earth's magnetic field and the ionosphere."

In November 1993, J. T. Gosling's seminal paper, *The Solar Flare Myth,* was published in the Space Physics section of the Journal of Geophysical Research [reference 13]. Gosling challenged this belief that solar flares were the sole cause of adverse changes in the Earth's magnetic field. He believed that coronal mass ejections, or CMEs, were separate from solar flares, and that coronal mass ejections and coronal holes were responsible for the adverse changes in the Earth's magnetic field.

This paper generated dissenting opinions followed by much discussion in the scientific community. In the end, Gosling's paper proved to be correct. In March 2002, the Space Weather Prediction Center (SWPC), an organization under the National Oceanic and Atmospheric Administration, reformatted the sources of adverse effects of the sun on propagation along the lines of Gosling's paper.

The current understanding of the sun's adverse effects on propagation on Earth, also known as disturbances to propagation, is three-fold: geomagnetic storms, solar radiation storms and radio blackouts. The information that follows comes from the Space Weather Prediction Center website at https://www.swpc.noaa.gov/noaa-scales-explanation. It's also important to understand that solar flares can occur without a concurrent CME, and CMEs can occur without a concurrent solar flare.

The Big Picture

Before digging into the details, it is instructional to step back and look at the big picture of disturbances to propagation. Figure 1.18 does this.

The image gives a very brief description of the impact of each of the three disturbances, and where and when they occur on a global scale.

Geomagnetic Storms

Geomagnetic storms, abbreviated **G** by SWPC, are caused by CMEs and coronal holes. Both explosively emit copious amounts of matter, and they can increase the solar wind speed from its average of around 400 km/sec. With the pressure on our atmosphere proportional to the number of particles times the square of the speed of the solar wind, the most critical factor with CMEs and coronal holes is the solar wind speed.

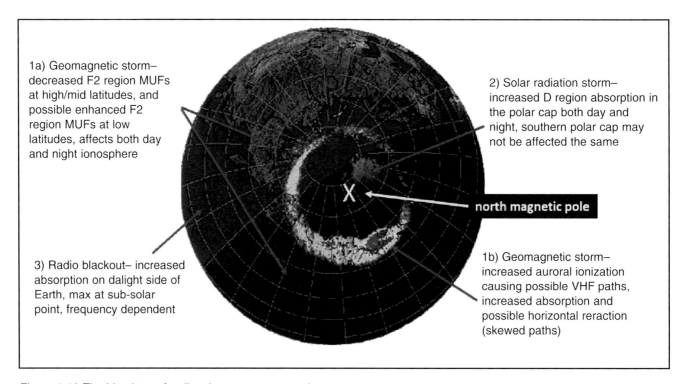

1a) Geomagnetic storm– decreased F2 region MUFs at high/mid latitudes, and possible enhanced F2 region MUFs at low latitudes, affects both day and night ionosphere

2) Solar radiation storm– increased D region absorption in the polar cap both day and night, southern polar cap may not be affected the same

north magnetic pole

3) Radio blackout– increased absorption on dalight side of Earth, max at sub-solar point, frequency dependent

1b) Geomagnetic storm– increased auroral ionization causing possible VHF paths, increased absorption and possible horizontal reraction (skewed paths)

Figure 1.18 The big picture for disturbances to propagation.

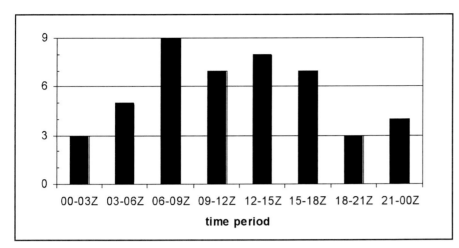

Figure 1.19 Kp Index on Nov. 24

CMEs occur most often at and just after solar maximum, but they can occur anytime in a solar cycle. Coronal holes mostly occur during the declining phase of a solar cycle, before solar minimum. CMEs and coronal holes can cause the Earth's magnetic field to become disturbed through an elevated *K* index. (The *K* index and the related *A* index are parameters defining the short-term and long-term variation of the Earth's magnetic field. See the accompanying sidebar, "Magnetic Indices.") This then disturbs the ionosphere, which can disrupt propagation at the high and mid latitudes. In general, CMEs and coronal holes disturb the ionosphere when the K index increases to 4 or higher.

CMEs and coronal holes must be Earth-directed to impact our ionosphere. A CME that is Earth-directed is called a halo CME, as the explosion is seen all around the occulting disc that is used to view the sun. A CME that goes off the side of the sun is not like-ly to impact Earth. Coronal holes tend to last longer than CMEs as they can persist for a complete solar rotation (and longer).

Let's take a look at the impact of a coronal mass ejection. We'll do this by looking at a contest log from Bill Tippett, W4ZV, who was doing a single-band 10-meter effort in the CQ World Wide CW DX Contest held Nov. 24-25 in 2001. Before the contest, a CME occurred concurrently with an M-class solar flare, magnitude M9.9 at 2330 UTC on Nov. 22. The shockwave of the CME arrived at Earth around 0600 UTC on Nov. 24, the contest's first day. Figure 1.19 shows the K index data.

With the K index increasing to 7 and greater from 0600 to 1800 UTC, the bands were adversely affected. Figure 1.20 is W4ZV's QSO rate on both days.

His QSO rate on the first day (when the K index was extremely high) only managed to get to a high of 70 QSOs per hour for a single one-hour period.

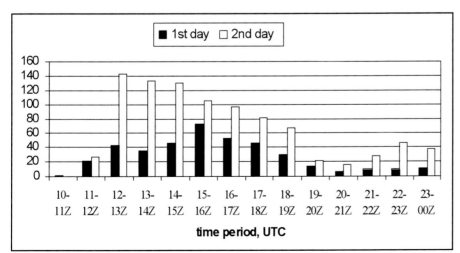

Figure 1.20 W4ZV QSO Rate

Magnetic Indices

Various chapters of this book cover how magnetic indices can affect ionospheric propagation. Here's a look at these indices amateur radio operators and other users of the HF spectrum most likely will encounter in their propagation studies.

The K index quantifies the maximum fluctuation in the horizontal component of the Earth's magnetic field observed on a magnetometer in a three-hour period at a specific observatory. The measure is relative to what would be observed on a "quiet" day. It ranges from 0, for quiet, to 9, for extremely disturbed, on a quasi-logarithmic scale. The Kp index – with the p standing for planetary - is the mean standardized K-index from 13 geomagnetic observatories located between 44 degrees and 60 degrees northern or southern geomagnetic latitude. The K index for various observatories is available as far back as 1932.

The A index is the mean, or average, of the eight K indices for an entire day at a given observatory. The index is computed on a linear scale. In other words, it is not a measured parameter – it is derived from the K index. Because the K index is a quasi-logarithmic parameter, you cannot simply add the eight three-hour K indices and divide by eight to determine the average. First, you must convert each K index to its linear equivalent a index. Then, when these eight a indices are averaged, the result is the daily A index. (A lowercase a indicates the linear equivalent of a three-hour K index while a capital A indicates the daily A index.) The A index ranges from 0, for quiet to 400, for extremely disturbed. A planetary A index—Ap—also can be computed for the A index. For more details on the K and A indices, visit https://k9la.us and read the paper "Where Do the A and K Indices Come From?" by clicking on the "General" icon on the left-hand side of the screen.

The AE (auroral electrojet) index is based on a linear scale. It was defined in 1966, and is primarily a measure of auroral zone magnetic activity produced by enhanced ionospheric currents flowing below and within the auroral oval. The AE index is measured every minute at various observatories.

The Dst (Disturbance – storm time) index (also based on a linear scale and known as the equatorial electrojet) was introduced in 1964. It is primarily a near-equatorial measurement of the current near the equator. The Dst index also is measured every minute at specific stations.

To see how the AE, ap and Dst indices are related, visit https://www.ann-geophys.net/15/1265/1997/.

Because the measurement of K (and, thus, A) only extends back to 1932, another index sometimes has been used to study geomagnetic activity. It is the antipodal a (aa) index, which extends back to 1868. Data for aa have been observed at two antipodal observatories and can help us understand propagation for dates before 1932 (for example: what type of geomagnetic activity existed during Marconi's experiments in 1901). Visit https://catalog.data.gov/dataset/aa-geomagnetic-activity-indices-from-two-antipodal-observatories-in-australia-and-england#sec-dates for more information.

Fortunately the K index decreased to low values later in the first day, and the ionosphere rapidly recovered to give very high QSO rates on the second day.

Solar Radiation Storms

Solar radiation storms, abbreviated as "**S**" by SWPC, are caused by intense solar flares – generally M-class and X-class. These intense solar flares can eject very energetic (high speed) protons. These protons then funnel into the polar caps — the area within the auroral oval — to cause increased D region absorption.

Since these disturbances affect the polar caps, propagation is adversely affected on over-the-pole paths, such as between North America and India. Since these protons come from outside the Earth's magnetosphere, the two polar caps may not be affected the same. So if short path over one pole is degraded, try the other way around – long path over the other pole.

Big solar flares generally tend to occur mostly around solar maximum. Be aware, though, that big solar flares have occurred throughout a solar cycle.

Radio Blackouts

Radio blackouts, abbreviated as "**R**" by SWPC, are also caused by intense solar flares. But instead of particles (protons) being the problem as in solar radiation storms, electromagnetic radiation at very short wavelengths is the problem for radio blackouts.

Electromagnetic radiation from the sun travels in a straight line, thus only the daylight side of Earth is affected. This radiation, being at very short wavelengths (0.1 – 10 nanometers), causes increased D region ionization on the daylight side of Earth. Since absorption is inversely proportional to the square of the frequency, it follows that radio blackouts do the most harm on the lower frequencies. Although their effect diminishes as the frequency is increased, they still can significantly affect the higher bands.

For example, Dan Reese, N9XX, traveled to the Cayman Islands in 2000 to do a single-band 10-meter low-power effort as ZF2RR in the CQ World Wide CW DX Contest. His QSO rate for the two days of the contest is shown in Figure 1.21.

The dip in the rate in the 1800-1900 UTC period on day one coincided with an X1.9 flare that erupted at 1836 UTC. The dip in the rate during the 1600-1700 UTC period on day two coincided with an X4.0 flare that erupted at 1638 UTC.

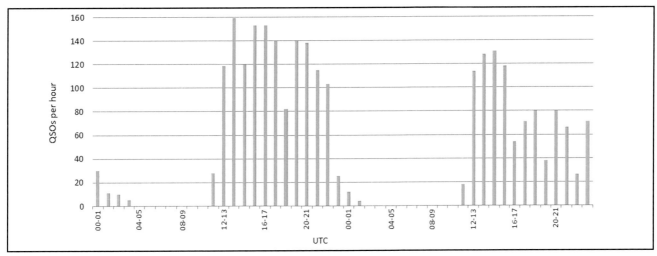

Figure 1.21 ZF2RR QSO Rate

The dip in rate in the 1900-2000 UTC and 2200-2300 UTC periods toward the end of the contest was due to ZF2RR looking for new multipliers (which sacrificed rate). ZF2RR ended up with 2,517 QSOs, 33 zones and 105 countries for a score of 851,736. That was about 32,000 below the North American 10-meter low power CW record that existed at the time. Adding in a conservative 100 more QSOs to compensate for the two flare periods might have allowed ZF2RR to set a new North American record.

Severity of Disturbances

Which of the three disturbances is the most detrimental to our amateur radio operations? Because of their disruptions to the ionosphere which can last several days or even longer, CMEs and coronal holes are the most severe. They can disrupt much of the worldwide ionosphere both day and night. Of these two, coronal holes are more detrimental because they can last for more than one solar rotation. If we look at a plot of the smoothed Ap index over a couple of solar cycles, we'll see where CMEs are most prevalent and where coronal holes are most prevalent. See Fig. 1.22.

The peak in the Ap index around the solar maximum of Cycle 23 (2000-2002 time frame) is due to CMEs, while the higher peak in Ap during the decline of Cycle 23 (2003-2007 time frame) is due to coronal holes. A similar pattern is seen in Cycle 24 – solar max (2012-2014 time frame) gave high Ap values, and the decline (2015-onward) gave even higher Ap due to

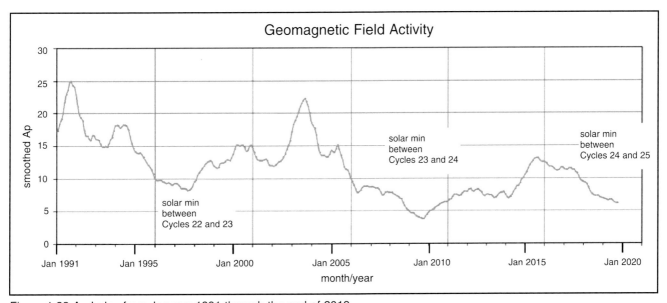

Figure 1.22 Ap Index from January 1991 through the end of 2019

```
Geomagnetic storms - G
        Most of the time a depleted F2 region
        Caused by CMEs (most prevalent at solar max) and coronal holes (most prevalent during
        the declining phase )

        Mitigation
                QSY to lower frequencies
                Look for enhanced low latitude paths
                Look for skewed paths on the lower bands
                Look for aurora at VHF

Radio blackouts - R
        Radiation at X -ray wavelengths
        Caused by M and X -Class solar flares (most prevalent at solar max )

        Mitigation
                QSY to higher frequencies (less loss & possible enhancement in ionization)
                Look for paths in darkness

Solar radiation storms - S
        Energetic protons into the polar cap
        Caused by M and X -Class solar flares (most prevalent at solar max )

        Mitigation
                Avoid polar paths
                Look other way around (long vs short path)
```

Figure 1.23 Mitigation for Disturbances to Propagation

coronal holes. The quietest time with respect to geomagnetic field activity, with lowest Ap, is right at solar minimum and during the initial rise of the new cycle.

Next in line for severity is the radio blackout since it affects all the frequencies to a certain extent. But it only does this on the daylight side of the Earth, and the ionosphere usually recovers in several hours.

The least severe of the disturbances is a solar radiation storm. Although it could last for several days, it only affects paths over the pole, across the polar cap.

Mitigation for Disturbances

When one of the disturbances occurs, there is some mitigation that can be applied as opposed to turning off your radio. Figure 1.23 summarizes these mitigating actions.

1.5   1989 and The Disturbed Sun

The influence of solar flares, CMEs and coronal holes on space and the Earth's atmosphere extends far beyond the interests of radio amateurs and other users of the HF spectrum.

In 1958, Dr. James Van Allen discovered the radioactive belts above the Earth that came to bear his name – the Van Allen Belts. These are two huge, doughnut–shaped belts of intense radiation that encircle the Earth. There is even evidence of a third belt. The Van Allen Belts consist of high-energy protons, electrons, other particles, and associated magnetic fields. With this discovery, theories of a benign space environment above the ionosphere had to be reconsidered and revised. Moreover, it subsequently was discovered that the radiation levels in these belts are greatly enhanced during solar disturbances.

The unusually high number of solar disturbances recorded during 1989 has earned it the unofficial title of "The Year of the Turbulent Sun." This coincided with the peak of sunspot Cycle 22. These disturbances not only were associated with a disturbed ionosphere, HF radio blackouts and degraded over-the-pole paths, but they also caused damage to satellite solar panels and caused errors in satellite tracking equipment – particularly to those satellites that passed through the Van Allen Belts [reference 14, 15]. Simply put, solar flares and CMEs, along with coronal holes prior to solar minimum, can affect satellite systems as well as terrestrial HF communications.

Although it was quite a few years ago, it is instructive to look at 1989 in some detail. An example of the turbulence of 1989 is in the number of Ground Level Events, or GLEs, that occurred that year. When the energy level of a solar proton event due to a big solar flare reaches or exceeds 500 MeV, energetic nuclei enter the Earth's upper atmosphere and collide with the atoms there. The result is a cascade of neutrons that arrive at the Earth's surface in the polar regions. There exists a global array of sensors to record these events in the two polar regions. It takes a very hard, intense solar flare to produce a GLE. Although no GLEs were recorded in the 11 years prior to 1989, there were seven during 1989! Each had associated space and terrestrial consequences.

When it first appeared on the solar disk on March 6, 1989, sunspot region 5395 gave hints of what was to come. It initially was observed as a massive, complex spot group and was classified at the highest level of complexity. Indeed, that day an X15 solar flare occurred, which is outside the normal range of solar flares – which is B, C, M and X. If there was a classification above X, this flare would have been 1.5 in the new category. This very active region maintained that complexity for the remaining 13.5 days of its passage on the solar disk. This volatile region was detected both before and after it came into view, and is noteworthy for the amount of activity it produced on its first and only passage. But what a passage it was!

Photo 1.C, provided by the National Solar Observatory in Sunspot, New Mexico, shows a nine–panel photograph of the CME on March 9, 1989. It was a massive particle ejection.

The pictures taken at 1555 UTC and 1605 UTC show a massive particle cloud being ejected from the CME region. Ionospheric effects from this CME were dramatic when it arrived at Earth on March 13 at 2:44 AM EST. It produced degradation on all HF systems. From March 6 through March 19, 11 X-Class flares and 48 M-Class flares erupted.

All this solar activity caused operational problems for LORAN navigation systems worldwide, and HF radio could not be used to notify ships at sea that there were environmental causes for their navigation problems. Low-altitude, high inclination satellites began to experience periods of uncontrolled tumbling as they transited regions of high magnetic-field gradients caused by field-aligned currents. During one large flare, satellite operators even indicated that they were not aware of any satellite anomalies because their communication links to the satellites were out of operation due to the storm!

During this period overhead aurora was observed as far south as Texas. The huge geomagnetic variations above Canada caused induction problems that disabled portions of that country's power distribution system. During magnetic storms on March 17 and 18, increased atmospheric drag caused orbiting satellites and "space junk" to change orbits, resulting in their positions being moved outside expected "windows" of observation.

Throughout all of these events, operators of satellites in geostationary orbit were kept quite busy re-initiating systems that were knocked out by energetic particles and performing station-keeping operations when the shock waves from large particle clouds knocked their satellites "off station." These solar disturbances also produced major HF blackouts and disturbances that lasted several days.

While the sun remained active during the next four months — April through July — even the large flares observed during that time seemed tame compared to those observed in March. Then, on Aug. 12, 1989 the first of six major flares occurred, with flares almost on a daily basis. Very high-energy protons reached the Earth's atmosphere anywhere from minutes to hours after each flare. On Aug. 16, a major flare launched a high-energy proton cloud that reached Earth minutes after this event occurred. During this event, half of the GOES-6 weather satellite telemetry system was lost. Users of satellite systems that employed star sensors for navigation reported spurious events as the sensors became confused by the solar particles. Many satellite systems operators reported having to reset or re-initiate their space-borne digital hardware.

On Sept. 29, a large flare produced another of the numerous GLEs seen in 1989. Very high-energy solar protons measured by monitors worldwide exhibited the largest increase measured in 33 years, since the start of the satellite age! Again, users of the

HF spectrum faced long periods of blackouts and severe disturbances. This event also had its effects on satellites in Earth orbit. For example, it was reported that photo-sensitive components on the Magellan space probe, on its way to Venus, were damaged; Geostationary Operational Environmental Satellite (GOES) power-panel outputs were permanently damaged; NOAA-10 experienced rare "phantom commands"; and numerous geostationary and orbiting satellites experienced "hits" in their digital systems.

Another series of solar flares and CMEs occurred between Oct. 19 and 26; they had a serious effect on

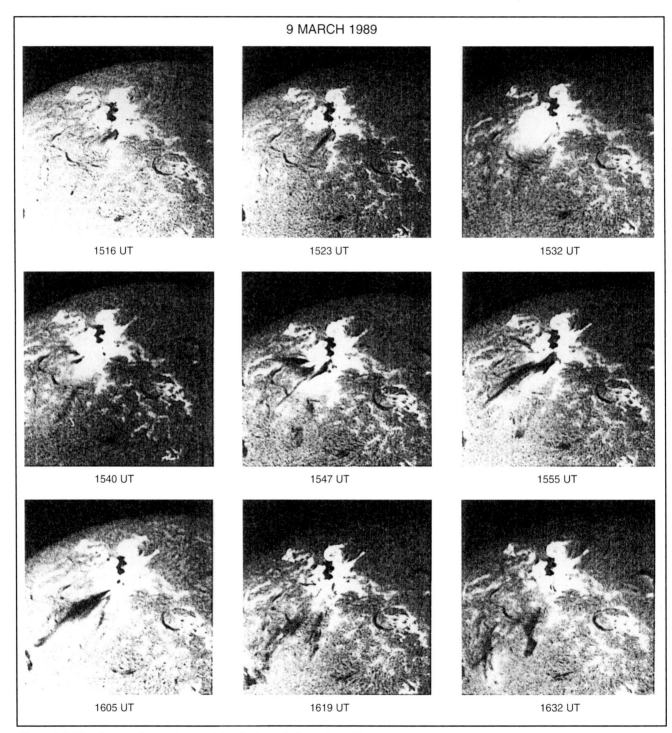

Photo 1.C The flare and massive particle ejection of March 9, 1989

terrestrial HF communication systems as well as on satellites. Specifically, a large number of satellites, including GOES-5, -6, and -7, were reported to have received severe damage to their solar-panel arrays. It also was reported that astronauts aboard the Shuttle Atlantis and cosmonauts aboard the Mir Space Station experienced physical effects. See Allen and Wilkinson [reference 15] for a more complete review of the effects caused by the unusually large solar events of 1989.

Summary of Record 1989 Solar Flare Activity

Marked by seven major solar events, 1989 was an unprecedented year for solar disturbances. The events were among the largest on record, as measured by the high degree of solar particle radiation ejected into space and, consequently, into the Earth's atmosphere.

By the time 1989 ended, HF propagation was completely or badly disturbed during one-third of the year, and a large number of space-borne satellite systems were damaged.

Figure 1.24 shows numerous space weather measurements for the period between March 10 and March 15. Included are X-ray flux, number of protons, number of neutrons and magnetic field readings.

The X-ray flux (top plot) shows an X7 flare at 1900 UTC on March 10. There are nine more flares at around X1 and numerous smaller flares during this period.

The number of protons in the solar wind (second plot down) peaked on March 13 at around 0700 UTC. These protons would result in a solar radio storm affecting the polar caps.

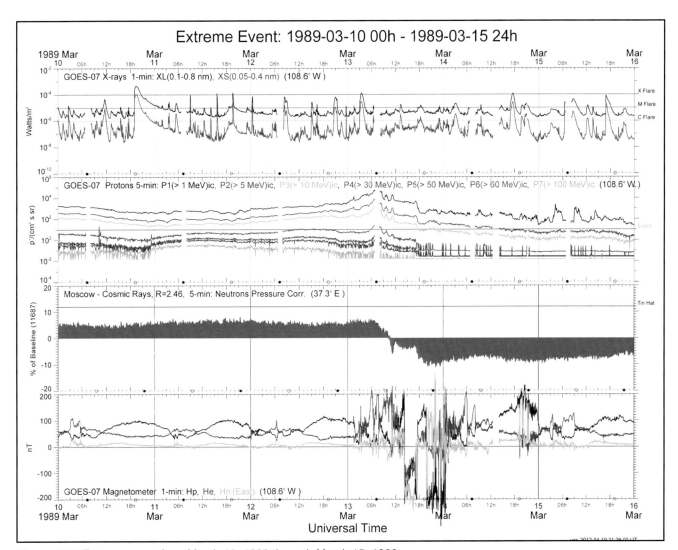

Figure 1.24 Extreme event from March 10, 1989 through March 15, 1989

The dark gray neutron count, also known as solar cosmic rays (third plot down), was quite normal until midday UTC on March 13.

The arrival of the March 9 CME caused wild variations in the Earth's magnetic field (bottom plot) – indicating elevated K indices.

1.6 References

The references given in this chapter's text are listed below. Additionally, at the end of this list, a handful of other general texts related to propagation [references 16-23] are cited for those interested in further research.

1. Solar Cycle Progression, https://www.swpc.noaa.gov/products/solar-cycle-progression

2. Kennelly, Arthur; *Electrical World and Engineer*, March 15, 1902.

3. Heaviside, Oliver; *The New Volume of the Encyclopedia Britannica*; No. XXIII; Dec. 19, 1902.

4. Kendrick, G.W., "The Kennelly-Heaviside Layer - Its Relationship to Our Everyday Communication Problems," G. W. Kendrick, *QST*, September 1936.

5. *Radiomans' Guide*; Theo. Audel & Co.; New York; 1939.

6. Reinisch, B.W., Dandenault, P.B., Galkin, I.A., Hamel, R., & Richards, P.G. (2018). Investigation of the electron density variation during the Aug. 21, 2017 solar eclipse. *Geophysical Research Letters*, 45, 1253-1261. https://doi.org/10.1002/2017GL076572.

7. Chapman and Milne, *Quarterly Journal of the Royal Meteorological Society*, Vol. 46, 1920, p. 357.

8. Rose, R. B., "High Resolution HF Time of Arrival Measurements (1981-1985)," *Radio Science*, Vol. 23, No. 3, May-June 1988, pp. 257-264.

9. Rose, R. B., and R. D. Hunsucker, "*Auroral-Observations: The First Year's Data*," NRaD Technical Document 2449, February 1993.

10. Davis, K., *Ionospheric Radio*, Peter Peregrinus Ltd., London, U.K., 1990.

11. "Sky-wave Field Strength at Frequencies between 2 and 30 MHz," Report 252-2, Radio Communications Sector, International Telecommunication Union (ITU), Place des Nations, Geneva, Switzerland.

12. *The ARRL Antenna Book*, 24th Edition, available from the American Radio Relay League, 225 Main Street, Newington, CT 06111.

13. Gosling, J.T., The Solar Flare Myth, Journal of Geophysical Research: Space Physics, Nov. 1, 1993, https://doi.org/10.1029/93JA01896

14. Cliffswallow, Maj. Willow, "Region 5395 of March 1989," NOAA Technical Memorandum ERL SEL-82, November 1993.

15. Allen, J.H., and D.C. Wilkinson, "Solar Terrestrial Activity Affecting Systems in Space and on Earth," NOAA, NGDC, 1991.

16. Goodman, John M., *HF Communications: Science and Technology*, Van Nostrand Reinhold, New York, 1992.

17. McNamara, Leo F., *Radio Amateurs Guide to the Ionosphere*, Krieger Publishing Company, Malabar, FL, 1994.

18. Brown, Robert R. NM7M (SK), *The Little Pistol's Guide to HF Propagation*, WorldRadio Books, March 1996, out-of-print but available at https://k9la.us

19. The Propagation chapter of *The ARRL Handbook for Radio Communications*, Ninety-Seventh Edition (dated 2020), available from the American Radio Relay League, 225 Main Street, Newington, CT 06111.

20. The Propagation chapter of the *The ARRL Antenna Book*, 24th Edition, available from the American Radio Relay League, 225 Main Street, Newington, CT 06111.

21. Nichols, Steve G0KYA, *Radio Propagation*, Radio Society of Great Britain (RSGB), 2016.

22. Hunsucker, R.D. and Hargreaves, J.K., *The High-Latitude Ionosphere and its Effects on Radio Propagation*, Cambridge University Press, 2003.

23. Kerr, Donald E., *Propagation of Short Radio Waves*, McGraw-Hill, 1951.

Sunspots and the Sunspot Cycle

When the Jesuit Friar Joseph Scheiner, one of the first specialists in solar research, saw his first sunspot with an early telescope in 1611, his fellow astronomers called it a stain on the lens of the telescope! Today, of course, we know sunspots are relatively cool regions on the sun's surface that are characterized by tremendous eruptions of whirling, electrified gases (plasma) associated with strong magnetic fields. Because these gases are cooled to temperatures below those of the sun's photosphere (the visible surface of the sun), they appear darker – and are called sunspots. We also know the number of sunspots on the solar surface rises and falls with a period of roughly 11 years, and because of the ultraviolet, extreme ultraviolet (EUV) and x-ray radiation associated with them, sunspots are responsible for forming the ionosphere, a region in the Earth's atmosphere that makes possible shortwave communications.

In this chapter we discuss sunspots and the sunspot cycle. In particular, using data on sunspot observations that have been collected since 1755, we examine the characteristics of the 24 cycles reported to date. Particular emphasis is placed on the most intense cycle to date (Cycle 19), on an average cycle (Cycle 20), on two big cycles that gave us great HF propagation (Cycles 21 and 22), on a cycle believed to be the start of several small cycles (Cycle 23), and on the current cycle (Cycle 24), which is the smallest in our lifetimes.

For those readers who would like to attempt their own studies of solar activity, we include complete listings of both the old (Version 1.0) and the new (Version 2.0) smoothed sunspot numbers recorded since 1749 by the Swiss Federal Observatory in Zurich, Switzerland, and more recently (since the second half of 1980), by the Royal Observatory of Belgium. More specifically, since July 1, 2015, the original sunspot data have been replaced by a new entirely revised series. On that occasion, the data were presented in a new array of files, containing additional values that were not present in the original series. For proper tracking of those changes, the present version was numbered V2.0. We will make every effort to distinguish between the two data sets in the discussions below. Going forward from July 2015, it is important to keep in mind, however, that sunspot counts are reported using the new numbering system.

2.1 Sunspots

Sunspots are thought to exist as a result of intense, localized magnetic fields that are trapped below the surface of the sun. Following is one explanation as to how sunspots form.

At solar minimum, spots associated with the new cycle appear at the middle solar latitudes. The magnetic fields are longitudinal, running north and south. However, as the sun rotates, the magnetic fields under the solar surface rotate at different speeds, with the equatorial region of the sun spinning at a slower rate than do regions at the higher latitudes. This causes the magnetic fields to distort and to realign slowly in an east–west direction. Tremendous energy builds up under the solar surface, starting at the higher (mid) latitudes and migrating toward the solar equator over the four to five-year period to solar maximum.

As these fields build in magnetic potential, they erupt through the surface, forming a huge magnetic loop. The solar surface, where this eruption appears, cools significantly, causing that region to be darker than the surrounding solar surface. At solar maxi-

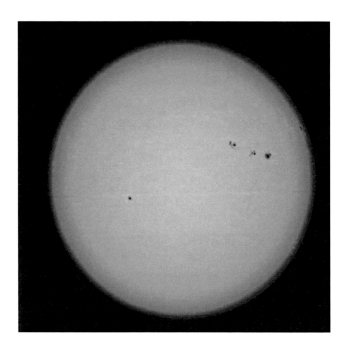

Photo 2.A Groups of sunspots seen on the solar disk.

mum the magnetic fields are almost completely latitudinal. From this point, sunspot activity begins its decline. At the end of roughly 11 years, the polarity at the poles associated with sunspots will reverse, the magnetic fields for spots associated with the new cycle will again be longitudinal, and the process starts over [reference 1].

The area around the sunspot, called a *plage* (a bright white region in the chromosphere of the sun, typically found in regions of the chromosphere near sunspots – the term itself is taken from the French word for "beach"), becomes an electromagnetic and cosmic-ray generator. Energy levels in the spectrum ranging from the visible through ultraviolet, EUV and x-ray emissions are elevated. When the magnetic field breaks down, a solar flare or CME (coronal mass ejection) results, emitting tremendous quantities of radiation and/or energetic particles. Photo 2.A was taken of the sun by NASA's Solar Dynamics Observatory (https://www.nasa.gov/mission_pages/sdo/multimedia/gallery/index.html). The sunspots appear as black spots on the solar surface.

Photo 2.B is an unprecedented close-up of a sunspot embedded in the solar surface by NASA.

Sunspots almost always appear in groups, probably the most notorious of which was Region 5395 in March 1989, which was accompanied by a series of large solar flares and CMEs. (What happened over the 14-day period as Region 5395 crossed the visible solar disk will be discussed later in this chapter.) Groups may range in size from small clusters of tiny specks a few hundred miles in diameter to enormous groups stretching nearly a quarter of a million miles across the sun's surface and containing individual spots as large as 80,000 miles in diameter . . . an area into which several planets the size of the Earth could easily disappear!

Sunspots, although embedded in the sun's surface, appear to move in an east to west direction as the sun rotates. If a spot is born on the side of the sun out of view from the Earth, it will first become visible as it crosses the sun's eastern edge. It will then drift westward across the visible face of the solar disk, and disappear out of sight behind the western edge in slightly more than 13 days, which corresponds roughly to half the period of rotation of the sun. The spot then enters the hidden side of the sun for the next 13 days.

The lifetime of a sunspot, or of a sunspot group, varies from a few days to several months. Larger sunspots often are visible during several solar rotations, reappearing roughly every 27 days. For this reason, many terrestrial phenomena that are believed to be influenced by sunspots tend to recur at intervals of about 27 days.

High-Flying Animal or Electro-Magnetic Eruption?

History vaguely records that sightings of sunspots before the invention of the telescope, if they drew any explanation at all, were usually thought to be

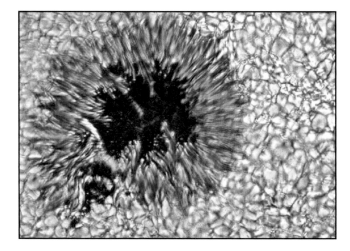

Photo 2.B Large sunspot embedded in the solar surface. Note the granular composition.

either slow, high-flying animals or far-away clouds. It was, in fact, Galileo, who in 1610 was the first to use the telescope to observe the heavens and record it, who offered the first serious explanation of sunspots. In 1613, he wrote:

"Having made repeated observations, I am at last convinced that the spots are objects close to the surface of the solar globe, where they are continually being produced and then dissolved, some quickly and some slowly; also, that they are carried around the sun by its rotation, which is completed in a period of about one lunar month. This is an occurrence of the first importance in itself, and still greater in its implications" [reference 2].

In this explanation, elementary as it was, Galileo was far closer to the truth than were many of his successors during the next 300 years.

During the 18th and 19th centuries various explanations for sunspots were given by noted astronomers. Some considered sunspots to be cold mountain peaks towering above the luminous surface of the sun; others, believing that a fiery, luminous cloud surrounded the sun, thought that sunspots were holes in this cloud, caused by hurricanes, through which could be seen the cool areas of the sun!

One of the most significant discoveries concerning sunspots took place in 1908. Using his newly invented spectro-heliograph, Dr. George E. Hale of the Mount Wilson Observatory in California photographed certain characteristics of the sun for the first time. From these he was able to demonstrate that large sunspots are frequently engulfed in whirling masses of gas, or vortices. Six years later, in 1914, Dr. Hale made another remarkable discovery. He proved that magnetic fields, often more powerful than the magnetic field surrounding the Earth, occur at the center of sunspots.

Working with these two important facts, that sunspots are engulfed in whirling masses of gas and that they are surrounded by magnetic fields, scientists have developed the explanation for the evolution of sunspots discussed earlier.

The Sunspot Cycle

Sunspots are known to have been observed by the Chinese many years before the birth of Christ. But it was not until 1611 that permanent records of sunspot activity were first made. In that year Galileo and his contemporaries began to draw pictures of the sun's surface by projecting telescopic views upon a white wall or screen. A number of Galileo's drawings of the solar disk made in 1612 still exist, and these show many large sunspots.

It was not until the middle of the 18th century, however, that many European astronomers independently began keeping sunspot records on a regular basis. To one of these, Samuel Heinrich Schwabe (a pharmacist from Dessau, Germany) who engaged in astronomy as a hobby, goes credit for the discovery of the sunspot cycle.

With the intellectual curiosity characteristic of a true scientist, Schwabe began his work on the sun in the early part of the 19th century, painstakingly counting the spots he saw with his small telescope, day after day and year after year. After several years he observed that the number of sunspots he saw varied over wide limits in a fairly regular manner. During some years he found the face of the sun almost completely free of sunspots, month after month. During other years he saw hundreds of spots day after day. After observing the sun almost every day for nearly 20 years, Schwabe concluded that sunspots came and went in a periodic fashion, varying from a minimum, to a maximum, and to a minimum again in about a decade's time. He published his findings in 1843.

Sunspot Numbers

Shortly after Schwabe's discovery, the director of the Zurich Solar Observatory, Rudolf Wolf, devised a means for all astronomers to describe relative sunspot activity in terms of a common standard. The Zurich Solar Observatory had been recording sunspot data on a regular basis since 1749, and Wolf realized the great importance of having other observatories and astronomers, who used various types and sizes of telescopes, report their observations according to a common standard.

Wolf called his standard a *sunspot number.* The sunspot number is obtained from daily solar observations of individual sunspot groups according to the following equation:

$$R = k(10g + s) \qquad \text{Equation 1}$$

where: R is Wolf's relative sunspot number;
g is the observed number of sunspot groups;

s is the total number of sunspots, either individually or in groups; and

k is a factor for bringing observations of many different observers into general agreement; it takes into account the type and power of telescope used, the viewing conditions, and observer biases.

The factor 10, which multiplies *g,* was selected by Wolf in order to give greater weight to the large active sunspot groups, which he intuitively judged to be a more important criterion of general activity, than to small spots of short duration. Thus, the sunspot number is more an index of solar activity than of the actual number of spots on the face of the sun.

From 1849 to 1981 the Zurich Observatory published daily sunspot numbers, recorded near mid-day, according to Equation 1. These numbers are known as the *Zurich Sunspot Numbers,* and they represent the official sunspot count upon which sunspot information is based. Because a record of daily sunspot observations, *R,* exhibits wide fluctuations, it is necessary to smooth the data in order that trends may be observed. The first smoothing is done by averaging the daily numbers over a one-month period; the result is the monthly mean sunspot number, R_m. Even the monthly mean numbers are subject to month-to-month fluctuations that tend to mask trends, and they do not correlate too well with general shortwave propagation conditions. As such, monthly means are further average into a *smoothed* number by taking a 12-month running average. The 12-month running smoothed sunspot number, R_{12} (also referred to as SSN) is derived from the following equation:

$$R_{12} = \frac{1/2R_{m1} + R_{m2} + \dots + R_{m12} + 1/2R_{m13}}{12}$$

Equation 2

where: R_{12} (or SSN) is the 12-month running smoothed sunspot number centered on R_{m7}; R_{m1} through R_{m13} are monthly mean relative sunspot numbers for 13 consecutive months. It should be noted, that some sources will refer to the value of the SSN computed using Equation 2 as the *13-month* SSN, given that data from 13 months are use. Regardless, there is no difference in what is being discussed.

As readers of *CQ* know from this magazine's "Propagation" column, following a long review and updating of all sunspot data by a distinguished committee of solar scientists, the Royal Observatory in Belgium began reporting a new Version 2 (V2.0) sunspot number in July 2015. The old sunspot numbers were named Version 1 (V1.0). The intent of the review was to correct for the number of observational and counting problems that had plagued the original data over time. For the discussion of the sunspot cycles through the cycle ending at this writing (near the end of Cycle 24), we will use the OLD values of the sunspot numbers with which we all are familiar. That is, the discussion below uses the V1.0 dataset for the 12-month running smoothed sunspot numbers. Following a review of the last six cycles, we'll then address the V2.0 dataset in detail and its impact going forward.

Values of *old* 12-month running smoothed sunspot numbers (again, the V1.0 dataset) reported since 1749 are given in the Appendix 1 (Section 2.11) of this chapter [reference 3] and are plotted in Figure 2.1. This data set from Reference 3 is in a file named "monthssn.dat".

It is the smoothed sunspot number, plotted over a long period of time, that exhibits the well-known solar cycle variation and that is used to define the sunspot cycle. The 12-month running smoothed sunspot number correlates closely with monthly median ionospheric parameters.

Wolf began publishing daily sunspot numbers in 1849. This effort, carried on by his successors at the Zurich Observatory, resulted in a long, unbroken, and very valuable series of solar data over more than a century's duration. In 1852, Wolf, using the sunspot records of earlier observers, reduced to sunspot numbers those data going back to 1749.

Beginning on Jan. 1, 1981, responsibility for the determination of the so-called Zurich sunspot numbers was officially transferred from the Swiss Federal Observatory to the Royal Observatory of Belgium in Brussels. Numbers are still based on observations made at the solar observatory in Locarno, Switzerland, thus assuring continuity between the pre-1981 sunspot numbers and those numbers prepared by the Royal Observatory. And again, as noted above, on July 1, 2015, the original sunspot data were replaced by a new entirely revised series.

Monthly average sunspot numbers and the corresponding smoothed values also appear each month in *CQ's* "Propagation" column.

While sunspots are now under daily scrutiny by the

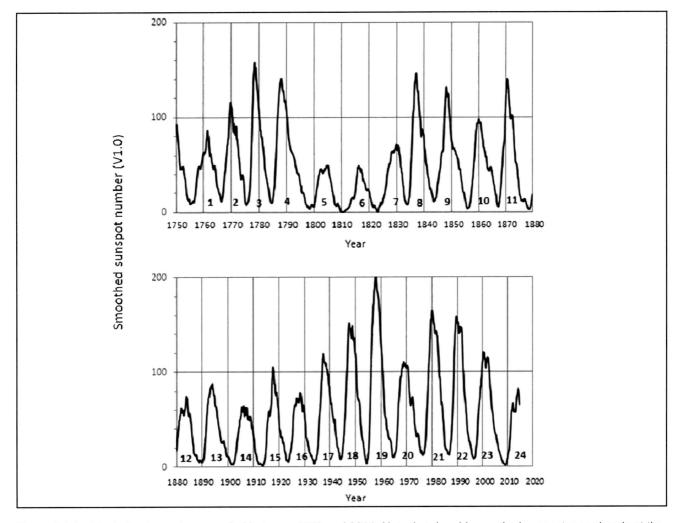

Figure 2.1 A plot of all solar cycles recorded between 1750 and 2014. Note that the old smoothed sunspot record ends at the end of 2014. The new smoothed sunspot record also goes back to the beginning, but continues to the present.

giant telescopes of dozens of solar observatories throughout the world, large sunspots often can be seen with the naked eye, **provided that a special aluminized Mylar filter, or some other suitable ray filter (e.g., a welder glass shade #14) is used to protect the eye's retina from serious damage by the sun's rays. Under no circumstances should the sun be viewed with the naked eye.**

Occasionally, at sundown or when light haze or fog obscures the sun's rays, large sunspots may be seen, often accidentally, without use of a telescope or sun filter. Such was the case in London some years ago, where the *Daily Telegraph* and *Morning Post* reported that thousands of persons were able to see two enormous spots on the face of the sun during a foggy sunset. It no doubt was due to accidental occurrences of this sort that history recorded the sightings of

sunspots by the Chinese, Greeks, and Egyptians more than 1000 years before the invention of the telescope.

Sunspots and the Ionosphere

From a radio communications viewpoint, perhaps the greatest discovery concerning sunspots was made during the early 1930s, when Edison Pettit and his associates at the Mount Wilson Observatory found a direct relationship between the smoothed sunspot number and the intensity of ultraviolet energy radiated by the sun.

Beginning in 1924, Dr. Pettit undertook daily systematic measurements of the intensity of ultraviolet radiation emanating from the sun. During the years from 1924 through 1928, he found a steady increase in the ultraviolet level as the smoothed sunspot numbers increased. After 1928, when the sunspot cycle

Characteristic	Average
Sunspot minimum	New cycle begins with 12-month running smoothed sunspot number between 0 and 12; 6 is average
Ascending period to maximum value	Varies between 2.6 and 6.9 years; 4.0 years is average
Maximum values	Ranges between 49 and 201; 112 is average
Descending period from maximum to minimum	Varies between 4 and 10.2 years; 6.8 years is average
Period from minimum to maximum to minimum	Average is 10.8 years
Interval between the maxima of two adjacent cycles	Ranges from 7.3 to 17.1 years; 10.9 years is average

Table 2.1 The "average" sunspot cycle (Cycles 1-23, inclusive).

began to decline, Dr. Pettit observed a corresponding decrease in ultraviolet radiation intensity.

Because ultraviolet radiation from the sun is mainly responsible for forming the ionosphere, which makes possible shortwave radio communications over long distances, Dr. Pettit's discovery was of paramount importance. In relating the sunspot number to the intensity of ultraviolet radiation, he also was relating it to the intensity of ionization in the upper atmosphere.

The more sunspots, or plage areas, that produce emissions that cause photo-ionization of the ionosphere, the denser will be the ionosphere and the higher will be the frequencies that it will propagate. During solar maximum, frequencies over 30 MHz will be propagated; during solar minimum, nothing much above 15-20 MHz is reliable. Simply put, the HF user loses at least the upper third of his spectrum during solar minimum, and sometimes he loses as much as half.

Sunspot Cycle Behavior

Figure 2.1, based on the V1.0 smoothed sunspot numbers computed since 1749, shows the cyclic nature of this solar index. In accordance with the Zurich Observatory's cycle numbering system, the cycle that began in 1755 is shown as Cycle 1. Since that time, 23 complete cycles have occurred, with this being written at the end of Cycle 24 (predicted to end in late 2019 or early 2020.

Inspection of Figure 2.1 (updated through Cycle 24) shows that sunspot activity varies in a periodic manner, resulting in alternate minima and maxima at intervals of several years. The number of years for a complete cycle of activity – from minimum, through maximum, and back to minimum again - varies somewhat with each cycle, but has an average period close to 11 years. For this reason, the variation in sunspot activity is called the 11-year sunspot cycle. It should be noted, however, that no two cycles are exactly

alike, and some cycles are as short as 9 years and others last as long as 14 years. The last complete cycle, Cycle 23, began in May 1996 and ended in November 2008. To reiterate, at the time of this writing Cycle 24 is still ongoing.

The average cycle determined from data for the first 23 recorded cycles (as just stated, Cycle 24 is still on-going) is summarized in Table 2.1 and Figure 2.2, and will serve to orient the reader to general sunspot cycle behavior. It must be emphasized, however, that there have been rather large deviations from these average values in the characteristics of many individual cycles.

In recent years, correlation between observed solar cycle and proxy data such as radiocarbon dating of soil sediments and ancient tree rings suggests that our relatively regular 11-year solar cycle over the last 250 years may well be anomalous when viewed using proxy data that date to about 3000 BC. Other indicators of past sunspot activity include auroral observations from high-latitude monasteries in Europe.

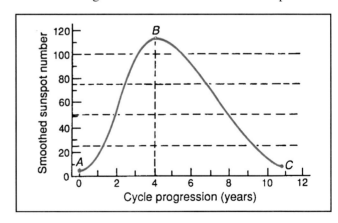

Figure 2.2 The average sunspot cycle based on the characteristics of 23 cycles which have taken place since 1750. At A, the minimum is 6. At B, the average maximum is 112. At C, the end of the cycle is at 10.8 years. The average time interval for the rising portion (A to B) is at 4.0 years while the average time interval for the descending portion (B to C) is 6.8 years.

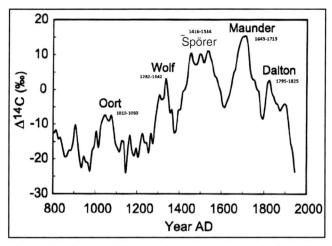

Figure 2.3 Carbon-14 in tree rings. A positive delta indicates a grand solar minimum period. A negative delta indicates a grand solar maximum period.

Most recently there is evidence that between 1645 and 1715, there was virtually no sunspot activity at all, and certainly there is no evidence for a solar cycle. This period was the early era of using telescopes for solar observation, and at first, this lack of sunspot observations was attributed to an inconsistent measurement program and poor equipment. It was Walter Maunder, upon reviewing the historical data in the 1890s, who pointed out that an extended minimum, in fact, had occurred. This period is now known as the "Maunder Minimum" [reference 4].

It also has been suggested that there was another extended sunspot minimum between approximately 1416 and 1534, called the "Spoerer Minimum." Radiocarbon dating indicates that there was a 200-year maximum between 1140 AD and 1340 AD (the "Medieval Maximum") and another 140-year maxi-

mum between 1 AD and 140 AD (the "Roman Maximum"). Compared to the last 5000 years, the last 23 solar cycles have been well behaved indeed! Figure 2.3 shows grand minimums and grand maximums from 800 AD to the mid-1900s.

The following sections will discuss the last six solar cycles and the highlights of each. Figure 2.4 shows the last six solar cycles in terms of the V1.0 data - Cycle 19 through the present one, Cycle 24. While Cycle 19 still is acknowledged as the "granddaddy" of modern solar maxima, Cycles 21 and 22 proved to be very exciting, too. Some of the events associated with the current cycle will be discussed in the section on Cycle 24.

2.2   Cycle 19 (1954-1964)

Solar Cycle 19 peaked during March 1958, and it exhibited the most intense level of solar activity ever recorded. It is this cycle to which all other cycles are at least qualitatively compared, and so, we briefly review Cycle 19 before proceeding with the review of the other cycles.

Unprecedented Activity

Cycle 19 officially began during April 1954, with a smoothed sunspot number of 3.3 (see Figure 2.5).

By November 1956, the cycle had already exhibited intense activity and had exceeded the previous record count of 159 that was recorded in May 1778 during Cycle 3. In the months that followed, solar activity continued to increase, and by March 1958, the smoothed sunspot number had reached an unprecedented peak of 201.

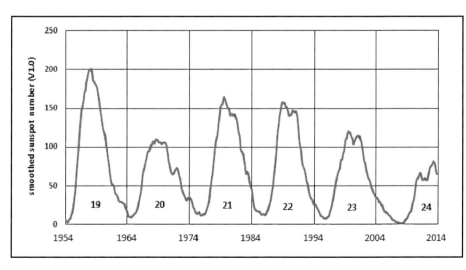

Figure 2.4 The last six solar cycles (19 thru 24).

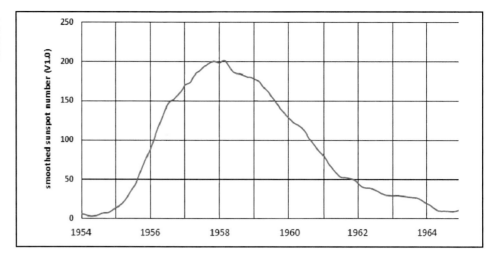

Figure 2.5 Sunspot Cycle 19, April 1954 to October 1964. The record-breaking peak occurred in March 1958 at a smoothed sunspot number of 201 (V1.0).

As a result of the unusually high level of solar activity, high-frequency radio conditions were better during the years 1957-1959 than they had ever been in the entire history of radio. Also in this time period, work in ionospheric sciences accelerated. The International Geophysical Year (IGY) in 1957 coordinated a global campaign to measure and correlate ionospheric characteristics. At about the same time, technology in electronics expanded in all directions, giving users of the shortwave spectrum the equipment they needed to exploit the exceptionally good propagation conditions. Together with the period of unprecedented activity, there came a new generation of HF users.

Once In a Lifetime Conditions

Because of the intense ionization of the ionosphere during the period 1957-1959, shortwave radio conditions - especially on the 20-, 15-, 11-, 10-, and 6-meter bands - were exceptionally good. Worldwide propagation was observed on 6 meters, while the 20-meter band was open around the clock. Ten meters was open from sunrise to sunset (and beyond, in some cases), and 25 watts of power on AM radiotelephone was sufficient to work the world. Then, too, direct reception of European and Latin American TV broadcasts in the 45-65 MHz bands, while amusing, caused considerable interference in the United States. Such conditions obviously occur very seldom ... perhaps only once in a lifetime.

The Decline

From its peak in March 1958, Cycle 19 slowly declined towards its minimum. It reached this point in

October 1964 with a smoothed sunspot number of 10. The cycle had lasted 11.5 years, and it had exhibited the most intense level of solar activity ever recorded since regular telescopic observations of the sun were begun in 1749. Even before Cycle 19 ended, however, the first spots of the new cycle were observed on the face of the sun (specifically, in September 1963), and they signaled the beginning of Cycle 20 activity.

2.3   Cycle 20 (1964-1976)

The 20th sunspot cycle recorded since solar records have been kept on a regular basis began in October 1964. Reaching its peak in November 1968, this cycle gave indications of paralleling the average sunspot cycle (Cycles 1-19) more closely than did any previous cycle. During its decline, however, Cycle 20 exhibited a prolonged decay in activity, and it continued on until June 1976, somewhat longer than the average cycle. Cycle 20's life span was 11.8 years.

Cycle 20 - The Beginning

Cycle 20 officially began during October 1964 with a smoothed sunspot number of 10. Cycle 20 began at a slightly higher-than-average level of solar intensity, and that it followed the average cycle almost exactly until reaching its peak in late 1968. In fact, the first four years of Cycle 20 paralleled that of the average cycle more closely than did any previous cycle.

Cycle 20 reached its peak during November 1968 with a smoothed sunspot number of 111. This peak is considerably lower than the peak values of the previous two cycles. Cycle 19, for example, soared to a record-breaking maximum of 201 during March

1958, while Cycle 18 peaked during June 1947, with a smoothed sunspot number of 152.

Unusual Behavior at the Maximum

Because its behavior paralleled so well the average sunspot cycle, it was expected to continue to follow the average cycle; that is, it was expected to decline in 6.7 years and to reach a minimum by July 1975. Such was not to be the case.

By July 1970, Cycle 20 had established a new type of record: it had stood practically still for 17 months! Specifically, the cycle hovered at the 106 mark, plus or minus 2, between March 1969 and July 1970. Yearlong plateaus have occurred occasionally during previous cycles, but always at lower levels of activity. For example, the longest plateau on record took place during Cycle 5, when the solar index remained in the 40s for more than three years, from January 1802 through mid-1805. Then, too, between December 1827 and April 1829, the cycle remained practically constant at 62. More recently a plateau occurred between November 1926 and December 1927, when solar activity remained at the 70 mark, plus or minus 2. Only once previously, however, has a year-long plateau occurred at a relatively high level of solar activity, and that was during Cycle 11, when a smoothed sunspot count around 100 was recorded during 1872.

By mid-1970, Cycle 20 had distinguished itself by displaying the longest, highest plateau ever recorded in the history of solar observations.

The plateau near Cycle 20's maximum ended in July 1970, when the running smoothed sunspot numbers started to decline once again. However, the

unexpected high solar activity observed during 1970 was most welcome, and it provided a continuation of the excellent HF propagation conditions observed during 1968 and 1969. During 1970, the 10-meter band continued in full bloom, with excellent DX openings to almost every corner of the world during the daylight hours of all but the summer months. Excellent worldwide conditions also were observed on 15 meters from shortly after sunrise through the early evening hours throughout almost the entire year. Twenty meters continued to be an around-the-clock DX band, with excellent openings possible at almost any hour. Good DX conditions during the hours of darkness also were observed on 40 and 80 meters throughout most of the year, and even some good 160-meter openings were recorded during the hours of darkness and the sunrise period, particularly during the winter, spring, and fall months.

The Decline

Between July 1970 and July 1971, Cycle 20's activity dropped off considerably - by a count of 40 in a span of one year. With this decline came some noticeable changes in shortwave radio propagation conditions. For example, regular F2-layer DX openings on 10 meters decreased considerably, and although excellent DX conditions held up on 15 meters, especially during the hours of daylight, the band opened less often than during the previous years of higher solar activity. A decrease in band openings also was observed on 20 meters during the hours of darkness, but the band continued to hold up well for daytime DX openings.

Then, in September 1971, Cycle 20 took another

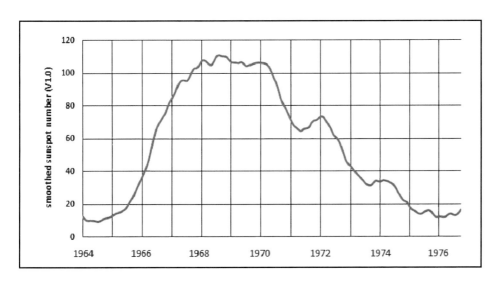

Figure 2.6 Sunspot Cycle 20, October 1964 to June 1976. The cycle began with a smoothed sunspot number of 10, peaked during November 1968 at a level of 111 and ended June 1976 with a smoothed sunspot number of 12.

strange turn - this time upward again! Solar activity increased from 65 in August 1971 to 73 in May 1972 before the count began to decline again (see Figure 2.6).

From May 1972 through December 1973, the 12-month running smoothed sunspot numbers declined steadily from a count of 73 to 32. Then, Cycle 20 hit another plateau, this one lasting from September 1973 through September 1974, a one-year period during which time solar activity remained practically constant at 33, plus or minus 2. By October 1974, the cycle once again began to decline, but very, very slowly. At times it stalled for a month or two, and at other times, it reversed direction and increased slightly.

Finally, in June 1976, Cycle 20 reached its minimum level of activity with a smoothed sunspot number of 12. This minimum level established a new record: it was the highest level of minimum activity ever recorded in the 225 years that sunspot records had been kept at the Swiss Federal Observatory. The lifespan of Cycle 20 was 11.8 years, one year longer than the average cycle.

Cycle 20 Summary

The smoothed sunspot values for Cycle 20 are plotted in Figure 2.6. Cycle 20 will be recorded as one of the most unusual cycles in the historical record because of its many plateaus and its unusually high level of minimum activity.

2.4   Cycle 21 (1976-1986)

Sunspot Cycle 21 started in June 1976 at a count of 12. During the minimum, scientists around the world made forecasts of the expected level of the next maximum. Early on, some scientists were forecasting a very low maximum smoothed sunspot number of approximately 50. Then, in 1976, Dr. Jay Hill at the Naval Ocean Systems Center in San Diego, California, working with Dr. Adolf Paul at ITS, Boulder, Colorado, predicted that the maximum for Cycle 21 would be substantially higher, somewhere in the range around an SSN of 150 [reference 5]. Predictions for Cycle 21 became an extremely controversial subject until independent studies in the U.K. and the U.S.S.R. produced essentially the same results as those developed by Hill and Paul. As history shows, these predictions were correct.

Cycle 21, shown in Figure 2.7, was 10.3 years long.

The rise, from June 1976 to the maximum SSN of 165 in December 1979, took 43 months. Sunspot numbers greater than 100 generally produce good propagation conditions over the entire HF band, and the activity of Cycle 21 was no exception! Ten meters was open almost every day, and virtually from sunrise to sunset in the fall and winter months. In fact, during this period, active DXers found daylight conditions superb on everything from 20 meters to 6 meters. Even if Cycle 21's numbers were not as high as those of Cycle 19, conditions were still excellent. Cycle 21 produced a maximum over which the SSNs were above 100 for 50 months, above 120 for 41 months, and above 150 for 17 months. Transpolar paths were especially reliable in the period 1979-1981. There were no really major sustained periods of solar disturbances, and when this is the case, HF propagation is excellent most of the time.

The only major plateau during Cycle 21 occurred between December 1980 and December 1981, when the sunspot number stalled at between 138 and 143

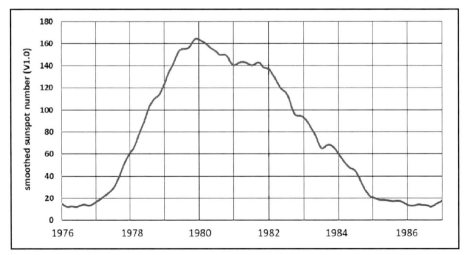

Figure 2.7 Sunspot Cycle 21, June 1976 to September 1986. The cycle began with a smoothed sunspot number of 12, peaked during December 1979 at a level of 165 and ended September 1986 with a smoothed sunspot number of 12.

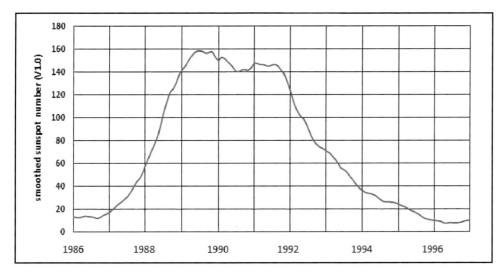

Figure 2.8 Solar Cycle 22, September 1986 to May 1996. The cycle began with a smoothed sunspot number of 12, peaked during June 1989 at a level of 158 and peaked again in January 1991, ended May 1996 with a smoothed sunspot number of 8.

(not a bad place to stall for 12 months!). In February 1982, the decline started from a SSN of 133, and the count steadily dropped over the next 52 months to the minimum of 12 in September 1986.

There were several large proton events during this cycle's maximum, although nothing that rivaled the August 1972 event (still considered a benchmark solar disturbance). However, manned space travel, such as the Apollo missions, had subsided, and there were few satellites in geostationary orbits. High frequency communications were falling from favor with the military, who opted instead for satellite communications, and interest in the space and ionospheric sciences was starting to wane. This solar maximum, however, was enjoyed by radio amateurs, by CBers and by short-wave broadcasters and their listeners. Between 1979 and 1982, Navy scientists in San Diego monitored and recorded the DL0IGI beacon on 10 meters. Review of these old strip charts indicates that during this period there were few times when it could not be heard, indicating stable and quiet conditions.

2.5   Cycle 22 (1986-1996)

Solar Cycle 22 will go on record as something of an enigma as far as these cycles go. It originally was predicted to have a maximum that probably would not exceed 100. But it did, and not just once, but twice! It had two peaks - the highest in June, July, and August 1989 with an SSN of 158, and a second peak in early 1991 at a count of 148. Overall, Cycle 22 had a volatile, broad maximum in which the smoothed sunspot numbers remained over 130 for 38 months. The decline of Cycle 22 began in November

1991, and the minimum occurred in May 1996. Figure 2.8 shows Cycle 22.

Cycle 22-The Beginning

Cycle 22 began in September 1986 with a sunspot number of 12. The rise took place over the next 33 months, until the first of two peaks occurred in June 1989 at an SSN of 158. The cycle's ascent was smooth, with amateurs starting to experience good band openings on 10 and 15 meters by mid-1988.

An Exciting Maximum

The twelve-month running smoothed sunspot numbers for Cycle 22 remained over 150 until April 1990, when they dipped into the low 140s for the remainder of the year. In January 1991, a second peak occurred, with the count rising to 148. It hovered in the mid-140s until November 1991, when the cycle decline abruptly commenced. Propagation conditions during this 40-month maximum were both exciting and volatile. While Cycle 19 was the most spectacular with respect to the sunspot numbers, Cycle 22 will be remembered as the most unpredictable and turbulent. Throughout its maximum it produced a record number of major solar disturbances, with one in 1989 (discussed in Chapter 1) leading the way. Monthly mean sunspot numbers varied wildly. For example, in June 1990, the monthly mean sunspot number dipped to around 105. It rose to 149 in the following month, and peaked in August 1990 with a monthly mean sunspot number of 200. Whereas the rise and fall of Cycle 21 was relatively smooth, with its peak accurately predicted by many

Figure 2.9 Solar Cycles with two peaks (Cycles 22, 23 and 24) are due to asymmetric sunspot generation in the two solar hemispheres.

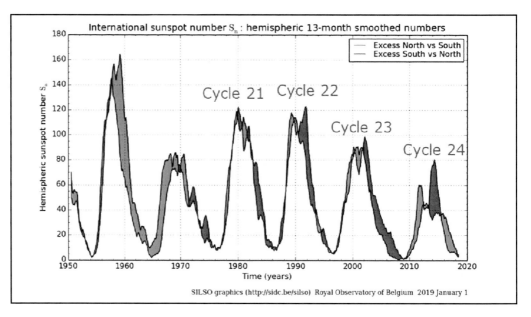

scientists, Cycle 22 was marked with large variations in monthly mean sunspot numbers.

Cycle 22 peaked during an era when the world had placed a lot of reliance on modem satellite communications in general and on space systems parked in geostationary orbit in particular. It is this orbit where there is no protection from solar radiation hazards. Initially, the susceptibility of modem communications to solar disturbances was thought to have diminished because there was less use of the narrow-bandwidth, disturbance-prone HF spectrum. However, in eliminating one vulnerability to solar disturbances, the modern communicator now was faced with a new one: space radiation hazards.

The Decline

Cycle 22 bottomed out in May 1996, and it will be remembered as the first in recorded history with a pronounced second peak. The cause of two peaks appears to be the two solar hemisphere not working in concert in generating sunspots. The first peak of Cycle 22 was the result of the northern solar hemisphere producing the most sunspots. The second peak was the result of the southern solar hemisphere producing the most sunspots. This can be seen in Figure 2.9, and shows subsequent cycles (Cycles 23 and 24) also exhibiting a pronounced second peak. Why the solar hemispheres are not working in concert is not understood.

2.6   Cycle 23 (1996-2008)

Cycle 23 turned out to be an average solar cycle in

terms of its amplitude. Beginning in mid-1996, it reached a maximum of 121 in April 2000.

But then, Cycle 23 took a dip and attained a second peak in November 2001 after a dip to about 100 in early 2001. The second peak was slightly smaller than the first peak – it was at a smoothed sunspot number of 116.

The second peak in late 2001 was fortuitous for high-band propagation. In fact, fall and winter in the northern hemisphere produce the highest MUFs in the northern hemisphere (the CQWW DX contests in October and November are timed for a reason!). Ten meter and 6 meter F2 propagation was excellent during this second peak.

After the second peak, Cycle 23 declined to solar minimum, with a smoothed sunspot number of 2 in November 2008. Figure 2.10 shows the progress of Cycle 23.

2.7   Cycle 24 (2008-2019)

Cycle 24 was extremely interesting with respect to the predictions for it. Solar scientists split pretty much down the middle – some believed it was going to be a small cycle (a smoothed sunspot number of about 90) and some believed it was going to be a large cycle (a smoothed sunspot number of about 140). This resulted, initially, in two predictions carried forth by the solar community.

What broke the tie was the length of the solar minimum between Cycles 23 and 24. For the past five solar minimums, the time below a smoothed sunspot

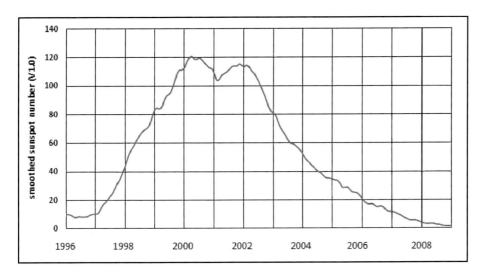

Figure 2.10 Solar Cycle 23, May 1996 to November 2008. The cycle began with a smoothed sunspot number of 8, peaked during April 2000 at a level of 121, peaked again in November 2001 at 116 and ended in November 2008 with a smoothed sunspot number of 2.

number 20 has been about 2 years. Thus, amateur radio operators were spoiled by short solar minimums. However, the solar minimum period between Cycles 23 and 24 exceeded 2 years in length, and it eventually lasted almost 5 years.

This brought solar scientists together, as history shows that the longer the solar minimum duration, the more likely the next maximum will be small. They now agreed that Cycle 24 was going to be a small cycle. Indeed it was. This was the smallest cycle observed in the past 100 years.

As was the case with Cycles 22 and 23, Cycle 24 had a second peak of 82 in early 2014. Again, 10- and 6-meter F2 propagation was excellent during this second peak. And to reiterate, solar scientists do not completely understand what a double peak means in terms of forecasting future solar cycles.

Figure 2.11 shows the progress of Cycle 24 in terms of the V1.0 and V2.0 sunspot numbers.

2.8 Solar Flux

Sunspots have been observed telescopically for more than 300 years, and daily records are available for observations made since the mid-20th century. Today sunspots are observed daily from a worldwide network of solar observatories. While the telescope at each participating observatory is carefully calibrated against a standard, results can vary between observatories because the measurements are strongly dependent on observer interpretation and experience, and on the visibility conditions in the Earth's atmosphere above the observing site. To compensate for differences, the daily international sunspot number is computed by the Royal Observatory of Belgium as a weighted average of

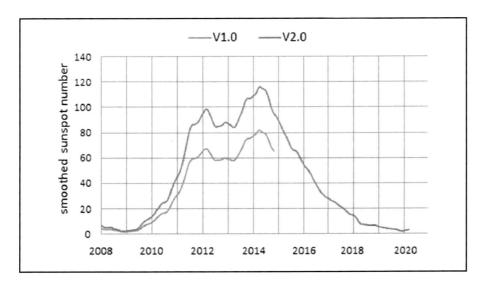

Figure 2.11 Solar Cycle 24, November 2008 and still ongoing. Cycle 24 began in November 2008 at a smoothed sunspot number of 2, peaked during February 2012 at a level of 67, peaked again in April 2014 at 82 and ended in December 2019.

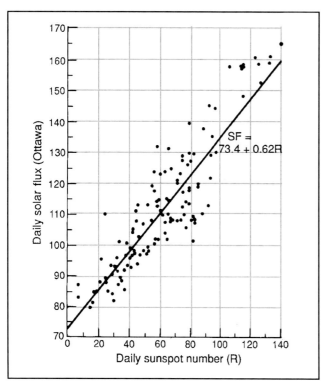

Figure 2.12 Daily solar flux versus daily sunspot number for April-May 1972, 1973.

measurements made from the network of participating observatories.

In addition to cosmic and ultraviolet radiation, the Sun is a massive generator of radio energy in the microwave range. This radio energy, or solar flux, changes gradually from day to day. These emissions are caused by a variety of phenomena in the solar atmosphere, including the random collisions of electrons.

Shortly after World War II, scientists found that changes in the level of solar flux were closely asso-ciated with the number and size of sunspot groups on the face of the sun. Using sophisticated and sensitive receiving equipment, with huge, high-gain antennas beamed towards the sun, many observatories throughout the world now measure solar flux levels on about a dozen selected frequencies between approximately one meter and one centimeter in wavelength. Canadian scientists have been leaders in this field, and they have measured the solar flux on 2,800 MHz (or 10.7 cm) daily at 1700 UTC since February 1947. Observations now are conducted at the Dominion Radio Astrophysical Observatory located at Penticton, British Columbia.

Solar flux measurements are more consistent, con-siderably less variable, and more objectively deter-mined than are the counts derived from telescopic viewing of sunspots by humans. There is a very close correlation between solar flux and old sunspot num-bers. Figure 2.12 shows the relationship between daily sunspots and daily 10.7 cm solar flux based on a long period of measurements.

Based on the data in Figure 2.12, a best-fit trend line to the relationship between the daily solar flux (SF) and the daily sunspot count (R) is linear:

$$SF = 73.4 + 0.62R \qquad \text{Equation 3}$$

But as can be seen in Figure 2.12, the actual val-ues in the plot do not give a unique mapping of a solar flux value to a sunspot number. For example, at a daily solar flux of 110, the daily sunspot number could be anywhere from 25 to 85. The difference in propagation between a sunspot number of 25 and a sunspot number of 85 would likely be significant.

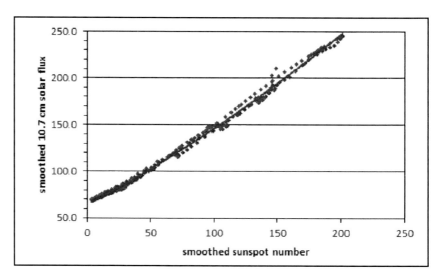

Figure 2.13 Smoothed solar flux versus smoothed sunspot number for August 1947 through December 2000. The trend line is a 2nd order polynomial.

A much better relationship between these two parameters uses smoothed values (smoothed 10.7 cm solar flux F_{12} and the smoothed sunspot number R_{12}). See Figure 2.13.

Note that a smoothed solar flux number maps more uniquely to a smoothed sunspot number. For example, at a smoothed solar flux of 110, the smoothed sunspot number would only be between about 45 and 55. The following 2nd-order polynomial equation is given by Leftin [reference 6] for smoothed 10.7 cm solar flux versus smoothed sunspot number.

$$F_{12} = 63.75 + 0.728R_{12} = 0.00089R_{12}^{2}$$

Equation 4

Again, remember: here we are working here with the *old* sunspot numbers (V1.0).

During low periods of solar activity, the flux never falls to zero because the sun emits some radio energy at all wavelengths, even when there are no visible sunspots. The lowest daily flux since 1947, as measured at a Canadian observatory, was 62.6 units on 3 November 1954. The highest observed value was 457.0, which occurred on 7 April 1947.

Solar flux measurements also have the advantage that they are broadcast daily at 18 minutes past each hour over National Institute of Standards and Technology (NIST) radio station WWV located in Colorado, and at 45 minutes past each hour from station WWVH located in Hawaii [reference 7]. Solar flux is rapidly becoming the favored measure of solar activity for use in preparing shortwave propagation predictions and forecasts because it is a more sensitive and objective measure of solar activity and because it

is more readily available to the general public than is the daily sunspot number. How solar flux indices and other propagation data transmitted by WWV and WWVH can be used to prepare updated shortwave propagation forecasts and predictions will be discussed in greater detail in Chapter 5.

Despite the increasing use of solar flux units to describe solar activity, telescopic observations of sunspots will continue. Solar flux data do not have the 300-year link with the past that sunspot numbers have. To keep that record unbroken and to provide additional solar and other solar-related cyclic data, sunspots will continue to be studied and counted by observatories throughout the world.

One last comment is in order. Both sunspots and 10.7 cm solar flux are *proxies* for the true ionizing radiation, which is in the range of wavelengths of 0.1 to 100 nanometers. Note that 10.7 cm is approximately one million times longer in wavelength that 100 nanometers. From Planck's Law, this says 10.7 cm radiation is about million times less energetic than radiation at 100 nanometers. Thus 10.7 cm solar flux does not do any ionizing of atmospheric constituents.

2.9 The NEW Sunspot Numbers (V2.0)

The monthly mean and 12-month smoothed sunspot numbers discussed thus far are from the original sunspot records; that is, they are from the V1.0 dataset. Realizing that these records go back to 1749, that telescopes have improved, and that there have been different "official" observers over the centuries, in the early 1990s, solar scientists began wondering about the quality of the data. Specifically, at that time, Douglas Hoyt

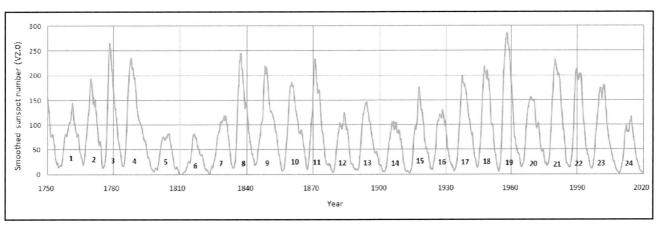

Figure 2.14 V2.0 sunspot numbers for all 24 solar cycles.

Figure 2.15 Old versus new smoothed sunspot numbers 1950-2014.

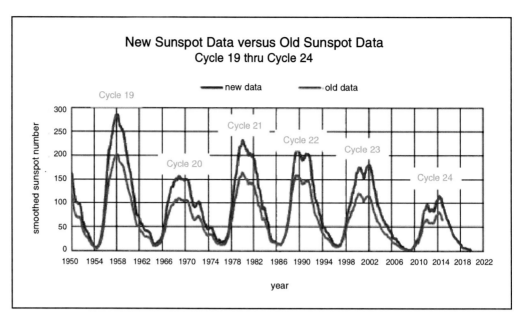

and Kenneth Schatten asked the simple question: "Do we have the correct reconstruction of solar activity?"

Their question came from the problem of counting the number of individual sunspots (as mentioned earlier, the observing conditions, the telescope used and the observer's bias play a big part in this determination). To get around individual sunspot number counts, Hoyt and Schatten devised the Group Sunspot Number, which is based solely on the number of

sunspot **groups** (sunspot areas) observed and normalized by a factor of 12 to match the Wolf numbers from 1874 to 1991. For more details on the Group Sunspot Number and the development of the new V2.0 sunspot numbers, visit http://sidc.oma.be/silso/datafiles.

The ratio of the group sunspot number to the Wolf sunspot number should ideally be 1.00. But the results of this effort showed two major times when the ratio changed significantly; these occurred when a new

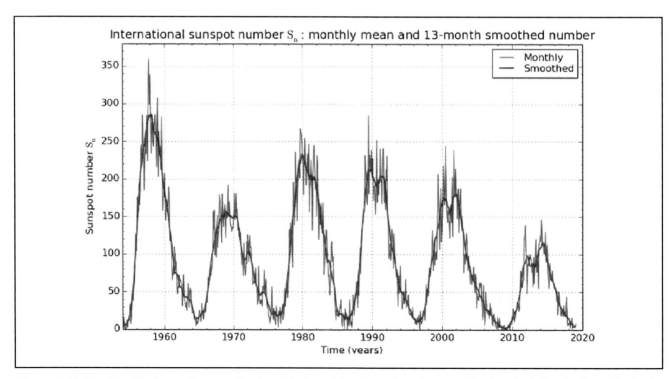

Figure 2.16 The Monthly Mean Sunspot Number (blue) and the Smoothed Sunspot Number (red) for the Last Six Cycles (http://sidc.oma.be/silso/ssngraphics).

"official" observer came onboard. These times were in 1885, when Wolfer and Brunner assumed responsibility, and again, in 1946, when Waldmeier took over.

After correcting for these issues, the ratio of the group sunspot number to the Wolf sunspot number was, for all intents and purposes, 1.00. As we've noted elsewhere, the old sunspot numbers are named Version 1.0 (V1.0) and the new sunspot numbers are named Version 2.0 (V2.0).

According to the International Astronomical Union (IAU), these data suggest the new (i.e., adjusted) record of solar activity "has no significant long-term upward trend in solar activity since 1700, as was previously indicated.

The Royal Observatory in Belgium began reporting the new V2.0 numbers on July 1, 2015. Figure 2.14 shows the entire solar cycle data to the present using the new V2.0 dataset.

Figure 2.15 compares the old V1.0 smoothed sunspot numbers to the V2.0 smoothed sunspot numbers starting in 1950 to the present.

Quite startling, isn't it?! For example, what we thought was an already extraordinary maximum of 201 in March 1958 is now seen as approaching a 12-month smoothed sunspot count of almost 300.

Finally, you may be interested in looking closely at the monthly mean and smoothed sunspot data for the last six solar cycles using the *new* V2.0 smoothed sunspot numbers. Figure 2.16 shows this data.

The new sunspot numbers are going to cause confusion with our propagation predictions. Make sure you know which version of sunspots you're using – V1.0 or V2.0. The propagation forecasts in this book were developed using a correlation between monthly median ionospheric parameters and the old V1.0 smoothed sunspot numbers. From the data in Figure 2.15, the monthly median MUF predictions may be off by up to one band now when using the new sunspot numbers (mostly around solar maximum where the difference in V1.0 and V2.0 is maximum). We will continue this discussion in Chapter 6 and show you how to compensate for the way the smoothed sunspot numbers now are reported.

2.10   Further Reading About Solar Cycles

Dr. David Hathaway, an astrophysicist formerly with NASA's Marshall Space Flight Center in Huntsville, AL and NASA Ames Research Center in Mountain View, CA, has written extensively about solar cycles.

In his 2015 document [reference 8], he reviews the solar cycle in detail. He discusses solar activity indicators that also vary in association with sunspots including; the 10.7cm radio flux, the total solar irradiance, the magnetic field, flares and coronal mass ejections, geomagnetic activity, galactic cosmic ray fluxes, and radioisotopes in tree rings and ice cores. He talks about characterizing solar cycles by their maxima and minima, cycle periods and amplitudes, cycle shape, the equatorward drift of the active latitudes, hemispheric asymmetries, and active longitudes. He reviews cycle-to-cycle variability including the Maunder Minimum, the Gleissberg Cycle, and the Gnevyshev-Ohl (even-odd) Rule. He discusses short-term variability including the 154-day periodicity, quasi-biennial variations, and double-peaked maxima.

2.11   References

1. Goodman, J. M., *HF Communications Science and Technology,* Van Nostrand Reinhold, New York, 1992

2. Galileo, "Three Letters on Sunspots," Academia dei Lincei, Rome, 1613

3. http://sidc.oma.be/silso/versionarchive

4. Eddy, J. A. (Ed), *The New Solar Physics,* West Press, Boulder, Colorado, 1978

5. Hill, J.R., "Long Term Solar Activity Forecasting Using High-Resolution Time Spectral Analysis," *Nature,* Vol. 266, No. 5598, March 10, 1977, pp. 151-153

6. M. Leftin, "Ionospheric Predictions. Volume 1 The Estimation of Maximum Usable Frequencies from World Maps of MUF(ZERO)F2, MUF(4000)F2 and MUF(2000)E, Institute for Telecommunication Science, Boulder, Colorado, September 1971.

7. https://www.nist.gov/pml/time-and-frequency-division/radio-stations/wwv/wwv-and-wwvh-digital-time-code-and-broadcast

8. Hathaway, David H., The Solar Cycle, *Living Reviews in Solar Physics,* 12 (2015), 4, 10.1007/lrsp-2015-4

2.12   Appendix 1

Tabulated here is the set of **old (V1.0)** 12-month running smoothed sunspot numbers from 1849 to 2014 (when the new sunspot numbers started being reported). These data were assembled by the Swiss Federal Observatory, Zurich Switzerland, and later, the Royal Observatory of Belgium in Brussels.

Year	Jan	Feb	Mar	Apr	May	Jun	Jul	Aug	Sep	Oct	Nov	Dec
1749							81.6	82.8	84.1	86.3	87.8	88.7
1750	89.0	90.2	92.3	92.6	88.2	83.8	83.3	81.8	78.6	75.4	72.9	69.6
1751	66.8	64.2	59.5	54.9	51.7	49.0	46.2	45.0	46.4	47.5	47.6	47.1
1752	47.2	46.4	45.3	46.4	47.8	48.0	48.2	47.8	46.0	44.1	42.2	40.9
1753	38.2	36.2	36.7	35.8	34.2	32.1	28.8	25.8	22.8	19.9	18.3	17.4
1754	17.1	15.8	13.9	13.0	12.7	12.3	12.6	13.4	14.0	13.9	12.7	10.7
1755	9.2	8.4	8.4	8.8	8.5	8.9	9.7	9.6	9.4	9.4	10.1	11.1
1756	11.5	11.4	11.3	10.6	10.7	10.6	10.3	10.9	12.4	14.1	16.0	17.1
1757	18.0	20.7	23.8	25.7	28.4	31.4	33.4	35.7	37.9	40.6	42.7	44.4
1758	46.5	46.8	47.2	48.4	47.7	47.2	48.0	48.2	47.7	46.6	45.6	46.0
1759	46.5	48.1	50.1	51.6	52.7	53.4	54.8	56.2	58.0	59.6	61.1	62.0
1760	62.5	63.3	62.8	61.8	62.0	62.7	63.0	64.4	66.0	66.8	68.8	72.4
1761	75.7	77.5	79.8	83.0	85.9	86.5	84.8	82.9	80.7	78.8	75.5	71.7
1762	68.3	64.8	62.5	60.4	59.0	59.8	61.7	60.5	58.3	56.7	55.3	53.2
1763	52.4	51.5	49.8	48.8	47.1	45.8	45.3	46.5	47.9	48.3	48.8	49.1
1764	47.8	46.9	45.4	43.0	40.8	37.8	34.9	32.0	29.9	28.8	27.3	25.8
1765	25.3	25.2	24.6	23.6	22.5	21.4	20.4	19.3	19.1	19.0	18.6	18.1
1766	16.4	14.4	12.8	12.0	11.2	11.2	12.1	13.5	14.5	15.9	17.2	18.6
1767	20.6	22.9	26.0	29.3	32.9	36.4	38.9	41.5	43.1	43.7	46.1	49.9
1768	53.0	55.4	57.8	60.6	63.5	67.4	70.7	71.5	72.1	75.1	77.2	77.8
1769	81.2	86.2	91.5	97.9	103.7	106.1	107.3	111.9	115.8	114.5	112.5	111.9
1770	111.1	110.9	109.3	105.2	102.3	101.2	98.0	91.1	85.7	84.9	88.9	93.9
1771	93.6	89.0	86.1	85.4	83.5	81.9	84.3	88.9	90.1	90.5	86.9	79.5
1772	77.3	77.6	75.4	72.8	70.7	67.8	64.6	60.1	58.3	56.7	54.3	53.3
1773	50.0	46.1	43.5	40.4	37.4	35.6	34.5	35.6	37.3	38.0	38.9	39.3
1774	38.9	38.2	37.1	35.6	34.2	31.9	28.9	24.4	19.8	16.6	13.3	10.6
1775	9.3	8.6	8.5	7.9	7.5	7.2	7.7	8.9	9.2	9.4	10.2	10.7
1776	11.0	11.7	12.9	14.5	16.3	18.5	20.8	22.8	25.2	29.6	35.6	41.0
1777	47.5	55.1	62.9	70.3	78.1	87.6	98.0	106.6	113.6	119.6	128.2	138.6
1778	144.8	148.4	151.9	156.3	158.5	156.5	151.8	151.5	153.2	152.5	148.4	141.9
1779	139.0	137.5	133.8	129.9	127.0	125.7	124.1	119.4	115.7	112.8	109.4	106.9
1780	103.5	100.0	98.2	95.5	91.3	86.9	86.0	86.2	83.4	80.4	79.2	79.5
1781	79.4	78.0	75.4	71.5	69.8	69.1	66.2	62.8	60.6	58.8	55.6	51.0
1782	47.0	44.5	42.9	42.0	40.4	38.7	37.4	36.3	36.0	35.0	33.2	31.3
1783	30.6	29.4	27.7	26.4	25.1	23.6	22.2	20.3	18.3	16.9	15.5	14.1
1784	12.3	10.8	10.0	9.7	9.8	10.0	9.9	9.6	9.5	9.7	10.5	11.9
1785	13.9	15.5	16.9	19.4	22.0	23.5	25.4	28.3	31.6	36.1	42.0	46.3
1786	49.6	54.5	60.7	66.7	72.6	79.3	86.9	93.4	97.5	100.9	104.4	107.9
1787	111.4	115.3	119.2	122.9	125.9	129.5	132.2	133.3	136.6	138.1	136.4	137.8
1788	140.7	141.2	140.4	139.1	136.6	132.8	129.9	128.7	127.6	127.3	128.3	127.3
1789	124.9	122.5	119.9	116.5	116.0	117.9	117.7	117.3	116.4	114.2	111.7	109.2
1790	106.0	103.4	101.2	99.6	97.2	92.5	88.6	84.6	81.0	79.4	77.8	75.9
1791	74.9	73.1	70.8	69.4	67.9	66.9	66.0	65.4	65.1	64.5	64.0	63.4
1792	62.2	61.9	62.2	61.8	61.3	60.5	60.0	59.5	58.8	57.6	56.2	55.4
1793	55.1	54.0	51.3	49.3	48.3	47.3	46.4	45.5	44.3	42.6	41.7	41.4
1794	40.7	40.7	40.7	39.3	39.6	40.8	40.0	38.9	37.6	36.2	34.7	32.7
1795	30.5	28.7	28.2	28.0	25.8	22.7	21.3	20.6	20.1	20.8	20.9	20.1
1796	20.2	19.8	19.0	18.8	17.8	16.6	15.7	14.6	13.3	11.6	9.9	9.5
1797	8.8	8.0	7.7	7.0	6.7	6.5	5.9	5.4	5.7	5.9	5.5	4.7
1798	4.1	3.8	3.5	3.2	3.2	3.8	4.0	4.4	5.1	5.8	6.5	7.3
1799	7.8	7.7	7.5	7.6	7.3	6.8	7.0	7.1	6.6	5.9	5.4	5.9
1800	7.2	8.8	10.1	10.9	11.5	13.2	15.3	17.0	18.5	20.4	22.8	24.3
1801	25.2	26.6	28.3	30.0	32.1	33.7	34.9	36.5	37.7	38.6	39.6	40.7

Year	Jan	Feb	Mar	Apr	May	Jun	Jul	Aug	Sep	Oct	Nov	Dec
1802	41.8	42.8	44.1	45.1	45.1	45.0	45.1	45.4	45.1	43.9	43.2	42.8
1803	42.4	41.7	40.8	41.2	42.5	43.1	42.9	42.6	43.2	45.1	45.7	45.2
1804	44.3	43.9	44.6	45.3	46.1	47.0	48.1	48.6	48.6	48.2	47.9	48.3
1805	48.9	49.2	48.8	47.1	44.9	43.1	41.3	39.8	38.4	37.2	36.3	35.2
1806	34.2	33.2	31.7	30.7	30.0	28.7	27.0	25.1	23.4	22.3	21.5	20.2
1807	18.9	17.6	16.3	14.7	13.0	11.1	9.5	8.7	8.0	7.1	6.8	7.0
1808	6.8	6.4	6.5	6.6	6.8	7.6	8.4	8.9	9.2	8.8	7.9	7.2
1809	6.7	6.1	5.3	4.6	4.0	3.0	2.2	1.6	1.1	1.0	0.8	0.4
1810	0.1	0.0	0.0	0.0	0.0	0.0	0.0	0.0	0.0	0.0	0.0	0.0
1811	0.3	0.6	0.7	1.0	1.3	1.4	1.9	2.4	2.5	2.6	2.6	2.7
1812	2.5	2.9	3.7	3.7	3.9	4.6	4.5	4.4	4.8	5.5	6.4	7.0
1813	8.1	8.6	8.7	10.1	11.5	12.0	13.1	14.1	14.3	14.8	15.1	15.3
1814	15.4	15.2	14.6	14.0	13.5	13.7	13.8	14.5	16.2	17.4	17.9	19.8
1815	22.2	24.8	27.6	29.2	30.7	33.5	35.7	37.5	41.0	44.1	46.7	47.6
1816	47.3	46.4	46.1	47.7	48.7	47.3	46.2	46.2	46.7	46.3	44.0	42.8
1817	43.2	44.5	45.0	43.2	41.6	41.1	41.0	39.5	35.0	32.4	34.1	35.3
1818	34.2	32.7	31.7	31.5	31.0	30.2	30.0	29.8	28.8	27.3	25.3	23.9
1819	24.0	23.9	23.2	22.6	23.0	23.8	23.4	23.1	23.4	23.4	23.7	23.1
1820	21.7	21.2	20.8	19.6	18.1	16.5	15.7	14.9	14.0	13.6	12.0	10.5
1821	9.4	7.8	6.8	7.2	7.5	7.0	5.7	4.7	5.0	5.6	5.8	5.9
1822	6.3	6.4	6.1	5.2	4.2	4.0	4.0	4.0	3.3	2.1	1.4	1.2
1823	0.6	0.2	0.1	0.1	0.1	0.9	2.7	4.0	4.5	5.3	6.2	6.3
1824	6.3	6.3	7.2	9.1	10.2	9.4	7.9	7.4	8.5	8.8	8.6	9.8
1825	11.7	14.0	14.9	14.3	14.3	15.7	17.1	17.8	18.5	19.9	21.5	23.1
1826	24.9	26.4	27.1	28.7	31.3	34.4	37.0	38.9	41.0	42.8	44.7	46.5
1827	46.9	47.1	48.9	50.4	51.0	50.5	50.3	51.8	52.8	53.7	55.7	58.8
1828	61.0	62.5	63.5	63.4	63.7	64.1	63.8	62.7	62.4	64.1	64.6	62.7
1829	63.2	64.8	65.0	65.2	65.7	66.6	67.3	68.7	70.1	71.1	71.5	71.1
1830	68.8	65.7	65.0	66.5	68.2	69.9	70.7	69.6	69.1	67.3	63.9	61.4
1831	60.2	60.4	59.6	57.0	53.8	50.0	47.1	46.7	45.3	42.6	41.5	41.4
1832	39.8	36.6	33.4	31.1	28.9	27.6	26.7	24.2	20.7	17.9	15.7	13.5
1833	12.1	11.7	11.7	11.3	10.3	9.3	8.3	8.1	7.9	7.5	7.3	7.4
1834	7.8	7.8	7.7	8.4	10.2	12.2	13.4	13.7	14.7	17.8	21.8	24.3
1835	27.5	31.9	37.9	44.6	50.4	55.1	60.2	67.1	73.8	80.5	86.7	93.3
1836	99.5	103.9	105.7	107.2	109.9	116.1	125.6	132.6	136.9	138.2	138.1	139.5
1837	142.8	145.8	146.9	146.4	145.3	141.5	136.5	130.9	127.4	127.2	127.8	126.2
1838	121.3	116.7	113.5	111.2	108.6	105.2	101.5	100.6	98.7	93.4	87.2	82.0
1839	79.4	80.6	85.3	87.7	87.4	86.3	84.7	83.0	82.0	81.8	82.6	83.0
1840	81.7	77.6	72.1	68.2	66.1	65.1	62.3	57.5	53.5	50.8	49.7	49.9
1841	49.0	47.0	44.6	42.0	39.4	37.4	36.6	36.1	35.4	34.6	32.2	29.0
1842	26.8	25.5	24.2	23.8	25.1	25.1	23.9	22.8	21.5	20.2	19.3	18.8
1843	18.2	17.5	16.3	14.3	12.0	10.9	10.6	10.9	11.6	12.3	12.3	11.7
1844	11.9	12.8	13.5	14.3	14.6	14.6	15.7	17.5	20.0	22.7	25.7	28.4
1845	29.9	30.7	32.0	33.7	35.7	38.5	40.6	41.5	42.6	44.0	45.0	46.9
1846	49.0	50.6	54.8	58.6	60.2	61.3	62.5	63.2	63.9	63.8	63.4	64.9
1847	66.0	69.8	75.6	83.0	91.5	96.6	102.5	109.3	113.0	116.6	120.3	123.2
1848	128.7	132.0	129.1	124.6	121.6	122.6	124.6	125.4	125.7	125.0	123.9	121.0
1849	116.4	111.2	108.2	105.4	102.2	98.9	93.0	88.0	85.7	82.7	79.4	78.2
1850	76.1	74.2	73.7	73.3	71.5	68.1	66.5	67.1	67.0	66.8	67.3	67.1
1851	66.7	66.4	65.4	64.3	63.8	64.1	64.2	62.3	60.5	60.8	60.8	59.8
1852	59.4	58.9	56.9	55.8	56.2	55.2	53.0	50.9	48.9	47.2	45.6	44.5
1853	44.4	45.0	45.2	44.0	41.9	40.0	38.0	35.9	34.3	32.7	31.4	30.1
1854	28.2	25.6	23.7	22.0	20.8	20.7	20.5	20.0	19.5	18.4	16.9	15.6

Year	Jan	Feb	Mar	Apr	May	Jun	Jul	Aug	Sep	Oct	Nov	Dec
1855	14.2	12.9	11.4	10.4	9.2	7.5	6.2	5.4	4.5	3.8	3.5	3.2
1856	3.3	3.6	3.9	3.9	3.8	4.1	4.9	5.5	5.8	6.2	7.6	9.2
1857	10.4	11.6	13.7	16.7	19.2	21.5	23.8	26.0	29.3	32.6	34.3	36.0
1858	38.6	41.7	44.8	48.5	51.5	53.6	56.7	60.7	64.3	67.6	71.7	75.5
1859	78.9	82.6	85.9	87.9	90.8	93.2	93.8	93.8	94.1	93.9	94.0	95.5
1860	97.3	98.0	97.1	95.5	94.5	95.2	95.0	93.7	93.3	94.5	93.6	90.6
1861	88.2	85.8	84.5	83.1	80.3	77.8	77.2	76.7	73.8	69.5	68.0	68.1
1862	67.7	66.7	65.3	63.7	62.5	60.8	58.5	57.5	58.2	58.6	57.6	55.3
1863	51.8	49.6	47.1	45.1	44.5	44.0	44.4	44.4	44.0	43.8	43.0	43.2
1864	44.8	46.0	46.6	46.6	47.2	47.5	46.6	45.9	44.4	43.1	42.5	41.3
1865	39.1	37.2	36.2	35.2	33.2	31.1	29.8	29.0	28.4	27.2	25.8	24.2
1866	22.8	21.0	19.4	18.7	17.9	16.8	15.0	12.1	9.9	8.7	7.8	6.7
1867	5.9	5.4	5.2	5.3	5.3	6.3	7.9	9.2	10.5	12.6	14.9	17.1
1868	19.3	21.6	24.4	27.9	32.0	35.8	39.5	43.2	46.1	47.4	50.8	57.3
1869	61.7	64.9	68.2	69.4	70.1	72.5	74.7	77.7	84.3	93.6	101.6	105.7
1870	109.9	116.1	121.5	127.4	133.9	137.9	139.4	140.3	140.1	139.6	138.5	135.4
1871	132.3	129.3	125.1	120.4	116.3	112.9	110.9	110.3	107.8	103.0	98.9	98.1
1872	98.9	98.3	99.0	101.0	101.9	101.9	101.9	101.6	101.5	100.8	97.3	92.1
1873	87.8	85.1	81.3	76.2	71.5	67.7	65.2	62.3	58.3	54.3	52.4	52.0
1874	51.7	51.5	50.4	49.1	47.4	45.5	42.7	39.0	36.7	36.1	34.6	32.6
1875	29.7	25.4	22.4	20.5	19.1	17.8	17.0	16.7	16.3	15.1	13.7	12.5
1876	11.7	11.5	11.6	12.0	11.7	11.3	11.7	11.8	10.8	10.6	11.8	13.1
1877	13.2	12.7	12.9	12.9	12.7	12.7	11.5	10.6	10.3	9.5	8.2	7.2
1878	6.6	6.1	5.4	4.7	4.0	3.5	3.3	3.0	2.4	2.3	2.5	2.2
1879	2.5	3.2	3.7	4.2	5.1	5.7	7.0	9.0	10.9	12.3	13.7	15.8
1880	17.7	19.8	23.9	27.6	29.7	31.3	32.8	34.4	36.8	39.5	41.6	43.6
1881	47.0	49.7	49.6	49.9	51.8	53.6	54.7	55.7	57.0	59.5	62.2	62.4
1882	60.5	58.4	57.8	57.8	58.8	59.8	60.3	60.0	58.0	56.5	54.5	54.5
1883	57.2	58.9	58.9	59.8	60.8	62.2	64.9	67.9	71.4	73.0	74.2	74.6
1884	72.4	71.7	72.5	71.4	67.9	64.7	61.5	58.8	56.6	54.2	53.6	55.2
1885	57.1	57.4	56.2	54.9	54.3	53.0	51.4	49.0	47.4	47.2	45.0	40.9
1886	37.0	34.1	32.0	30.0	27.4	25.8	24.6	23.3	20.5	16.8	14.8	13.9
1887	13.1	13.0	12.6	12.0	12.1	12.7	13.2	13.0	12.9	13.0	12.4	11.5
1888	10.3	8.6	7.9	7.8	7.8	7.3	6.3	5.8	5.8	5.8	5.5	5.3
1889	5.5	6.5	7.2	7.1	6.7	6.2	6.4	6.3	5.9	5.7	5.7	5.6
1890	5.4	5.0	5.0	5.8	6.6	7.0	7.4	8.6	9.8	10.8	13.1	16.5
1891	20.5	23.4	26.0	29.2	32.2	34.6	37.9	42.5	46.4	50.0	53.7	56.5
1892	58.4	62.0	65.2	66.4	68.1	71.0	73.2	73.3	73.9	75.3	76.3	77.1
1893	78.1	79.8	81.6	82.6	83.4	84.5	85.4	86.3	86.2	85.3	85.8	86.8
1894	87.9	86.2	83.2	82.6	81.6	79.4	77.2	75.6	75.3	75.4	73.8	71.3
1895	67.7	65.2	64.8	64.2	63.5	63.5	62.5	60.7	59.9	58.2	55.1	52.5
1896	51.5	49.6	48.0	46.6	44.5	43.0	42.3	41.6	39.5	38.0	37.1	35.3
1897	33.0	32.0	31.2	30.1	28.3	26.6	25.8	25.7	26.3	26.0	25.6	26.3
1898	26.0	25.6	25.4	25.7	27.5	27.6	26.3	24.7	22.7	21.9	21.1	20.3
1899	20.4	19.4	17.1	15.1	13.2	12.2	11.7	11.5	11.2	10.9	11.3	11.3
1900	10.7	10.5	10.6	10.6	10.4	9.9	9.1	8.2	7.6	6.8	5.9	5.4
1901	4.8	4.4	3.9	3.2	2.8	2.8	3.0	3.1	3.3	3.6	3.3	2.8
1902	2.7	2.7	3.1	3.9	4.7	5.0	5.2	6.0	6.7	7.9	9.5	10.6
1903	12.3	14.5	15.8	16.9	19.3	22.5	25.4	26.6	27.9	29.6	31.4	33.5
1904	35.5	37.7	39.7	41.1	41.5	41.6	42.9	46.4	49.8	50.4	50.6	51.3
1905	52.5	53.5	54.5	56.6	60.5	63.4	63.1	60.4	58.5	59.5	60.6	61.6
1906	63.4	64.2	63.8	61.3	55.9	53.5	55.1	59.6	62.7	62.4	61.7	60.1
1907	56.9	55.0	56.4	59.6	62.5	62.8	60.5	55.8	51.4	50.3	50.4	50.6
1908	50.5	51.6	53.2	51.9	49.9	48.9	49.3	50.5	52.6	53.1	51.9	50.6
1909	49.4	46.4	41.6	40.7	42.2	43.3	42.6	40.7	38.2	35.4	33.8	32.8

Year	Jan	Feb	Mar	Apr	May	Jun	Jul	Aug	Sep	Oct	Nov	Dec
1910	31.5	30.1	29.1	27.7	24.7	20.6	17.6	15.7	14.2	14.0	13.8	12.8
1911	12.0	11.2	10.0	7.5	6.0	5.9	5.6	5.1	4.6	4.0	3.3	3.1
1912	3.2	3.0	3.1	3.4	3.4	3.4	3.7	3.9	3.8	3.5	3.2	2.8
1913	2.6	2.5	2.2	1.8	1.7	1.5	1.5	1.5	1.6	2.4	3.3	4.0
1914	4.6	5.0	5.8	6.5	7.4	8.8	10.4	12.9	16.1	18.6	20.7	24.3
1915	29.4	34.8	38.9	42.3	45.3	46.9	48.3	49.8	51.5	53.9	56.9	58.6
1916	57.8	55.6	54.0	53.7	54.6	56.3	58.3	60.2	62.1	63.3	65.1	68.7
1917	73.4	81.2	89.7	94.1	96.3	100.7	104.8	105.4	104.2	103.5	102.2	98.3
1918	95.5	92.8	88.5	87.0	87.0	83.5	78.6	77.2	77.5	76.1	75.4	78.0
1919	78.4	75.2	72.8	70.4	67.4	64.6	63.7	62.8	61.9	60.5	56.7	51.4
1920	46.8	43.2	40.3	39.4	38.7	37.9	36.8	34.9	32.1	31.0	31.3	30.6
1921	31.0	31.7	31.1	29.0	27.3	26.5	25.3	24.4	25.5	25.8	24.3	22.5
1922	20.1	18.1	16.9	15.8	14.9	14.4	13.9	12.6	9.4	7.1	6.7	6.6
1923	6.4	5.9	6.0	6.6	6.9	6.4	5.6	5.6	5.7	5.8	6.8	8.1
1924	9.8	11.6	12.9	14.0	15.1	16.1	16.9	17.9	19.3	20.8	22.6	24.5
1925	25.9	27.1	29.4	32.6	36.0	40.9	47.1	51.8	55.6	57.7	58.9	60.9
1926	62.5	64.1	65.1	65.2	65.4	64.7	64.3	65.7	66.9	69.5	72.4	72.4
1927	71.9	71.7	71.7	71.7	71.6	70.5	69.1	68.4	68.2	68.4	67.7	69.0
1928	72.1	75.2	77.3	78.1	77.4	77.2	77.2	76.1	74.2	71.6	69.7	68.1
1929	66.1	64.2	61.1	58.5	59.5	62.8	64.7	64.0	62.9	61.6	60.1	57.4
1930	53.6	49.9	48.1	47.2	44.5	39.1	33.6	31.2	30.7	30.2	29.4	28.4
1931	27.6	26.9	25.9	24.3	22.6	21.6	21.1	19.7	17.5	15.9	14.8	14.8
1932	14.8	14.2	13.3	12.6	12.1	11.4	11.2	11.6	12.1	11.7	10.7	9.4
1933	8.4	7.9	7.6	7.4	6.9	6.1	5.3	4.3	3.5	3.6	4.6	5.4
1934	5.7	6.3	6.6	6.7	7.1	8.1	9.3	10.5	11.8	12.6	13.0	14.9
1935	17.6	19.5	22.0	25.6	29.9	34.1	37.9	42.0	46.5	51.3	55.1	57.2
1936	59.0	62.1	65.9	68.8	72.4	77.2	82.6	87.8	90.3	92.1	96.1	101.2
1937	107.6	113.5	116.7	119.2	119.0	115.8	113.0	111.2	110.9	110.7	110.8	109.8
1938	109.3	109.2	107.9	106.3	107.2	109.4	108.8	106.3	103.6	103.1	103.0	102.8
1939	100.1	96.9	97.4	97.9	95.2	90.9	87.5	85.5	85.5	84.3	79.6	76.3
1940	74.3	73.0	71.1	67.8	66.0	66.7	67.6	66.8	64.6	61.9	59.7	57.7
1941	56.6	54.7	52.8	52.4	51.2	48.9	47.1	47.0	47.7	49.2	50.1	47.9
1942	43.9	40.2	36.5	33.3	31.9	31.1	29.6	27.7	25.6	23.0	21.1	20.5
1943	20.2	19.9	19.6	18.8	17.5	16.5	16.0	14.4	12.5	10.8	9.2	8.6
1944	8.2	7.7	7.8	8.4	8.8	9.2	10.2	11.3	12.3	14.0	16.5	19.0
1945	21.9	23.8	25.1	28.1	31.7	33.1	34.3	38.6	43.9	48.1	52.1	56.0
1946	60.6	67.0	72.9	76.8	81.4	88.6	95.3	100.1	104.3	109.6	117.6	126.2
1947	131.7	136.8	143.4	149.0	151.8	151.7	151.2	148.9	145.5	145.7	146.2	145.3
1948	144.8	142.8	140.5	138.2	135.8	135.3	136.6	141.1	147.7	148.5	143.9	139.2
1949	136.6	134.5	133.2	133.0	134.8	136.0	134.4	130.0	124.4	121.0	119.6	118.0
1950	115.0	111.9	106.4	99.5	92.9	86.6	82.2	79.0	75.3	72.2	71.4	72.3
1951	71.7	69.5	69.8	70.7	70.2	69.8	68.6	66.3	63.3	59.2	53.0	46.8
1952	43.2	42.0	39.5	36.1	33.6	31.9	30.8	29.4	28.2	27.6	27.1	26.0
1953	24.1	21.6	19.9	18.9	17.4	15.2	12.8	11.5	11.4	10.4	8.8	7.4
1954	6.4	5.6	4.2	3.4	3.7	4.2	5.4	7.2	7.8	7.9	9.5	12.0
1955	14.2	16.4	19.5	23.4	28.8	35.1	40.1	46.5	55.5	64.4	73.0	81.0
1956	88.8	98.5	109.3	118.7	127.4	136.9	145.5	149.6	151.5	155.8	159.6	164.3
1957	170.2	172.2	174.3	181.0	185.5	187.9	191.4	194.4	197.3	199.5	200.8	200.0
1958	199.0	200.9	201.3	196.8	191.4	186.8	185.2	184.9	183.8	182.2	180.7	180.5
1959	178.6	176.9	174.5	169.2	165.1	161.4	155.8	151.3	146.3	141.1	137.2	132.5
1960	128.9	125.0	121.6	119.6	117.0	113.9	108.6	102.4	97.9	93.3	87.9	83.7
1961	80.2	74.8	68.9	64.3	60.1	55.8	53.1	52.5	52.3	51.4	50.5	48.7
1962	45.2	41.8	39.8	39.4	39.2	38.3	36.8	34.9	32.7	30.8	30.0	29.8

Year	Jan	Feb	Mar	Apr	May	Jun	Jul	Aug	Sep	Oct	Nov	Dec
1963	29.4	29.8	29.7	29.1	28.7	28.2	27.7	27.2	26.9	26.0	23.8	21.3
1964	19.5	17.8	15.4	12.7	10.8	10.2	10.3	10.2	9.9	9.6	10.2	11.1
1965	11.7	12.0	12.5	13.6	14.6	15.0	15.5	16.4	17.4	19.7	22.3	24.5
1966	27.7	31.3	34.5	37.4	40.7	44.7	50.3	56.7	63.1	67.6	70.2	72.7
1967	75.0	78.8	82.2	84.6	87.5	91.3	94.1	95.3	95.3	95.0	97.1	100.6
1968	102.6	102.9	104.7	107.2	107.6	106.6	105.2	104.8	107.0	109.9	110.6	110.1
1969	110.0	109.6	108.0	106.4	106.2	106.1	105.9	106.5	105.4	104.1	104.6	104.9
1970	105.6	106.0	106.2	106.1	105.8	105.3	103.9	101.0	97.2	93.9	89.4	84.1
1971	80.4	77.8	74.4	70.9	68.1	66.7	65.4	64.6	65.8	66.2	66.8	69.4
1972	70.8	71.2	72.4	73.4	72.9	70.5	68.2	65.5	62.2	60.6	58.7	55.1
1973	50.9	46.5	44.2	42.7	40.7	39.1	37.5	36.1	34.4	32.6	31.8	31.5
1974	32.7	34.4	34.0	33.9	34.6	34.5	34.0	33.1	32.1	30.2	27.5	25.2
1975	23.0	22.1	21.2	18.6	16.8	16.0	15.0	14.3	14.4	15.4	16.1	16.3
1976	15.2	13.2	12.2	12.6	12.5	12.2	12.9	14.0	14.3	13.5	13.5	14.8
1977	16.7	18.1	20.0	22.2	24.2	26.3	29.0	33.4	39.1	45.6	51.9	56.9
1978	61.3	64.5	69.6	76.9	83.2	89.3	97.4	104.0	108.4	111.1	113.3	117.7
1979	123.7	130.9	136.5	141.1	147.3	153.0	155.0	155.4	155.7	157.8	162.3	164.5
1980	163.9	162.6	160.9	158.7	156.3	154.7	152.8	150.3	150.1	150.2	147.7	142.7
1981	140.3	141.5	143.0	143.4	142.9	141.5	140.3	141.1	142.8	142.2	138.8	137.8
1982	137.0	133.3	129.2	124.3	119.9	117.3	115.2	109.4	101.0	95.7	94.7	94.6
1983	92.8	90.3	85.9	81.5	77.1	70.5	65.5	65.8	67.9	68.2	66.8	64.0
1984	60.2	56.4	53.1	49.8	47.5	46.5	44.2	39.6	33.9	28.9	24.7	21.7
1985	20.5	19.6	18.6	18.3	18.3	18.0	17.4	17.1	17.3	17.3	16.8	15.3
1986	13.8	13.1	13.0	13.7	14.3	13.8	13.7	13.2	12.3	13.2	14.9	16.3
1987	17.6	19.6	22.1	24.4	26.5	28.4	31.3	34.8	39.0	43.6	46.7	51.3
1988	58.2	64.6	71.3	77.5	83.8	93.7	104.3	113.7	121.2	125.3	130.4	137.6
1989	142.0	145.0	149.7	153.5	156.9	158.4	158.5	157.7	156.6	157.4	157.5	153.5
1990	150.6	152.9	152.0	149.3	147.0	143.8	140.6	140.5	142.1	142.1	141.7	143.9
1991	147.6	147.6	146.6	146.5	145.5	145.2	146.3	146.6	144.9	141.7	138.1	131.7
1992	123.7	115.4	108.2	103.3	100.3	97.1	90.7	84.0	79.5	76.4	74.4	73.2
1993	71.4	69.3	66.6	63.6	59.9	56.1	54.7	52.3	48.4	44.9	41.2	38.4
1994	36.6	34.8	34.1	33.7	32.5	30.8	28.5	26.8	26.6	26.5	26.2	25.6
1995	24.2	23.0	22.1	20.6	19.2	18.2	17.0	15.4	13.4	12.1	11.3	10.8
1996	10.4	10.1	9.7	8.5	8.0	8.5	8.4	8.3	8.4	8.8	9.8	10.4
1997	10.5	11.0	13.5	16.5	18.3	20.3	22.6	25.0	28.3	31.8	35.0	39.0
1998	43.7	48.9	53.4	56.5	59.4	62.5	65.5	67.8	69.5	70.5	73.0	77.9
1999	82.6	84.6	83.8	85.5	90.5	93.1	94.3	97.5	102.3	107.8	111.0	111.1
2000	112.9	116.8	119.9	120.8	119.0	118.7	119.8	118.6	116.3	114.5	112.7	112.0
2001	108.7	104.0	104.8	107.5	108.6	109.8	111.7	113.6	114.1	114.0	115.5	114.6
2002	113.5	114.6	113.3	110.5	108.8	106.2	102.7	98.7	94.6	90.5	85.2	82.0
2003	80.8	78.3	74.0	70.1	67.6	65.0	61.8	60.0	59.5	58.2	56.7	54.8
2004	52.0	49.3	47.1	45.5	43.8	41.6	40.2	39.2	37.5	35.9	35.3	35.2
2005	34.6	33.9	33.5	31.6	28.9	28.8	29.1	27.4	25.8	25.5	24.9	23.0
2006	20.8	18.6	17.4	17.1	17.3	16.3	15.2	15.6	15.5	14.2	12.6	12.1
2007	11.9	11.5	10.7	9.8	8.6	7.6	6.9	6.0	5.9	6.0	5.7	4.9
2008	4.2	3.6	3.3	3.4	3.5	3.3	2.8	2.7	2.3	1.8	1.7	1.7
2009	1.8	1.9	2.0	2.2	2.3	2.7	3.6	4.8	6.2	7.1	7.6	8.3
2010	9.3	10.6	12.3	14.0	15.5	16.4	16.7	17.4	19.6	23.2	26.5	28.8
2011	30.9	33.4	36.9	41.8	47.6	53.2	57.3	59.0	59.5	59.9	61.1	63.4
2012	65.5	66.9	66.8	64.6	61.7	58.9	57.8	58.2	58.1	58.6	59.7	59.6
2013	58.7	58.4	57.6	57.9	59.9	62.6	65.5	68.9	73.0	74.9	75.3	75.9
2014	77.3	78.3	80.8	81.9	80.5	79.7	78.5	75.5	70.8	67.3	65.4	

2.13 Appendix 2

Tabulated here are the **new (V2.0)** 12-month running smoothed sunspot numbers from 1749 to the present. These values are available from the file "13-month smoothed monthly total sunspot number (1/1749 –present)" found at http://sidc.oma.be/silso/datafiles.

Year	Jan	Feb	Mar	Apr	May	Jun	Jul	Aug	Sep	Oct	Nov	Dec
1749							135.9	137.9	140.2	143.8	146.4	147.9
1750	148.4	150.3	153.9	154.3	147.0	139.7	138.8	136.3	131.0	125.7	121.5	116.0
1751	111.3	106.9	99.2	91.6	86.2	81.6	77.0	75.0	77.3	79.2	79.4	78.5
1752	78.6	77.3	75.5	77.3	79.6	79.9	80.3	79.7	76.7	73.4	70.3	68.1
1753	63.6	60.4	61.1	59.7	57.0	53.4	48.1	43.0	37.9	33.2	30.4	29.0
1754	28.5	26.4	23.2	21.7	21.2	20.5	21.1	22.3	23.3	23.1	21.2	17.9
1755	15.3	14.0	14.0	14.7	14.2	14.8	16.1	16.0	15.6	15.7	16.8	18.5
1756	19.1	19.0	18.8	17.7	17.7	17.7	17.1	18.2	20.6	23.5	26.7	28.5
1757	29.9	34.6	39.6	42.8	47.4	52.4	55.7	59.5	63.2	67.7	71.2	74.0
1758	77.6	78.0	78.7	80.7	79.5	78.7	80.1	80.3	79.6	77.6	76.1	76.6
1759	77.4	80.2	83.5	86.0	87.8	89.0	91.3	93.7	96.7	99.4	101.8	103.3
1760	104.2	105.5	104.7	103.0	103.3	104.5	105.0	107.3	109.9	111.3	114.7	120.7
1761	126.1	129.2	133.0	138.4	143.1	144.1	141.3	138.2	134.5	131.3	125.8	119.6
1762	113.8	108.0	104.2	100.6	98.4	99.7	102.8	100.8	97.2	94.5	92.1	88.8
1763	87.3	85.9	83.0	81.3	78.6	76.3	75.4	77.6	79.9	80.4	81.3	81.7
1764	79.7	78.2	75.7	71.7	68.0	63.1	58.1	53.3	49.9	48.0	45.4	43.1
1765	42.2	41.9	41.1	39.2	37.4	35.7	34.0	32.1	31.9	31.6	30.9	30.2
1766	27.4	24.0	21.4	19.9	18.7	18.6	20.1	22.5	24.2	26.6	28.6	30.9
1767	34.3	38.2	43.4	48.8	54.9	60.7	64.9	69.2	71.9	72.8	76.8	83.2
1768	88.4	92.4	96.4	101.0	105.8	112.4	117.8	119.1	120.2	125.2	128.7	129.6
1769	135.4	143.7	152.5	163.2	172.8	176.8	178.9	186.4	193.0	190.9	187.5	186.5
1770	185.1	184.9	182.2	175.3	170.4	168.7	163.3	151.9	142.9	141.5	148.2	156.5
1771	156.1	148.4	143.5	142.3	139.1	136.4	140.5	148.1	150.1	150.9	144.8	132.5
1772	128.9	129.4	125.7	121.4	117.9	113.0	107.6	100.1	97.2	94.5	90.6	88.8
1773	83.4	76.9	72.4	67.3	62.3	59.4	57.4	59.4	62.2	63.3	64.8	65.5
1774	64.8	63.7	61.8	59.4	56.9	53.2	48.1	40.6	33.0	27.7	22.1	17.7
1775	15.4	14.4	14.1	13.2	12.5	12.0	12.9	14.9	15.3	15.7	16.9	17.9
1776	18.4	19.5	21.5	24.1	27.2	30.8	34.7	38.0	42.0	49.4	59.3	68.4
1777	79.2	91.8	104.9	117.1	130.2	146.0	163.4	177.6	189.3	199.3	213.7	231.1
1778	241.4	247.4	253.2	260.5	264.3	260.9	252.9	252.5	255.3	254.2	247.3	236.4
1779	231.7	229.1	222.9	216.5	211.7	209.5	206.8	199.0	192.9	188.0	182.3	178.2
1780	172.5	166.7	163.7	159.2	152.2	144.9	143.3	143.7	139.0	134.0	131.9	132.4
1781	132.2	130.0	125.6	119.2	116.3	115.1	110.4	104.7	101.0	98.0	92.6	85.0
1782	78.3	74.2	71.5	70.0	67.3	64.5	62.3	60.6	59.9	58.3	55.3	52.2
1783	51.0	49.0	46.2	44.1	41.9	39.4	37.0	33.8	30.6	28.2	25.7	23.4
1784	20.5	18.0	16.7	16.2	16.3	16.7	16.5	16.0	15.9	16.2	17.6	19.8
1785	23.1	25.9	28.1	32.4	36.7	39.2	42.3	47.2	52.6	60.1	69.9	77.2
1786	82.7	90.8	101.1	111.2	121.0	132.2	144.9	155.7	162.5	168.2	174.0	179.8
1787	185.7	192.1	198.6	204.9	209.8	215.8	220.3	222.1	227.6	230.2	227.4	229.7
1788	234.4	235.3	234.1	231.9	227.6	221.3	216.5	214.6	212.7	212.1	213.8	212.2
1789	208.1	204.1	199.8	194.2	193.3	196.4	196.1	195.5	194.0	190.3	186.1	182.0
1790	176.7	172.3	168.7	166.0	162.0	154.1	147.7	141.1	135.0	132.2	129.7	126.5
1791	124.8	121.9	118.1	115.7	113.1	111.5	109.9	109.1	108.4	107.6	106.7	105.6
1792	103.7	103.1	103.7	103.0	102.2	100.8	99.9	99.2	98.0	95.9	93.7	92.3
1793	91.9	90.1	85.5	82.2	80.5	78.9	77.4	75.9	73.9	71.0	69.5	69.1
1794	67.8	67.9	67.7	65.6	65.9	67.9	66.7	64.8	62.7	60.3	57.9	54.5
1795	50.8	47.9	47.1	46.6	43.0	37.8	35.5	34.4	33.5	34.6	34.9	33.4

Year	Jan	Feb	Mar	Apr	May	Jun	Jul	Aug	Sep	Oct	Nov	Dec
1796	33.7	33.0	31.6	31.4	29.6	27.6	26.2	24.3	22.1	19.4	16.5	15.9
1797	14.6	13.3	12.8	11.6	11.1	10.8	9.8	8.9	9.5	9.9	9.2	7.9
1798	6.8	6.3	5.9	5.3	5.4	6.3	6.7	7.3	8.6	9.7	10.8	12.1
1799	13.0	12.9	12.5	12.6	12.1	11.4	11.6	11.8	11.0	9.9	9.1	9.8
1800	12.0	14.6	16.8	18.1	19.2	21.9	25.5	28.3	30.8	34.0	38.1	40.5
1801	42.0	44.3	47.1	50.1	53.5	56.1	58.1	60.8	62.8	64.3	65.9	67.8
1802	69.7	71.4	73.4	75.1	75.2	74.9	75.2	75.6	75.1	73.1	72.0	71.3
1803	70.6	69.5	68.0	68.6	70.9	71.9	71.4	70.9	72.0	75.1	76.1	75.3
1804	73.9	73.3	74.4	75.5	76.7	78.3	80.2	81.0	80.9	80.3	79.8	80.5
1805	81.5	82.0	81.4	78.5	74.8	71.9	68.9	66.3	64.0	62.1	60.5	58.6
1806	57.0	55.4	52.8	51.2	49.9	47.8	45.0	41.9	39.1	37.2	35.8	33.7
1807	31.6	29.4	27.1	24.5	21.6	18.4	15.9	14.6	13.4	11.9	11.3	11.7
1808	11.4	10.7	10.8	11.0	11.3	12.7	14.1	14.9	15.3	14.7	13.2	12.0
1809	11.1	10.1	8.8	7.7	6.7	5.1	3.7	2.6	1.9	1.6	1.3	0.7
1810	0.1	0.1	0.0	0.0	0.0	0.0	0.0	0.0	0.0	0.0	0.0	0.0
1811	0.5	0.9	1.1	1.7	2.2	2.3	3.1	4.1	4.2	4.3	4.4	4.5
1812	4.2	4.9	6.1	6.2	6.5	7.6	7.5	7.3	7.9	9.2	10.6	11.6
1813	13.6	14.3	14.5	16.9	19.1	20.0	21.9	23.5	23.9	24.7	25.2	25.5
1814	25.7	25.3	24.4	23.3	22.6	22.8	23.0	24.2	27.0	29.0	29.8	33.0
1815	37.0	41.3	46.0	48.6	51.2	55.9	59.5	62.5	68.4	73.6	77.8	79.4
1816	78.8	77.3	76.8	79.5	81.2	78.8	77.1	77.0	77.8	77.1	73.3	71.4
1817	71.9	74.2	75.0	72.1	69.3	68.5	68.3	65.8	58.4	54.0	56.8	58.8
1818	57.0	54.6	52.9	52.6	51.7	50.3	50.0	49.7	48.1	45.6	42.3	39.9
1819	40.0	39.9	38.7	37.6	38.3	39.6	39.0	38.5	38.9	38.9	39.6	38.6
1820	36.1	35.3	34.6	32.7	30.2	27.5	26.2	24.8	23.3	22.7	20.0	17.5
1821	15.6	12.9	11.4	12.0	12.5	11.6	9.5	7.8	8.3	9.3	9.5	9.8
1822	10.4	10.6	10.1	8.5	6.9	6.6	6.6	6.5	5.4	3.4	2.4	1.9
1823	1.0	0.3	0.2	0.2	0.2	1.6	4.5	6.7	7.4	8.7	10.3	10.5
1824	10.4	10.5	12.0	15.2	17.0	15.6	13.1	12.3	14.2	14.6	14.4	16.4
1825	19.6	23.4	24.8	23.8	23.9	26.2	28.6	29.6	30.8	33.2	35.8	38.4
1826	41.4	43.9	45.1	47.8	52.1	57.2	61.6	64.8	68.3	71.3	74.5	77.5
1827	78.2	78.5	81.6	84.1	85.0	84.1	83.8	86.3	88.0	89.5	92.9	98.0
1828	101.7	104.1	105.8	105.7	106.2	106.9	106.3	104.6	104.0	106.9	107.7	104.5
1829	105.4	108.0	108.3	108.6	109.5	110.9	112.3	114.5	116.9	118.5	119.2	118.6
1830	114.7	109.5	108.3	110.9	113.7	116.4	117.9	116.0	115.1	112.1	106.6	102.4
1831	100.3	100.7	99.3	95.0	89.7	83.4	78.6	77.8	75.5	70.9	69.2	69.0
1832	66.4	61.0	55.7	51.9	48.1	46.0	44.5	40.3	34.5	29.8	26.2	22.4
1833	20.1	19.4	19.5	18.7	17.2	15.4	13.8	13.5	13.2	12.6	12.2	12.4
1834	13.0	13.0	12.9	14.1	17.0	20.4	22.3	22.9	24.4	29.7	36.2	40.4
1835	45.7	53.1	63.1	74.2	83.9	91.7	100.4	111.8	123.0	134.1	144.5	155.6
1836	165.9	173.2	176.2	178.7	183.1	193.5	209.3	221.0	228.2	230.4	230.1	232.4
1837	237.9	243.0	244.9	244.0	242.1	235.8	227.5	218.2	212.3	211.9	212.9	210.3
1838	202.1	194.5	189.1	185.3	180.9	175.4	169.2	167.7	164.6	155.7	145.4	136.8
1839	132.4	134.4	142.1	146.2	145.6	143.9	141.1	138.4	136.7	136.3	137.6	138.3
1840	136.2	129.4	120.2	113.6	110.1	108.4	103.8	95.8	89.1	84.7	82.8	83.2
1841	81.6	78.2	74.4	69.9	65.7	62.2	61.0	60.2	59.0	57.6	53.7	48.3
1842	44.6	42.4	40.3	39.7	41.8	41.8	39.8	38.0	35.8	33.7	32.2	31.3
1843	30.4	29.1	27.1	23.8	20.1	18.2	17.6	18.1	19.3	20.4	20.5	19.4
1844	19.7	21.4	22.4	23.7	24.3	24.3	26.0	29.2	33.3	37.9	42.9	47.3
1845	49.9	51.1	53.3	56.2	59.5	64.1	67.7	69.1	71.0	73.3	75.0	78.2
1846	81.7	84.4	91.3	97.8	100.3	102.1	104.2	105.4	106.5	106.3	105.7	108.2
1847	110.0	116.4	126.1	138.4	152.5	161.0	170.8	182.1	188.4	194.3	200.5	205.4

Year	Jan	Feb	Mar	Apr	May	Jun	Jul	Aug	Sep	Oct	Nov	Dec
1848	214.5	219.9	215.2	207.6	202.6	204.4	209.2	213.3	216.0	216.7	216.7	213.4
1849	207.4	200.1	196.7	193.6	189.9	186.4	176.8	167.2	162.7	157.0	150.9	148.5
1850	144.6	141.0	139.9	139.3	135.7	129.4	126.3	127.4	127.3	126.8	127.9	127.4
1851	126.6	126.1	124.3	122.2	121.2	121.7	121.9	118.3	114.9	115.4	115.5	113.6
1852	112.8	111.8	108.0	106.0	106.6	104.8	100.6	96.6	92.9	89.6	86.6	84.5
1853	84.2	85.4	85.9	83.6	79.6	75.9	72.1	68.3	65.1	62.1	59.6	57.3
1854	53.6	48.7	45.1	41.9	39.5	39.3	38.9	38.0	37.0	35.0	32.1	29.6
1855	26.9	24.5	21.7	19.7	17.5	14.2	11.8	10.3	8.5	7.3	6.7	6.0
1856	6.3	6.9	7.5	7.4	7.3	7.9	9.3	10.5	11.1	11.8	14.5	17.6
1857	19.8	22.1	26.0	31.8	36.6	40.8	45.2	49.4	55.7	62.0	65.1	68.4
1858	73.4	79.1	85.2	92.2	97.8	101.8	107.6	115.3	122.1	128.5	136.1	143.4
1859	149.8	157.0	163.1	167.0	172.4	177.1	178.1	178.1	178.8	178.4	178.5	181.5
1860	185.0	186.2	184.6	181.5	179.7	180.9	180.4	178.0	177.3	179.6	177.8	172.2
1861	167.5	163.0	160.6	157.9	152.6	147.8	146.7	145.7	140.1	132.0	129.1	129.4
1862	128.7	126.7	124.1	121.0	118.8	115.4	111.1	109.3	110.5	111.3	109.4	105.1
1863	98.5	94.1	89.4	85.7	84.5	83.5	84.3	84.3	83.5	83.1	81.7	82.0
1864	85.1	87.4	88.5	88.5	89.6	90.2	88.5	87.1	84.4	81.8	80.8	78.4
1865	74.3	70.7	68.8	66.9	63.0	59.1	56.5	55.1	53.8	51.7	49.1	46.0
1866	43.3	39.9	36.8	35.4	34.0	31.9	28.5	23.0	18.8	16.6	14.8	12.8
1867	11.3	10.3	9.9	10.0	10.0	11.9	14.9	17.0	19.1	22.4	26.2	29.8
1868	33.5	37.1	41.6	47.3	53.9	60.0	65.8	72.1	77.0	79.1	84.8	95.5
1869	103.0	108.2	113.7	115.9	117.0	120.9	124.6	129.5	140.7	156.2	169.5	176.4
1870	183.4	193.6	202.6	212.5	223.4	230.0	232.5	234.0	233.7	232.9	231.0	225.8
1871	220.7	215.6	208.7	200.8	193.9	188.2	184.9	183.9	179.7	171.8	164.9	163.6
1872	165.0	164.0	165.2	168.5	169.9	169.9	170.0	169.6	169.3	168.2	162.3	153.6
1873	146.4	142.0	135.6	127.1	119.3	112.9	108.7	103.9	97.4	90.7	87.4	86.7
1874	86.3	85.9	84.1	81.9	79.2	75.9	71.3	65.2	61.3	60.2	57.7	54.4
1875	49.6	42.5	37.5	34.2	31.9	29.8	28.4	27.9	27.3	25.2	22.9	20.9
1876	19.5	19.3	19.4	20.1	19.6	19.0	19.5	19.8	18.1	17.7	19.8	21.8
1877	22.0	21.2	21.5	21.4	21.2	21.1	19.2	17.6	17.2	15.8	13.6	12.0
1878	11.0	10.2	8.9	7.8	6.7	5.9	5.6	5.0	4.0	3.9	4.1	3.7
1879	4.1	5.4	6.2	7.0	8.4	9.5	11.6	15.1	18.3	20.5	22.9	26.4
1880	29.4	33.0	39.8	46.1	49.4	52.2	54.6	57.3	61.3	65.8	69.4	72.6
1881	78.3	82.8	82.6	83.2	86.4	89.3	91.1	92.8	95.1	99.2	103.7	104.1
1882	100.8	97.4	96.5	96.4	98.1	99.8	100.5	100.0	96.7	94.1	90.9	90.8
1883	95.4	98.2	98.2	99.6	101.3	103.7	108.2	113.1	119.0	121.7	123.7	124.4
1884	120.8	119.5	120.9	119.0	113.2	107.8	102.5	98.0	94.4	90.3	89.3	92.0
1885	95.1	95.7	93.7	91.6	90.5	88.4	85.7	81.6	79.0	78.7	75.0	68.2
1886	61.7	56.9	53.3	50.0	45.7	43.0	41.0	38.8	34.2	28.0	24.7	23.1
1887	21.9	21.7	21.0	19.9	20.2	21.2	21.9	21.7	21.5	21.6	20.6	19.1
1888	17.1	14.4	13.2	13.0	12.9	12.2	10.4	9.7	9.7	9.5	9.2	8.8
1889	9.2	10.9	12.0	11.8	11.1	10.4	10.7	10.5	9.8	9.5	9.5	9.3
1890	9.1	8.4	8.3	9.7	10.9	11.7	12.3	14.4	16.2	17.9	21.7	27.5
1891	34.1	39.0	43.3	48.7	53.7	57.7	63.2	70.8	77.3	83.5	89.5	94.2
1892	97.4	103.3	108.7	110.6	113.6	118.4	122.0	122.2	123.1	125.5	127.2	128.5
1893	130.2	133.0	136.0	137.7	139.0	140.8	142.4	143.8	143.6	142.3	142.9	144.7
1894	146.5	143.7	138.7	137.6	136.0	132.4	128.6	126.0	125.4	125.7	123.0	118.8
1895	112.8	108.7	108.0	106.9	105.8	105.9	104.2	101.2	99.9	96.9	91.9	87.5
1896	85.8	82.7	80.1	77.6	74.2	71.7	70.5	69.4	65.8	63.4	62.0	58.8
1897	55.0	53.4	52.1	50.2	47.1	44.4	43.1	42.8	44.0	43.5	42.7	43.9
1898	43.3	42.7	42.4	42.9	45.8	46.0	43.8	41.2	37.9	36.4	35.2	33.8
1899	34.0	32.3	28.5	25.2	22.1	20.3	19.5	19.1	18.8	18.2	18.9	18.8

Year	Jan	Feb	Mar	Apr	May	Jun	Jul	Aug	Sep	Oct	Nov	Dec
1900	17.9	17.6	17.7	17.7	17.5	16.5	15.2	13.7	12.7	11.3	9.8	9.0
1901	8.1	7.3	6.5	5.4	4.7	4.6	5.0	5.2	5.5	6.1	5.6	4.8
1902	4.5	4.6	5.2	6.5	7.8	8.4	8.6	10.0	11.3	13.1	15.8	17.6
1903	20.5	24.2	26.3	28.1	32.1	37.6	42.3	44.4	46.6	49.4	52.3	55.8
1904	59.1	62.7	66.1	68.5	69.1	69.3	71.5	77.4	83.0	84.1	84.4	85.5
1905	87.6	89.1	90.9	94.4	100.9	105.7	105.1	100.7	97.5	99.1	100.9	102.6
1906	105.7	107.1	106.4	102.2	93.2	89.1	91.9	99.4	104.5	104.0	102.8	100.2
1907	94.9	91.6	94.0	99.4	104.2	104.6	100.8	93.1	85.7	83.8	84.0	84.4
1908	84.3	86.1	88.7	86.6	83.1	81.5	82.2	84.3	87.8	88.6	86.5	84.4
1909	82.4	77.4	69.4	67.9	70.4	72.1	71.0	67.9	63.7	58.9	56.3	54.6
1910	52.4	50.1	48.4	46.2	41.2	34.4	29.4	26.2	23.7	23.3	23.0	21.4
1911	20.0	18.7	16.6	12.6	10.1	9.8	9.3	8.5	7.7	6.6	5.5	5.3
1912	5.4	5.1	5.2	5.7	5.6	5.7	6.1	6.5	6.4	5.8	5.2	4.7
1913	4.3	4.2	3.6	2.9	2.8	2.6	2.5	2.5	2.6	4.0	5.5	6.6
1914	7.7	8.5	9.8	10.9	12.4	14.8	17.5	21.6	26.8	31.0	34.6	40.5
1915	49.1	58.0	64.8	70.5	75.5	78.1	80.5	83.0	85.8	89.9	94.9	97.7
1916	96.4	92.7	90.0	89.5	91.0	93.9	97.2	100.4	103.4	105.6	108.5	114.6
1917	122.4	135.3	149.5	156.8	160.4	167.9	174.7	175.7	173.6	172.5	170.3	163.8
1918	159.1	154.6	147.5	145.0	145.0	139.2	131.0	128.6	129.2	126.9	125.7	130.0
1919	130.6	125.4	121.4	117.4	112.3	107.7	106.2	104.6	103.1	100.8	94.4	85.6
1920	78.0	71.9	67.2	65.7	64.4	63.1	61.3	58.2	53.4	51.6	52.1	51.0
1921	51.6	52.9	51.8	48.3	45.5	44.2	42.2	40.7	42.5	42.9	40.5	37.6
1922	33.5	30.2	28.2	26.4	24.9	24.0	23.2	21.0	15.7	11.8	11.1	11.0
1923	10.7	9.8	10.0	10.9	11.5	10.7	9.4	9.4	9.5	9.8	11.3	13.6
1924	16.3	19.3	21.5	23.3	25.1	26.9	28.2	29.8	32.2	34.7	37.7	40.8
1925	43.2	45.2	48.9	54.4	59.9	68.2	78.5	86.3	92.6	96.2	98.2	101.4
1926	104.2	106.8	108.5	108.7	109.0	107.8	107.2	109.4	111.6	115.9	120.7	120.8
1927	120.0	119.6	119.6	119.5	119.4	117.5	115.2	114.0	113.7	113.9	112.9	115.0
1928	120.2	125.3	128.9	130.2	128.9	128.7	128.7	126.9	123.7	119.4	116.1	113.5
1929	110.2	107.0	101.9	97.5	99.2	104.7	107.9	106.7	104.7	102.7	100.2	95.7
1930	89.3	83.2	80.2	78.6	74.1	65.2	56.0	52.0	51.2	50.4	49.0	47.2
1931	46.0	44.9	43.1	40.5	37.7	35.9	35.2	32.8	29.2	26.5	24.6	24.7
1932	24.6	23.6	22.1	21.0	20.2	19.0	18.6	19.4	20.1	19.5	17.9	15.7
1933	14.0	13.1	12.7	12.4	11.5	10.2	8.8	7.2	5.8	6.0	7.7	9.0
1934	9.5	10.5	11.0	11.1	11.9	13.5	15.6	17.5	19.7	21.1	21.7	24.9
1935	29.3	32.6	36.7	42.7	49.8	56.9	63.1	69.9	77.4	85.5	91.8	95.3
1936	98.3	103.5	109.8	114.7	120.7	128.6	137.7	146.3	150.5	153.4	160.1	168.6
1937	179.2	189.2	194.4	198.6	198.3	193.0	188.3	185.2	184.8	184.4	184.6	183.0
1938	182.2	182.1	179.8	177.2	178.7	182.3	181.4	177.2	172.8	171.8	171.8	171.4
1939	166.9	161.5	162.4	163.3	158.8	151.5	145.9	142.6	142.6	140.6	132.7	127.1
1940	123.8	121.7	118.5	113.0	110.0	111.1	112.6	111.3	107.7	103.2	99.5	96.1
1941	94.4	91.2	88.0	87.3	85.3	81.6	78.5	78.3	79.4	81.9	83.6	79.9
1942	73.1	67.0	60.8	55.5	53.1	51.8	49.4	46.2	42.6	38.4	35.2	34.2
1943	33.6	33.2	32.7	31.4	29.2	27.5	26.6	24.0	20.9	18.0	15.4	14.4
1944	13.6	12.9	13.0	13.9	14.6	15.3	17.0	18.9	20.4	23.4	27.5	31.7
1945	36.4	39.7	41.7	46.8	52.8	55.2	57.1	64.3	73.2	80.1	86.9	93.2
1946	101.0	111.7	121.5	128.0	135.7	147.7	157.7	163.1	167.3	173.3	182.8	193.4
1947	199.2	204.1	211.2	217.2	218.7	216.1	214.1	210.9	206.0	206.3	207.1	205.7
1948	205.0	202.3	198.9	195.7	192.2	191.6	193.5	199.8	209.1	210.3	203.8	197.1
1949	193.4	190.4	188.5	188.4	190.9	192.5	190.3	184.1	176.1	171.4	169.4	167.1
1950	162.8	158.5	150.7	141.0	131.6	122.6	116.4	111.9	106.7	102.3	101.2	102.4
1951	101.6	98.5	98.9	100.2	99.5	98.9	97.3	94.0	89.8	84.0	75.3	66.5
1952	61.5	59.8	56.2	51.4	48.0	45.5	44.0	42.1	40.3	39.5	38.8	37.3

Year	Jan	Feb	Mar	Apr	May	Jun	Jul	Aug	Sep	Oct	Nov	Dec
1953	34.6	31.0	28.6	27.2	25.0	22.0	18.5	16.7	16.6	15.1	12.8	10.8
1954	9.3	8.2	6.3	5.1	5.5	6.3	7.9	10.5	11.4	11.6	13.8	17.4
1955	20.5	23.7	28.0	33.5	41.2	50.0	57.0	66.0	78.8	91.3	103.5	114.8
1956	125.8	139.4	154.7	168.1	180.4	193.9	206.1	211.8	214.5	220.6	226.0	232.7
1957	241.1	243.8	246.8	256.3	262.7	266.1	271.1	275.3	279.3	282.5	284.4	283.3
1958	281.8	284.5	285.0	278.7	271.0	264.5	262.3	261.9	260.3	258.1	255.9	255.6
1959	252.9	250.4	247.1	239.7	233.9	228.5	220.6	214.2	207.1	199.7	194.2	187.6
1960	182.5	177.0	172.1	169.4	165.7	161.3	153.8	145.0	138.6	132.1	124.5	118.5
1961	113.6	105.9	97.5	91.1	85.1	79.1	75.3	74.4	74.3	73.0	71.7	69.1
1962	64.2	59.4	56.7	56.1	55.9	54.6	52.5	49.8	46.7	44.0	42.9	42.6
1963	42.1	42.6	42.6	41.6	41.1	40.4	39.7	39.0	38.6	37.4	34.2	30.7
1964	28.1	25.7	22.3	18.6	16.0	15.0	15.2	15.1	14.6	14.3	15.0	16.2
1965	17.2	17.7	18.4	19.9	21.2	21.8	22.6	23.8	25.2	28.4	32.1	35.2
1966	39.7	44.8	49.2	53.3	57.9	63.4	71.4	80.3	89.5	95.8	99.4	103.0
1967	106.2	111.6	116.5	119.8	123.9	129.4	133.3	135.0	134.9	134.5	137.6	142.5
1968	145.3	145.7	148.2	151.8	152.4	150.9	148.9	148.4	151.5	155.5	156.6	156.0
1969	155.7	155.1	152.9	150.7	150.4	150.1	149.9	150.7	149.2	147.4	148.0	148.5
1970	149.5	150.1	150.3	150.3	149.8	149.1	147.0	143.0	137.6	132.9	126.5	119.0
1971	113.8	110.1	105.3	100.4	96.5	94.5	92.7	91.5	93.2	93.8	94.7	98.3
1972	100.3	100.9	102.6	104.0	103.3	99.9	96.6	92.9	88.2	85.9	83.3	78.2
1973	72.3	66.1	62.8	60.8	57.9	55.6	53.4	51.4	49.0	46.6	45.4	45.0
1974	46.8	49.1	48.5	48.3	49.4	49.3	48.6	47.3	45.8	43.2	39.3	36.1
1975	33.0	31.8	30.6	26.8	24.2	23.2	21.8	20.7	20.9	22.3	23.3	23.6
1976	22.1	19.2	17.8	18.4	18.3	17.9	18.8	20.5	20.8	19.7	19.7	21.6
1977	24.3	26.3	28.8	31.9	34.7	37.7	41.4	47.6	55.8	64.8	73.7	80.7
1978	86.9	91.5	98.7	109.0	117.8	126.6	138.0	147.3	153.6	157.3	160.4	166.7
1979	175.2	185.4	193.3	199.9	208.5	216.7	219.5	220.1	220.4	223.4	229.8	232.9
1980	232.0	230.2	227.9	224.6	221.3	219.1	216.1	212.0	211.5	211.9	209.1	202.8
1981	199.6	202.2	205.4	205.7	204.1	200.9	198.5	199.9	202.7	201.4	196.0	194.1
1982	192.7	186.6	180.0	173.4	167.5	164.0	161.5	153.5	141.4	133.3	131.3	130.5
1983	127.9	123.9	117.1	110.5	104.5	95.9	89.1	88.9	91.7	92.0	89.7	85.5
1984	80.5	75.8	71.2	66.8	63.5	61.7	58.3	52.2	44.3	37.2	31.6	27.4
1985	25.2	23.5	21.7	21.3	21.4	20.8	19.9	19.6	19.8	19.7	19.1	17.3
1986	15.2	14.3	14.3	15.1	15.8	15.2	15.1	14.4	13.5	14.7	16.6	18.3
1987	19.9	22.3	25.5	28.0	30.3	32.7	36.2	40.5	45.3	51.0	55.1	60.9
1988	69.2	76.9	84.9	93.0	101.4	114.3	128.5	141.1	151.2	156.9	164.4	176.1
1989	184.8	190.7	198.0	203.8	209.5	212.1	212.0	211.1	210.5	212.4	212.5	206.2
1990	201.2	202.4	200.9	198.1	195.1	192.0	190.1	191.6	194.6	195.2	195.2	197.8
1991	202.8	204.4	203.9	203.8	202.9	202.8	203.5	203.3	200.9	196.7	191.4	183.1
1992	172.6	161.1	151.8	146.0	142.1	137.1	128.5	119.3	113.0	109.0	106.3	104.5
1993	101.9	99.3	95.4	90.2	84.2	78.6	76.5	73.6	68.3	63.2	58.4	55.1
1994	52.6	50.2	49.4	49.6	48.7	46.4	42.7	40.1	39.7	39.4	38.7	37.6
1995	35.6	33.7	32.0	29.4	27.3	25.9	24.4	22.0	19.0	17.0	15.9	15.1
1996	14.5	14.2	13.7	12.0	11.2	11.6	11.3	11.2	11.3	12.0	13.4	14.3
1997	14.5	15.2	18.3	22.0	24.4	27.2	30.4	33.6	38.2	43.1	47.1	52.0
1998	58.4	65.4	72.0	76.9	80.8	85.4	89.8	93.5	96.4	98.2	102.3	110.4
1999	118.4	122.5	122.3	125.0	132.6	136.3	138.1	142.9	150.5	159.3	164.1	164.0
2000	166.1	170.6	174.3	175.2	172.9	172.7	174.2	172.8	168.8	165.3	163.1	162.7
2001	158.3	152.5	155.1	160.7	163.7	167.4	172.0	175.8	177.1	177.3	180.3	179.1
2002	177.6	179.7	178.2	174.4	171.3	166.9	161.5	155.4	149.5	143.9	136.0	131.4
2003	129.6	125.7	118.7	111.9	107.0	101.7	96.0	92.9	91.8	89.1	86.9	84.1
2004	80.1	76.4	73.2	71.0	69.5	67.1	64.8	63.0	60.2	57.9	56.6	55.7
2005	54.5	53.2	52.3	49.3	45.0	44.5	44.6	41.9	39.4	38.9	38.4	36.0

Year	Jan	Feb	Mar	Apr	May	Jun	Jul	Aug	Sep	Oct	Nov	Dec
2006	33.0	29.7	27.4	27.0	27.4	26.2	25.0	25.9	26.0	23.7	21.1	20.2
2007	19.8	19.0	17.7	16.4	14.4	12.8	11.6	9.9	9.6	9.9	9.2	7.9
2008	6.6	5.6	5.1	5.1	5.4	4.8	4.0	3.8	3.2	2.4	2.3	2.2
2009	2.5	2.7	2.9	3.3	3.5	4.1	5.5	7.4	9.5	10.9	11.7	12.7
2010	14.0	16.1	18.5	20.8	23.1	24.6	25.2	26.4	29.5	34.5	39.1	42.5
2011	45.7	48.8	53.8	61.1	69.3	77.2	83.6	86.3	86.6	87.4	89.4	92.5
2012	95.5	98.1	98.3	95.1	90.9	86.6	84.5	85.1	85.3	85.8	87.7	88.1
2013	86.8	86.1	84.4	84.3	87.0	90.9	94.6	99.0	104.6	107.0	106.9	107.6
2014	109.3	110.5	114.3	116.4	115.0	114.1	112.6	108.3	101.9	97.3	94.7	92.2
2015	89.3	86.1	82.1	78.9	76.1	72.1	68.3	66.4	65.9	64.3	61.2	57.8
2016	54.4	52.5	50.4	47.8	44.8	41.5	38.5	36.0	33.2	31.5	29.9	28.5
2017	27.8	26.5	25.7	24.8	23.3	22.2	21.0	19.6	18.3	16.7	15.4	15.1
2018	14.2	12.6	9.9	7.8	7.5	7.2	7.0	6.7	6.5	6.8	6.7	6.0
2019	5.4	5.0	4.6	4.3	3.9	3.7	3.5	3.5	3.1	2.6	2.0	1.8
2020	2.2	2.8	3.0	3.5								

Chapter 3

Sunspot Cycle Predictions

Since the discovery of the sunspot cycle by Samuel Heinrich Schwabe in the middle of the 19th century, considerable interest has been shown in forecasting future cycles. For years, predicting the next sunspot cycle was somewhat of a sport for mathematicians, statisticians, and those who had a flair for studying the cycles. Until 1928, these predictions were primarily of academic interest.

With the discovery of the relationship between sunspot numbers and ultraviolet radiation, however, these predictions have taken on even broader importance. Since the beginning of the space age, the sunspot numbers have been used to guide the extent to which semiconductors used in satellites should be "hardened" against galactic radiation.

If a cycle is predicted to have a relatively low maximum, satellite designers will not harden the circuitry as much as they might otherwise believe necessary because the additional hardware can add weight and cost to the satellite. It also will require more fuel to launch the satellite and keep it in orbital position. If the sunspot cycle prediction proves wrong and the maximum smoothed sunspot number is higher than predicted or a higher-than-expected number of solar proton events occur, accumulated radiation damage will occur in the satellite. In the extreme, that may cause the satellite to fail. This is what happened during Cycle 22. The maximum was under-predicted by most experts and several satellites suffered major damage.

Knowing the level of solar activity also is important for astronaut safety, performance of the Global Positioning Service, or GPS, and other earth navigation systems, electric power transmission grids, satellite drag calculations, and, in extreme cases, even human safety on Earth.

In the 1950s, new technology allowed scientists to view the sun at the frequency of the red spectral line emitted by hydrogen. Newly developed filters, called H-alpha filters, were used to produce what appears to be a larger solar image. This is because the layer above the sun's photosphere — the region we see as white light — could now be observed. This layer is called the chromosphere. The chromosphere emits massive amounts of extreme ultraviolet, or EUV, radiation, which is responsible for forming the ionosphere's F2 region. The chromosphere also is where the features of active regions around sunspots can better be studied. The use of H-alpha filters yields more consistent sunspot counts and more detailed information on the complexity of sunspots than do data produced using "white light."

This chapter addresses the question: "Just what *is* a solar cycle prediction?" The answer is multifold: (1) a prediction is when to expect a minimum condition of solar activity, when the sun is virtually featureless; (2) when to expect a maximum condition, when the mid-latitudes of the solar surface are literally covered with dark spots; and (3) to determine the amplitude of the maximum . . . that is, the maximum 12-month smoothed sunspot number.

The first part of this chapter, Section 3.1, will be a high-level review of prediction techniques. The end of the section contains detailed open-access references for those who want to dig deeper into the various predic-

What Kinds of Predictions?

- **Climatological (statistical):** Future is an average of the past
    - —One example: The upcoming solar maximum will be 115 ± 40 the long term average of all prior maxima
    - —Should be obsolete!

- **Spectral:** Evolution of Fourier coefficients

- **Precursor:** Look for other variables that are leading indicators of activity
    - —Polar magnetic field at minimum ~level of activity at next maximum
    - —Flares are anticipated by the appearance of a sigmoid

- **Physics-based models:** Forecasts produced by models capable of integrating conservation equations, possibly using data-assimilation

Figure 3.1 Common methods for producing solar cycle predictions.

tion techniques cited. Section 3.2 will discuss the accuracy of predictions for Cycle 24, and Section 3.3 will review the predictions available for Cycle 25.

3.1 Prediction Methods

There are a variety of ways in which predictions can be made. Some of the more important ones are listed and briefly described in Figure 3.1 [reference 1].

Climatological (Statistical)

The climatological, or statistical, method is almost totally based on data observed from previous cycles. These statistical, or empirical, prediction methods fall into two categories: those which consider each solar cycle as an independent event, and those which assume solar activity to be a periodic phenomenon. Some attempts also have been made to predict solar behavior based on the assumption that the alignment of the planets determines solar activity. This will be discussed toward the end of this section.

Independent Event Theory

The independent event theory makes no assumptions as to the existence of long-term periodicities. It considers each rise and subsequent fall to be inde-

pendent from all the other cycles. In this method, extensive studies on the behavior of previous cycles are used to derive empirical relationships between the various solar cycle parameters.

For example, the following empirical law derived by Max Waldmeier [reference 2] relates the time in years between the maximum and the minimum of a given cycle to the maximum smoothed sunspot number Rs for the cycle [note: We are referring here to the old smoothed sunspot numbers, V1.0)]:

$$\text{time in years} = 3 + 0.03 \times Rs \qquad \text{Equation 1}$$

Working through an example, the maximum smoothed sunspot number for Cycle 20 was 111 in November 1968. Using that value in Equation 1 yields a decay time of roughly 6.3 years. As such, this method predicts that the minimum for Cycle 20 should have occurred early in 1975; it actually occurred in June 1976.

Let's work through a more recent example using Equation 1. The maximum smoothed sunspot number for the recent Cycle 24 was 82 — again, using the V1.0 data — in April 2014, which was the second peak of Cycle 24. Equation 1 says the minimum for Cycle 24 should occur 5.5 years after solar maximum. That puts it in October 2019. That is very close to reality, as Cycle 24 ended in December 2019.

Another empirical method developed by George Jacobs, W3ASK, is interesting to consider. In using this method, one first selects about five or six cycles that more or less are similar to the cycle under study. The average of the decline of these five or six cycles is then applied to the current cycle to predict its decline.

For Cycle 21, application of Jacobs' technique in 1981 suggested that the minimum should be reached in September 1986, with an expected minimum smoothed sunspot number of 9. The actual minimum did, in fact, occur in September 1986 and had a smoothed sunspot number of 12. This prediction was very good.

In June 1992, based on matching characteristics of Cycle 22 with similar characteristics of Cycles 11, 18, 19, and 21, Jacobs [reference 3] predicted the most likely date for Cycle 22's minimum would be January 1997, with a smoothed sunspot count of approximately 7. The actual minimum occurred in May 1996 with a smoothed sunspot number of 8. With the actual minimum occurring 8 months earlier than predicted, this prediction was not as good.

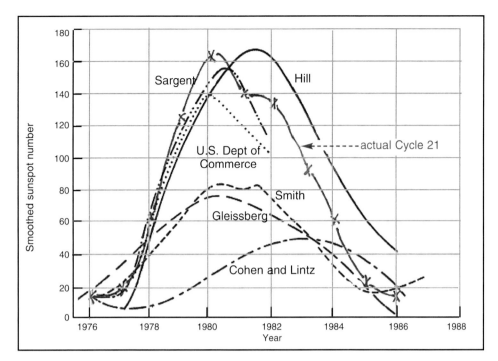

Figure 3.2 Comparison of six predictions using the periodic phenomenon theory to actual data for Cycle 21. Data shown are for old smoothed sunspot numbers (V1.0)

These two results suggest solar cycles may not be entirely independent. This leads to the periodic phenomenon theory and, ultimately, to other methods.

Periodic Phenomenon Theory

Methods for predicting solar activity that are based on the periodic behavior of the solar cycle seek to describe the short- and long-period recurrence behavior of previous cycles and to extrapolate these results to portions of the current and future cycles.

The last edition of this book, in 1995, discussed six of these methods using the periodic phenomenon theory. Figure 3.2 shows the results of these methods for Cycle 21.

The predictions by H. H. Sargent III, J. Hill and the U.S. Department of Commerce were decent compared to the actual Cycle 21 results, displayed in red. The other three under-predicted Cycle 21 by a significant amount. A search of literature has shown no predictions of later solar cycles by Sargent or Hill. Space weather personnel in the National Oceanic and Atmospheric Administration, one of the bureaus under the Commerce Department, continue to make solar cycle predictions.

Spectral

Spectral analysis of the sunspot number record is used for predictions under the assumption that the main reason for the solar cycle's variability is a long-term modulation due to one or more periods. Fourier analysis of

the entire solar cycle record reveals there is the dominant 11-year peak, a 22-year peak and more peaks.

Precursor

The precursor method generally uses a parameter around solar minimum to predict the next solar maximum. Precursor forecasts are the most commonly used category of predictions. Two types of precursors dominate this category: geomagnetic field activity and the magnitude of the solar polar magnetic field.

The most-used precursor index of geomagnetic field activity is the ap index (the three-hour linear equivalent of the Kp index).

The magnitude of the solar polar magnetic field at solar minimum is representative of the poloidal field that is sheared off by differential rotation to produce the toroidal field that erupts as active regions – sunspots — during the following cycle. Knowing the magnitude of the polar fields allows for predictions of the next cycle. But measuring the polar fields is difficult and data do not go back far enough to assess previous solar cycle predictions. There is evidence the magnitude of the solar polar field at minimum can be an indicator of the level of activity at the next solar maximum.

Physics-Based Models

A physics-based model attempts to "describe" what actually goes on inside the sun. This involves the alpha-effect, the lifting and twisting that converts the toroidal field into the poloidal field, which depends nonlinearly on the sun's magnetic field itself. These solar dynamo models — flux transport models — have been developed to include the kinematic effects of the sun's meridional circulation because it can play a significant role in the magnetic dynamo. In these models, the speed of the meridional circulation sets the cycle period, which influences both the strength of the polar fields and the amplitudes of following cycles.

Much effort is ongoing using physics-based modeling techniques. Ultimately, they should provide the best results of all methods . . . if the models are accurate!

Neural Networks

This is a relatively new technique to predict solar cycles. Neural networks are algorithms constructed using a large number of small, interconnected units known as neurons. Each neuron is capable of performing only a simple, nonlinear operation on an input signal. To identify the optimal values of thresholds and weights parameterizing the functions of each neuron, an algorithm is employed that minimizes the error between the predicted and observed values in a process called "training" the network. This is done with or without human guidance. Once the network has been correctly trained, it is capable of further predictions.

Planetary Alignment

The gravitational force F of one body on another body is given by:

$$F = G \frac{m1 \times m2}{r^2} \qquad \text{Equation 2}$$

where G is the gravitational constant
        m1 is the mass of one body
        m2 is the mass of the other body
        r is the distance between the two bodies

When Equation 2 is applied with m1 being the mass of the sun and m2 being the masses of all the other planets, the three planets that most affect the sun are Venus, Earth and Jupiter. When these planets are in alignment with the sun — in a straight line or near-straight line through all of them — the gravitational force on the sun is at a maximum.

This alignment of the sun, Venus, Earth and Jupiter occurs every 11.07 years. Because this time period is

so close to the length of a solar cycle, much research has gone on to determine whether this could be a driving force for a solar cycle period.

Many researchers have examined this phenomenon. Frank Stefani, Andre Giesecke and Tom Weier [reference 4] have looked at this alignment in relation to this solar dynamo model. Gravitational pull could be an important related consideration.

More References about Prediction Techniques

Detailed information about solar cycle prediction techniques can be found in K. Petrovay [reference 5], D.H. Hathaway [reference 6] and W. D. Pesnell [reference 7].

Additionally, publications from the American Geophysical Union (AGU) (https://agupubs.onlinelibrary. wiley.com/), the Journal of Atmospheric and Solar-Terrestrial Physics (https://www.sciencedirect.com/ journal/journal-of-atmospheric-and-solar-terrestrial-physics), Advances in Space Research (https://www. sciencedirect.com/journal/advances-in-space-research), the European Geosciences Union (EGU) (https://www.ann-geophys.net/volumes.html) and other organizations have articles about solar cycle predictions. The EGU articles are open-access, but the others may require membership or may require payment.

3.2   How Good Were the Predictions for Cycle 24?

Given the different methods employed, it may not come as a surprise that scientists still have trouble predicting a solar cycle's magnitude. As seen in Figure 3.3, the predictions made for Cycle 24 are a great example of the problem [reference 8]. Remember we are referring to the old sunspot numbers, V1.0.

Of the more than 100 predictions displayed, the smallest prediction was for a smoothed sunspot number of 40 and the largest prediction was for a smoothed sunspot number of 185. The colored vertical bars are the different methods – even the same method created wildly different predictions.

Because of the range of results, initially the NOAA/ NASA Solar Cycle 24 Prediction Panel, consisting of 12 well-respected individuals in the solar science community, was split. Half of the panelists believed Cycle 24 would be small and the other half believed it would be big. Visit https://www.swpc.noaa.gov/content/april-

Figure 3.3 Predictions for Cycle 24

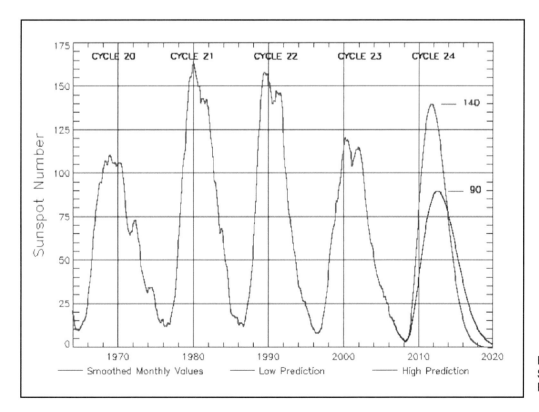

105 Predictions of Solar Cycle 24

2007-press-release for this announcement. Figure 3.4 shows the two predictions of Cycle 24 that NOAA/NASA carried for a couple of years.

Note that the large-cycle prediction (in red, at a max of 140 +/- 20 in October 2011) has a peak earlier than the small-cycle prediction (in green, at a max of 90 +/- 10 in August 2012). This comes from the fact that our historical data show that a large cycle rises a bit faster than does a small cycle.

As Cycle 23 continued its decline through 2007 and 2008, it became apparent the solar minimum between Cycles 23 and 24 was going to be very long – longer than anything we've seen in our lifetimes.

Based on these new data, the Solar Cycle 24 Pre-

Figure 3.4 NOAA/NASA Solar Cycle 24 Prediction Panel forecast of 2007

Figure 3.5 Next maximum vs. duration of previous minimum.

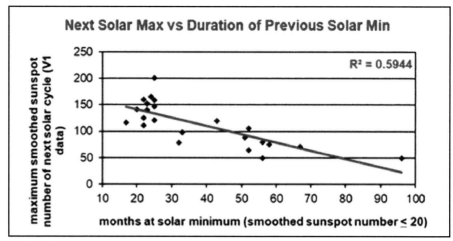

Figure 3.6 Cycle 24 actual results

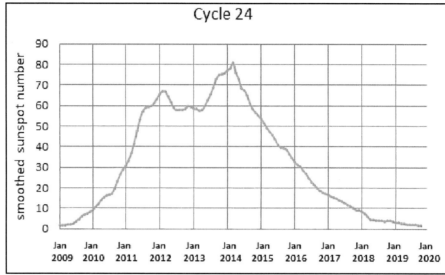

diction Panel came to a consensus in 2009 that Cycle 24 was going to be small. Their new prediction was for a maximum smoothed sunspot number of 90 in early 2013.

This was reasonable, taking into consideration the plot of Figure 3.5 [reference 9] of solar minimum duration versus maximum of the next cycle.

The red linear trend line strongly suggests the longer the solar minimum period, the smaller the maximum of the next cycle. The correlation isn't perfect, but there is an obvious trend.

So, how did the predictions of Figure 3.3 and the prediction by the NOAA/NASA Solar Cycle 24 Prediction Panel in Figure 3.4 do compared to the actual Cycle 24 results? Figure 3.6 shows the actual Cycle 24 results in terms of the V1.0 smoothed sunspot cycle.

A handful of the predictions in Figure 3.3 were around the actual maximum of 82 in the second peak.

These "good" predictions fell into the climatological, or statistical method and the dynamo model method, which is physics-based. The NOAA/NASA Solar Cycle 24 Prediction Panel wasn't far off: 90 versus 82.

The most obvious feature of Cycle 24 is its double peak. Cycles 22 and 23 also had pronounced double peaks (see Figures 2.8 and 2.10 in Chapter 2). None of the predictions for Cycle 24 had foreseen two peaks. It is likely that the only method that will predict this double peak will be a physics-based model that accurately addresses what's going on inside the sun with respect to plasma flow and magnetic fields.

3.3 Predicting Cycle 25

The nature of the next solar cycle, known as Cycle 25, is of utmost importance to all users of the high-frequency spectrum, the range between 3 and 30 MHz. It's the radiation from the active sun, after all,

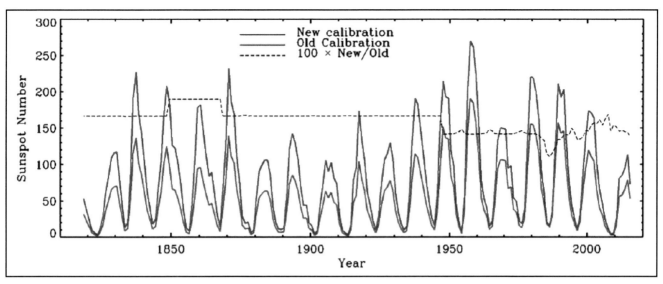

Figure 3.7 As seen here for the revised sunspot data (called "V2.0"; blue line), the new smoothed sunspot numbers (SSN) are significantly higher in value than those previously stated in the old "V1.0" (red line) dataset.

that controls the strength of the Earth's ionosphere and our ability to use this naturally occurring phenomenon for long-distance communications. As we go to press, as seen in Figure 3.6, we just went through the end of Cycle 24 in December 2019, which is the smallest solar cycle in our lifetimes.

First you *must* understand that the 12-month running smoothed sunspot numbers, or SSN, now reported

have been "recalibrated" as of July 2015. At that time, **the entire sunspot database was republished using recalibrated numbers.** This may not have made much of a difference in the numbers you have been seeing reported in various publications, given we are near a solar minimum and the sunspot counts have been low. But look at the maximum in March 1958. Remember that cycle? The old method of reporting SSNs, produc-

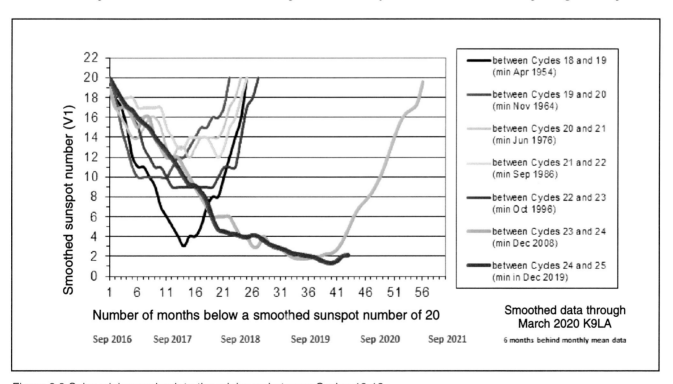

Figure 3.8 Solar minimums back to the minimum between Cycles 18-19.

Figure 3.9 Distribution of Cycle 25 predictions.

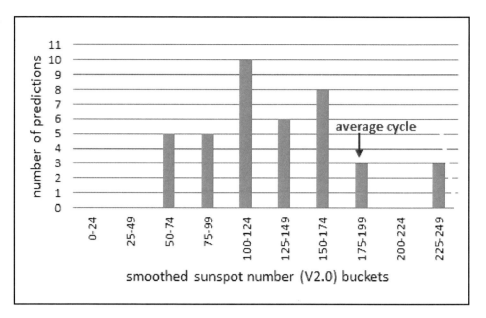

ing V1.0, had the 12-month running SSN at 201; the new calibration puts Cycle 19's maximum just under 300. The lesson here is to be aware of what SSNs are being discussed in any given presentation. Your *CQ* magazine "Propagation" editor will be reminding you of this from time to time as well. Figure 3.7 [reference 10] compares the V2.0 numbers to the V1.0 numbers.

Note this figure includes the ratio of the V2.0 data over the V1.0 data (the dashed line). It's not a single correction factor. It has changed over the years. We'll look at this in more detail in Chapter 4.

As we saw in Figure 3.6, we are at solar minimum. It's instructive to take a closer look at this minimum before looking at the Cycle 25 predictions and to compare this minimum to the six previous solar minimums. Figure 3.8 [reference 11] does this for us.

The early data indicates we've been spoiled. The minimums between Cycles 18 and19 through Cycles 22 and 23 were short. In this figure, the definition of solar minimum is when the smoothed sunspot number was below 20. On average, we experienced solar minimum durations of two years. That was a small price to pay for the bigger-than-average solar cycles we've seen in our lifetimes (Cycles 19, 21 and 22 – and even Cycle 18, if you're a real old-timer). But the minimum between Cycles 23 and 24 – the thick green line — broke that mold by a long shot. It lasted almost five years.

The thick red line shows the progress of the current solar minimum. Now it appears this solar minimum will be even longer than the last one. By how much?

The next few months of data will give us the clues we need to answer this question.

Although our current solar minimum period is very long, there is good news. Figure 3.8 shows that the smoothed sunspot number (the thick red line) minimized and appears to be headed up. This resulted in NASA and NOAA announcing in the September 16, 2020 daily report at spaceweather.com that the official solar minimum was in December 2019.

So, back to the original question: where might we be going in Cycle 25? Reference 5 (published in early 2020) listed 15 predictions for Cycle 25. Reference 12 in late 2020 identified 38 predictions for Cycle 25. Two more predictions surfaced after Reference 12 was published. Figure 3.9 is the distribution of all 40 predictions. Be advised that there will likely be some more predictions as Cycle 25 ascends.

The average smoothed sunspot number for all 24 solar cycles is 179 as indicated by the red arrow. Note that 34 of the 40 predictions (85%) are for a Cycle 25 that is below average. There are three predictions for a Cycle 25 around the average value. And for 12-meter, 10-meter and 6-meter aficionados, there are 3 predictions for a big Cycle 25. Representative examples of these 40 predictions are cited in References 13, 14, 15, 16 and 17.

One of the big cycle predictions is from McIntosh, et al [reference 18], and has received much publicity in the scientific community and the amateur radio community. If this prediction and the other two big predictions prove to be the most accurate, we will enjoy 10-meter and 6-meter propagation rivaling Cycles 21 (maximum in December 1979) and 22 (first maximum in July 1989 and a smaller second peak in early 1991). But we have to temper our expectation for a big cycle with the data in Figure 3.5; the longer the solar minimum period, the smaller the next cycle.

Knowing that big cycles rise faster than small cycles, we may have an indication of where Cycle 25 is going before we actually reach solar maximum around 2024 or 2025. Otherwise, we'll just have to wait to see what actually occurs. Hopefully, the more objective physics-based models will improve [for example, reference 13] to the point where our predictions can be refined to reflect more accurately what actually can be expected.

3.4   References

1. Pesnell_SC_Pred_GSFC_SWx_Jun_2017.pdf.

2. Waldmeier, M. "A Prediction of the Next Maximum of Solar Activity," Terrestrial Magnetism and Atmospheric Electricity, Vol. 51, 1946.

3. Jacobs, G., "Propagation" column, CQ, August 1992.

4. F. Stefani, A. Giesecke, T. Weier, A Model of a Tidally Synchronized Solar Dynamo, Solar Physics volume 294, Article number: 60 (2019).

5. Petrovay, K., Solar cycle prediction, Living Reviews in Solar Physics, Volume 17, Article Number 2, 2020, open access, https://link.springer.com/article/10.1007/s41116-020-0022-z.

6. Hathaway, D. H., The Solar Cycle, Living Reviews in Solar Physics, Volume 12, Article Number 4, 2015, open access, https://link.springer.com/article/10.1007/lrsp-2015-4.

7. Pesnell, W. D., Solar Cycle Predictions, NASA Technical Reports Server, Document ID 20120008362.

8. See reference 1.

9. Luetzelschwab, R. C., K9LA, personal data.

10. http://www.spaceclimate.fi/SC6/presentations/session2a/Dean_Pesnell_SC6.pdf.

11. Luetzelschwab, R. C., K9LA, personal data.

12. Pesnell, W. D., Sun Climate, Tucson, January 2020.

13. Shepherd, S. J., Zharkov, S. I., V. Zharkova, V. V., Prediction of Solar Activity from Solar Background Magnetic Field Variations in Cycles 21–23, The Astrophysical Journal, 795:46 (8pp), 2014 November 1, doi:10.1088/0004-637X/795/1/46.

14. Javaraiah, J, Will Solar Cycles 25 and 26 Be Weaker than Cycle 24?, Solar Physics, Volume 292, Article Number 172, November 2017.

15. Miao, J., Wang, X., Ren, T.-L., and Li1, Z.-L, Prediction verification of solar cycles 18–24 and a preliminary prediction of the maximum amplitude of solar cycle 25 based on the Precursor Method, Volume 20, Number 1, 2020, https://iopscience.iop.org/article/10.1088/1674-4527/20/1/4/meta.

16. Bhomik, P., and Nandy, D., Prediction of the strength and timing of sunspot cycle 25 reveal decadal-scale space environmental conditions, Nature Communications, open access, https://doi.org/10.1038/s41467-018-07690-0.

17. https://www.swpc.noaa.gov/news/solar-cycle-25-forecast-update.

18. McIntosh, S. W., S. Chapman, R. J. Leamon, R. Egeland and N. W. Watkins, Overlapping Magnetic Activity Cycles and the Sunspot Number: Forecasting Sunspot Cycle 25 Amplitude, Solar Physics, https://arxiv.org/abs/2006.15263.

Chapter 4

Do-It-Yourself Propagation Predictions and Master Propagation Charts

This chapter is the heart of the book for those of you who want to make your own propagation forecasts and determine for yourselves the best band and best time to make a contact over a given path. Worldwide propagation predictions and short-skip propagation predictions are presented in tabular format for all phases of a solar cycle, for the four seasons, and for the 160-, 80-, 40-, 20-, 15-, 10-, and 6-meter ham bands. These charts were prepared for the first edition of this book, which was published before the so-called WARC bands (30, 17 and 12 meters) or the 60-meter band were allocated for amateur use. Nonetheless, these predictions may be interpolated for these bands as well as the international shortwave broadcast bands. Also, additional comments on propagation on 160 meters (1.8 to 2.0 MHz) and 6 meters (50 to 54 MHz) are provided in this chapter. Propagation on 2200 meters (135.7 to 137.8 kHz) and 630 meters (472 to 479 kHz) is discussed in Chapter 8.

No previous knowledge of the ionosphere or ionospheric propagation is required to use the charts discussed in this chapter. However, it is strongly suggested that you read Chapter 1 to get a basic background and better understand the predictions that are of interest to you.

Detailed instructions are given here on how to use the tables and interpret the results. In addition, discussions of band conditions for worldwide and short-skip propagation are discussed on a band-by-band basis during the various phases of a solar cycle, and a top-level summary of the bands over a solar cycle, over the seasons, and for day/night conditions is provided.

These charts make the task of predicting either DX or short-skip HF propagation conditions relatively easy for both the beginner and advanced user of the shortwave bands.

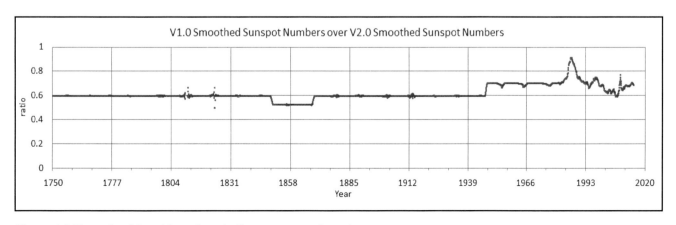

Figure 4.1 The ratio of the old numbers to the new sunspot numbers

The Master DX Propagation Charts and the Master Short-Skip Propagation Charts contained in Sections 4.3 to 4.6 of this chapter make it possible for users of the HF radio spectrum to predict propagation conditions from most areas of the U.S. and Canada to just about any spot on Earth, given the frequency, time of day, season of the year, and phase of the solar cycle. The charts have been derived from a computer analysis of hundreds of DX and short-skip paths, and they have been well-tested for utility and accuracy over a period of more than 40 years through the monthly "Propagation" column in *CQ* magazine [reference 1]. The Master Propagation Charts provide everything that is required to make do-it-yourself HF propagation predictions of relatively high accuracy within a few moments.

An Important Reminder

First, we should review an important issue discussed in Section 2.9 of Chapter 2: the new sunspot numbers. Our propagation predictions are based on the correlation between the smoothed sunspot number and monthly median ionospheric parameters. When this correlation was established, all we had were the V1.0 smoothed sunspot numbers. The predictions in the 1995 handbook — and in most propagation prediction software packages — were created using the V1.0 smoothed sunspot numbers. Using the V2.0 smoothed sunspot numbers will result in overly optimistic predictions. When we work with the propagation charts, we must use the V1.0 smoothed sunspot numbers. There are two scenarios to be considered.

The first scenario is for predictions beginning with December 2014. The last time the old smoothed sunspot numbers were reported was November 2014. Recall Figure 3.7 from Chapter 3. It showed the old smoothed sunspot numbers versus the new smoothed sunspot numbers, and it included the ratio of the new data to the old data. What we really want to know is the ratio of the old sunspot data to the new data. Then we can multiply the new smoothed sunspot numbers by this ratio to determine the old smoothed sunspot numbers. Figure 4.1 shows this ratio over the entire smoothed sunspot number record.

Since December 2014, the ratio has been close to 0.7. Download the current smoothed sunspot number from the Royal Observatory of Belgium at http://sidc. oma.be/silso/datafiles) and multiply the data by 0.7 to

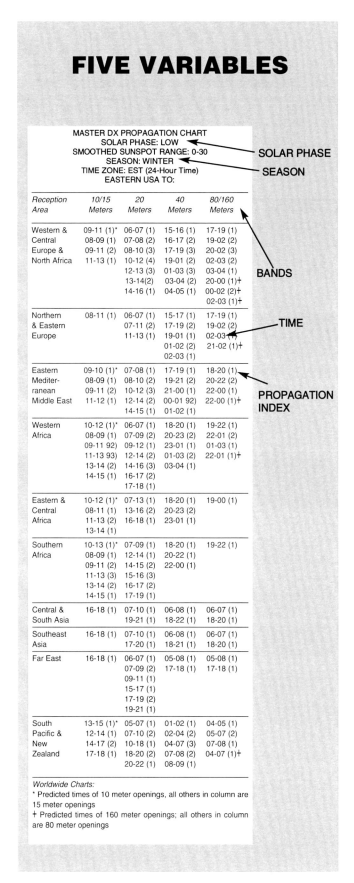

FIVE VARIABLES

MASTER DX PROPAGATION CHART
SOLAR PHASE: LOW → SOLAR PHASE
SMOOTHED SUNSPOT RANGE: 0-30
SEASON: WINTER → SEASON
TIME ZONE: EST (24-Hour Time)
EASTERN USA TO:

Reception Area	10/15 Meters	20 Meters	40 Meters	80/160 Meters
Western & Central Europe & North Africa	09-11 (1)* 08-09 (1) 09-11 (2) 11-13 (1)	06-07 (1) 07-08 (2) 08-10 (3) 10-12 (4) 12-13 (3) 13-14(2) 14-16 (1)	15-16 (1) 16-17 (2) 17-19 (3) 19-01 (2) 01-03 (3) 03-04 (2) 04-05 (1)	17-19 (1) 19-02 (2) 20-02 (3) 02-03 (2) 03-04 (1) 20-00 (1)+ 00-02 (2)+ 02-03 (1)+
Northern & Eastern Europe	08-11 (1)	06-07 (1) 07-11 (2) 11-13 (1)	15-17 (1) 17-19 (2) 19-01 (1) 01-02 (2) 02-03 (1)	17-19 (1) 19-02 (2) 02-03 (1) 21-02 (1)+
Eastern Mediterranean Middle East	09-10 (1)* 08-09 (1) 09-11 (2) 11-12 (1)	07-08 (1) 08-10 (2) 10-12 (3) 12-14 (2) 14-15 (1)	17-19 (1) 19-21 (2) 21-00 (1) 00-01 92) 01-02 (1)	18-20 (1) 20-22 (2) 22-00 (1) 22-00 (1)+
Western Africa	10-12 (1)* 08-09 (1) 09-11 92) 11-13 93) 13-14 (2) 14-15 (1)	06-07 (1) 07-09 (2) 09-12 (1) 12-14 (2) 14-16 (2) 16-17 (2) 17-18 (1)	18-20 (1) 20-23 (2) 23-01 (1) 01-03 (2) 03-04 (1)	19-22 (1) 22-01 (2) 01-03 (1) 22-01 (1)+
Eastern & Central Africa	10-12 (1)* 08-11 (1) 11-13 (2) 13-14 (1)	07-13 (1) 13-16 (2) 16-18 (1)	18-20 (1) 20-23 (2) 23-01 (1)	19-00 (1)
Southern Africa	10-13 (1)* 08-09 (1) 09-11 (2) 11-13 (3) 13-14 (2) 14-15 (1)	07-09 (1) 12-14 (1) 14-15 (2) 15-16 (3) 16-17 (2) 17-19 (1)	18-20 (1) 20-22 (1) 22-00 (1)	19-22 (1)
Central & South Asia	16-18 (1)	07-10 (1) 19-21 (1)	06-08 (1) 18-22 (1)	06-07 (1) 18-20 (1)
Southeast Asia	16-18 (1)	07-10 (1) 17-20 (1)	06-08 (1) 18-21 (1)	06-07 (1) 18-20 (1)
Far East	16-18 (1)	06-07 (1) 07-09 (2) 09-11 (1) 15-17 (1) 17-19 (2) 19-21 (1)	05-08 (1) 17-18 (1)	05-08 (1) 17-18 (1)
South Pacific & New Zealand	13-15 (1)* 12-14 (1) 14-17 (2) 17-18 (1)	05-07 (1) 07-10 (2) 10-18 (1) 18-20 (2) 20-22 (1)	01-02 (1) 02-04 (2) 04-07 (3) 07-08 (2) 08-09 (1)	04-05 (1) 05-07 (2) 07-08 (1) 04-07 (1)+

→ BANDS
→ TIME
→ PROPAGATION INDEX

Worldwide Charts:
* Predicted times of 10 meter openings, all others in column are 15 meter openings
+ Predicted times of 160 meter openings; all others in column are 80 meter openings

Table 4.1 Sample Master DX Propagation Chart

Solar Phase	V1.0 Smoothed Sunspot Number Range	10.7 cm Solar Flux Range	Section in Which Charts Appear
LOW	0-30	<70-90	4.3
MODERATE	30-60	90-110	4.4
HIGH	60-90	110-130	4.5
VERY HIGH	90-120	130-160	4.6
INTENSE	>120	>160	Use 4.6

Table 4.2 Major phases of a solar cycle in terms of the V1.0 dataset.

determine the equivalent, old smoothed sunspot number to use in your application of the propagation charts. You can click on "Total Sunspot Number" and then download from the text file labeled "13-month smoothed monthly total sunspot number [1/1749 - now]."

The second scenario is for predictions for November 2014 and earlier. This would be for use in historical analyses of propagation. The easiest way to get the V1.0 smoothed sunspot number is to use the data in section 2.12, Appendix 1, of Chapter 2. These are the V1.0 smoothed sunspot numbers; when using these in this handbook's charts, no corrections are necessary.

For this second scenario, you could also download the new smoothed sunspot numbers from the SIDC website referenced above and multiply by the ratio in Figure 4.1 depending on the date. Note the small gap in the ratio for 1810. Both the old smoothed sunspot numbers and the new smoothed sunspot numbers were extremely low during 1810. For many months, they were zero. This was during the solar minimum between Cycles 5 and 6, part of the Dalton Minimum seen in Figures 2.1 and 2.3 in Chapter 2. The best solution here might be to go around 1810 and use the old smoothed sunspot numbers from Appendix 1 in Chapter 2. Of course, with the smoothed sunspot number so low in 1810, it really won't matter which version you use.

You might wonder why the ratio of the V1.0 sunspots to the V2.0 sunspots isn't constant. The reason is that there were several corrections to the old record – not just one correction. And these corrections were not independent in time – they overlapped. One major correction was backing out the 0.6 factor that A. Wolfer applied to R. Wolf's sunspot numbers when he took over as Director of the Zürich Observatory upon R. Wolf's death. A. Wolfer applied it because he counted more sunspots than R. Wolf, and wanted to align his count to the long series built by R. Wolf. Another correction is known as the "Waldmeier" jump from 1947

to 1980, when M. Waldmeier, the last director of the Zürich Observatory, introduced a new counting method. For detailed information on all the corrections, go to https://www.researchgate.net/publication/283247356_The_New_Sunspot_Number_Assembling_All_Corrections

4.1 How To Use The Master DX Propagation Charts

Table 4.1 is a sample of a portion of a Master DX Propagation Chart. These DX charts are intended for stations in the U.S. and Canada to use in communications with other parts of the world. The chart contains five variables that require explanation: *solar phase, season, frequency, time,* and *propagation index.*

Solar Phase: Sets of charts have been prepared for the major phases of a solar cycle, as shown in Table 4.2.

Note that the smoothed sunspot numbers in Table 4.2 are the V1.0 values. The V2.0 values will need to be converted for accurate predictions.

Assuming the maximum of Cycle 25 will be per the NOAA/NASA prediction of 115 in Figure 3.9 in Section 3.3 in Chapter 3 (it's roughly between the low and high predictions), we need to convert the V2.0 115 value to a V1.0 value by multiplying 115 by 0.7. This results in a maximum of 81 for Cycle 25 in terms of the V1.0 data. Based on that value, only the low, moderate and high phases are expected to occur in Cycle 25 per Table 4.3.

In using the Master DX Propagation Charts, it's advisable to check for the latest smoothed sunspot

LOW	mid 2020 to mid 2022
MODERTE	mid 2022 to mid 2023
HIGH	mid 2023 to mid 2027
MODERATE	mid 2027 to mid 2029
LOW	mid 2029 to late 2033

Table 4.3 Solar phases expected during Cycle 25.

number [reference 2] and multiply it by 0.7 rather than relying on the information in Table 4.3, because actual solar activity may differ from predicted values. Charts for a very high phase of solar activity also may be used during an intense period of solar activity. Once a smoothed sunspot number is known, or is assumed from Table 4.3, the Master DX Propagation Chart for the appropriate solar phase can be selected from Sections 4.3 through 4.6.

Season: As shown in Table 4.4, there are three sets of charts covering the four seasons. Select the appropriate seasonal chart from Table 4.4 depending upon the month for which the prediction is to be made.

Frequency: Predictions are contained in the charts for the 10-, 15-, 20-, 40-, 80-, and 160-meter amateur bands. The charts also can be used with the 60-meter, 30-meter, 17-meter and 12-meter bands, along with the HF shortwave broadcasting bands, as shown in Tables 4.5 and 4.6, respectively. We will look at the 2200-meter and 630-meter ham bands in a later chapter.

SUMMER Charts—for use during May, June, July and
  August
WINTER Charts—for use during November, December,
  January and February
SPRING & FALL Charts (Equinox)—for use during March,
  April, September and October

Table 4.4 Months during which seasonal propagation charts can be used

---

For 12-meter openings, interpolate between 10- and 15-
  meter openings
For 17-meter openings, interpolate between 15- and 20-
  meter openings
For 30-meter openings, interpolate between 20- and 40-
  meter openings
For 60-meter openings, use 80-meter openings

Table 4.5 How to apply the Master DX Propagation Charts to 12, 17, 30 and 60 meters

---

11-meter SWL band—use 10 meters
13- and 16-meter SWL bands—use 15 meters
19- and 25-meter SWL bands—use 20 meters
31-, 41- and 49-meter SWL bands—use 40 meters
60-, 75- and 90-meter SWL bands—use 80 meters
120-meter SWL bands—use 160 meters

Table 4.6 How to apply the Master DX Propagation Charts to the shortwave broadcast bands

---

Time: Time in the charts is given by the 24-hour system. Charts are available for four sets of time zones: EST, CST and MST, and PST. Standard time is used throughout. Table 4.7 can be used to convert from 24-hour to regular time, to daylight time during the months when it is applicable, and to UTC.

Propagation Index: This is the number that appears in parentheses after the time of each predicted opening shown in the charts. The propagation index indicates the number of days during a month for which the predicted opening is expected to occur, as shown in Table 4.8.

The higher the propagation index, the better is the chance for the opening to occur. In other words, the higher the propagation index, the more days the path is expected to be open. Unfortunately, the propagation index does not indicate the specific days on which the opening is likely to occur. In Chapter 5, we'll discuss how our propagation predictions were developed, and we'll look at methods to assess propagation on a short-term basis.

The Master DX Propagation Charts are based on an effective radiated power (ERP) of 1,000 watts. For example, 1,000 watts ERP could be 100 watts into an antenna with 10 dB gain. For each 10 dB gain above the 1,000-watt ERP reference, the propagation index will increase by roughly one level; for each 10 dB drop, it will decrease by roughly one level. Remember that the calculation of ERP also should take feedline loss into account.

The following are several examples that illustrate the ease with which the Master DX Propagation Charts can be used.

Example 1: It is November 2020, and you want to work a radio amateur friend in France at noon. You live in Washington, D.C. What is the best band to use?

1. From Table 4.3, November 2020 is expected to correspond to a low solar phase. From Table 4.2, Master Propagation Charts for low solar phase are found in Section 4.3 of this chapter.

2. From Table 4.4, the winter seasonal chart should be used for November. Because Washington, D.C. is in the EST zone, the EST chart should be used. From Table 4.7, noon EST corresponds to 12 in the 24-hour time system. *Note that the times in the Master DX Propagation Charts are local times for the indicated time zone – they are not UTC times.*

3. From the appropriate Master DX Propagation Chart contained in Section 4.3 (for EST, winter, low

EST ZONE				CST ZONE			
24-hour Time	EST	EDT	UTC	24-hour Time	CST	CDT	UTC
00	Midnight	1 AM	0500	00	Midnight	1 AM	0600
01	1 AM	2 AM	0600	01	1 AM	2 AM	0700
02	2 AM	3 AM	0700	02	2 AM	3 AM	0800
03	3 AM	4 AM	0800	03	3 AM	4 AM	0900
04	4 AM	5 AM	0900	04	4 AM	5 AM	1000
05	5 AM	6 AM	1000	05	5 AM	6 AM	1100
06	6 AM	7 AM	1100	06	6 AM	7 AM	1200
07	7 AM	8 AM	1200	07	7 AM	8 AM	1300
08	8 AM	9 AM	1300	08	8 AM	9 AM	1400
09	9 AM	10 AM	1400	09	9 AM	10 AM	1500
10	10 AM	11 AM	1500	10	10 AM	11 AM	1600
11	11 AM	Noon	1600	11	11 AM	Noon	1700
12	Noon	1 PM	1700	12	Noon	1 PM	1800
13	1 PM	2 PM	1800	13	1 PM	2 PM	1900
14	2 PM	3 PM	1900	14	2 PM	3 PM	2000
15	3 PM	4 PM	2000	15	3 PM	4 PM	2100
16	4 PM	5 PM	2100	16	4 PM	5 PM	2200
17	5 PM	6 PM	2200	17	5 PM	6 PM	2300
18	6 PM	7 PM	2300	18	6 PM	7 PM	0000
19	7 PM	8 PM	0000	19	7 PM	8 PM	0100
20	8 PM	9 PM	0100	20	8 PM	9 PM	0200
21	9 PM	10 PM	0200	21	9 PM	10 PM	0300
22	10 PM	11 PM	0300	22	10 PM	11 PM	0400
23	11 PM	Midnight	0400	23	11 PM	Midnight	0500
24	Midnight	1 AM	0500	24	Midnight	1 AM	0600

MST ZONE				PST ZONE			
24-hour Time	MST	MDT	UTC	24-hour Time	PST	PDT	UTC
00	Midnight	1 AM	0700	00	Midnight	1 AM	0800
01	1 AM	2 AM	0800	01	1 AM	2 AM	0900
02	2 AM	3 AM	0900	02	2 AM	3 AM	0900
03	3 AM	4 AM	1000	03	3 AM	4 AM	1100
04	4 AM	5 AM	1100	04	4 AM	5 AM	1200
05	5 AM	6 AM	1200	05	5 AM	6 AM	1300
06	6 AM	7 AM	1300	06	6 AM	7 AM	1400
07	7 AM	8 AM	1400	07	7 AM	8 AM	1500
08	8 AM	9 AM	1500	08	8 AM	9 AM	1600
09	9 AM	10 AM	1600	09	9 AM	10 AM	1700
10	10 AM	11 AM	1700	10	10 AM	11 AM	1800
11	11 AM	Noon	1800	11	11 AM	Noon	1900
12	Noon	1 PM	1900	12	Noon	1 PM	2000
13	1 PM	2 PM	2000	13	1 PM	2 PM	2100
14	2 PM	3 PM	2100	14	2 PM	3 PM	2200
15	3 PM	4 PM	2200	15	3 PM	4 PM	2300
16	4 PM	5 PM	2200	16	4 PM	5 PM	0000
17	5 PM	6 PM	0000	17	5 PM	6 PM	0100
18	6 PM	7 PM	0100	18	6 PM	7 PM	0200
19	7 PM	8 PM	0200	19	7 PM	8 PM	0300
20	8 PM	9 PM	0300	20	8 PM	9 PM	0400
21	9 PM	10 PM	0400	21	9 PM	10 PM	0500
22	10 PM	11 PM	0500	22	10 PM	11 PM	0600
23	11 PM	Midnight	0600	23	11 PM	Midnight	0700
24	Midnight	1 AM	0700	24	Midnight	1 AM	0800

Table 4.7 This table simplifies converting from 24 hour time shown in the Master Proagation Charts to standard time, and from standard time to daylight time and UTC, for each of the continental U.S.A. time zones.

propagation index	expected openings
(4)	more than 22 days of the month
(3)	from 14 to 22 days of the month
(2)	from 7 to 13 days of the month
(1)	fewer than 7 days of the month

Table 4.8 Propagation index in relation to the number of days an opening is expected to occur during a month.

solar phase), or in this case, from the sample contained in Table 4.1, you find under "Western and Central Europe and North Africa" a propagation index of (1) for 15 meters at 12 hours; a propagation index of (3) for 20 meters at 12 hours; and no entries for 12 hours for 40, 80, or 160 meters. The best band to use, therefore, would be 20 meters since it has the highest propagation index.

Example 2: You live in California, and you want to try to hear an elusive shortwave broadcast station located in Liberia, Western Africa, that operates around the clock in the 25-meter shortwave broadcast band. It is June, and you have determined that the V1.0 smoothed sunspot number is 80. When would be the best time to listen for the station?

1. From Table 4.2, a smoothed sunspot number of 80 is found to correspond to a high solar phase, and appropriate charts will be found in Section 4.5 of this chapter.

2. From Table 4.4, the summer seasonal chart should be used for June, and the PST zone chart would be applicable for California.

3. From Table 4.6, it is found that the 25-meter broadcast band corresponds to the 20-meter amateur band.

4. From the appropriate Master DX Propagation Chart found in Section 4.5 (summer, PST, high solar phase), you find at the intersection of "20 meters" and "West and Central Africa" that the highest propagation index is (4), and that this occurs between 19 and 21 hours. This would be the best time to listen for the desired station. From Table 4.7, this corresponds to between 8 and 10 p.m. PDT.

Example 3: It is 3 p.m. in Denver on a day in March, and you want to operate on the HF bands for an hour or so. From what areas of the world can you expect the strongest signals on 15 meters and on 20 meters? You already know that the V1.0 smoothed sunspot number is around 40.

1. From Table 4.3, you find that a smoothed sunspot number of 40 corresponds to a moderate

solar phase, and that the appropriate charts for this phase can be found in Section 4.4 of this chapter.

2. From Table 4.4, for the month of March, the appropriate seasonal chart to use would be for spring and fall. For Denver, the CST and MST zones chart would be applicable. From Table 4.7, you find that 3 p.m. MST corresponds to 15 hours in the 24-hour time system used in the charts.

3. From the appropriate Master DX Propagation Chart contained in Section 4.4 (moderate, spring and fall, CST and MST zones), your find for "15 meters" that the highest propagation index shown for anywhere in the world at 15 hours is (4), to the "Caribbean, Central America and Northern Countries of South America" and (4), also, to "Peru, Bolivia, Paraguay, Brazil, Chile, Argentina and Uruguay."

4. For "20 meters," the highest propagation index shown at 15 hours is a (4), for "West and Central Africa."

4.2   How To Use The Master Short-Skip Propagation Charts

Table 4.9 is a sample of a Master Short-Skip Propagation Chart.

The Short-Skip Charts are intended for use within the United States and Canada over distances ranging as far as 2,300 miles; this is considered to be the maximum possible distance for one-hop F2-layer propagation.

The explanations given for solar phase, season and frequency in Section 4.1 for the Master DX Propagation Charts also apply to the Master Short-Skip Propagation Charts. The Short-Skip Charts are found following the DX Charts given in Sections 4.3 through 4.6. Tables 4.2 through 4.7 also are applicable to the Short-Skip Charts.

The explanation for the Propagation Index given in Table 4.8 also applies to the Short-Skip Charts *except* that often, two numerals are shown within a single set of parentheses. Where this is the case, the first number applies to the shorter distance of the distance range shown while the second is for the greater distance.

In the Short-Skip Charts, appropriate standard time is given in the 24-hour time system, but it applies at the path midpoint rather than at the receiving or transmitting ends. For example, on an opening between Maine and Florida, the local time at the path midpoint would be EST; on an opening between New York and

Colorado, the local time in the chart would be CST, because the path midpoint falls in this time zone.

The following are several examples that illustrate the use of the Master Short-Skip Propagation Charts.

Example 1: You live in Los Angeles and you want to contact another radio amateur in California, 350 miles away. You want to set up a schedule every Saturday during March 2023 at noon PST. You have no idea what the smoothed sunspot number might be. What is the best band to use?

1. From Table 4.3, March 2023 is expected to correspond to a moderate solar phase. From Table 4.2, Master Propagation Charts for a moderate solar phase can be found in Section 4.4 of this chapter. The Short-Skip Charts follow the DX Charts.

2. From Table 4.4, the spring and fall seasonal chart should be used for March. Because the path midpoint in this example falls in the PST zone, the charts will give results in PST. From Table 4.7, noon PST corresponds to 12 hours.

3. From the appropriate Master Short-Skip Propagation Chart contained in Section 4.4 (moderate, spring and fall), or in this case, from the sample chart shown in Table 4.9, you find that under the range 250-750 miles between stations, the highest propagation index occurring at 12 hours is a (4-2) for "40 meters." The "4" applies to the shorter distance. This means 40 meters would be the best band to use for contacting a station 350 miles away at noon PST during March 2023.

Example 2: What would be the best time to keep a regular schedule on 15 meters between a station in New York City and one in Denver during the winter months when the V1.0 smoothed sunspot number is expected to be around 70?

1. From Table 4.2, a smoothed sunspot number of around 70 corresponds to a high solar phase, and appropriate Short-Skip Charts can be found in Section 4.5.

2. The distance between New York City and Denver is measured on a map to be 1,600 miles. The path midpoint falls in the CST zone.

3. Finding the appropriate Short-Skip Chart in Section 4.5 (high, winter), enter the chart under the column heading marked "Distance Between Stations (miles)" for the range 1,300-2,300 miles. Note the propagation index shown next to each opening at the intersection of this column and the one marked "15 meters." The highest propagation index, (4), occurs between 11 and 16 hours. From Table 4.7, this corresponds to 11 a.m. to 4 p.m. CST.

This means that the best time to make contact between New York City and Denver during the winter of high solar activity on 15 meters would be between 11 a.m. and 4 p.m. CST. This would be

MASTER SHORT-SKIP PROPAGATION CHART
SOLAR PHASE: MODERATE
SMOOTHED SUNSPOT RANGE: 30-60
SEASONS: SPRING & FALL
TIME ZONES: LOCAL STANDRAD AT PATH MID-POINT
(24-Hour Time)

Band (Meters)	Distance Between Stations (Miles)			
	50-250	250-750	650-1300	1300-2300
10	Nil	Nil	08-09 (0-1)	08-09 (1-0)
			09-12 (0-2)	09-12 (2-1)
			12-14 (0-3)	12-14 (3-2)
			14-16 (0-2)	14-16 (2)
			16-18 (0-1)	16-17 (1-2)
				17-18 (1)
				18-20 (0-1)
15	Nil	08-09 (1)	07-08 (0-1)	07-08 (1-0)
		09-15 (0-2)	08-09 (1)	08-09 (1)
		15-17 (0-1)	09-10 (2)	09-10 (2-3)
			10-15 (2-4)	10-15 (4)
			15-17 91-3)	15-17 (3)
			17-18 (0-2)	17-18 (2-3)
			18-20 (0-1)	18-20 (1-2)
				20-21 (0-1)
20	11-13 (0-1)	07-10 (0-1)	06-08 91-2)	06-07 (2-1)
	13-15 (0-2)	10-11 (0-2)	08-10 (1-3)	07-08 (2)
	15-16 (0-1)	11-13 (1-3)	10-13 (3-4)	08-10 (3)
		13-15 (2-4)	13-15 (4)	10-15 (4-3)
		15-16 (1-3)	15-18 (3-4)	15-18 (4)
		16-18 (0-3)	18-20 (2-3)	18-20 (3-4)
		18-20 (0-2)	20-22 (1-2)	20-22 (2-3)
		20-07 (0-1)	22-06 (1)	22-02 (1-2)
				02-06 (1)
40	06-07 (1-2)	06-07 (2-3)	06-07 (3-2)	06-08 (2-1)
	07-09 (2-3)	07-09 (3-4)	07-08 (4-2)	08-15 (1-0)
	09-18 (3-4)	09-11 (4-3)	08-09 (4-1)	15-16 (2-0)
	18-19 (2-3)	11-13 (4-2)	09-11 (3-1)	16-17 (2-1)
	19-21 (1-2)	13-15 (4-3)	11-13 (2-1)	17-19 (3-2)
	21-00 (0-1)	15-18 (1)	13-15 (3-1)	19-21 (4-3)
		18-19 (3-4)	15-17 (4-2)	21-22 (4)
		19-20 (2-4)	17-19 (4-3)	22-00 (3-4)
		20-21 (2-3)	19-20 (4)	00-02 (3)
		21-00 (1-2)	20-12 (3-4)	02-05 (2-3)
		00-06 (0-1)	21-00 (2-3)	05-06 (2)
			00-02 (1-3)	
			02-06 (1-2)	
80	07-08 (2-3)	07-08 (3-2)	07-08 (2-1)	07-08 (1-0)
	08-11 (3-4)	08-11 (4-1)	08-11 (1-0)	08-16 (0)
	11-18 (4-3)	11-16 (3-0)	11-16 (0)	16-18 (1-0)
	18-20 (3-4)	16-18 (4-3)	16-18 (2-1)	18-20 (2-1)
	20-22 (2-3)	18-20 (4-3)	18-20 (3-2)	20-22 (1-2)
	22-02 (1-2)	20-22 (3-4)	20-02 (4)	22-02 (4-3)
	02-05 (1)	22-02 (2-4)	02-05 (2-3)	02-05 (3-2)
	05-07 (1-2)	02-05 (1-2)	05-07 (2)	05-07 (2-1)
		05-07 (2)		
160	05-07 (4-2)	05-06 (2-1)	05-06 (1)	05-06 (1)
	07-09 (3-1)	06-07 (2-0)	06-19 (0)	06-19 (0)
	09-17 (2-0)	07-09 (1-0)	19-20 (2-1)	19-20 (1-0)
	17-19 (3-1)	09-17 (0)	20-22 (3-2)	20-22 (2-1)
	19-20 (4-2)	17-19 (1-0)	22-03 (4-2)	22-03 (2)
	20-05 (4)	19-20 (2)	03-05 (3-2)	03-05 (2-4)
		20-22 (4-3)		
		22-03 (4)		
		03-05 (4-3)		

Table 4.9 Sample Master Short Skip Propagation Chart.

between noon and 5 p.m. EST in New York City and between 10 a.m. and 3 p.m. MST in Denver.

Example 3: You live in Boston and you want to set up a three-way schedule with a radio amateur in Washington, D.C., about 500 miles away, and with another in central North Carolina, about 750 miles away. What would be the best band to use at 7 p.m. EDT during the summertime when solar activity is at a moderate level? In this case, all stations must be able to work each other.

1. From Table 4.2, Short-Skip Charts for the summer season of a moderate solar phase can be found in Section 4.4. From Table 4.7, 7 p.m. EDT corresponds to 18 hours EST in 24-hour time. Because all three stations are in the EST Zone, the results in the chart also will be in EST.

2. Finding the appropriate Short-Skip Chart in Section 4.4 (moderate, summer), enter the chart under the column heading marked "Distance Between Stations (miles)" for the distance range that corresponds to the 500 miles between Boston and Washington, D.C. The highest propagation index at 18, (4), occurs on 40 meters. Next, do the same for the range that corresponds to the distance of 750 miles between Boston and central North Carolina. On 40 meters at 18 hours for this distance, the propagation index also is (4), so there should be no problem communicating between Boston and Washington, D.C., and Boston and central North Carolina. Now, to finish the network, check 40 meters at 18 hours for the 250 miles between Washington, D.C., and central North Carolina. Here, again, the propagation index is found to be (4), so this three-way contact should work out very well. Don't forget that 18 hours is 7 p.m. in the summer in the Eastern Standard Time Zone.

4.3 Master Propagation Charts – Low Solar Phase Smoothed Sunspot Number Range 0-30

Band-By-Band Summary

10 meters – DX possibilities in this band are very poor, although an occasional F2 layer opening should be possible toward South America and other tropical areas during the daylight hours of the fall, winter, and early spring months. During the summer months, when sporadic-E ionization is at a maximum, fairly regular short-skip openings should be possible from a few hundred miles up to a distance of approximately 1,300 miles. When sporadic-E ionization is particularly intense and widespread, multi-hop openings to distances considerably beyond this range also may occur.

12 meters – Interpolate between 10 and 15 meter openings.

15 meters – Summer: DX openings in this band are expected to be fairly good, and somewhat regular, particularly on circuits into the Southern Hemisphere. Because of relatively high sporadic-E activity, short-skip activity should be good to excellent at distances from 300 to 1,300 miles.

15 meters – Winter: Through the daylight hours, DX openings generally should be fair to good, particularly during the period from noon to around sunset. Short-skip should be fairly consistent from around sunrise to sunset, but not much can be expected at night, when critical frequencies are depressed.

15 meters – Equinox: About the only consistent DX in this band in the spring and fall occurs on circuits to Africa and Latin America from the Northern Hemisphere. Short–skip openings may be fairly good over distances of 1,000 miles or more.

17 meters – Interpolate between 15 and 20 meters.

20 meters – Summer: During the summer in the low part of the sunspot cycle, the 20-meter band is the best band for consistent daytime DX to all parts of the world. It should remain open from sunrise to sunset, and often, to as late as midnight. Peak conditions can be expected for an hour or two after sunrise and again during the late afternoon. In addition to DX, the seasonal increase in sporadic-E activity should make short-skip openings a frequent occurrence over distances ranging from a few hundred miles to approximately 2,300 miles.

20 meters – Winter: Although the hours of daylight are considerably fewer than during the summer, what daylight hours there are will be good for DX activity in the 20-meter band. Peak conditions, with openings possible to all areas of the world, should occur for several hours after sunrise and again during the early afternoon. The band normally will close for DX an hour or so after sundown, but it may occasionally remain open to midnight for openings toward South America and Antarctica. Short-skip openings from a few hundred miles to approximately 2,300 miles should be possible throughout the daylight hours.

20 meters – Equinox: Again, this should be the best band for DX openings to all areas of the world between sunrise and sunset. The band should remain open from time to time well past sunset, particularly for long openings into the Southern Hemisphere. Excellent short-skip openings between distances of a few hundred and approximately 2,300 miles should be possible during the daylight hours.

30 meters – Interpolate between 20 and 40 meters.

40 meters – Summer: In the summertime, because of greater thunderstorm activity, there is an increase in the static level on most shortwave bands; as the frequency is lowered, the noise becomes more pronounced. In spite of increased static in the 40-meter band, nighttime DX openings should be numerous and consistent from just before sunset to just after sunrise to all parts of the world. Daytime short-skip should range between distances of 100 and approximately 1,000 miles. Nighttime short-skip should be possible between distances of 500 and 2,300 miles.

40 meters – Winter: Forty meters should open for DX in an easterly direction toward Europe and Africa during the late afternoon and toward the south just after sundown, after which time the MUF will fall below 7 MHz to many areas of the world. Openings toward the South Pacific and in a westerly direction should be possible after midnight and should peak just before sunrise. Short-skip openings during the daytime should range between distances of approximately 100 and 1,000 miles, and between 1,000 and 2,300 miles at night.

40 meters – Equinox: The band should remain open for DX from just before sunset, through the hours of

---

MASTER DX PROPAGATION CHART
SOLAR PHASE: LOW
SMOOTHED SUNSPOT RANGE: 0-30
SEASON: SUMMER
TIME ZONE: EST (24-Hour time)
EASTERN USA TO:

Reception Area	10/15 Meters	20 Meters	40 Meters	80/160 Meters
Western & Central Europe & North Africa	15-18 (1)	05-06 (1) 06-09 (3) 09-13 (2) 13-15 (3) 15-17 (4) 17-19 (3) 19-20 (2) 20-21 (1)	19-22 (1) 22-00 (2) 00-02 (1)	21-23 (1) 23-00 (2) 00-01 (1) 23-01 (1)
Northern & Eastern Europe	Nil	05-07 (1) 07-09 (2) 09-14 (1) 14-16 (2) 16-19 (1)	22-00 (1)	22-00 (1)
Eastern Mediterranean & East Africa	11-13 (1)	05-06 (1) 06-07 (2) 07-09 (1) 09-11 (2) 11-15 (1) 15-17 (1) 17-19 (1)	20-00 (1)	21-23 (1)
Western Africa	14-17 (1)	04-06 (1) 06-08 (2) 08-15 1) 15-16 (2) 16-18 (3) 18-19 (2) 19-21 (1)	21-00 (1) 00-02 (2) 02-04 (1)	00-02 (1)
Central & South Africa	Nil	05-06 (1) 06-07 (2) 07-14 (1) 14-16 (2) 16-18 (1) 01-03 (1)	22-23 (1) 23-01 (2) 01-03 (1)	23-01 (1)
Central & South Asia	Nil	05-08 (1) 18-21 (1)	Nil	Nil
Southeast Asia	Nil	05-06 (1) 06-08 (2) 08-10 (1) 18-21 (1)	Nil	Nil
Far East	Nil	06-07 (1) 07-08 (2) 08-11 (1) 20-23 (1)	Nil	Nil
South Pacific & New Zealand	18-20 (1)	16-22 (1) 22-00 (2) 00-06 (1) 06-09 (2) 08-11 (1)	01-02 (1) 02-05 (2) 05-06 (1)	02-05 (1) 02-04 (1)+
Australasia	19-22 (1)	15-22 (1) 22-00 (2) 00-06 (1) 06-09 (2) 08-11 (1)	01-02(1) 02-05(2) 05-06 (1)	03-05 (1) 03-04 (1)+
Carribbean, Central America & Northern Countries of South America	13-15 (1) 15-17 (2) 17-18 (1)* 08-09 (1) 08-11 (3) 11-13 (2) 13-14 (3) 14-17 (4) 17-19 (3) 19-21 (1)	06-07 (3) 07-09 (4) 08-11 (3) 11-16 (2) 16-18 (3) 18-21 (4) 21-22 (3) 22-00 (2) 00-06 (1)	18-21 (1) 21-00 (2) 00-03 (3) 03-05 (2) 05-06 (1)	22-01 (1) 01-04 (2) 04-05 (1) 01-03 (1)+
Peru, Bolivia, Paraguay, Brazil, Chile, Argentina & Uruguay	14-17 (1)* 08-11 (1) 11-14 (2) 14-15 (3) 15-16 (4) 16-17 (3) 17-18 (2) 18-20 (1)	05-06 (1) 06-10 (2) 10-14 (1) 14-17 (2) 17-18 (3) 18-20 (4) 20-22 (3) 22-23 (2) 23-01 (1)	21-00 (1) 00-02 (2) 02-06 (1)	00-04 (1) 02-04 (1)+
McMurdo Sound, Antarctica	14-17 (1)	14-16 (1) 16-18 (2) 18-22 (1)	03-07 (1)	Nil

---

MASTER DX PROPAGATION CHART
SOLAR PHASE: LOW
SMOOTHED SUNSPOT RANGE: 0-30
SEASON: SUMMER
TIME ZONE: CST & MST (24-Hour time)
CENTRAL USA TO:

Reception Area	10/15 Meters	20 Meters	40 Meters	80/160 Meters
Western & Central Europe & North Africa	15-17 (1)	05-06 (1) 06-08 (2) 08-12 (1) 12-14 (2) 14-17 (3) 17-19 (2) 19-20 (1)	20-22 (1) 22-00 (2) 00-01 (1)	21-23 (1)
Northern & Eastern Europe	Nil	05-07 (1) 07-09 (2) 09-13 (1) 13-15 (2) 15-18 (1)	21-23 (1)	Nil
Eastern Mediterranean & East Africa	Nil	05-06 (1) 06-07 (2) 07-14 (1) 14-16 (2) 16-18 (1)	20-23 (1)	Nil
Western Africa	Nil	05-06 (1) 06-09 (2) 09-14 (1) 14-16 (2) 16-17 (3) 17-18 (2) 18-20 (1)	21-00 (1) 00-01 (2) 01-03 (1)	00-01 (1)
Central & South Africa	Nil	05-06 (1) 06-07 (2) 07-14 (1) 14-16 (2) 16-18 (1) 00-02 (1)	22-23 (1) 23-00 (2) 00-02 (1)	22-00 (1)
Central & South Asia	Nil	05-09 (1) 18-21 (1)	Nil	Nil
Southeast Asia	Nil	05-06 (1) 06-09 (2) 09-11 (1) 18-20 (1) 20-22 (1) 22-23 (1)	Nil	Nil
Far East	21-23 (1)	06-07 (1) 07-10 (2) 10-20 (1) 20-22 (2) 22-00 (1)	04-06 (1}	Nil
South Pacific & New Zealand	14-18 (1) 18-20 (2) 20-22 (1)	02-06 (1) 06-09 (2) 09-17 (1) 17-19 (2) 19-22 (3) 20-02 (1)	00-02 (1) 02-06 (2) 06-07 (1)	01-06(1) 03-05 (1)+
Australasia	15-17 (1) 17-19 (2) 19-22 (1)	06-07 (1) 07-09 (2) 09-13 (1) 13-15 (2) 15-18 (1) 18-20 (2) 20-23 (3) 23-01 (1) 01-03 (1)	00-02 (1) 02-05 (2) 05-07 (1)	02-03 (1) 03-05 (2) 05-06 (1) 03-05 (1)+

darkness and until just after sunrise. Signals from the east should peak between sunset and midnight; signals from all other directions should peak between midnight and sunrise. Daytime short-skip distances should range between distances of 100 and 1,000 miles; nighttime short-skip should range between 1,000 and 2,300 miles.

60 meters – Interpolate between 40 and 80 meters.

80 meters – Summer: Generally fair DX to many areas of the world is possible on this band during the hours of darkness although static levels will be high. During daylight hours, short-skip openings to distances up to 250 miles should be likely, ranging from 200 to approximately 2,300 miles during the night.

80 meters – Winter: This should be the best band for DX during most of the hours of darkness. DX to most areas of the world should be possible from sundown to sunrise, with peaks at about midnight and again just before sunrise. Short-skip openings to distances as far as about 500 miles should be possible during the day, and between distances of 750 and 2,300 miles at night.

80 meters – Equinox: Fairly good DX conditions to most areas of the world should be possible between sundown and sunrise. Excellent short-skip openings should be possible during the day over distances up to about 350 miles. During the hours of darkness, short-skip openings should range between 500 and 2,300 miles.

160 meters – Summer: During the daylight hours, high levels of static and solar absorption will prevent any short-skip openings. During the hours of darkness, short-skip openings should be possible at ranges out to approximately 1,000 miles and, at times, to greater distances. Conditions do not favor DX openings on this

---

(Continuation table)

Reception Area	10/15 Meters	20 Meters	40 Meters	80/160 Meters
Caribbean, Central America & Northern Countries of South America	14-15 (1)*, 15-16 (2)*, 16-17 (1)*, 08-10 (1), 10-12 (3), 12-14 (3), 14-16 (4), 16-18 (3), 18-19 (2), 19-20 (1)	06-07 (3), 07-09 (4), 09-11 (3), 11-16 (2), 16-18 (3), 18-20 (4), 20-22 (3), 22-00 (2), 00-06 (1)	19-21 (1), 21-23 (2), 23-02 (3), 02-04 (2), 04-05 (1)	21-23 (1), 23-02 (2), 02-04 (1), 00-02 (1)+
Peru, Bolivia, Paraguay, Brazil, Chile, Argentina & Uruguay	13-16 (1)*, 08-11 (2), 11-13 (2), 13-14 (3), 14-16 (4), 16-17 (3), 17-18 (2), 18-19 (1)	05-06 (1), 06-09 (2), 09-14 (1), 14-16 (2), 16-17 (3), 17-19 (4), 19-21 (3), 21-22 (2), 22-00 (1)	20-23 (1), 23-01 (2), 01-05 (1)	23-04 (1), 01-03 (1)+
McMurdo Sound, Antarctica	13-15 (1)	12-16 (1), 16-18 (2), 18-21 (1)	03-07 (1)	Nil

MASTER DX PROPAGATION CHART
SOLAR PHASE: LOW
SMOOTHED SUNSPOT RANGE: 0-30
SEASON: SUMMER
TIME ZONE: PST (24-Hour Time)
WESTERN USA TO:

Reception Area	10/15 Meters	20 Meters	40 Meters	80/160 Meters
Western & Central Europe & North Africa	Nil	20-22 (1), 05-06 (1), 06-08 (2), 08-13 (1), 13-16 (2), 16-17 (1)	19-23 (1)	Nil
Northern & Eastern Europe	Nil	05-07 (1), 07-09 (2), 09-16 (1), 20-22 (1)	20-22 (1)	Nil
Eastern Mediterranean & East Africa	Nil	06-11 (1), 11-14 (2), 14-16 (1), 20-22 (1)	Nil	Nil
Western & Central Africa	09-11 (1)	21-23 (1), 05-06 (1), 06-08 (2), 08-13 (1), 13-16 (3), 16-17 (2), 17-18 (1)	20-23 (1)	Nil
Southern Africa	Nil	05-07 (1), 07-08 (2), 08-13 (1), 21-23 (1)	19-21 (1), 20-21 (2), 21-22 (1)	19-21 (1)
Central & South Asia	Nil	07-11 (1), 17-18 (1), 18-20 (2), 20-21 (1)	Nil	Nil
Southeast Asia	20-22 (1)	06-08 (1), 08-09 (2), 09-13 (1), 19-21 (1), 21-23 (2), 23-00 (1)	02-06 (1)	Nil
Far East	12-14 (1), 20-22 (1)	06-07 (1), 07-09 (2), 09-18 (1), 18-20 (2), 20-22 (1), 22-00 (2), 00-02 (1)	01-02 (1), 02-05 (2), 05-07 (1)	01-04 (1)
South Pacific & New Zealand	14-17 (1), 17-20 (2), 20-21 (1)	02-07 (1), 07-09 (2), 09-11 (1), 11-17 (2), 17-18 (3), 18-22 (4), 22-00 (3), 00-02 (2)	23-01 (1), 01-04 (3), 04-06 (2), 06-07 (1)	23-01 (1), 01-04 (2), 04-06 (1), 02-04 (1)+
Australasia	14-17 (1), 17-20 (2), 20-22 (1)	01-07 (1), 07-09 (2), 09-12 (1), 12-14 (2), 14-18 (1), 18-20 (1), 20-23 (3), 23-01 (2)	23-01 (1), 01-04 (2), 04-07 (1)	00-02 (1), 02-04 (2), 04-06 (1), 02-04 (1)+
Caribbean, Central America & Northern Countries of South America	14-17 (1)*, 08-10 (1), 10-12 (2), 12-14 (3), 14-16 (4), 16-18 (2), 18-19 (1)	06-08 (3), 08-10 (1), 10-13 (1), 13-15 (2), 15-17 (3), 17-20 (4), 20-22 (3), 22-23 (2), 23-04 (1), 04-06 (2)	19-21 (1), 21-23 (2), 23-01 (3), 01-03 (2), 03-04 (1)	20-22 (1), 22-00 (2), 00-03 (1), 00-02 (1)+
Peru, Bolivia, Paraguay, Brazil, Chile, Argentina & Uruguay	12-14 (1)*, 08-11 (1), 11-12 (2), 12-13 (3), 13-15 (4), 15-16 (2), 16-18 (1)	05-06 (1), 06-08 (2), 08-14 (1), 14-16 (2), 16-18 (4), 18-20 (2), 20-22 (1)	20-22 (1), 22-01 (2), 01-04 (1)	22-04 (1), 00-02 (1)+
McMurdo Sound, Antarctica	12-16 (1)	11-16 (1), 16-18 (2), 18-20 (1)	19-21 (1), 02-07 (1)	

MASTER DX PROPAGATION CHART
SOLAR PHASE: LOW
SMOOTHED SUNSPOT RANGE: 0-30
SEASON: WINTER
TIME ZONE: EST (24-Hour Time)
EASTERN USA TO:

Reception Area	10/15 Meters	20 Meters	40 Meters	80/160 Meters
Western & Central Europe & North Africa	09-11 (1)*, 08-09 (1), 09-11 (2), 11-13 (1)	06-07 (1), 07-08 (2), 08-10 (3), 10-12 (4), 12-13 (3), 13-14 (2), 14-16 (1)	15-16 (1), 16-17 (2), 17-19 (3), 19-01 (2), 01-03 (3), 03-04 (2), 04-05 (1)	17-19 (1), 19-20 (2), 20-02 (3), 02-03 (2), 03-04 (1), 20-00 (1)+, 00-02 (2)+, 02-03 (1)+
Northern & Eastern Europe	08-11 (1), 07-11 (2), 11-13 (1)	06-07 (1)	15-17 (1), 17-19 (2), 19-01 (1), 01-02 (2), 02-03 (1)	17-19 (1), 19-02 (2), 02-03 (1), 21-02 (1)+
Eastern Mediterranean & Middle East	09-10 (1)*, 08-09 (1), 09-11 (2), 11-12 (1)	07-08 (1), 08-10 (2), 10-12 (3), 12-14 (2), 14-15 (1)	17-19 (1), 19-21 (2), 21-00 (1), 00-01 (2), 01-02 (1)	18-20 (1), 20-22 (2), 22-00 (1), 22-00 (1)
Western Africa	10-12 (1)*, 08-09 (1), 09-11 (2), 11-13 (3), 13-14 (2), 14-15 (1)	06-07 (1), 07-09 (2), 09-12 (2), 12-14 (2), 14-16 (3), 16-17 (2), 17-18 (1)	18-20 (1), 20-23 (2), 23-01 (1), 01-03 (2), 03-04 (1)	19-22 (1), 22-01 (2), 01-03 (1), 22-01 (1)
Eastern & Central Africa	10-12 (1)*, 08-11 (1), 11-13 (2), 13-14 (1)	07-13 (1), 13-16 (2), 16-18 (1)	18-20 (1), 20-23 (2), 23-01 (1)	19-00 (1)
Southern Africa	10-13 (1)*, 08-09 (1), 09-11 (2), 11-13 (3), 13-14 (2), 14-15 (1)	07-09 (1), 12-14 (1), 14-15 (2), 15-16 (3), 16-17 (2), 17-19 (1)	18-20 (1), 20-22 (1), 22-00 (1)	19-22 (1)

Reception Area	10/15 Meters	20 Meters	40 Meters	80/160 Meters
Central & South Asia	16-18 (1) 19-21 (1)	07-10 (1)	06-08 (1) 18-22 (1)	06-07 (1) 18-20 (1)
Southeast Asia	16-18 (1)	07-10 (1) 17-20(1)	06-08 (1) 18-21 (1)	06-07 (1) 18-20 (1)
Far East	16-18 (1)	06-07 (1) 07-09 (2) 09-11 (1) 15-17 (1) 17-19 (2) 19-21 (1)	05-08 (1) 17-18 (1)	05-08 (1) 17-18 (1)
South Pacific & New Zealand	13-15 (1) 12-14 (1) 14-17 (2) 17-18 (1)	05-07 (1) 07-10 (2) 10-18 (1) 18-20 (1) 20-22 (1)	01-02 (1) 02-04 (2) 04-07 (3) 07-08 (2) 08-09 (1)	04-05 (1) 05-07 (2) 07-08 (1) 04-07 (1)+
Australasia	14-16 (1)* 12-15 (1) 15-17 (2) 17-18 (1)	06-07 (1) 07-10 (1) 10-12 (1) 15-16 (1) 16-19 (2) 19-21 (1)	03-05 (1) 05-08 (2) 08-09 (1) 17-19 (1)	05-06 (1) 06-07 (2) 07-08 (1) 17-18 (1) 05-07 (1)+
Caribbean, Central America & Northern Countries of South America	10-15 (1)* 08-09 (1) 09-12 (2) 12-16 (3) 16-17 (2) 17-18 (1)	05-07 (1) 07-08 (3) 08-09 (4) 09-11 (2) 11-15 (2) 15-17 (2) 17-18 (4) 18-19 (3) 19-20 (2) 20-02 (1)	17-18 (1) 18-19 (2) 19-21 (3) 21-03 (2) 03-06 (3) 06-07 (2) 07-08 (1)	18-20 (1) 20-21 (2) 21-04 (3) 04-06 (2) 06-07 (1) 21-03 (1)+ 03-05 (2)+ 05-06 (1)+
Peru, Bolivia, Paraguay, Brazil, Chile, Argentina & Uruguay	11-15 (1)* 08-09 (1) 09-11 (2) 11-13 (1) 13-14 (2) 14-16 (3) 16-17 (2) 17-18 (1)	06-07 (1) 07-09 (2) 09-10 (1) 12-14 (1) 14-15 (2) 15-16 (3) 16-18 (4) 18-19 (3) 19-20 (2) 20-22 (1) 22-00 (2) 00-02 (1)	19-21 (1} 21-02 (2) 02-05 (1) 05-06 (2) 06-07 (1)	21-03 (1) 03-05 (2) 05-06 (1) 03-05 (1)+
McMurdo Sound, Antarclica	15-17 (1)	07-09 (1) 17-18 (1) 18-20 (2) 20-22 (1) 22-00 (2) 00-02 (1)	22-00 (1) 00-02 (2) 02-06 (1)	Nil

MASTER DX PROPAGATION CHART
SOLAR PHASE: LOW
SMOOTHED SUNSPOT RANGE: 0-30
SEASON: WINTER
TIME ZONES: CST & MST (24-HOUR TIME)
CENTRAL USA TO:

Reception Area	10/15 Meters	20 Meters	40 Meters	80/160 Meters
Western Europe & North Africa	08-09 (1) 09-11 (2) 11-12 (1)	06-08 (1) 08-10 (2) 10-12 (3) 12-13 (2) 13-15 (1)	15-17 (1) 17-19 (2) 19-12 (3) 23-01 (1) 01-02 (1)	17-19 (1) 19-00 (2) 00-01 (1) 20-01 (1)+
Northern, Central, & Eastern Europe	08-11 (1)	07-08 (1) 08-11 (2) 11-12 (1)	16-18 (1) 18-19 (2) 19-22 (1) 22-00 (2) 00-01 (1)	18-00 (1) 20-00 (1)+
Eastern Mediterranean & Middle East	08-11 (1)	07-09 (1) 09-12 (2) 12-14 (1) 22-00 (1)	17-19 (1) 19-22 (2) 22-23 (1)	19-22 (1)
Western Africa	09-12 (1)* 08-09 (1) 09-11 (2) 11-13 (3) 13-14 (2) 14-15 (1)	06-07 (1) 07-09 (2) 09-11 (2) 11-13 (2) 13-15 (3) 15-16 (2) 16-18 (1) 22-00 (1)	17-20 (1) 20-23 (2) 23-01 (1)	19-22 (1) 22-23 (2) 23-00 (1) 21-23 (1)+
Eastern & Central Africa	10-12 (1)* 08-1 1(1) 11-13 (2) 13-14 (1)	06-12 (1) 12-14 (2) 14-16 (3) 16-17 (1)	18-19 (1) 19-21 (2) 21-23 (1)	19-22 (1)

Reception Area	10/15 Meters	20 Meters	40 Meters	80/160 Meters
Southern Africa	10-12 (1) 08-10 (1) 10-13 (2) 13-14 (1)	07-13 (1) 13-15 (2) 15-16 (3) 16-17 (2) 17-18 (1) 22-00 (1)	18-19 (1) 19-21 (2) 21-23 (1)	19-22 (1)
Central & South Asia	17-19 (1)	07-10 (1) 19-22 (1)	06-08 (1) 18-21 (1)	06-07 (1) 18-20 (1)
Southeast Asia	17-19 (1)	06-07 (1) 07-09 (2) 09-12 (1) 17-20 (1)	06-08 (1) 17-19 (1)	06-07 (1) 17-19 (1)
Far East	17-19 (1)	06-07 (1) 07-09 (2) 09-11 (1) 15-17 (1) 17-19 (2) 19-20 (1)	01-03 (1) 03-07 (2) 07-08 (1)	02-04 (1) 04-06 (2) 06-07 (1) 04-06 (1)+
South Pacific & New Zealand	12-16 (1)* 11-13 (1) 13-15 (2) 15-17 (3) 17-18 (2) 18-19 (1)	06-07 (1) 07-11 (2) 11-16 (1) 16-17 (2) 17-19 (1) 19-20 (2) 20-22 (1)	23-01 (1) 01-02 (2) 02-06 (3) 06-07 (2) 07-09 (1)	00-01 (1) 01-06 (2) 06-08 (1) 13-07 (1)
Australasia	14-17 (1) 11-15 (1) 15-18 (2) 18-19 (1)	06-07 (1) 07-11 (2) 11-18 (1) 18-21 (2) 21-22 (1)	01-03 (1) 03-07 (3) 07-08 (2) 08-09 (1)	03-05 (1) 05-07 (2) 07-08 (1) 04-07 (1)
Caribbean, Central America & Northern Countries of South America	10-15 (1)* 07-08 (1) 08-10 (2) 10-13 (3) 13-15 (4) 15-16 (3) 16-18 (1)	04-06 (1) 06-07 (2) 07-10 (3) 10-14 (2) 14-16 (3) 16-18 (4) 18-19 (3) 19-20 (2) 20-22 (1) 22-00 (2) 00-02 (1)	18-20 (1) 20-22 (2) 22-00 (3) 00-04 (2) 04-06 (3) 06-07 (1)	19-21 (1) 21-05 (1) 05-06 (1) 23-05 (1)
Peru, Bolivia, Paraguay, Brazil, Chile, Argentina & Uruguay	11-15 (1)* 07-09 (1) 09-11 (2) 11-13 (1) 13-14 (2) 14-16 (3) 16-17 (2) 17-18 (1)	06-07 (1) 07-09 (2) 09-13 (1) 13-14 (2) 14-15 (3) 15-17 (4) 17-18 (3) 18-19 (2) 19-21 (2) 21-23 (2) 23-00 (1)	19-21 (1) 21-02 (2) 02-04 (1) 04-06 (2) 06-07 (1)	21-05 (1) 00-04 (1)
McMurdo Sound, Antarctica	15-17 (1)	06-07 (1) 07-09 (2) 09-11 (1) 17-18 (1) 18-20 (2) 20-22 (1) 22-00 (2) 00-02 (1)	22-00 (1) 00-02 (2) 02-06 (1)	Nil

MASTER DX PROPAGATION CHART
SOLAR PHASE: LOW
SMOOTHED SUNSPOT RANGE: 0-30
SEASON: WINTER
TIME ZONE: PST (24-How Time)
WESTERN USA TO:

Reception Area	10/15 Meters	20 Meters	40 Meters	80/160 Meters
Western Europe & North Africa	08-10 (1)	06-07 (1) 07-11 (2) 11-13(1) 23-01 (1)	17-21 (1) 21-23 (2) 23-01 (1)	18-20 (1) 20-22 (2) 22-23 (1) 19-22 (1)+
Northern, Central & Eastern Europe	08-10 (1)	06-07 (1) 07-10 (2) 10-12 (1) 23-01 (1)	17-00 (1)	19-22 (1) 19-21 (1)+
Eastern Mediterranean & Middle East	08-10 (1)	07-10 (1) 10-12 (2) 12-13 (1) 21-23 (1)	06-08 (1) 18-22 (1)	06-08 (1) 18-21 (1)

Reception Area	10/15 Meters	20 Meters	40 Meters	80/160 Meters
Western Africa	09-11 (1)* 08-09 (1) 09-12 (2) 12-13 (1)	07-10(1) 10-13 (2) 13-16 (3) 16-17 (2) 17-18 (1)	18-23(1)	19-22(1)
Eastern & Central Africa	09-11 (1)	08-10 (1) 13-16 (2) 21-23 (1)	06-08 (1) 18-22 (1)	06-08 (1) 18-21 (1)
Southern Africa	08-10 (1) 10-12 (2) 12-14 (1)	09-13 (1) 13-16 (2) 16-18 (1) 23-01 (1)	18-21 (1)	18-20 (1)
Central & South Asia	17-19 (1)	08-10 (1) 17-18 (1) 18-19 (2) 19-20 (1)	15-08 (1) 17-19 (1)	05-07 (1)
Southeast Asia	14-16 (1)* 14-15 (1) 15-17 (2) 17-18 (1)	08-09 (1) 09-11 (2) 11-16 (1) 16-19 (2) 19-20 (1)	01-04 (1) 04-07 (2) 07-09 (1)	04-07 (1)
Far East	14-15 (1) 15-17 (2) 17-19 (1)	08-10 (1) 13-14 (1) 14-15 (2) 15-17 (3) 17-18 (2) 18-19 (1)	22-00 (1) 00-02 (2) 02-06 (3) 06-08 (2) 08-10 (1)	23-01 (1) 01-06 (2) 06-08 (1) 01-06 (1)+
South Pacific & New Zealand	14-16 (1)* 11-13 (1) 13-14 (2) 14-16 (3) 16-18 (2) 18-19 (1)	07-08 (1) 08-13 (2) 13-15 (1) 15-16 (2) 16-18 (4) 18-19 (2) 19-21 (1)	20-22 (1) 22-00 (2) 00-07 (3) 07-08 (2) 08-09 (1)	00-03 (1) 03-06 (2) 06-08 (1) 03-06 (1)+
Australasia	14-16 (1)* 10-13 (1) 13-15 (2) 15-17 (3) 17-18 (1)	07-08 (1) 08-11 (2) 11-17 (1) 17-18 (2) 18-19 (3) 19-20 (2) 20-22 (1)	01-03 (1) 03-05 (2) 05-07 (3) 07-08 (2) 08-09 (1)	03-05 (1) 05-06 (2) 06-08 (1) 04-07 (1)+
Caribbean, Central America & Northern Countries of South America	10-14 (1)* 07-08 (1) 08-10 (2) 10-12 (3) 12-14 (4) 14-15 (3) 15-16 (2) 16-17 (1)	04-06 (1) 06-07 (2) 07-09 (3) 09-13 (2) 13-15 (3) 15-17 (4) 17-18 (3) 18-19 (2) 19-21 (1) 21-23 (2) 23-01 (1)	18-20 (1) 20-21 (2) 21-23 (3) 23-01 (2) 01-03(3) 03-04 (1) 04-05(1)	19-21 (1) 21-03 (2) 03-04 (1) 21-03 (1)+
Peru, Bolivia, Paraguay, Brazil Chile, Argentina & Uruguay	11-14 (1)* 08-10 (1) 10-12 (2) 12-14 (3) 14-16 (2) 16-17 (1)	05-07 (1) 07-09 (2) 09-13 (1) 13-15 (2) 15-16 (3) 16-17 (4) 17-18 (3) 18-19 (2) 19-20 (1) 22-00 (1)	19-21 (11 21-00 (2) 00-02 (1) 02-04 (2) 04-06 (2)	22-05 (1) 00-04 (1)+
McMurdo Sound, Antarctica	14-16 (1) 07-09 (2)	06-07 (1) 00-02 (2) 09-11 (1) 15-17 (1) 17-19 (2) 19-21 (2) 23-01 (1)	21-00 (1) 02-05 (1)	Nil

MASTER DX PROPAGATION CHART
SOLAR PHASE: LOW
SMOOTHED SUNSPOT RANGE: 0-30
SEASONS: SPRING & FALL
TIME ZONE: EST (24-Hour Time)
EASTERN USA TO:

Reception Area	10/15 Meters	20 Meters	40 Meters	80/160 Meters
Western & Central Europe & North Africa	08-10 (1) 10-12 (2) 12-14 (1)	06-07 (1) 07-08 (2) 08-12 (3) 12-13 (4) 13-14 (3) 14-15 (2) 15-18 (1)	16-18 (1) 18-19 (2) 19-23 (3) 23-02 (2) 02-05 (1)	18-20 (1) 20-23 (2) 23-01 (1) 01-03 (1) 20-23 (1)+ 23-01 (2)+ 01-02 (1)+

Central USA (continued)

Reception Area	10/15 Meters	20 Meters	40 Meters	80/160 Meters
Northern & Eastern Europe	09-12 (1)	06-07 (1) 07-10 (2) 10-14 (1)rn	18-02 (1)	20-00 (1) 21-23 (1)+
Eastern Mediterranean & East Africa	09-11 (1)	06-11 (1) 11-13 (2) 13-15 (1)	18-20 (1) 20-21 (2) 21-23(1)	19-23 (1) 20-22 (1)+
Western Africa	08-10 (1) 10-12 (3) 12-13 (2) 13-16 (1)	06-07 (1) 07-09 (2) 09-12 (1) 12-14 (2) 14-16 (3) 16-17 (2) 17-19 (1)	18-19 (1) 19-22 (2) 22-01 (1)	19-21 (1) 21-22 (2) 22-00 (1) 20-22 (1)+
Central & South Africa	10-13 (1)* 07-10 (1) 10-12 (2) 12-14 (3) 14-15 (2) 15-18 (1)	07-14 (1) 14-15 (2) 15-17 (3) 17-18 (2) 18-21 (1)	18-20 (1) 20-22 (2) 22-00 (1)	19-22 (1) 19-21 (1)+
Central & South Asia	Nil	06-07 (1) 07-09 (2) 09-11 (1) 19-22 (1)	05-07 (1) 18-21 (1)	Nil
Southeast Asia	17-19 (1)	06-07 (1) 07-09 (2) 09-11 (1) 17-2 0(1)	06-08 (1) 17-20 (1)	Nil
Far East	16-19 (1)	06-07 (1) 07-09 (2) 09-11 (1) 17-20 (1)	05-08 (1)	06-07 (1)
South Pacfic & New Zealand	15-17 (1)* 12-16 (1) 16-18 (2) 18-20 (1)	07-09 (2) 09-20 (1) 20-22 (2) 22-07 (1)	00-02 (1) 02-06 (3) 06-07 (2) 07-08 (1)	02-03 (1) 03-05 (2) 05-07 (1) 02-06 (1)+
Australasia	12-16 (1) 16-18 (2) 18-20 (1)	06-07 (1) 07-09 (2) 09-15 (1) 20-23 (1)	03-05 (1) 05-07 (2) 07-09 (1)	04-05 (1) 05-07 (2) 07-08 (1) 05-07 (1)+
Caribbean, Central America & Northern Countries of South America	12-16 (1)* 07-08 (1) 08-09 (2) 09-11 (4) 11-13 (2) 13-15 (4) 15-16 (3) 16-18 (2) 18-20 (1)	00-06 (1) 06-07 (2) 07-10 (3) 10-15 (2) 15-17 (3) 17-19 (4) 19-21 (3) 21-00 (2)	18-19 (1) 19-20 (2) 20-03 (3) 03-05 (2) 05-07 (1)	19-21 (1) 00-02 (2) 02-06 (1) 00-04 (1)+
Peru, Bolivia. Paraguay, Brazil, Chile, Argentina & Uruguay	12-15 (1)* 07-09 (1) 09-11 (2) 11-13 (1) 13-15 (2) 15-17 (3) 17-19 (1)	06-07 (1) 07-10 (2) 10-14 (1) 14-16 (2) 16-18 (3) 18-20 (4) 20-22 (2) 22-03 (1)	19-21 (1) 21-03 (2) 03-07 (1)	21-06 (1) 01-04 (1)+
McMurdo Sound, Antarctica	15-17 (1)	16-18 (1) 18-20 (2) 20-23 (1) 06-07 (1) 07-09 (2) 09-11 (1)	23-05 (1)	Nil

MASTER DX PROPAGATION CHART
SOLAR PHASE: LOW
SMOOTHED SUNSPOT RANGE: 0-30
SEASONS: SPRING & FALL
TIME ZONES: CST & MST (24-Hour Time)
CENTRAL USA TO:

Reception Area	10/15 Meters	20 Meters	40 Meters	80/160 Meters
Western & Central Europe & North Africa	06-08 (1) 08-09 (1) 09-12 (2) 12-14 (1)	06-08 (1) 08-12 (2) 12-14 (3) 14-15 (2) 15-17(1)	16-19 (1) 22-02 (1)	18-20 (1) 20-22 (2) 22-00 (1) 20-00 (1)+
Northern & Eastern Europe	08-12 (1)	07-08 (1) 08-10 (2) 10-13 (1)	19-01 (1)	20-23 (1)
Eastern Mediterranean & East Africa	09-12 (1)	07-11 (1) 11-13 (2) 13-15 (1)	19-23 (1)	20-22 (1)

Western USA

Reception Area	10/15 Meters	20 Meters	40 Meters	80/160 Meters
Western Africa	08-10 (1) 10-12 (2) 12-15 (1)	06-07 (1) 07-09 (2) 09-11 (1) 11-13 (2) 13-15 (3j 15-17 (2) 17-18 (1)	18-19 (1) 21-00 (1)	19-20 (1) 20-22 (2) 22-23 (1) 20-22 (1)+
Central & South Africa	11-13 (1)* 08-10 (1) 10-12 (2) 12-14 (3) 14-15 (2) 15-18 (1)	07-14 (1) 14-15 (2) 15-16 (2) 16-17 (2) 17-20 (1)	18-20 (1) 20-22 (2) 22-0 0(1)	19-22 (1) 19-21 (1)+
Central & South Asia	Nil	06-07 (1) 07-09 (2) 09-11 (1) 19-21 (1)	06-08 (1) 19-21 (1)	Nil
Southeast Asia	10-14 (1) 17-20 (1)	06-07 (1) 07-09 (2) 09-12 (1) 19-21 (1)	06-08 (1) 17-19 (1)	Nil
Far East	16-19 (1)	06-07 (1) 07-09 (2) 09-11 (1) 16-18 (1) 18-20 (2) 20-22 (1)	02-09 (1)	05-07 (1)
South Pacfic & New Zealand	14-17 (1)* 12-16 (1) 16-18 (2) 18-21 (1)	18-19 (1) 19-21 (3) 21-00 (2) 00-06 (1) 06-09 (2) 09-18 (1)	22-01 (1) 01-06 (3) 06-07 (2) 07-09 (1)	00-03 (1) 03-06 (2) 06-07 (1) 03-07 (1)+
Australasia	12-16 (1) 16-18 (2) 18-2 0(1)	06-07 (1) 07-09 (2) 09-14 (1) 17-19 (1) 19-21 (2) 21-23 (1)	02-04 (1) 04-07 (2) 07-09(1)	04-05 (1) 05-07 (2) 07-08 (1) 05-01 (1)+
Caribbean, Central America & Northern Countries of South America	11-15 (1)* 07-08 (1) 08-09 (2) 09-11 (3) 11-13 (2) 13-15 (4) 15-17 (2) 17-19 (1)	00-06 (1) 06-07 (2) 07-09 (3) 09-14 (2) 14-16 (3) 16-18 (4) 18-20 (3) 20-00 (2)	18-19 (1) 19-20 (2) 20-02 (3) 02-04 (2) 04-0 6(1)	20-21 (1) 21-02 (2) 02-06 (1) 00-03 (1)+
Peru, Bolivia, Paraguay, Brazil. Chile, Argentina & Uruguay	12-14 (1)* 07-08 (1) 08-10 (2) 10-12 (1) 12-13 (2) 13-16 (3) 16-17 (2) 17-19 (1)	06-07(1) 07-09 (2) 09-13 (1) 13-15 (2) 15-17 (3) 17-19 (4) 19-21 (2) 21-02 (1)	19-21 (1) 21-03 (2) 03-06 (1)	21-05 (1) 01-04 (1)+
McMurdo Sound, Antarctica	15-17 (1)	16-18 (1) 18-20 (2) 20-00 (1) 06-07 (1) 07-09 (2) 09-11 (1)	00-07(1)	Nil

MASTER DX PROPAGATION CHART
SOLAR PHASE: LOW
SMOOTHED SUNSPOT RANGE 0-30
SEASONS: SPRING & FALL
TIME ZONE: PST (24-Hour Time)
WESTERN USA TO:

Reception Area	10/15 Meters	20 Meters	40 Meters	80/160 Meters
Western & Central Europe & North Africa	09-11 (1)	23-01 (1) 06-08 (1) 08-11 (2) 11-15 (1)	18-00 (1)	19-22 (1) 19-21 (1)+
Northern & Eastern Europe	07-10 (1)	23-01 (1) 06-07 (1) 07-09 (2) 09-12 (1)	18-23 (1)	20-23(1)
Eastern Mediterranean & East Africa	Nil	07-12 (1) 19-21 (1)	18-21 (1)	Nil

West USA / short-skip (continued)

Reception Area	10/15 Meters	20 Meters	40 Meters	80/160 Meters
West & Central Africa	07-08 (1) 08-10 (2) 10-13 (1)	06-10 (1) 13-15 (3) 15-16 (2) 16-18 (1)	18-22 (1)	19-21 (1) 19-21 (1)+
Southern Africa	09-11 (1) 07-10 (1) 10-13 (2) 13-15 (1)	05-14 (1) 14-17 (2) 17-18 (1) 23-01 (1)	19-22 (1)	20-21 (1)
Central & South Asia	17-19 (1)	07-09 (1) 16-18 (1) 18-20 (2) 20-21 (1)	05-08 (I)	Nil
Southeast Asia	11-15 (1) 15-17 (2) 17-19 (1)	07-09 (1) 09-11 (2) 11-13 (1) 19-22 (1)	02-05 (1) 05-07 (2) 07-09 (1)	Nil
Far East	12-14 (1) 14-18 (2) 18-20 (1)	07-12 (1) 12-14 (2) 14-16 (2) 16-17 (2) 17-19 (3) 19-20 (2) 20-22 (1)	22-00 (1) 00-02 (2) 02-06 (3) 06-08 (2) 08-0 (1)	00-02 (1) 02-05 (2) 05-07 (1) 03-06 (1)+
South Pacific & New Zealand	15-17 (1)* 10-13 (1) 13-15 (2) 15-17 (4) 17-18 (2) 18-20 (1)	07-08 (1) 08-10 (2) 10-16 (3) 16-17 (2) 17-19 (4) 19-21 (2)	21-22 (1) 22-05 (3) 05-07 (2) 07-09 (1)	22-00 (1) 00-05 (2) 05-07 (1) 02-06 (1)+
Australasia	15-17 (1)* 13-17 (2) 17-19 (3) 19-20 (1)	07-08 (1) 08-10 (2) 10-17 (3) 17-18 (2) 18-20 (3) 20-21 (2) 21-22 (1)	00-03 (1) 03-05 (3) 05-07 (2) 07-08 (1)	02-03 (1) 03-05 (2) 05-07 (1) 04-06 (1)+
Caribbean, Central America & Northern Countries of South America	10-14 (1)* 06-08 (1) 08-13 (2) 13-15 (3) 15-16 (2) 16-18 (1)	00-05 (1) 05-06 (2) 06-08 (3) 08-14 (2) 14-16 (3) 16-18 (4) 18-20 (3) 20-00 (2)	18-20 (1) 20-00 (3) 00-03 (2) 03-05 (1)	20-21 (1) 21-01 (2) 01-04 (2) 23-02(1)+
Peru, Bolivia, Paraguay, Brazil, Chile, Argentina & Uruguay	10-14 (1)* 06-08 (1) 08-10 (2) 10-12 (1) 12-13 (2) 13-15 (3) 15-16 (2) 16-18 (1)	05-07 (1) 07-09 (2) 09-13 (1) 13-15 (2) 15-17 (3) 17-19 (2) 19-00 (1)	19-21 (1) 21-02 (2) 02-05 (1)	21-04 (1) 00-03(1)+
McMurdo Sound, Antarctica	08-10 (1) 14-16 (1)	15-17 (1) 17-19 (3) 19-00 (1) 05-00 (1) 06-08 (2) 08-11 (1)	00-06 (1)	Nil

MASTER SHORT-SKIP PROPAGATION CHART
SOLAR PHASE: LOW
SMOOTHED SUNSPOT RANGE: 0-30
SEASON: SUMMER
TIME ZONES: LOCAL STANDARD AT PATH MID-POINT
(24-Hour Time)

Band (Meters)	Distance Between Stations (Miles) 50-250	250-750	650-1300	1300-2300
10	Nil	07-09 (0-1)* 09-13 (0-3)* 13-17 (0-1)* 17-21 (0-2)* 21-23 (0-1)*	07-09 (1)* 09-13 (3)* 13-17 (1-2)* 17-21 (2-3)* 21-07 (1)*	07-09 (1-0)* 09-13 (3-0)* 13-17 (2-0) 17-21 (3-0)* 21-07 (1-0)*
15	Nil	07-09 (0-2)* 09-13 (0-3)* 13-17 (0-2)* 17-19 (0-3)* 19-21 (0-2)* 21-07 (0-1)*	07-09 (2)* 09-13 (3)* 13-17 (2)* 17-19 (3)* 19-21 (2)* 21-23 (1-2)* 23-07 (1)*	07-09 (2-0) 09-13 (3-2) 13-17 (2-0) 17-19 (3-1) 19-20 (2-1) 20-23 (2-0) 23-07 (1-0)

Worldwide Chart — Left (Winter)

Band	50-250 / col1	col2	col3	col4
20	09-00 (0-1)*	06-09 (0.2)* 09-15 (0-4)* 15-20 (0-3)* 20-00 (0-2)* 00-06 (0-1)*	06-09 (2-3)* 09-16(4)* 16-21 (3-4)* 21-00 (2-3)* 00.06 (1-2)*	06-09 (2-0) 09-15 (3-2) 15-16 (4-2) 16-21 (4) 21-23 (3) 23-00 (3-2) 00-06 (2-1)
40	07-09 (1-2)* 09-15(1-4)* 15-19 (2-4)* 19-22 (1-2) 22-07 (0-1)* 19-22 (2-4) 22-07 (1-3)*	07-09 (2)* 09-11 (4-2) 11-15 (4-1) 15-17 (4-3) 17-19 (4) 20-22 (4) 22-05 (3-4) 05-07 (3)	07-09 (2-1) 09-11 (2-0) 11-15 (1-0) 15-17 (3-1) 17-20 (4-3) 05-07 (3-1)	07-09 (1-0) 09-15 (0) 15-17 (1-0) 17-20 (3-2) 20-05 (4)
80	06-09 (3-4) 09-17 (4-3) 17-21 (4) 21-04 (3-4) 04-06 (3)	07-09 (4-1) 09-17 (3-0) 17-19 (4-0) 19-21 (4-2) 21-23 (4-3) 23-04 (4) 04-06 (3) 06-07 (4-2)	07-09 (1-0) 09-19 (0) 19-21 (2-1) 21-23(3) 23-04 (4) 04-06 (3) 06-07 (2-1)	07-19 (0) 19-21 (1) 21-23 (3) 23-03 (4-3) 03-04 (4-2) 04-05 (3-2) 05-06 (3-1) 06-07 (1)
160	17-18 (1-0) 18-19 (1) 19-21 (3-1) 21-23 (4-2) 23-05 (4-3) 05-07 (3-2) 07-09 (1-0)	18-20 (1-0) 20-21 (1) 21-22 (2-1) 22-23 (2) 23-05 (3-0) 05-06 (2-1) 06-07 (2-0)	20-22 (1) 22-00 (2-1) 00-02 (2) 02-06 (2-1)	20-22 (1-0) 22-00 (1) 00-02 (2-1) 02-05 (1)

MASTER SHORT-SKIP PROPAGATION CHART
SOLAR PHASE: LOW
SMOOTHED SUNSPOT RANGE: 0-30
SEASON: WINTER
TIME ZONES: LOCAL STANDARD AT PATH MID-POINT
(24-Hour Time)

Band (Meters)	Distance Between Stations (Miles) 50-250	250-750	650-1300	1300-2300
10	Nil	Nil	11-16 (0-1)	11-16 (1-0)
15	Nil	10-16 (0-1)	09-10 (0-1) 10-12 (1) 12-16 (1-2) 16-17 (0-1)	09-10 (1) 10-12 (1-3) 12-14 (2-4) 14-15 (2-3) 15-16 (2) 16-17 (1) 17-18 (0-1)

Worldwide Chart — Middle (Spring & Fall)

Band	col1	col2	col3	col4
20	Nil	08-11 (0-1) 11-16 (0-2) 16-19 (0-1)	08-09 (0-1) 08-11 (1-4) 11-16 (2-4) 16-17 (1-3) 17-18 (1-2) 18-19 (1) 19-21 (0-1)	07-08 (0-1) 08-09 (1-3) 08-11 (4) 11-15 (4-3) 15-16 (4) 16-17 (3) 17-18 (2-3) 18-19 (1-2) 19-20 (1)
40	07-09 (0-1) 08-10 (1-3) 10-15 (3-4) 15-16 (2-3) 16-18 (1-2) 18-20 (0-1)	07-09 (1-3) 08-10 (3) 10-15 (4-3) 15-16 (3-4) 16-18 (2-4) 18-20 (1-2) 20-00 (0-2) 00-07 (0-1)	07-09 (3) 08-14 (3-1) 14-15 (3-2) 15-16 (3) 16-18 (4) 18-20 (2-4) 20-22 (2-3) 22-00 (2) 00-04 (1-2) 04-07 (1-3)	07-08 (3-2) 08-09 (3-1) 08-14 (1-0) 14-15 (2-0) 15-16 (3-1) 16-17 (4-2) 17-18 (4-3) 18-20 (4) 20-22 (3-4) 22-00 (2-3) 02-04 (2-3) 04-06 (3)
80	08-16 (4) 16-18 (2-4) 18-20 (1-3) 20-06 (1-2) 06-08 (2-3)	08-09(4-2) 08-16 (4-1) 16-18 (4-2) 20-06 (2-4) 06-07 (3-4) 07-08 (3)	08-09 (2-1) 09-16 (1-0) 16-18 (2-1) 18-20 (4-3) 20-06 (4) 06-07 (4-2) 07-08 (3-1)	08-09 (1-0) 09-16 (0) 16-18 (1-0) 18-20 (3-2) 20-04 (4-3) 04-06 (4-2) 06-07 (2-1) 07-08 (1)
160	07-09 (3-2) 09-11 (2-0) 11-17 (1-0) 17-19 (3-2) 19-07 (4)	07-09 (2-1) 09-17 (0) 17-19 (2-1) 19-04 (4) 04-05 (4-3) 05-07 (4-2)	06-07 (2-1) 07-09 (1-0) 17-19 (1-0) 19-20 (4-2) 20-21 (4-3) 21-04 (4) 04-06 (3-2)	06-07 (1-0) 07-19 (0) 19-20 (2-1) 20-21 (3-2) 21-04 (4-2) 04-06 (2-1)

MASTER SHORT-SKIP PROPAGATION CHART
SOLAR PHASE: LOW
SMOOTHED SUNSPOT RANGE: 0-30
SEASONS: SPRING & FALL
TIME ZONES: LOCAL STANDARD AT PATH MID-POINT
(24-Hour Time)

Band (Meters)	Distance Between Stations (Miles) 50-250	250-750	650-1300	1300-2300
10	Nil	09-13 (0-1)	07-09 (1) 09-13 (1-2) 13-21 (0-1)	07-09 (1-0) 09-11 (2-0) 11-13(2-1) 13-17 (1) 17-21 (1-0)

Worldwide Chart — Right

Band	col1	col2	col3	col4
15	Nil	07-09 (0-1) 09-13 (0-2) 13-21 (0-1)	07-09 (1) 09-13 (2) 13-17 (1-2) 17-21 (1) 21-07 (0-1)	07-09(1) 09-15 (2) 15-17 (2-1) 17-19 (1) 19-07 (1-0)
20	Nil	07-09 (0-1) 09-11 (0-2) 11-14 (0-4) 14-16 (0-3) 16-18 (0-2) 19-07 (0-1)	07-09 (1-2) 09-11 (2-4) 11-14 (4) 14-16 (3-4) 16-18 (2-4) 18-20 (1-3) 20-22 (1-2) 22-07 (1)	07-09 (2) 09-13 (4-2) 13-15 (4-3) 15-18 (4) 18-20 (3) 20-22 (2) 22-00 (1) 00-05 (1-0) 05-07 (1)
40	07-09 (0-2) 09-11 (2-4) 11-15 (3-4) 15-17 (2-3) 17-19 (1-2) 19-21 (0-1)	07-09 (2-3) 09-11 (4-3) 11-15 (4-2) 15-17 (3) 17-19 (2-4) 19-21 (4) 21-23 (0-3) 23-02 (0-2) 02-05 (0-1) 05-07 (0-2)	07-09 (3-2) 09-11 (3-1) 11-15 (2-1) 15-17 (3-2) 17-19 (4-3) 19-21 (4) 21-23 (3-4) 23-02 (2-3) 02-05(1-2) 05-07 (2-4)	07-09 (2-1) 09-15 (1-0) 15-17 (2-1) 17-19 (3-2) 19-23 (4) 23-02 (3-4) 02-05 (2-3) 05-07 (4-2)
80	06-08 (3-4) 08-21 (4) 21-03 (3-4) 03-06 (2-3)	06-08 (4-2) 08-16 (4-1) 16-18 (4-2) 18-21 (4-3) 21-03 (4) 03-05 (3-4) 05-06 (3)	06-08 (2-1) 08-16 (1-0) 16-18 (2-1) 18-21 (3-2) 21-03 (4) 03-05 (4-2) 05-06 (3-2)	06-08 (1) 08-16 (0) 16-18 (1) 18-21 (2) 21-03 (4-3) 03-06 (2)
160	16-18 (1-0) 18-20 (2-1) 20-05 (4) 05-07 (3-2) 07-09 (2-1) 09-11 (1-0)	17-19 (1-0) 19-20 (1) 20-02 (4-3) 02-05 (3-2) 05-07 (2-1) 07-09 (1-0)	19-20 (1-0) 20-22 (3-1) 22-02 (3) 02-05 (2-1) 05-07 (1)	20-22 (1-0) 22-02 (3-2) 02-05 (1) 05-07 (1-0)

FOOTNOTES

Worldwide Charts:
• Predicted times of 10 meter openings: all others in column are 15 meter openings.
+ Predicted times of 160 meter openings; all others in column are 80 meter openings.

Short Skip Charts:
• Predominately sporadic-E openings.

---

band during the summer although an occasional opening may be possible during the hours of darkness.

160 meters – Winter: In spite of low sunspot conditions, solar absorption rules out any skip during the daylight hours. Around sunset, the band will begin to open for skip. Regular short-skip openings to distances as far as 1,500 miles should be possible, with frequent openings as far as 2,300 miles. DX openings should be possible, with conditions peaking toward Europe and the east near midnight, and toward the west, south, and other directions just before sunrise.

160 meters – Equinox: No daylight skip is possible, but look for short-skip and DX openings during the hours of darkness. Expect short-skip openings regularly to distances of as much as 1,200 miles and occasionally to 2,300 miles. DX openings are expected to some areas of the world, with conditions expected to peak around midnight and again just before sunrise.

4.4 Master Propagation Charts – Moderate Solar Phase Smoothed Sunspot Number Range: 30-60

Band-By-Band Summary

10 meters – Summer: Some north-south DX openings should be possible during the afternoon hours, but in general, DX opportunities on this band will only be poor to fair. Short-skip openings due to sporadic-E ionization, however, should provide communications on paths as far as 1,300 miles during most days throughout this season. When sporadic-E ionization is intense and widespread, multi-hop openings over considerably greater distances should also be possible.

10 meters – Winter: DX activity in the 10-meter band should be fair. While F2-layer openings will occur only during the daytime hours, possibilities exist for occasional morning openings to Europe, fairly frequent midday openings to South America and Africa, and late afternoon openings to the South Pacific and Australia. Then, too, short-skip openings to distances between 1,000 and 2,300 miles also should be possible.

10 meters – Equinox: Some fairly good north-south daytime openings should be possible on the 10-meter band during the spring and fall months, particularly during the afternoon. Further, some F2-layer DX openings should be possible on east-west paths, especially to Africa, and to the South Pacific and New Zealand. An occasional opening to Europe also may be possible earlier in the day. Some fairly good short-skip propagation should be possible to distances between approximately 1,300 and 2,300 miles, particularly during the afternoon hours.

12 meters – Interpolate between 10 and 15 meters.

15 meters – Summer: Watch for fairly good DX openings on a regular basis toward the Southern Hemisphere during daylight hours. Peak conditions should occur, along with an occasional east-west opening toward Europe and Africa, during the afternoon hours. Then, too, sporadic-E peaks during this season, and it should provide excellent short-skip propagation to distances between 750 and 1,300 miles, and often beyond.

15 meters – Winter: Worldwide DX conditions should be very good during daytime hours. The band should peak toward Europe and the east a few hours after sunrise, toward the Southern Hemisphere during the early afternoon, and toward the South Pacific, the Far East and in a generally westerly direction during the late afternoon. Consistent short-skip openings also should be possible during the daylight hours to distances of between approximately 1,000 and 2,300 miles.

15 meters – Equinox: Expect fairly good DX openings to all areas of the world, with excellent propagation from the Northern Hemisphere to Africa, South America, and the South Pacific during the hours of daylight; signals should peak during the afternoon. Good short-skip openings should be possible over distances greater than approximately 1,000 miles.

17 meters – Interpolate between 15 and 20 meters.

20 meters – Summer: 20 meters should be the best band for worldwide propagation. The band, which will open shortly after sunrise and remain open until well after sunset, should provide good openings to all areas of the world on most of the days during this season. Look for peak conditions for an hour or two after

sunrise and again during the late afternoon and early evening. Excellent short-skip openings should be possible for distances beyond approximately 500 miles.

20 meters – Winter: While the band will not be open as long as it is during other times of the year, 20 meters should provide excellent DX openings to all areas of the world between sunrise and sunset. Excellent short-skip openings should also be possible during the daylight hours over distances beyond approximately 500 miles.

20 meters – Equinox: Expect very good DX openings to all areas of the world from sunrise through the early hours of darkness. Openings should peak for an hour or two after sunrise and again during the afternoon. Further, short-skip openings should provide excellent propagation conditions over distances beyond approximately 750 miles during daylight hours.

30 meters – Interpolate between 20 and 40 meters.

40 meters – Summer: Good DX openings should be possible on this band during the evening, nighttime, and sunrise hours; however, atmospheric noise – static — generated by thunderstorms will frequently limit activity. Peak conditions should occur at about midnight for openings toward Europe and the east, and just before sunrise for openings in other directions. Short-skip openings over ranges as far as approximately 1,000 miles should be possible during the daytime, and between 500 and 2,300 miles at night.

40 meters – Winter: The band should first open toward Europe and the east during the late afternoon, and remain open to different areas of the world during the hours of darkness and until just after sunrise. This should be the best band for DX during the nighttime hours. Excellent short-skip openings should be possible during the daytime for distances as far as approximately 1,000 miles, and during the hours of darkness to distances beyond 1,000 miles.

40 meters – Equinox: Expect fairly good worldwide DX openings from early evening through sunrise. Short-skip openings should occur during the daylight hours in the range from 100 to 1,000 miles, and during the hours of darkness to distances beyond 1,000 miles.

60 meters – Interpolate between 40 and 80 meters

80 meters – Summer: Due to high daytime ionospheric absorption and generally high static levels, expect no daytime DX openings. Some fairly good openings should be possible, however, during the hours of darkness and just before sunrise to some areas of the world. Short-skip openings should be possible to ranges as far as 250 miles during the day, and to approximately 2,300 miles at night.

80 meters – Winter: Fairly good DX openings should be possible to almost all areas of the world between sunset and sunrise, with peaks expected around midnight for signals from Europe and an easterly direction, and just before sunrise for signals from all other directions. Excellent daytime short-skip openings should be possible over distances as far as approximately 500 miles, with nighttime openings ranging between 500 and 2,300 miles.

80 meters – Equinox: Expect fairly good DX openings to many areas of the world, particularly to the Southern Hemisphere, during the hours of darkness and the sunrise period. Excellent daytime short-skip

MASTER DX PROPAGATION CHART
SOLAR PHASE: MODERATE
SMOOTHED SUNSPOT RANGE: 30-60
SEASON: SUMMER
TIME ZONE: EST (24-Hour Time)
EASTERN USA TO:

Reception Area	10/15 Meters	20 Meters	40 Meters	80/160 Meters
Western & Central Europe & North America	Nil	14-18 (1)	06-08 (2) 08-11 (1) 11-13 (2) 13-15 (3) 15-19 (4) 19-20 (3) 20-21 (2) 21-06 (1)	19-21 (1) 21-22 (2) 22-00 (3) 00-01 (2) 01-02 (1) 21-23 (1)* 23-00 (2)* 00-01 (1)*
Northern & Eastern Europe	Nil	14-17 (1)	08-14 (1) 14-18 (2) 18-22 (3) 22-00 (2) 00-05 (1) 05-08 (2)	20-21 (1) 21-23 (2) 23-01 (1) 20-23 (1)*
Eastern Mediterranean & Middle East	Nil	15-17 (1)	11-13 (1) 13-17 (2) 17-23 (3) 23-00 (2) 00-05 (1) 05-07 (2) 07-09 (1)	19-21 (1) 21-23 (2) 23-00 (1) 21-23 (1)*
Western Africa	Nil	10-13 (1) 13-16 (2) 16-18 (1)	00-06 (1) 06-08 (2) 08-14 (1) 14-16 (2) 16-18 (3) 18-21 (4) 21-23 (3) 23-00 (2)	19-21 (1) 21-23 (2) 23-01 (1)
East & Central Africa	Nil	12-14 (1) 14-16 (2) 16-18 (1)	13-15 (1) 15-17 (2) 17-20 (3) 20-21 (2) 21-23 (1) 23-01 (2) 01-05 (1)	20-23 (1)
Southern Africa	Nil	09-12 (1)	23-00 (1) 00-03 (2) 03-06 (1) 14-15 (1) 15-17 (2) 17-18 (1)	20-21 (1) 21-23 (2) 23-01 (1) 22-00 (1)*
Central & South Asia	Nil	Nil	16-19 (1) 19-21 (2) 21-23 (1) 06-08 (1)	18-20 (1)
Southeast Asia	Nil	Nil	05-06 (1) 06-08 (2) 08-10 (1) 18-20 (1)	Nil
Far East	Nil	Nil	05-06 (1) 06-09 (2) 09-11 (1) 19-23 (1)	Nil
South Pacific & New Zealand	17-20 (1)	15-17 (1) 17-20 (2) 20-21 (1)	17-20 (1) 20-22 (2) 22-02 (3) 02-05 (2) 05-08 (1)	00-02 (1) 02-05 (2) 05-07 (1) 03-05 (1)*

Reception Area	10/15 Meters	20 Meters	40 Meters	80/160 Meters
Australasia	Nil	18-21 (1)	22-00 (1) 00-01 (2) 01-03 (3) 03-04 (2) 04-07 (1) 07-09 (1) 09-11 (1) 15-17 (1)	02-03 (1) 03-05 (2) 05-06 (1) 03-05 (1)*
Caribbean, Central America & Northern Countries of South America	10-14 (1) 14-16 (2) 16-17 (1)	07-08 (1) 08-14 (2) 14-15 (3) 15-17 (4) 17-19 (3) 19-20 (2) 20-21 (1)	05-06 (2) 06-07 (3) 07-09 (4) 09-11 (3) 11-15 (2) 15-17 (3) 17-21 (4) 21-23 (3) 23-00 (2) 00-05 (1)	20-22 (1) 22-03 (2) 03-05 (1) 22-03 (1)
Peru, Bolivia, Paraguay, Brazil, Chile, Argentina & Uruguay	13-14 (1) 14-16 (2) 16-17 (1)	07-08 (1) 08-10 (2) 10-14 (1) 14-15 (2) 15-16 (3) 16-17(4) 17-18 (3) 18-20 (2) 20-21 (1)	15-16 (1) 16-18 (2) 18-19 (3) 19-21 (4) 21-23 (3) 23-01 (2) 01-06 (1) 06-08 (2) 08-10 (1)	22-00 (1) 00-03 (2) 03-05 (1) 00-04 (1)*
McMurdo Sound, Antarctica	Nil	14-17 (1)	16-18 (1) 18-22 (2) 22-00 (1)	02-04 (1)

MASTER DX PROPAGATION CHART
SOLAR PHASE: MODERATE
SMOOTHED SUNSPOT RANGE: 30-60
SEASON: SUMMER
TIME ZONES: CST & MST (24-Hour Time)
CENTRAL USA TO:

Reception Area	10/15 Meters	20 Meters	40 Meters	80/160 Meters
Western & Central Europe & North Africa	Nil	14-17 (1)	05-06 (1) 06-08 (2) 08-12 (1) 12-14 (2) 14-19 (3) 19-21 (2) 21-23 (1)	19-22 (1) 22-00 (2) 00-01 (1) 21-23 (1)
Northern & Eastern Europe	Nil	14-16 (1)	04-06 (1) 06-08 (2) 08-15(1) 15-21 (2) 21-23 (1)	19-23 (1)
Eastern Medterranean & Middle East	Nil	13-15 (1)	12-16 (1) 16-18 (2) 18-20 (3) 20-22 (2) 22-00 (1) 06-08 (1)	20-23 (1)
West & Central Africa	Nil	09-12 (1) 12-15 (2) 15-17 (1)	13-15 (1) 15-17 (2) 17-20 (3) 20-22 (2) 22-00 (1) 04-07 (1)	19-23 (1) 22-23 (1)*
East Africa	Nil	11-15 (1)	14-17 (1) 17-20 (2) 20-23 (1) 05-07 (1)	19-22 (1)
Southern Africa	Nil	09-11 (1)	21-23 (1) 23-02 (2) 02-06 (1) 12-14 (1)	20-22 (1) 22-23 (1) 23-00 (1) 22-00 (1)*

Reception Area	10/15 Meters	20 Meters	40 Meters	80/160 Meters
Central & South Asia	Nil	Nil	16-18 (1) 18-21 (2) 21-23 (1) 04-06 (1) 06-08 (2) 08-09 (1)	Nil
Southeast Asia	Nil	19-21 (1)	04-06 (1) 06-09 (2) 09-10 (1) 20-23 (1)	Nil
Far East	Nil	19-22 (1)	06-07 (1) 07-09 (3) 09-10 (2) 20-21 (1) 21-23 (2) 23-00 (1)	03-04 (1) 04-05 (2) 05-08 (1)
South Pacific & New Zealand	17-19 (1)	12-15 (1) 15-17 (2) 17-20 (3) 20-21 (2) 21-22 (1)	16-18 (1) 18-21 (2) 21-22 (3) 22-00 (4) 00-02 (3) 02-06 (2) 06-08 (3) 08-10 (2) 10-12 (1)	22-00 (1) 00-02 (2) 02-04 (3) 04-06 (2) 06-07 (1) 00-06 (1)*
Australasia	Nil	13-14 (1) 14-16 (2) 16-18 (1) 18-20 (2) 20-22 (1)	21-23 (1) 23-00 (2) 00-02 (3) 02-06 (2) 06-08 (3) 08-10 (2)	00-02 (1) 02-06 (2) 06-07 (1) 03-06 (1)*
Caribbean, Central America & Northern Countries of South America	10-14 (1) 14-16 (2) 16-17 (1)	07-08 (1) 08-10 (2) 10-15 (3) 15-17 (4) 17-18 (3) 18-19 (2) 19-20 (1)	01-04 (1) 04-05 (2) 05-06 (3) 06-08 (4) 08-10 (3) 10-15 (2) 15-17 (3) 17-21 (4) 21-23 (3) 23-01 (2)	20-22 (1) 22-03 (2) 03-05 (1) 23-02 (1)*
Peru, Bolivia, Paraguay, Brazil, Chile, Argentina & Uruguay	13-17 (1)	06-07 (1) 07-09 (2) 09-13 (1) 13-14 (2) 14-15 (3) 15-17 (4) 17-18 (3) 18-20 (2) 20-21 (1)	13-15 (1) 15-16 (2) 16-17 (3) 17-21 (4) 21-23 (3) 23-02 (2) 02-04 (1) 04-06 (2) 06-09 (1)	21-22 (1) 22-01 (2) 01-04 (1) 23-03 (1)*
McMurdo Sound, Antarctica	Nil	14-17 (1)	16-18 (1) 18-22 (2) 22-00 (1)	02-05 (1)

MASTER DX PROPAGATION CHART
SOLAR PHASE: MODERATE
SMOOTHED SUNSPOT RANGE: 30-60
SEASON: SUMMER
TIME ZONE: PST (24-Hour Time)
WESTERN USA TO:

Reception Area	10/15 Meters	20 Meters	40 Meters	80/160 Meters
Western Europe & North Africa	Nil	14-16 (1)	04-05 (1) 05-07 (1) 07-14 (1) 14-16 (2) 16-18 (2) 18-21 (2) 21-23 (1)	19-22 (1)

MASTER DX PROPAGATION CHART
SOLAR PHASE: MODERATE
SMOOTHED SUNSPOT RANGE: 30-60
SEASON: WINTER
TIME ZONE: EST (24-Hour Time)
EASTERN USA TO:

Reception Area	10/15 Meters	20 Meters	40 Meters	80/160 Meters
Central, Northern & Eastern Europe	Nil	Nil	04-05 (1) 05-07 (2) 07-09 (1) 09-12 (1) 12-16 (1) 16-21 (2) 21-22 (1)	19-21 (1)
Eastern Mediterranean & Middle East	Nil	Nil	16-19 (1) 19-21 (2) 21-22 (1) 05-07 (1)	Nil
West & Central Africa	Nil	09-11 (1) 11-14 (2) 14-15 (1)	14-17 (1) 17-19 (2) 19-21 (3) 21-23 (2) 23-02 (1) 06-08 (1)	20-23 (1)
East Africa	Nil	12-15 (1)	16-19 (1) 19-21 (2) 21-22 (1)	Nil
Southern Africa	Nil	09-11 (1)	14-16 (1) 21-22 (1) 22-00 (2) 00-01 (1)	19-22 (1)
Central & South Asia	Nil	Nil	04-06 (1) 06-08 (2) 08-10 (1) 16-20 (1) 20-22 (2) 22-00 (1)	Nil
Southeast Asia	Nil	19-21 (1)	20-22 (1) 22-00 (1) 00-06 (1) 06-08 (2) 08-10 (1)	02-06 (1)
Far East	Nil	19-21 (1)	17-19 (1) 19-21 (2) 21-23 (3) 23-01 (4) 01-03 (2) 03-06 (1) 06-09 (2) 09-11 (1)	01-02 (1) 02-05 (2) 05-06 (1) 02-04 (1)*
South Pacific & New Zealand	15-10 (1)	10-12 (1) 12-16 (2) 16-20 (3) 20-22 (2) 22-23 (1)	16-18 (1) 18-20 (2) 20-00 (4) 00-02 (3) 02-07 (2) 06-07 (1) 07-09 (3) 09-10 (2) 10.12 (1)	21-22 (1) 22-00 (2) 00-05 (3) 05-06 (2) 06-07 (1) 23-01 (1)* 01-04 (2)* 04-06 (1)*
Australasia	Nil	12-14 (1) 14-17 (2) 17-20 (3) 20-21 (2) 21-22 (1)	19-21 (1) 21-23 (2) 23-00 (3) 00-06 (2) 06-08 (3) 08-09 (2) 09-12 (1) 12-14 (2) 14-15 (1)	23-01 (1) 01-03 (2) 03-05 (3) 05-06 (2) 06-07 (1) 01-06 (1)*
Caribbean, Central America & Northern Countries at South America	10-14 (1) 14-16 (2) 16-18 (1)	07-10 (1) 10-12 (2) 12-14 (3) 14-16 (4) 16-17 (3) 17-18 (2) 18-20 (1)	08-10 (2) 10-13 (1) 13-15 (2) 15-17 (3) 17-21 (4) 21-23 (3) 23-01 (2) 01-03 (1) 03-06 (2) 06-08 (3)	20-22 (1) 22-03 (2) 03-05 (1) 22-03 (1)*
Peru, Bolivia, Paraguay, Brazil, Chile, Argentina & Uruguay	11-16 (1)	07-10 (1) 10-13 (2) 13-14 (3) 14-16 (4) 16-17 (3) 17-19 (2) 19-20 (1)	13-15 (1) 15-17 (2) 17-18 (3) 18-20 (4) 20-22 (3) 22-00 (2) 00-04 (1) 04-06 (1) 06-09 (1)	21-23 (1) 23-01 (2) 01-03 (1) 23-02 (1)*
McMurdo Sound, Antarctica	Nil	13-17 (1)	16-18 (1) 18-20 (2) 20-22 (1)	02-06 (1)

Reception Area	10/15 Meters	20 Meters	40 Meters	80/160 Meters
Western & Central Europe & North Africa	09-11 (1)	07-08 (1) 08-09 (3) 09-11 (4) 11-12 (3) 12-13 (2) 13-14 (1)	06-07 (1) 07-09 (4) 09-11 (3) 11-13 (4) 13-14 (3) 14-15 (2) 15-17 (1)	15-16 (1) 16-17 (2) 17-19 (3) 19-00 (4) 00-04 (2) 04-05 (1) 17-19 (1)* 19-20 (2)* 20-02 (3)* 02-03 (2)* 03-04 (1)*
Northern & Eastern Europe	08-10 (1)	07-08 (1) 09-10 (2) 10-12 (1)	06-07 (1) 07-09 (3) 09-12 (2) 12-14 (1)	16-19 (1) 19-23 (2) 23-03 (1) 19-02 (1)*
Eastern Mediterranean & Middle East	08-10 (1)	07-08 (1) 08-09 (2) 09-10 (3) 10-11 (2) 11-12 (1)	06-09 (1) 09-10 (2) 10-12 (3) 12-14 (2) 14-17 (1) 19-21 (1)	18-20 (1) 20-22 (2) 22-00 (1) 20-23 (1)*
Western & Central Africa	09-11 (1) 11-13 (2) 13-15 (1)	07-08 (1) 08-09 (2) 09-12 (3) 12-14 (4) 14-15 (3) 15-16 (2) 16-17 (1)	06-07 (1) 07-09 (2) 09-13 (1) 13-15 (2) 15-17 (4) 17-18 (3) 18-19 (2) 19-20 (1)	18-22 (1) 22-02 (2) 02-03 (1) 00-02 (1)*
East Africa	10-13 (1)	08-10 (1) 10-12 (2) 12-14 (3) 14-15 (2) 15-16 (1)	07-13 (1) 13-15 (2) 15-18 (3) 18-19 (2) 19-20 (1) 00-02 (1)	18-00 (1)
Southern Africa	09-10 (1) 10-12 (2) 12-13 (1)	07-09 (1) 09-12 (2) 12-14 (3) 14-16 (2) 16-17 (1)	06-09 (1) 12-14 (1) 14-15 (2) 15-17 (3) 17-18 (2) 18-20 (1)	18-19 (1) 19-21 (2) 21-00 (1) 19-22 (1)*
Central & South Asia	Nil	08-10 (1) 17-19 (1)	06-07 (1) 07-09 (2) 09-11 (1) 18-21 (1)	06-08 (1) 20-22 (1)
Southeast Asia	Nil	08-11 (1) 17-19 (1)	06-07 (1) 07-09 (2) 09-12 (1) 19-21 (1)	06-08 (1) 20-22 (1)
Far East	Nil	16-17 (1) 17-19 (2) 19-20 (1)	06-07 (1) 07-09 (2) 09-11 (1) 16-18 (1) 18-20 (2) 20-21 (1)	05-08 (1) 05-07 (1)*
South Pacific & New Zealand	13-17(1)	11-14 (1) 14-15 (2) 15-17 (3) 17-18 (2) 18-20 (1)	03-07 (1) 07-09 (2) 09-11 (1) 16-18 (1) 18-20 (2) 20-22 (1)	01-02 (1) 02-04 (2) 04-07 (3) 07-08 (2) 08-09 (1) 04-05 (1)* 05-07 (2)* 07-08 (1)*
Australasia	16-18 (1)	09-12 (1) 15-16 (1) 16-18 (2) 18-20 (1)	06-07 (1) 07-10 (2) 10-14 (1) 14-16 (2) 16-18 (1) 18-20 (2) 20-22 (1)	03-05 (1) 05-07 (2) 07-09 (1) 05-08 (1)*

Reception Area	10/15 Meters	20 Meters	40 Meters	80/160 Meters
Caribbean, Central America & Northern Countries of South America	09-10 (1) 10-12 (2) 12-14 (1) 14-16 (2) 16-17 (1)	07-08 (1) 08-11 (3) 11-13 (2) 13-15 (4) 15-16 (3) 16-17 (2) 17-18 (1)	06-07 (2) 07-09 (4) 09-11 (3) 11-15 (3) 15-17 (3) 17-18 (4) 18-19 (3) 19-20 (2) 20-22 (1) 22-00 (2) 00-06 (1)	17-18 (1) 19-21 (3) 21-04 (4) 04-05 (3) 05-06 (2) 06-07 (1) 19-20 (1)* 20-22 (2)* 22-02 (3)* 02-04 (2)* 04-06 (1)*
Peru, Bolivia, Paraguay, Brazil, Chile, Argentina & Uruguay	09-12 (1) 12-15 (2) 15-16 (1)	07-08 (1) 08-10 (2) 10-12 (1) 12-14 (2) 14-16 (4) 16-17 (3) 17-18 (1)	13-14 (1) 14-15 (2) 15-17 (3) 17-18 (4) 18-19 (3) 19-20 (2) 20-22 (1) 22-00 (2) 00-03 (1) 05-06 (1) 06-08 (2) 08-09 (1)	19-21 (1) 21-02 (2) 02-05 (1) 21-03 (1)*
McMurdo Sound, Antarctica	Nil	07-10 (1) 16-18 (1)	07-09 (1) 17-18 (1) 18-22 (1) 22-00 (1) 00-02 (2) 02-03 (1)	00-05 (1)

MASTER DX PROPAGATION CHART
SOLAR PHASE: MODERATE
SMOOTHED SUNSPOT RANGE: 30-60
SEASON: WINTER
TIME ZONES: CST & MST (24-Hour Time)
CENTRAL USA TO:

Reception Area	10/15 Meters	20 Meters	40 Meters	80/160 Meters
Western & Southern Europe & North Africa	09-11 (1)	07-08 (1) 08-09 (2) 09-11 (3) 11-12 (2) 12-13 (1) 12-13 (1)	06-08 (1) 08-09 (2) 09-12 (2) 12-13 (2) 13-15 (1) 22-00 (1)	16-18 (1) 18-20 (2) 20-00 (1) 00-02 (2) 02-03 (1) 17-22 (1)* 22-01 (2)* 01-02 (1)*
Northern, Central & Eastern Europe	Nil	07-08 (1) 08-10 (2) 10-12 (1)	07-08 (1) 08-11 (2) 11-13 (1) 23-01 (1)	17-19 (1) 19-22 (2) 22-01 (1) 19-00 (1)*
Eastern Mediterranean & Middle East	Nil	08-11 (1)	06-09 (I) 09-12 (2) 12-14 (2) 22-00 (1)	18-20 (1) 20-22 (2) 22-23 (1) 20-22 (1) *
West & Central Africa	08-10 (1) 10-12 (2) 12-13 (1)	07-09 (1) 09-11 (2) 11-13 (3) 13-14 (2) 14-15 (1)	06-11 (1) 11-13 (2) 13-16 (2) 16-17 (2) 17,19 (1) 22-02 (1)	18-22 (1) 22-23 (2) 23-01 (1) 19-22 (1)*
East Africa	10-12 (1)	07-11 (1) 11-13 (2) 13-14 (1)	06-12 (1) 12-14 (2) 14-16 (3) 16-17 (2) 17-19 (1)	19-23 (1)
Southern Africa	08-09 (1) 09-12 (2) 12-13 (1)	07-09 (1) 09-11 (2) 11-13 (3) 15-16 (1)	07-13 (1) 13-15 (2) 15-17 (3) 17-18 (2) 18-20 (1) 23-01 (1)	18-19 (1) 19-21 (2) 21-23 (1)
Central & South Asia	Nil	08-10 (1) 19-21 (1)	06-07 (1) 07-09 (2) 09-11 (1) 19-22 (1)	06-08 (1) 19-21 (1)
Southeast Asia	Nil	08-11 (1) 17-20 (1)	07-08 (1) 08-10 (2) 10-12 (1) 16-17 (1) 17-19 (2) 19-20 (1)	04-07 (1)

Reception Area	10/15 Meters	20 Meters	40 Meters	80/160 Meters
Far East	Nil	07-09 (1) 16-17 (1) 17-19 (2) 19-20 (1)	06-07 (1) 07-09 (2) 09-11 (2) 15-17 (1) 17-19 (2) 19-21 (1)	02-01 (1) 04-06 (2) 06-07 (1) 04-07 (1)*
South Pacific & New Zealand	12-14 (1) 14-16 (2) 16-18 (1)	10-12 (1) 12-14 (2) 14-17 (3) 17-19 (2) 19-20 (1)	06-07 (1) 07-09 (3) 09-12 (2) 12-15 (1) 15-17 (2) 17-20 (3) 20-21 (2) 21-22 (1) 02-04 (1)	23-01 (1) 01-02 (2) 02-06 (3) 06-07 (1) 07-08 (1) 03-07 (1)*
Australasia	14-15 (1) 15-17 (2) 17-18 (1)	09-11 (1) 13-15 (1) 15-17 (3) 17-19 (2) 19-20 (1)	06-07 (1) 07-08 (2) 08-10 (3) 10-12 (2) 12-18 (1) 18-21 (2) 21-22 (1)	02-04 (1) 04-07 (2) 07-09 (1) 03-06 (1)*
Caribbean, Central America & Northern Countries of South America	08-10 (1) 10-14 (2) 14-16 (1)	07-08 (1) 08-09 (2) 09-13 (3) 13-16 (3) 16-17 (2) 17-19(1)	06-07 (2) 07-11 (3) 11-14 (2) 14-16 (3) 16-18 (4) 18-19 (3) 19-20 (2) 20-22 (1) 22-00 (2) 00-06 (1)	18-20 (1) 20-22 (2) 22-03 (3) 03-05 (2) 05-07 (1) 19-21 (1)* 21-01 (2) 01-04 (1)*
Peru, Bolivia, Paraguay, Brazil, Chile, Argentina & Uruguay	08-11 (1) 11-15 (2) 15-17 (1)	07-08 (1) 08-13 (2) 13-15 (4) 15-16 (3) 16-17 (2) 17-19 (1)	05-06 (1) 06-08 (2) 08-10 (1) 12-14 (1) 14-15 (2) 15-17 (3) 17-19 (4) 19-20 (2) 20-22 (1) 22-00 (2) 00-03 (1)	19-21 (1) 21-02 (2) 02-05 (1) 21-04 (1)*
McMurdo Sound, Antarctica	Nil	07-09(1) 16-18 (1)	06-07 (1) 07-09 (2) 09-11 (1) 17-18 (1) 18-22 (2) 22-00 (1) 00-02 (2) 02-03 (1)	22-05 (1)

MASTER DX PROPAGATION CHART
SOLAR PHASE: MODERATE
SMOOTHED SUNSPOT RANGE: 30-60
SEASON: WINTER
TIME ZONE: PST (24-Hour Time)
WESTERN USA TO:

Reception Area	10/15 Meters	20 Meters	40 Meters	80/160 Meters
Western Europe & North Africa	07-09 (1)	07-08 (1) 08-10 (2) 10-11 (1)	05-07 (1) 07-10 (2) 10-12 (1) 23-01 (1)	18-20 (1) 20-23 (2) 23-01 (1) 19-23 (1)*
Northern, Central & Eastern Europe	Nil	07-09 (1)	06-07 (1) 07-10 (2) 10-13 (1) 23-01 (1)	17-00 (1) 19-23 (1)*
Eastern Mediterranean & Middle East	Nil	07-09 (1)	06-07 (1) 07-09 (2) 09-11 (1) 21-23 (1)	18-21 (1)
West & Central Africa	09-12 (1)	07-09 (1) 09-10 (2) 10-12 (3) 12-13 (2) 13-14 (1)	06-10 (1) 10-13 (2) 13-16 (3) 16-18 (2) 18-19 (1)	18-22 (1)
East Africa	Nil	08-11 (1)	08-10 (1) 13-16 (1) 21-23 (1)	18-20 (1)

Reception Area	10/15 Meters	20 Meters	40 Meters	80/160 Meters
Southern Africa	08-11 (1)	06-08 (1) 08-10 (2) 10-12 (3) 12-13 (2) 13-14 (1)	07-11 (1) 11-13 (2) 13-16 (3) 16-18 (2) 18-19 (1) 00-02 (1)	18-20 (1)
Central & South Asia	Nil	09-11 (1) 17-19 (1)	08-10 (1) 17-19 (1) 19-20 (2) 20-21 (1)	05-07 (1) 18-20 (1)
Southeast Asia	15-18 (1)	09-11 (1) 15-16 (1) 16-18 (2) 18-19 (1)	07-09 (1) 09-11 (2) 11-16 (1) 16-19 (2) 19-20 (1)	03-08 (1)
Far East	15-17 (1)	14-15 (1) 15-16 (2) 16-17 (3) 17-18 (3) 18-19 (1)	08-10 (1) 13-14 (2) 14-15 (2) 15-18 (3) 18-19 (2) 19-21 (1)	00-01 (l) 01-03 (2) 03-06 (3) 06-08 (2) 08-10 (1) 02-08 (1)*
South Pacific: & New Zealand	12-14 (1) 14-16 (2) 16-17 (1)	09-12 (1) 12-14 (2) 14-16 (4) 16-17 (3) 17-18 (2) 18-20 (1)	07-08 (1) 08-10 (2) 10-15 (1) 15-16 (2) 16-18 (4) 18-19 (3) 19-20 (2) 20-22 (1) 03-05(1)	22-00 (1) 00-03 (2) 03-06 (3) 06-07 (2) 07-08 (1) 00-03(1)* 03-06 (2)* 06-07 (1)*
Australasia	13-15 (1) 15-17 (2) 17-18 (1)	08-12 (1) 12-15 (2) 15-17 (3) 17-18 (2) 18-19 (1)	07-08 (1) 08-10 (3) 10-12 (2) 12-17 (1) 17-18 (2) 18-20 (3) 20-21 (2) 21-22 (1)	01-0 3(1) 03-06 (2) 06-08 (1) 01-03 (1)* 03-06 (2)* 06-07 (1)*
Caribbean, Central America & Northern Countries of South America	09-11 (1) 11-14 (2) 14-16 (1)	06-07 (1) 07-08 (2) 08-12 (3) 12-14 (4) 14-15 (3) 15-16 (2) 16-17 (1)	06-07 (2) 07-09 (3) 09-13 (3) 13-15 (3) 15-17 (4) 17-18 (3) 18-20 (2) 20-22 (1) 22-00 (2) 00-06 (1)	18-20 (1) 20-22 (2) 22-02 (3) 02-04 (2) 04-05 (1) 19-21 (1)* 21-01 (2)* 01-04 (1)*
Peru, Bolivia, Paraguay, Brazil, Chile, Argentina & Uruguay	10-12 (1) 12-14 (2) 14-15 (1)	07-10 (1) 10-12 (2) 12-13 (3) 13-15 (4) 15-16 (2) 16-18 (1)	08-14 (1) 14-15 (2) 15-16 (3) 16-18 (4) 18-19 (3) 19-20 (2) 20-23 (1) 23-01 (2) 01-06 (1) 06-08 (2)	20-22 (1) 22-01 (2) 01-04 (1) 22-02 (1)
McMurdo Sound, Antarctica	Nil	07-09 (1) 12-15 (1) 15-17 (2) 17-18 (1)	16-18 (1) 18-19 (2) 19-22 (3) 22-01 (2) 01-03 (1) 07-09 (1)	23-05 (1)

MASTER DX PROPAGATION CHART
SOLAR PHASE: MODERATE
SMOOTHED SUNSPOT RANGE: 30-60
SEASONS: SPRING & FALL
TIME ZONE: EST (24-Hour Time)
EASTERN USA TO:

Reception Area	10/15 Meters	20 Meters	40 Meters	80/160 Meters
Western & Central Europe & North Africa	09-12 (1)	08-09 (1) 09-10 (2) 10-13 (3) 13-14 (2) 14-15 (1)	06-07 (1) 07-09 (3) 09-11 (2) 11-12 (3) 12-14 (4) 14-15 (3) 15-17 (2) 17-19 (1)	17-18 (1) 18-19 (2) 19-22 (3) 22-01 (4) 01·02 (3) 02·03 (2) 03-04 (1) 19-21 (1)* 21-00 (2)* 00-02 (1)"

Reception Area	10/15 Meters	20 Meters	40 Meters	80/160 Meters
Northern & Eastern Europe	08-11(1)	08-09 (1) 09-12 (2) 12-13 (1)	06-07 (1) 07-09 (3) 09-11 (2) 11-13 (1) 13-15 (2) 15-17 (1) 00-03 (1)	17-19 (1) 19-02 (2) 02-03 (1) 20-01 (1)*
Eastern Mediterranean & Middle East	08-11 (1)	08-09 (1) 09-11 (2) 11-13(1)	06-07 (1) 07-09 (2) 09-12 (1) 12-15 (2) 15-16 (3) 16-18 (2) 18-20 (1) 00-02 (1)	18-20 (1) 20-23 (2) 23-00 (1) 20-23 (1)*
West & Central Africa	09-11 (1) 11-13 (2) 13-14 (1)	07-09 (1) 09-10 (2) 10-12 (3) 12-14 (4) 14-15 (3) 15-16 (2) 16-17 (1)	05-06(1) 06-08 (2) 08-13 (1) 13-14 (2) 14-15 (3) 15-17 (4) 17-18 (3) 18-20 (2) 20-22 (1)	18-21 (1) 21-01 (2) 01-03 (1) 22-02(1)*
Southern Africa	09-10 (1) 10-12 (2) 12-14 (1)	07-10 (1) 10-13 (2) 13-15 (1) 15-17 (2) 17-18 (1)	07-14 (1) 14-16 (2) 16-18 (3) 18-20 (2) 20-22 (1) 22-00 (2) 00-01 (1)	18-20 (1) 20-23 (2) 23-00 (1) 21-23 (1)*
East Africa	10-13 (1)	07-09 (1) 09-11 (2) 11-13 (3) 13-14 (2) 14-16 (1)	12-14 (1) 14-16 (2) 16-18 (3) 18-19 (2) 19-20 (1)	19-23 (1) 23-01 (2) 01-02 (1)
Central & South Asia	08-11 (1) 19-21 (1)	08-10 (1) 19-21 (1)	06-07 (1) 07-09 (2) 09-11 (1) 19-21 (1)	19-22 (1) 04-06 (1)
Southeast Asia	10-13 (1) 18-20 (1)	08-10(1) 17-19 (1)	06-07 (1) 07-09 (2) 09-11 (1) 19-21 (1)	05-07 (1) 19-22(1)
Far East	17-19 (1)	16-17 (1) 17-19 (2) 19-20 (1)	06-07 (1) 07-09 (2) 09-11 (1) 17-18 (1) 18-20 (2) 20-22 (1)	05-08 (1) 05-07 (1)*
South Pacific & New Zealand	12-14 (1) 14-16 (2) 16-18 (1)	10-14 (1) 14-16 (2) 16-18 (3) 18-19 (2) 19-20 (1)	09-11 (1) 11-19 (1) 19-23 (2) 23-06 (1) 06-07 (2) 07-09 (3)	00-01 (1) 01-02 (2) 02-05 (3) 05-07 (2) 07-08 (1) 03-07 (1)*
Australasia	09-11 (1) 16-18 (1)	08-12 (1) 14-16 (1) 16-19 (2) 19-21 (1)	06-07 (1) 07-09 (3) 09-10 (2) 10-14 (1) 14-16 (2) 16-19 (1) 19-22 (2) 22-00 (1)	02-04 (1) 04-06 (2) 06-08 (1) 04-06 (1)*
Caribbean, Central America & Northern Countries of South America	09-11 (1) 11-12 (2) 12-14 (3) 14-16 (2) 16-18 (1)	07-08 (1) 08-09 (2) 09-11 (4) 11-13 (2) 13-16 (4) 16-17 (3) 17-18 (2) 18-20 (1)	22-00 (2) 00-06 (1) 06-07 (2) 07-09 (4) 09-10 (3) 10-14 (2) 14-16 (3) 16-19 (4) 19-22 (3)	18-19 (1) 19-20 (2) 20-03 (4) 03-05 (2) 05-06 (2) 06-07 (1) 20-22 (1)* 22-03 (2)* 03-05 (1)*
Peru, Bolivia, Paraguay, Brazil, Chile, Argentina & Uruguay	09-11 (1) 11-14 (2) 14-16 (3) 16-17 (2) 17-18 (1)	07-08 (1) 08-10 (2) 10-13 (3) 13-15 (4) 15-16 (3) 16-17 (4) 17-18 (2) 18-19 (1)	13-15 (1) 15-16 (2) 16-18 (3) 18-20 (2) 20-21 (3) 21-23 (2) 23-06 (1) 06-08 (2) 08-10 (1)	19-21 (1) 21-03 (2) 03-06 (1) 21-05 (1)'
McMurdo Sound, Antarctica	Nil	14-17 (1) 17-19 (2) 19-20 (1)	17-19 (1) 19-23 (2) 23-01 (1) 06-08 (1)	22-00 (1) 00-04 (2) 04-06 (1)

MASTER DX PROPAGATION CHART
SOLAR PHASE: MODERATE
SMOOTHED SUNSPOT RANGE: 30-60
SEASONS: SPRING & FALL
TIME ZONES: CST & MST (24-Hour Time)
CENTRAL USA TO:

Reception Area	10/15 Meters	20 Meters	40 Meters	80/160 Meters
Western & Central Europe & North Africa	09-11 (1), 09-13 (2), 13-14 (1)	08-09 (1), 07-09 (2), 09-11 (1), 11-13 (2), 13-15 (3), 15-16 (2), 16-18 (1), 22-00 (1)	00-07 (1), 19-22 (2), 22-00 (3), 00-01 (2), 01-02 (1)	17-19 (1), 19-22 (2), 20-22 (1)*, 22-0 0(2)*, 00-01 (1)*
Northern & Eastern Europe	09-11 (1)	07-09 (1), 09-11 (2), 11-12 (1)	06-07 (1), 07-10 (2), 10-12 (2), 12-13 (2), 13-15 (3), 23-01 (1)	19-22 (1), 22-00 (2), 00-02 (1), 22-01 (1)*
Eastern Mediterranean & Middle East	09-11 (1)	07-09 (1), 09-11 (2), 11-13 (1)	07-12 (1), 12-15 (2), 15-17 (1), 22-00 (1)	19-22 (1), 20-22 (1)*
West & Central Africa	09-10 (1), 10-12 (2), 12-14 (1)	07-09 (1), 09-10 (2), 10-12 (3), 12-13 (4), 13-15 (3), 15-16 (2), 16-17 (1)	06-12 (1), 12-14 (2), 14-15 (3), 15-16 (4), 16-17 (3), 17-19 (2), 19-21 (1)	18-20 (1), 20-23 (2), 23-01 (1), 21-00 (1)*
East Africa	09-12 (1)	09-11 (1), 11-15 (2), 15-17 (1)	06-12 (1), 12-14 (2), 14-16 (3), 16-18 (2), 18-19 (1)	19-22 (1)
Southern Africa	08-09 (1), 09-12 (2)	07-09 (1), 09-11 (2), 12-13 (1), 14-15 (2), 15-16 (1)	05-07 (2), 07-13 (1), 11-14 (3), 15-17 (3), 17-18 (2), 18-20 (1), 23-01 (1)	19-22 (1), 20-21 (1)*, 13-15 (2)
Central & South Asia	07-09 (1), 17-19 (1)	08-10 (1), 19-21 (1)	06-07 (1), 07-09 (2), 09-11 (1), 19-21 (1)	05-07 (1), 18-20 (1)
Southeast Asia	09-10 (1)	09-12 (1), 18-20 (1), 17-19 (2), 19-20 (1)	06-07 (1), 16-17 (1), 10-12 (1), 16-18 (1), 18-20 (2), 20-21 (1)	04-07 (1), 07-10 (2)
Far East	16-19 (1)	14-16 (1), 16-18 (2), 18-20 (1)	06-07 (1), 07-09 (2), 09-11 (1), 16-18 (1), 18-21 (2), 21-23 (1)	02-04 (1), 04-06 (2), 06-08 (1), 05-07 (1)*
South Pacific & New Zealand	11-13 (1), 13-14 (2), 14-15 (3), 15-16 (2), 16-17 (1)	10-12 (1), 12-15 (2), 15-17 (3), 17-19 (2), 19-20 (1)	06-07 (1), 07-09 (3), 09-11 (2), 11-18 (1), 18-20 (2), 20-22 (3), 22-00 (2), 00-02 (1)	22-00 (1), 00-01 (2), 01-06 (3), 06-07 (2), 07-08 (1), 00-02 (1)*, 02-05 (2)*, 05-07 (1)*
Australasia	14-15 (1), 15-16 (2), 16-18 (1)	08-14 (1), 14-16 (2), 16-18 (3), 18-19 (2), 19-21 (1)	06-07 (1), 07-09 (3), 09-12 (2), 12-15 (1), 15-17 (1), 17-19 (1), 19-21 (2), 21-01 (1)	02-04 (1), 04-06 (3), 06-07 (2), 07-08 (1), 04-05 (1)*, 05-06 (2)*, 06-07 (1)*
Caribbean, Central America & Northern Countries of South America	08-09 (1), 09-10 (2), 10-14 (3), 14-15 (2), 15-16 (1)	07-08 (1), 09-09 (2), 09-13 (3), 13-16 (4), 16-17 (3), 17-18 (2), 18-19 (1)	07-09 (4), 09-11 (3), 11-15 (2), 15-16 (3), 16-18 (4), 18-21 (3), 21-00 (2), 00-06 (1), 06-07 (2)	18-19 (1), 19-20 (2), 20-00 (3), 00-02 (4), 02-03 (3), 03-04 (2), 04-06 (1), 19-21 (1)*, 21-03 (2)*, 03-05 (1)*
Peru, Bolivia, Paraguay, Brazil, Chile, Argentina & Uruguay	08-11 (1), 11-14 (2), 14-16 (3), 16-17 (2)	07-08 (1), 08-13 (2), 13-14 (3), 14-16 (4), 17-18 (1), 16-17 (3), 17-18 (1), 18-20 (1)	14-15 (2), 15-16 (3), 16-19 (4), 19-20 (3), 16-17 (3), 00-02 (1), 04-06 (1), 06-08 (2), 08-14 (1)	19-20 (1), 20-02 (2), 02-05 (1), 21-03 (1), 20-00 (2)
McMurdo Sound, Antarctica	Nil	13-16 (1), 16-18 (2), 18-20 (1)	16-19 (2), 19-23 (3), 23-02 (1), 07-09 (1)	22-02 (1), 02-04 (2), 04-06 (1)

MASTER DX PROPAGATION CHART
SOLAR PHASE: MODERATE
SMOOTHED SUNSPOT RANGE: 30-60
SEASONS: SPRING & FALL
TIME ZONE: PST (24-Hour Time)
WESTERN USA TO:

Reception Area	10/15 Meters	20 Meters	40 Meters	80/160 Meters
Western Europe & North Africa	09-11 (1)	08-09 (1), 09-12 (2), 12-14 (1)	05-07 (1), 07-09 (2), 09-11 (1), 11-13 (2), 13-14 (3), 14-16 (2), 16-18 (1), 22-00 (1)	19-20 (1), 20-22 (2), 22-00 (1), 20-22 (1)*
Northern, Central & Eastern Europe	Nil	07-08 (1), 08-10 (2), 10-12 (1)	06-07 (1), 07-09 (2), 09-12 (1), 12-13 (2), 13-15 (1), 22-00 (1)	19-21 (1), 21-23 (2), 23-00 (1), 21-23 (1)*
Eastern Mediterranean & Middle East	Nil	07-08 (1), 08-10 (2), 10-12 (1)	07-12 (1), 12-14 (2), 14-17 (1), 22-02 (1)	18-21 (1)
West & Central Africa	08-10 (1)	07-09 (1), 10-12 (2), 12-14 (2), 15-16 (2), 16-17 (1)	04-06 (1), 09-12 (2), 12-15 (2), 12-14 (2), 14-17 (3), 17-19 (2), 19-21 (1)	18-22 (1), 06-08 (2), 08-12 (1)
East Africa	09-12 (1)	08-10 (1), 10-13 (3), 13-14 (1)	06-08 (1), 12-14 (1), 14-16 (2), 16-18 (1)	18-20 (1)
Southern Africa	09-12 (1)	07-10 (1), 10-14 (2), 14-15 (1)	06-08 (2), 08-13 (2), 13-15 (2), 15-17 (3), 17-18 (2), 18-19 (1), 23-01 (1)	18-21 (1)
Central & South Asia	17-19 (1)	07-09 (1), 16-17 (1), 17-19 (2), 19-20 (1)	16-18 (1), 18-20 (2), 20-22 (1), 06-07 (1), 07-09 (2), 09-12 (1)	05-07 (1), 19-21 (1)
Southeast Asia	09-11 (1), 17-19 (1)	08-10 (1), 15-17 (1), 17-19 (2), 19-22 (1)	07-08 (1), 08-11 (2), 11-13 (1), 20-22 (1), 22-00 (2), 00-02 (1)	00-02 (1), 02-05 (2), 05-07 (1)
Far East	15-17 (1)	12-14 (1), 14-17 (2), 17-18 (3), 18-19 (2), 19-20 (1)	06-07 (1), 07-09 (2), 09-11 (1), 11-13 (2), 13-15 (1), 15-17 (2), 17-20 (3), 20-22 (2), 22-02 (1)	00-02 (1), 02-07 (2), 07-08 (1), 02-06 (1)*
South Pacific & New Zealand	12-15 (1), 15-17 (2), 17-18 (1)	10-14 (1), 14-16 (2), 16-19 (3), 19-21 (2), 21-22 (1)	06-07 (1), 07-09 (2), 09-11 (2), 11-17 (1), 17-19 (2), 19-20 (3), 20-22 (4), 22-00 (3), 00-02 (2), 02-04 (1)	19-21 (1), 21-22 (2), 22-23 (3), 23-05 (4), 05-06 (3), 06-07 (2), 07-08 (1), 22-01 (1)*, 01-05 (2)*, 05-06 (1)*
Australasia	12-15 (1), 15-17 (1), 17-18 (1)	09-12 (1), 12-16 (2), 16-19 (3), 19-20 (2), 20-21 (1)	07-08 (1), 08-10 (3), 10-12 (2), 12-17 (1), 17-19 (2), 19-22 (3), 22-01 (2), 01-04 (1)	00-01 (1), 01-02 (2), 02-05 (3), 05-06 (2), 06-08 (1), 02-04 (1)*, 04-06 (2)*, 06-07 (1)*
Caribbean, Central America & Northern Countries of South America	09-11 (1), 11-12 (2), 12-14 (3), 14-15 (2), 15-16 (1)	06-07 (1), 07-09 (2), 09-12 (3), 12-15 (4), 15-16 (3), 16-17 (2), 17-18 (1)	06-07 (2), 07-09 (3), 09-14 (2), 14-16 (3), 16-19 (4), 19-21 (3), 21-23 (2), 23-06 (1)	18-20 (1), 20-01 (3), 01-03 (2), 03-06 (1), 19-21 (1)*, 21-02 (2)*, 02-04 (1)*
Peru, Bolivia, Paraguay, Brazil, Chile, Argentina & Uruguay	09-11 (1), 11-13 (2), 13-15 (3), 15-16 (2)	07-08 (1), 08-09 (2), 09-11 (1), 11-13 (2), 16-17 (1), 15-16 (4), 16-17 (3), 17-18 (2), 18-19 (1)	12-14 (1), 14-15 (2), 15-16 (3), 16-18 (4), 13-15 (3), 20-23 (2), 23-05 (1), 05-07 (2), 07-09 (1)	18-20 (1), 20-01 (2), 22-02 (1)*, 18-20 (3)
McMurdo Sound, Antarctica	13-16 (1), 15-18 (2), 18-20 (1)	12-15 (1), 19-20 (2), 20-22 (3), 22-00 (2), 00-02 (1), 05-06 (1), 06-08 (2), 08-10 (1)	16-19 (1), 19-20 (2), 20-22 (3)	22-02 (1), 02-04 (2), 04-06 (1)

MASTER SHORT-SKIP PROPAGATION CHART
SOLAR PHASE: MODERATE
SMOOTHED SUNSPOT RANGE: 30-60
SEASON: SUMMER
TIME ZONES: LOCAL STANDARD AT PATH MID-POINT (24-Hour Time)

Band (Meters)	Distance Between Stations (Miles) 50-250	250-750	650-1300	1300-2300
10	Nil	07-09 (0-1)*, 09-13 (0-3)*, 13-17 (0-1)*, 17-21 (0-2)*, 21-23 (0-1)*	07-09 (1)*, 09-13 (3)*, 13-17 (1-2)*, 17-21 (2-3)*, 21-07(1)*	07-09 (1-0), 09-13 (3-1), 13-17 (2-1), 17-21 (3-1), 21-07 (1-0)
15	Nil	07-09 (0-2)*, 09-13 (0-3)*, 13-17 (0-2)*, 17-19 (0-3)*, 19-21 (0-2)*, 21-07 (0-1)*	07-09 (3)*, 09-13 (3)*, 13-17 (3)*, 17-19 (3)*, 19-21 (2)*, 21-23 (1-2)*, 23-07 (1)*	07-09 (2-1), 09-13 (3-2), 13-17 (2-2), 17-19 (3), 19-21 (2), 21-23 (2-1), 23-07 (1-0)
20	09-00 (0-1)*, 00-06 (0-1)*	06-09 (0-2)*, 09-15 (1-4)*, 15-20 (1-3)*, 20-00 (1-2)*, 00-06 (1-2)*	06-09 (2-3)*, 09-16 (4)*, 16-21 (3-4)*, 21-00 (2-3)*, 00-06 (2-1)	06-09 (3-2), 09-15 (4-2), 15-16 (4-3), 16-21 (4), 21-00 (3-2), 00-06 (2-1)
40	07-11 (1-2)*, 11-16 (2-4), 16-20 (3-4), 20-22 (1-2), 22-07 (0-1)*, 22-07 (1-3)*	07-09 (2-3)*, 09-11 (2), 11-16 (4-2), 16-17 (4-3), 17-20(4), 20-22 (2-4), 22-05 (3-4)	07-0 9(3-1), 09-16 (2-1), 16-17 (3-1), 17-20 (4-3), 20-22 (4), 05-07 (3)	07-17 (1-0), 17-20 (3-2), 20-05 (4), 05-07 (3-1)
80	06-11 (3-4), 11-15 (4-3), 15-21 (4), 21-04 (3-4), 04-06 (3)	07-09 (4-1), 09-11 (4-0), 11-15 (3-0), 15-17 (4-1), 17-19 (4-2), 19-21 (4-3), 21-04 (4), 04-06 (3), 06-07 (4-2)	07-09 (1-0), 09-15 (0), 15-17 (1-0), 17-19 (2-1), 19-21 (3-1), 21-04 (4), 04-06 (3), 06-07 (2-1)	07-17 (0), 17-19 (1-0), 19-21 (1-0), 21-03 (4-3), 03-04 (4-2), 04-05 (4-3), 05-06 (3-1), 06-07 (1)

160			
17-18 (1-0)	18-19 (1-0)	20-21 (1)	20-22 (1-0)
18-19 (1)	19-20 (2-0)	21-00 (2-1)	22-00 (1)
19-21 (3-2)	20-21 (2-1)	00-03 (2)	00-05 (2-1)
21-23 (4-3)	21-23 (3-2)	03-05 (3-2)	05-06 (1-0)
23-05 (4)	23-03 (4-2)	05-06 (1)	
05-07 (3-2)	03-05 (4-3)	06-07 (1-0)	
07-08 (1)	05-07 (2-1)		
08-09 (1-0)	07-08 (1-0)		

MASTER SHORT-SKIP PROPAGATION CHART
SOLAR PHASE: MODERATE
SMOOTHED SUNSPOT RANGE: 30-60
SEASON: WINTER
TIME ZONES: LOCAL STANDARD AT PATH MID-POINT
(24-How Time)

Band (Meters)	Distance Between Stations (Miles)			
	50-250	250-750	650-1300	1300-2300
10	Nil	Nil	11-16 (0-1)	09-11 (0-1)
				11-15 (1-2)
				15-16 (1)
				16-17 (0-1)
15	Nil	10-12 (0-1)	08-10 (0-1)	07-09 (1)
		12-14 (0-2)	10-11 (1-2)	09-11 (2-3)
		14-16 (0-1)	11-12 (1-3)	11-12 (3-4)
			12-14 (2-4)	12-14 (4)
			14-15 (1-3)	14-15 (3)
			15-16 (1-2)	15-16 (2-3)
			16-18 (0-1)	16-17 (1-2)
				17-18 (1)
				18-19 (0-1)
20	Nil	07-09 (0-1)	07-08 (1)	06-07 (1)
		09-11 (0-2)	08-09 (1-3)	07-08 (1-2)
		11-14 (0-4)	09-11 (2-4)	08-09 (3)
		14-15 (0-3)	11-14 (4)	09-15 (4-3)
		15-17 (0-2)	14-15 (3-4)	15-17 (4)
		17-20 (0-1)	15-17 (2-4)	17-18 (3)
			17-18 (1-3)	18-20 (2-3)
			18-20 (1-2)	20-22 (1)
			20-22 (0-1)	
40	07-08 (0-1)	07-08 (1-3)	07-09 (3)	07-08 (3-2)
	08-09 (1-2)	08-09 (2-3)	09-14 (3-1)	08-09 (3-1)
	09-16 (3-4)	09-16 (4-3)	14-16 (3-2)	09-14 (1-0)
	16-17 (2-3)	16-17 (3-4)	16-18 (4)	14-16 (2-0)
	17-18 (1-2)	17-18 (2-4)	18-20 (3-4)	17-18 (4-3)
	18-20 (0-1)	18-20 (1-3)	20-22 (2-3)	18-20 (4)
		20-02 (0-2)	22-02 (2)	20-22 (3-4)
		02-07 (0-1)	02-04 (1-2)	22-00 (2-3)
			04-07 (1-3)	00-02 (2)
				02-04 (2-3)
				04-07 (3)

80			
08-18 (4)	08-09 (4-2)	08-09 (2-0)	08-16 (0)
18-19 (3-4)	09-16 (4-1)	09-16 (1-0)	16-18 (1-0)
19-00 (1-2)	16-18 (4-2)	16-18 (2-1)	18-20 (3-2)
00-07 (1-3)	18-19 (4-3)	18-19 (3)	20-04 (4-3)
07-08 (2-3)	19-00 (2-4)	19-20 (4-3)	04-06 (3-2)
	00-07 (3-4)	20-04 (4)	06-07 (2-1)
	07-08 (3)	04-06 (4-3)	07-08 (1)
		06-07 (4-2)	
		07-08 (3-1)	

160			
07-09 (3-2)	07-09 (2-0)	07-09 (1-0)	06-19 (0)
09-11 (2-0)	09-17 (0)	09-17 (0)	19-20 (2-1)
11-17 (1-0)	17-19 (2-1)	17-19 (1-0)	20-21 (3-2)
17-19 (3-2)	19-04 (4)	19-20 (4-2)	21-04 (4-2)
19-07 (4)	04-06 (4-2)	20-21 (4-3)	04-06 (1)
	06-07 (4-1)	21-04 (4)	
		04-06 (2-1)	
		06-07 (1-0)	

MASTER SHORT-SKIP PROPAGATION CHART
SOLAR PHASE: MODERATE
SMOOTHED SUNSPOT RANGE: 30-60
SEASONS: SPRING & FALL
TIME ZONES: LOCAL STANDARD AT PATH MID-POINT
(24-Hour Time)

Band (Meters)	Distance Between Stations (Miles)			
	50-250	250-750	650-1300	1300-2300
10	Nil	Nil	08-09 (0-1)	08-09 (1-0)
			09-12 (0-2)	09-12 (2-1)
			12-14 (0-3)	12-14 (3-2)
			14-16 (0-2)	14-16 (2)
			16-18 (0-1)	16-17 (1-2)
				17-18 (1)
				18-20 (0-1)
15	Nil	08-09 (1)	07-08 (0-1)	07-08 (1-0)
		09-15 (0-2)	08-09 (1)	08-09 (1)
		15-17 (0-1)	09-10 (2)	09-10 (2-3)
			10-15 (2-4)	10-15 (4)
			15-17 (1-3)	15-17 (3)
			17-18 (0-2)	17-18 (2-3)
			18-20 (0-1)	18-20 (1-2)
				20-21 (0-1)
20	11-13 (0-1)	07-10 (0-1)	06-08 (1-2)	06-07 (2-1)
	13-15 (0-2)	10-11 (0-2)	08-10 (1-3)	07-08 (2)
	15-16 (0-1)	11-13(1-3)	10-13 (3-4)	08-10 (3)
		13-15(2-4)	13-15(4)	10-15 (4-3)
		15-16 (1-3)	15-18 (3-4)	15-18 (4)
		16-18 (0-3)	18-20 (2-3)	18-20 (3-4)
		18-20 (0-2)	20-22 (1-2)	20-22 (2-3)
		20-07 (0-1)	22-06 (1)	22-02 (1-2)
				02-06 (1)

40			
06-07 (1-2)	06-07 (2-3)	06-07 (3-2)	06-08 (2-1)
07-09 (2-3)	07-09 (3-4)	07-08 (4-2)	08-15 (1-0)
09-18 (3-4)	09-11 (4-3)	08-09 (4-1)	15-16 (2-0)
18-19 (2-3)	11-13 (4-2)	09-11 (3-1)	16-17 (2-1)
19-21 (1-2)	13-15 (4-3)	11-13 (3-1)	17-19 (3-2)
21-00 (0-1)	15-18 (1)	13-15 (3-1)	19-21 (4-3)
00-06 (0-1)	15-17 (4-2)	15-17 (4-2)	21-22 (4)
	19-20 (2-4)	17-19 (4-3)	22-00 (3-4)
	20-21 (2-3)	19-20 (4)	00-02 (3)
	21-00 (1-2)	20-21 (3-4)	02-05 (2-3)
	00-06 (0-1)	21-00 (2-3)	05-06 (2)
		00-02 (1-3)	
		02-06 (1-2)	

80			
07-08 (2-3)	07-08 (3-2)	07-08 (2-1)	07-08 (1-0)
08-11 (3-4)	08-11 (4-1)	08-11 (1-0)	08-16 (0)
11-18 (4-3)	11-16 (3-0)	11-16 (0)	16-18 (1-0)
18-20 (2-3)	16-18 (3-2)	16-18 (2-1)	18-20 (2-1)
20-22 (2-3)	18-20 (4-3)	18-20 (3-2)	20-22 (1-2)
22-02 (1-2)	20-22 (3-4)	20-02 (4)	22-02 (4-3)
02-05 (1)	22-02 (2-4)	02-05 (2-3)	02-05 (3-2)
05-07 (1-2)	02-05 (1-2)	05-07 (2)	05-07 (2-1)
	05-07 (2)		

160			
05-07 (4-2)	05-06 (2-1)	05-06 (1)	05-06 (1)
07-09 (3-1)	07-09 (2-0)	06-19 (0)	06-19 (0)
09-17 (2-0)	07-09 (1-0)	19-20 (3-2)	19-20 (1-0)
17-19 (3-1)	09-17 (0)	20-22 (3-2)	20-22 (2-1)
19-20 (4-2)	17-19 (1-0)	22-03 (4-2)	22-03 (2)
20-05 (4)	19-20 (2)	03-05 (3-2)	03-05 (2-4)
	20-22 (4-3)		
	22-03 (4)		
	03-05 (4-3)		

FOOTNOTES

Worldwide Charts:
• Predicted times of 80 meter openings. Openings on 160 meters are also likely to occur during those times when 80 meter openings are shown with a forecast rating of (2) or higher.

Short Skip Charts:
• Predominately sporadic-E openings.

openings should be possible over distances as far as approximately 350 miles, while nighttime openings should range between 500 and 2,300 miles.

160 meters – Summer: Due to intense solar absorption, no ionospheric propagation will be possible on this band during daylight hours. An occasional DX opening may be possible during the hours of darkness and the sunrise period, but high static levels often will make it difficult, if not impossible, to communicate. During the nighttime hours, short-skip openings over distances up to approximately 1,000 miles may often be possible, despite heavy static.

160 meters – Winter: No ionospheric propagation is expected during the daytime, but by late afternoon, conditions should begin to improve and some fairly good DX openings should be possible to many parts of the world during the hours of darkness and the pre-dawn period. Short-skip openings should be possible over dis-

tances as far as approximately 1,500 miles during the nighttime hours, and at times, as far as 2,300 miles.

160 meters – Equinox: Expect no daytime openings, but fairly good openings to some areas of the world should be possible during the nighttime hours and the pre-dawn period. Nighttime short-skip openings should provide communications on paths up to 1,200 miles long on a regular basis, and often out to distances as great as 2,300 miles. Conditions should peak around midnight, and again just before dawn.

4.5 Master Propagation Charts - High Solar Phase Smoothed Sunspot Number Range: 60-90

Band-By-Band Summary

10 meters – Summer: Fairly good daytime DX should be possible on north-south paths, particularly into the

Southern Hemisphere. Conditions should peak during the afternoon. Plenty of short-skip openings due to sporadic-E ionization should be possible between distances of approximately 500 and 1,300 miles, and considerably beyond this range when intense and widespread sporadic-E ionization permits multi-hop propagation.

10 meters – Winter: Excellent worldwide DX conditions are expected during the daytime hours. Conditions should peak before noon for openings toward Europe, Africa, and the east; during the early afternoon for openings toward the south and during the late afternoon for openings toward the northwest and west. There also should be frequent short-skip openings from just after sunrise until shortly before sunset over distances ranging between approximately 1,000 and 2,300 miles.

10 meters – Equinox: Some fairly good openings should be possible toward Europe and the east before noon, and toward Africa shortly after noon. Good openings also should be possible toward South America, into the South Pacific, and to other areas in the Southern Hemisphere during the afternoon. Expect fairly good short–skip openings during most of the day over distances of between 1,000 and 2,300 miles.

12 meters – Interpolate between 10 and 15 meters.

15 meters – Summer: Fairly good worldwide DX propagation should be possible on most days from a few hours after sunrise until sunset. Conditions should peak to most areas of the world during the afternoon. Short-skip openings should be possible during the hours of daylight over distances of 500 to 2,300 miles.

15 meters – Winter: Excellent DX conditions are expected to most areas of the world from shortly after sunrise until past sunset. Openings should peak toward Europe and the east before noon; toward Africa and South America during the early afternoon; and toward the Far East, the South Pacific, and areas in a westerly direction during the late afternoon and early evening. Regular short-skip openings should be possible at ranges of beyond approximately 750 miles.

15 meters – Equinox: Excellent daytime DX is expected to almost all areas of the world, particularly to the Southern Hemisphere. Signals should peak toward Europe before noon, but to most other areas of the world during the afternoon. Excellent short-skip openings should be possible beyond a range of about 1,000 miles.

17 meters – Interpolate between 15 and 20 meters.

20 meters – Summer: This band should remain open for DX around the clock. It should peak for signals from practically all directions for an hour or two after sunrise and again during early evening. Daytime short-skip openings should range between 500 and 2,300 miles; nighttime, between 1,000 and 2,300 miles.

20 meters – Winter: DX conditions should be excellent from sunrise, through the hours of daylight, and until a few hours after sunset. Openings can be expected to all areas of the world, particularly during peak periods, for an hour or two after sunrise and again during the late afternoon. Some DX openings into the Southern Hemisphere should also be possible during the hours of darkness. Daytime short-skip openings should be excellent over a range of between 500 and 2,300 miles.

20 meters – Equinox: Excellent DX conditions can be expected from sunrise, through the daylight hours, and well into the evening. It should be possible to work into all areas of the world on 20 meters, particularly during peak periods, which should occur for an hour or two after sunrise and again during the late afternoon and early evening. The band should remain open fairly regularly during the hours of darkness as well, particularly toward the Southern Hemisphere. The range for short skip during the daylight hours should extend out to between 500 and 2,300 miles.

30 meters – Interpolate between 20 and 40 meters.

40 meters – Summer: Good DX conditions should be possible to most areas of the world from sunset, through the hours of darkness, until just after sunrise, despite seasonally high static levels. Excellent short–skip openings should be possible during the hours of daylight between distances of approximately 100 and 1,000 miles and during the hours of darkness to distances between 500 and 2,300 miles.

40 meters – Winter: This band should be an optimum band for worldwide DX during the hours of darkness and the sunrise period. The band should be open in the late afternoon toward Europe and the east, with signals peaking toward the east and south after sundown. Signals from the northwest and west should begin to build up by midnight, and reach a peak just before sunrise. Expect excellent short-skip openings between distances of 100 and 1,000 miles during the day, and between 750 and 2,300 miles at night.

40 meters – Equinox: Expect good DX to most parts of the world, particularly into the Southern

MASTER DX PROPAGATION CHART
SOLAR PHASE: HIGH
SMOOTHED SUNSPOT RANGE: 60-90
SEASON: SUMMER
TIME ZONE: EST (24-Hour Time)
EASTERN USA TO:

Reception Area	10 Meters	15 Meters	20 Meters	40/80 Meters
Western & Central Europe & North Africa	Nil	07-08 (1) 08-11 (2) 11-14 (1) 14-17 (2) 17-19 (1)	08-13 (1) 13-14 (2) 14-16 (3) 16-21 (4) 21-00 (3) 00-04 (2) 04-06 (3) 06-06 (2)	19-21 (1) 21-22 (2) 22-00 (3) 00-01 (2) 01-02 (1) 21-23 (1)* 23-00 (2)* 00-01 (1)*
Northern & Eastern Europe	Nil	10-13 (1) 13-15 (2) 15-18 (1)	08-14 (1) 14-16 (2) 16-17 (3) 17-20 (4) 20-23 (3) 23-01 (2) 01-06 (1) 06-08 (2)	20-21 (1) 21-23 (2) 23-01 (1) 20-23 (1)*
Eastern Mediterranean & Middle East	Nil	10-12 (1) 12-16 (2) 16-17 (3) 17-18 (2) 18-19 (1)	11-13 (1) 13-15 (2) 15-18 (3) 19-22 (4) 22-00 (3) 00-02 (2) 02-05 (1) 05-07 (2) 07-09 (1)	19-21 (1) 21-23 (2) 23-00 (1) 21-23 (1)*
Western Africa	10-12 (1) 15-18 (1)	09-11 (1) 11-13 (2) 13-14 (3) 14-16 (4) 16-18 (3) 19-19 (2) 19-21 (1)	13-14 (1) 14-15 (2) 15-17 (3) 17-22 (4) 22-01 (3) 01-03 (2) 03-06 (1)	19-21 (1) 21-23 (2) 23-01 (1)
East & Central Africa	09-11 (1)	08-11 (1) 15-17 (1) 11-13 (2) 13-15 (3) 15-16 (4) 16-17 (3) 17-19 (2) 19-20 (1)	13-15 (1) 11-13 (2) 16-17 (3) 17-20 (4) 20-23 (3) 23-02 (2) 02-05 (1)	20-23 (1) 15-16 (2)
Southern Africa	09-12 (1)	07-08 (1) 09-10 (2) 10.12 (3) 12-13 (2) 13-14 (1)	23-00 (1) 00-02 (3) 02-04 (2) 04-07 (3) 12-13 (1) 13-15 (2) 15-17 (1)	20-21 (1) 21-23 (2) 23-01 (1) 22-00 (1)*
Central & South Asia	Nil	08-10 (1) 13-18 (1) 19-21 (2) 21-22 (1)	16-19 (1) 19-22 (2) 22-02 (1) 02-05 (2) 05-07 (1)	19-20 (1)
Southeast Asia	Nil	09-12 (1) 15-18 (1) 19-20 (2) 20-21 (1)	05-06 (1) 06-06 (2) 08-10 (1) 15-18 (1) 19-20 (2) 20-23 (1) 23-01 (2) 01-02 (1)	Nil
Far East	Nil	09-11 (1) 15-17 (1) 17-19 (2) 19-21 (1)	05-06 (1) 06-08 (3) 08-09 (2) 09-11 (1) 17-19 (1) 23-01 (1)	Nil
South Pacific & New Zealand	14-17 (1) 17-19 (2) 19-21 (1)	08-10 (1) 13-15(1) 15-18 (2) 19-22 (3) 22-23 (2) 23-00 (1)	17-20 (1) 20-22 (2) 22-00 (3) 00-03 (4) 03-04 (3) 04-06 (2) 06-08 (3) 08-09 (2) 09-11 (1)	00-02 (1) 02-05 (2) 05-07 (1) 03-05 (1)*
Australasia	18-20 (1)	08-10 (1) 16-17 (1) 17-19 (2) 19-21 (3) 21-22 (2) 22-23 (1)	22-00 (1) 00-02 (2) 02-04 (3) 04-07 (2) 07-09 (3) 09-11 (2) 11-13 (1)	02-03 (1) 03-05 (2) 05-06 (1) 03-05 (1) 03-05 (1)*
Caribbean, Central America & Northern Countries of South America	10-13 (1) 13-15 (2) 15-17 (3) 17-18 (2) 18-19 (1)	07-08 (1) 08-10 (2) 10-15 (3) 15-19 (4) 19-21 (3) 21-23 (2) 23-00 (1)	05-06 (3) 06-08 (4) 09-10 (3) 10-15 (2) 15-17 (3) 17.00 (4) 00-03 (3) 03-05 (2)	20-22 (1) 22-03 (2) 03-05 (1) 22.03 (1)*
Peru, Bolivia, Paraguay, Brazil, Chile, Argentina & Uruguay	10-13 (1) 13-15 (2) 15-17 (3) 17-18 (2) 18-19 (1)	06-07 (1) 07-10 (2) 10-14 (1) 14-15 (2) 15-16 (3) 16-19 (4) 19-22 (3) 22-00 (2) 00-01 (1)	15-16 (1) 16-18 (2) 18-19 (3) 19-00 (4) 00-02 (3) 02-04 (2) 04-06 (1) 06-08 (2) 08-10 (1)	23-05 (1) 00-04 (1)*
McMurdo Sound, Antarctica	Nil	13-15 (1) 15-19 (2) 19-20 (1)	16-18 (1) 18-22 (2) 22-02 (3) 02-06 (2) 06-08 (1)	01-04 (1)

MASTER DX PROPAGATION CHART
SOLAR PHASE: HIGH
SMOOTHED SUNSPOT RANGE: 60-90
SEASON: SUMMER
TIME ZONES: CST & MST (24-Hour Time)
CENTRAL USA TO:

Reception Area	10 Meters	15 Meters	20 Meters	40/80 Meters
Western & Central Europe & North Africa	Nil	10-15(1) 15-17 (2) 17-19 (1) 22-00 (1)	00-04 (1) 04-06 (2) 06-15 (1) 15-16 (2) 16-17 (3) 17-19 (4) 19-22 (3) 22.00 (2)	19-22 (1) 22-00 (2) 00-01 (1) 21-23(1)*
Northern & Eastern Europe	Nil	08-11 (1) 11-15 (1) 15-17 (1)	01-06 (1) 06-08 (2) 08-14 (1) 14-17 (2) 17-21 (3) 21-01 (2)	19-23 (1)
Eastern Mediterranean & Middle East	Nil	12-14 (1) 14-17 (2) 17-19 (1)	12-15 (1) 15-17 (2) 17-21 (3) 21-23 (2) 23-00 (1) 06-08 (1)	20-23 (1)
Western Africa	09-11 (1) 15-17 (1)	09-11 (1) 11-14 (2) 14-16 (3) 16-18 (2) 18-20 (1)	13-14 (1) 14-15 (2) 15-17 (3) 17-21 (4) 21-23 (3) 23-02 (2) 02-04 (1)	19-23 (1) 22-23 (1)*
East & Central Africa	15-18 (1)	12-14 (1) 14-15 (2) 15-17 (3) 17-18 (2) 18-19 (1)	14-16 (1) 16-17 (2) 17-19 (3) 19-21 (4) 21-22 (3) 22-00 (2) 00-01 (1)	19-22 (1)
Southern Africa	09-11 (1)	23-01 (1) 07-09 (1) 09-11 (2) 11-12 (1) 12-14 (2) 14-16 (1)	22-23 (1) 23-01 (2) 01-04 (1) 10-12 (1)	20-22 (1) 22-23 (2) 23-00 (1) 22-00(1)*
Central & South Asia	Nil	14-17 (1) 17-20 (2) 20-22 (1) 08-10 (1)	16-18 (1) 18-21 (2) 21-05 (1) 05-07 (2) 07-09 (1)	Nil
Southeast Asia	Nil	09-12 (1) 16-18 (1) 18-20 (1) 20-22 (1)	02-06 (1) 06-09 (2) 09-10 (1) 21-22 (1) 22-00 (2) 00-01 (1)	Nil
Far East	Nil	08-10 (1) 12-14 (1) 17-19 (1) 19-22 (2) 22-00 (1)	00-03 (1) 03-05 (2) 05-09 (3) 09-10 (2) 10-12 (1)	03-04 (1) 04-05 (2) 05-08 (1)
South Pacific & New Zealand	12-17 (1) 17-19 (2) 19-20 (1)	12-15 (1) 15-17 (2) 17-19 (3) 19-21 (4) 21-22 (3) 22-23 (2) 23-00 (1)	16-18 (1) 18-22 (2) 22-00 (4) 00-04 (3) 04-06 (2) 06-08 (4) 08-10 (2) 10-12 (1)	22-00 (1) 00-02 (2) 02-04 (3) 04-06 (2) 06-07 (1) 00-06 (1)*
Australasia	16-20 (1)	13-14 (1) 14-16(2) 16-18 (1) 18-19 (2) 19-21 (3) 21-22 (2) 22-23 (1)	21-23 (1) 23-00 (2) 00-02 (2) 02-04 (3) 04-06 (2) 06-08 (4) 08-10 (2) 10-11 (1)	00-02 (2) 02-06 (2) 06-07 (1) 03-06 (1)*
Caribbean, Central America & Northern Countries of South America	10-12 (1) 12-14 (2) 14-16 (3) 16-17 (2) 17-18 (1)	07-08 (1) 08-10 (2) 10-15 (3) 15-18 (4) I8-19 (3) 19-20 (2) 20-22 (1)	02-04 (2) 04-06 (3) 06-08 (4) 08-10 (3) 10-15 (2) 15-17 (3) 17-22 (4) 22-02 (3)	20-22 (1) 22-03 (2) 03-05 (1) 22-04 (1) 23-02 (1)*
Peru, Bolivia, Paraguay, Brazil, Chile, Argentina & Uruguay	08-12 (1) 12-15 (2) 15-18 (3) 18-19 (2) 19-20 (1)	06-07 (1) 07-09 (2) 09-13 (1) 13-15 (2) I5-16 (3) 16-19 (4) 19-20 (3) 20-22 (2) 22-00 (1)	13-15 (1) 15-17 (2) 17-18 (3) 18-22 (4) 22-00 (3) 00-02 (2) 02-04 (1) 04-06 (2) 06-09 (1)	21-22 (1) 22-01 (2) 01-04 (1) 23-03 (1)*
McMurdo Sound, Antarctica	Nil	13-15 (1) 15-18 (2) 18-20 (1)	13-16 (1) 16-18 (2) 18-23 (3) 23-02 (2) 02-06 (1) 06-08 (1) 08-09 (1)	22-03 (1)

MASTER DX PROPAGATION CHART
SOLAR PHASE: HIGH
SMOOTHED SUNSPOT RANGE: 60-90
SEASON: SUMMER
TIME ZONE: PST (24-Hour Time)
WESTERN USA TO:

Reception Area	10 Meters	15 Meters	20 Meters	40/80 Meters
Western Europe & North Africa	Nil	07-08 (1) 08-10 (2) 10-14 (1) 14-16 (2) 16-17 (1) 20-22 (1)	23-05 (1) 05-07 (2) 07-14 (1) 14-16 (2) 16-21 (3) 21-23 (2)	19-22 (1)
Northern, Central & Eastern Europe	Nil	06-08 (1) 13-16 (1) 20-22 (1)	13-15 (1) 15-20 (2) 20-22 (3) 22-00 (2) 00-07 (1)	19-21 (1)

Reception Area	10 Meters	15 Meters	20 Meters	40/80 Meters
Eastern Mediterranean & Middle East	Nil	07-09 (1) 09-11 (2) 11-14 (1) 19-21 (1)	12-15 (1) 15-19 (2) 19-21 (3) 21-23 (2) 23-00 (1) 05-07 (1)	Nil
West & Central Africa	07-10 (1)	06-10 (1) 10-12 (2) 12-16 (1) 16-18 (2) 18-19 (1)	12-14 (1) 14-17 (2) 17-19 (3) 19-21 (4) 21-23 (3) 23-03 (2) 03-07 (1)	20-23 (1)
East Africa	Nil	08-12 (1) 12-15 (1) 15-16 (1) 19-21 (1)	14-16 (1) 16-18 (2) 18-21 (3) 21-23 (2) 23-00 (1)	Nil
Southern Africa	Nil	07-09 (1) 09-11 (2) 11-12 (1) 22-00 (1)	14-16 (1) 21-22 (1) 22-00 (2) 00-06 (1) 06-08 (2) 08-10 (1)	19-22 (1)
Central & South Asia	Nil	07-09 (1) 09-11 (2) 11-13 (1)	22-04 (1) 04-08 (2) 08-11 (1) 17-19 (1) 19-21 (2) 21-22 (1)	Nil
Southeast Asia	Nil	07-08 (1) 08-10 (2) 10-12 (1) 16-19 (1) 19-21 (2) 21-22 (1)	22-00 (1) 00-02 (2) 02-04 (3) 04-06 (2) 06-08 (3) 08-10 (2) 10-13 (1)	02-06 (1)
Far East	13-15 (1)	08-09 (1) 09-11 (2) 11-13 (1) 13-14 (2) 14-16 (3) 16-18 (2) 18-21 (1)	18-20 (1) 20-22 (2) 22-00 (3) 00-02 (4) 02-03 (3) 03-06 (2) 06-09 (3) 09-11 (2) 11-14 (1)	01-02 (1) 02-05 (2) 05-06 (1) 02-04 (1)*
South Pacific & New Zealand	11-13 (1) 13-18 (2) 18-19 (1)	08-10 (1) 10-11 (2) 11-13 (3) 13-15 (2) 15-17 (3) 17-19 (4) 19-20 (3) 20-21 (2)	16-18 (1) 18-20 (2) 20-01 (4) 01-05 (2) 05-06 (2) 05-07 (4) 07-10 (2) 10-12 (1) 04-06 (1)* 21-22 (1)	21-22 (1) 22-00 (2) 00-05 (3) 05-06 (2) 06-07 (1) 23-01 (1)* 01-04 (2)*
Australasia	13-16 (1) 16-19 (2) 19-21 (1)	06-08 (1) 12-14 (1) 14-17 (2) 17-19 (3) 19-21 (4) 21-22 (3) 22-00 (2)	19-21 (1) 21-23 (2) 23-04 (4) 04-06 (3) 06-08 (4) 08-09 (2) 09-12 (1) 00-02 (1)	23-01 (1) 01-03 (2) 03-05 (3) 05-06 (2) 06-07 (1) 01-06 (1)*
Caribbean, Central America & Northern Countries of South America	08-10 (1) 10-12 (2) 12-14 (1) 14-16 (2) 16-17 (1)	07-08 (1) 08-12 (2) 12-14 (3) 14-17 (4) 17-18 (3) 18-19 (2) 19-20 (1)	08-10 (2) 10-13 (1) 13-15 (2) 15-17 (3) 17-22 (4) 22-00 (3) 00-05 (2) 05-08 (3)	20-22 (2) 22-03 (2) 03-05 (1) 22-03 (1)*
Peru, Bolivia, Paraguay, Brazil, Chile, Argentina & Uruguay	08-12 (1) 12-14 (2) 14-16 (3) 16-18 (2) 18-20 (1)	05-06 (1) 06-08 (2) 08-12 (1) 12-14 (2) 14-16 (3) 16-19 (4) 19-20 (3) 20-21 (2) 21-22 (1)	13-15 (1) 15-17 (2) 17-18 (3) 18-22 (4) 22-00 (3) 00-02 (2) 02-04 (1) 04-06 (2) 06-09 (1)	21-23 (1) 23-01 (2) 01-03 (1) 23-02 (1)*
McMurdo Sound, Antarctica	Nil	14-16 (1) 16-20 (2) 20-21 (1)	15-17 (1) 17-18 (2) 18-00 (3) 00-03 (2) 03-06 (1)	21-04 (1)

MASTER DX PROPAGATION CHART
SOLAR PHASE: HIGH
SMOOTHED SUNSPOT RANGE: 60-90
SEASON: WINTER
TIME ZONE: EST (24-Hour Time)
EASTERN USA TO:

Reception Area	10 Meters	15 Meters	20 Meters	40/80 Meters
Western & Central Europe & North Africa	08-09 (1) 09-10 (2) 10-12 (1)	07-08 (1) 08-09 (3) 09-11 (4) 11-12 (3) 12-13 (2) 13-15 (1)	05-07 (1) 07-09 (4) 09-13 (3) 13-14 (4) 14-15 (3) 15-17 (2) 17-19 (1)	15-17 (1) 17-19 (2) 19-00 (4) 00-03 (2) 03-04 (1) 19-23 (1)* 23-01 (2)* 01-02 (1)*
Northern & Eastern Europe	08-11 (1)	07-08 (1) 08-11 (2) 11-13 (1)	05-07 (1) 07-09 (3) 09-12 (2) 12-16 (1)	16-19 (1) 19-23 (2) 23-03 (1) 19-02 (1)*
Eastern Mediterranean & Middle East	08-09 (1) 09-10 (2) 10-11 (1)	07-08 (1) 08-10 (3) 10-13 (1)	01-03 (1) 05-07 (1) 07-09 (2) 09-11 (1) 11-14 (2) 14-17 (1)	19-00 (1) 20-23 (1)*
East Africa	08-09 (1) 09-11 (2) 11-15 (1)	07-08 (1) 08-12 (2) 12-15 (3) 15-16 (2) 16-17 (1)	06-07 (1) 07-09 (2) 09-12 (1) 12-15 (2) 15-18 (3) 18-20 (2) 20-22 (1)	19-00 (1) 22-00 (1)*
West & Central Africa	08-09 (1) 09-13 (2) 13-16 (1) 12-14 (4)	07-08(1) 08-09 (2) 09-12 (3) 09-12 (1) 14-15 (3) 15-16 (2) 16-17 (1)	01-03 (1) 06-07 (1) 07-09 (2) 00-02 (1)* 12-14 (2) 14-15 (3) 15-17 (4) 17-18 (3) 18-19 (2) 19-21 (1)	18-22 (1) 22-01 (2) 01-02(1)
Southern Africa	08-09 (1) 09-13 (2) 13-15 (1)	07-09 (1) 09-12 (2) 12-14 (3) 14-16 (2) 16-17 (1)	05-14 (1) 14-15 (2) 15-17 (3) 17-19 (2) 19-23 (1) 23-01 (2) 01-03 (1)	18-19 (1) 19-21 (2) 21-00 (1) 19-22 (1)*
Central & South Asia	Nil	08-10 (1) 17-20 (1)	06-07 (1) 07-09 (2) 09-11 (1) 18-22 (1)	06-08 (1) 20-22 (1)
Southeast Asia	08-10 (1) 18-20 (1)	08-11 (1) 17-20 (1)	06-07 (1) 07-09 (2) 09-12 (1) 18-21 (1)	06-08 (1)
Far East	17-19 (1)	07-09 (1) 16-17 (1) 17-19 (2) 19-20 (1)	06-07 (1) 07-09 (2) 09-11 (1) 17-19 (1) 19-21 (2) 21-23 (1)	05-08 (1) 07-09 (1)*
South Pacific & New Zealand	12-13 (1) 13-15 (2) 15-17 (1)	11-13 (1) 13-15 (2) 15-17 (1) 17-19 (1) 19-20 (1)	05-07 (1) 07-09 (3) 09-11 (2) 11-19 (1) 19-22 (2) 22-00 (1)	01-02 (1) 02-04 (2) 04-07 (3) 07-08 (1) 08-09 (1) 04-05 (1)* 05-07 (2)* 07-08 (1)*
Australasia	09-11 (1) 16-18 (1)	08-12 (1) 15-17 (1) 17-19 (1) 19-21 (1)	06-07 (1) 07-09 (3) 09-10 (2) 10-13(1) 13-15 (1) 15-19 (1) 19-22 (2) 22-23 (1)	04-06 (1) 06-08 (2) 08-09 (1) 05-08 (1)*

Reception Area	10 Meters	15 Meters	20 Meters	40/80 Meters
Caribbean, Central America & Northern Countries of South America	07-09 (1) 09-11 (2) 11-14 (3) 14-15 (2) 15-16 (1)	07-08 (1) 08-11 (3) 11-14 (2) 14-16 (4) 16-17 (3) 17-18 (2) 18-20 (1)	05-06 (1) 06-07 (2) 07-09 (4) 09-11 (3) 11-15 (2) 15-17 (3) 17-19 (4) 19-20 (3) 20-02 (2) 02-05 (1)	18-20 (1) 20-22 (2) 22-00 (3) 00-04 (2) 04-07 (1) 19-21 (1)* 21-02 (2)* 02-05 (1)*
Peru, Bolivia, Paraguay, Brazil, Chile, Argentina & Uruguay	08-12 (1) 12-15 (2) 15-17 (1)	07-08 (1) 08-14 (2) 14-16 (4) 16-17 (3) 17-18 (2) 18-19 (1)	01-06 (1) 06-07 (2) 07-08 (3) 08-09 (2) 09-15 (1) 15-16 (2) 16-17 (3) 17-19 (4) 19-20 (3) 20-01 (2)	19-21 (1) 21-02 (2) 02-05 (1) 21-03 (1)*
McMurdo Sound, Antarctica	08-11 (1)	08-15 (1) 15-17 (2) 17-19 (1)	06-07 (1) 07-09 (2) 09-12 (1) 15-18 (1) 18-20 (1) 20-23 (3) 23-01 (2) 01-03 (1)	22-00 (1) 00-02 (2) 02-05 (1)

MASTER DX PROPAGATION CHART
SOLAR PHASE: HIGH
SMOOTHED SUNSPOT RANGE: 60-90
SEASON: WINTER
TIME ZONES: CST & MST (24-Hour Time)
CENTRAL USA TO:

Reception Area	10 Meters	15 Meters	20 Meters	40/80 Meters
Western & Central Europe & North Africa	08-11 (1)	07-08 (1) 08-09 (2) 09-11 (3) 11-13 (3) 13-14 (1)	05-07 (1) 07-09 (3) 09-11 (2) 11-13 (3) 13-15 (2) 15-17 (1)	15-17 (1) 17-23 (2) 23-03 (1) 19-23 (1)* 23-00 (2)* 00-01 (1)*
Northern & Eastern Europe	08-10 (1)	07-09 (1) 09-10 (2) 10-12 (1)	06-07 (1) 07-09 (2) 09-11 (1) 11-12 (2) 12-14 (1)	18-01 (1) 19-00 (1)*
Eastern Mediterranean & Middle East	08-11 (1)	07-08 (1) 08-10 (2) 10-12 (1)	23-02 (1) 07-10 (1) 10-12 (2) 12-15 (1)	18-23 (1) 20-02 (1)*
East Africa	09-11 (1)	07-11 (1) 11-15 (2) 15-17 (1)	06-11 (1) 11-14 (2) 14-17 (1) 17-18 (2) 18-22 (1)	19-23 (1)
West & Central Africa	08-09 (1) 09-12 (2) 12-15 (1)	07-08 (1) 08-10 (2) 10-12 (3) 12-14 (4) 14-15(3) 15-16 (2)	05-11 (1) 11-13 (2) 13-15 (3) 15-17 (4) 17-19 (2) 19-21 (1) 16-17 (1)	18-21 (1) 21-23 (2) 23-00 (1) 22-00 (1)*
Southern Africa	08-09 (1) 09-12 (2) 12-13 (1)	07-09 (1) 09-11 (2) 11-14 (3) 14-15 (2) 15-16 (1)	06-13 (1) 13-15 (2) 15-17 (3) 17-19 (2) 19-21 (1) 00-02 (1)	18-20 (1) 20-22 (2) 19-22 (1)*
Central & South Asia	Nil	08-10 (1) 19-21 (1)	06-07 (1) 07-09 (2) 09-11 (1) 19-22 (1)	06-08 (1) 19-21 (1)
Southeast Asia	08-10 (1) 18-20 (1)	08-11 (1) 16-17 (1) 17-19 (2) 19-20 (1)	06-07 (1) 07-09 (2) 09-12 (1) 17-18 (1) 18-20 (1) 20-21 (1)	06-08 (1)

Reception Area | 10 Meters | 15 Meters | 20 Meters | 40/80 Meters

Reception Area	10 Meters	15 Meters	20 Meters	40/80 Meters
Far East	16-18 (1)	07-09 (1)	06-07 (1)	03-09 (1)
		14-16 (1)	07-09 (2)	04-07(1)*
		16-19 (2)	09-11 (1)	
		19-20 (1)	15-17 (1)	
			17-20 (2)	
			20-22 (1)	
South Pacific & New Zealand	12-13 (1)	10-12 (1)	06-07 (1)	22-00 (1)
	13-15 (2)	12-14 (2)	07-09 (3)	00-02 (2)
	15-17 (1)	14-17 (3)	09-11 (2)	02-06 (3)
		17-19 (2)	11-15 (3)	06-07 (2)
		19-20 (1)	15-17 (2)	07-09 (1)
			17-20 (3)	02-04 (1)*
			20-21 (2)	04-06 (2)*
			21-22 (1)	06-08 (1)*
Australasia	04-15 (1)	08-14 (1)	06-07 (1)	02-05 (1)
	15-16 (2)	14-18 (2)	07-11 (2)	05-07 (3)
	16-17 (1)	18-21 (1)	11-16 (1)	07-09 (1)
			16-17 (2)	04-07 (1)*
			17-21 (3)	
			21-22 (2)	
			22-23 (1)	
Caribbean, Central America & Northern Countries of South America	08-10 (1)	06-07 (1)	06-07 (2)	19-21 (1)
	10-13 (2)	07-08 (2)	07-11 (3)	21-23 (2)
	13-14 (3)	08-12 (3)	11-14 (2)	23-01 (3)
	14-15 (2)	12-16 (4)	14-16 (3)	01-03 (2)
	15-16 (1)	16-17(3)	16-18 (4)	03-06 (1)
		17-18 (2)	18-20 (3)	19-21 (1)*
		18-19 (1)	20-22 (2)	21-01 (2)*
			22-00 (1)	01-04 (1)*
			00-02 (2)	
			02-06 (1)	
Peru, Bolivia, Paraguay, Brazil, Chile, Argentina & Uruguay	08-11 (1)	07-08 (1)	06-07 (2)	19-21 (1)
	11-15 (2)	08-13 (2)	07-08 (3)	21-02 (2)
	15-17 (1)	13-16 (4)	08-09 (2)	02-05 (1)
		16-17 (3)	09-14 (2)	21-05 (1)*
		17-18 (2)	14-16 (2)	
		18-19 (1)	16-18 (4)	
			18-21 (3)	
			21-23 (2)	
			23-06 (1)	
McMurdo Sound, Antarctica	08-11 (1)	07-14 (1)	06-07 (1)	22-00 (1)
		14-16 (2)	07-09 (2)	00-02 (2)
		16-19 (1)	09-12 (1)	02-05 (1)
			15-18 (1)	
			18-20 (2)	
			20-22 (3)	
			22-00 (2)	
			00-03 (1)	

**MASTER DX PROPAGATION CHART
SOLAR PHASE: HIGH
SMOOTHED SUNSPOT RANGE: 60-90
SEASON: WINTER
TIME ZONE: PST (24-Hour Time)
WESTERN USA TO:**

Reception Area	10 Meters	15 Meters	20 Meters	40/80 Meters
Western & Central Europe & North Africa	07-09 (1)	06-07 (1)	05-07 (1)	17-19 (1)
		07-08 (2)	07-10 (2)	19-22 (2)
		08-09 (3)	10-12 (3)	22-00 (1)
		09-10 (2)	12-13 (2)	19-23 (1)*
		10-11 (1)	13-15 (1)	
			00-03 (1)	
Northern & Eastern Europe	Nil	07-09 (1)	06-08 (1)	17-00 (1)
			08-10 (2)	19-23 (1)*
			10-13 (1)	
			00-04 (1)	
Eastern Mediterranean & Middle East	Nil	07-09 (1)	06-07 (1)	18-21 (1)
			07-09 (2)	
			09-13 (1)	
Western Africa	08-10 (1)	06-08 (1)	05-10 (1)	18-22 (1)
	10-12 (2)	08-10 (2)	10-13 (2)	19-21 (1)*
	12-13 (1)	10-12 (3)	13-15 (3)	
			12-14 (4)	15-17 (4)
			14-16 (2)	17-19 (2)
			16-17 (1)	19-21 (1)
East & Central Africa	08-09 (1)	06-11 (1)	05-11 (1)	18-21 (1)
	09-11 (2)	09-11 (2)	11-13 (2)	
	11-12 (2)	12-14 (3)	13-17 (3)	
		14-15 (2)	17-19 (2)	
		15-16 (1)	19-20 (1)	
Southern Africa	08-09 (1)	06-08 (1)	07-11 (1)	18-21 (1)
	09-10 (2)	09-11 (2)	11-14 (2)	
	10-12 (1)	11-13 (3)	14-17 (3)	
		13-15 (2)	17-19 (2)	
		15-16 (1)	19-20 (1)	
			00-02 (1)	
Central & South Asia	Nil	08-10 (1)	06-07 (1)	05-07 (1)
		16-17 (1)	07-09 (2)	18-20 (1)
		17-19 (2)	09-11 (1)	
		19-20 (1)	17-19 (1)	
			19-20 (2)	
			20-21 (1)	
Southeast Asia	14-15 (1)	09-11 (1)	07-09 (1)	00-02 (1)
	15-17 (2)	15-16 (1)	09-11 (2)	02-07 (2)
	17-18 (1)	16-17 (2)	11-13 (1)	07-08 (1)
		17-18 (3)	13-15 (2)	04-06 (1)*
		18-19 (2)	15-18 (1)	
		19-20 (1)	18-20 (2)	
			20-21 (1)	
Far East	14-15 (1)	13-15 (1)	08-10 (1)	00-03 (1)
	15-16 (2)	15-16 (2)	13-14 (1)	03-08 (2)
	16-18 (1)	16-17 (3)	14-17 (3)	08-10 (1)
		17-18 (2)	17-19 (2)	02-08 (1)*
		18-20 (1)	19-21 (1)	
South Pacific & New Zealand	12-14 (1)	09-10 (1)	07-08 (1)	20-22 (1)
	14-16 (2)	10-13 (2)	08-10 (2)	22-00 (2)
	16-17 (1)	13-14 (3)	10-15 (3)	00-05 (3)
		14-16 (4)	15-16 (2)	05-07 (2)
		16-17 (3)	16-18 (4)	07-09 (1)
		17-18 (2)	18-20 (3)	00-03 (1)*
		18-20 (1)	20-21 (2)	03-06 (2)*
			21-22 (1)	06-08 (1)*
Australasia	14-15 (1)	08-12 (1)	07-08 (1)	01-03 (1)
	15-16 (2)	12-15 (2)	08-10 (3)	03-05 (2)
	16-18 (1)	15-17 (3)	10-12 (2)	05-07 (3)
		17-18 (2)	12-16 (4)	07-09 (1)
		18-19 (1)	16-17 (2)	03-05 (1)*
			17-19 (4)	05-06 (2)*
			19-20 (3)	06-08 (1)*
			20-22 (2)	
			22-23 (1)	
Caribbean, Central America & Northern Countries of South America	08-10 (1)	06-07 (1)	06-07 (2)	20-22 (1)
	10-15 (2)	07-08 (2)	07-09 (3)	22-01 (2)
	15-16 (1)	08-12 (3)	09-10 (2)	01-04 (1)
		12-15 (4)	10-13(1)	22-06 (1)*
		15-16 (3)	13-15 (2)	
		16-17 (2)	15-18 (4)	
		17-18 (1)	18-20 (3)	
			20-22 (2)	
			22-06 (1)	
Peru, Bolivia, Paraguay, Brazil, Chile, Argentina & Uruguay	08-10 (1)	07-10 (1)	05-06 (1)	20-22 (1)
	10-14 (2)	10-12 (2)	06-08 (2)	22-01 (2)
	14-16 (1)	12-13 (3)	08-14 (1)	01-04 (1)
		13-15 (4)	14-15 (2)	22-06 (1)*
		15-16 (3)	15-17 (4)	
		16-17 (2)	17-19 (2)	
		17-18 (1)	19-20 (1)	
McMurdo Sound, Antarctica	08-11 (1)	07-14 (1)	06-07 (1)	21-00 (1)
		14-16 (2)	07-09 (2)	00-02 (2)
		16-19 (1)	09-12 (1)	02-05 (1)
			16-18 (1)	
			18-19 (2)	
			19-21 (2)	
			21-23 (2)	
			23-03 (1)	

**MASTER DX PROPAGATION CHART
SOLAR PHASE: HIGH
SMOOTHED SUNSPOT RANGE: 60-90
SEASONS: SPRING & FALL
TIME ZONE: EST (24-Hour Time)
EASTERN USA TO:**

Reception Area	10 Meters	15 Meters	20 Meters	40/80 Meters
Western & Central Europe & North Africa	09-11 (1)	07-08 (1)	04-07 (1)	17-19 (1)
	11-13 (2)	08-09 (3)	07-09 (4)	19-20 (2)
	13-14 (1)	09-12 (4)	09-12 (3)	20-01 (1)
		12-13 (3)	12-15 (4)	01-02 (2)
		13-15(2)	15-17 (3)	02-03 (1)
		15-16 (1)	17-19 (2)	19-21 (1)*
			19-21 (1)	21-22 (2)*
				22-23 (3)*
				23-00 (2)*
				00-01(1)*
Northern & Eastern Europe	08-12 (1)	07-08 (1)	05-07 (1)	18-20 (1)
		08-11 (2)	07-09 (3)	20-22 (2)
		11-14 (1)	09-11 (2)	22-02 (2)
			11-13 (3)	20-00 (1)*
			13-14 (1)	
			14-18 (1)	
Eastern Mediterranean & Middle East	09-13 (1)	08-09 (1)	07-09 (1)	19-20 (1)
		09-11 (3)	09-12 (1)	20-22 (2)
		11-13 (2)	12-14 (2)	22-23 (1)
		13-15 (1)	14-16 (1)	20-22 (1)*
			16-18 (3)	
			18-22 (2)	
			22-23 (1)	
			04-07 (1)	
East Africa	10-13 (1)	07-08 (1)	06-07 (1)	19-00 (1)
	13-15 (2)	08-13 (2)	07-09 (2)	21-23 (1)*
	15-16 (1)	13-16 (3)	09-13 (1)	
		16-17 (2)	13-18 (2)	
		17-18 (1)	18-21 (3)	
			21-23 (2)	
			23-01 (1)	
West & Central Africa	11-14 (1)	07-08 (1)	07-09 (2)	18-20 (1)
	14-16 (2)	08-09 (2)	09-12 (1)	20-22 (2)
	16-17 (1)	09-11 (3)	12-13 (2)	22-01 (1)
		11-14 (4)	13-15 (3)	21-23 (1)*
		14-16 (3)	15-18 (4)	
		16-17 (2)	18-19 (3)	
		17-19 (1)	19-22 (2)	
			22-07 (1)	
Southern Africa	10-11 (1)	07-09 (1)	05-14 (1)	21-23 (1)
	11-12 (2)	09-13 (3)	14-16 (2)	23-00 (2)
	12-14 (1)	13-15 (3)	16-18 (3)	00-01 (1)
		15-17 (2)	18-20 (2)	23-01 (1)*
		17-18 (1)	20-23 (1)	
			23-01 (2)	
			01-03 (1)	
Central & South Asia	Nil	07-09 (1)	07-10 (1)	05-07 (1)
		18-20 (1)	19-22 (1)	19-21 (1)
Southeast Asia	Nil	07-09 (1)	06-07 (1)	06-08 (1)
		18-20 (1)	07-09 (2)	17-20 (1)
			09-10 (1)	
			19-21 (1)	
Far East	17-19 (1)	07-09 (1)	06-07 (1)	05-08 (1)
		16-17 (1)	07-09 (2)	06-07 (1)*
		17-19 (2)	09-11 (1)	
		19-21 (1)	17-20 (1)	
			20-22 (2)	
			22-00 (1)	
South Pacific & New Zealand	13-15 (1)	12-15 (1)	01-07 (1)	00-02 (1)
	15-17 (2)	15-17 (2)	07-10 (2)	02-06 (3)
	17-18 (1)	17-19 (3)	10-19 (1)	06-07 (2)
		19-20 (2)	19-01 (2)	07-08 (1)
		20-21 (1)		02-03 (1)*
				03-05 (2)*
				05-06 (1)*
Australasia	16-18 (1)	08-12 (1)	00-03 (1)	03-05 (1)
		15-17 (1)	03-07 (1)	05-07 (2)
		17-20 (2)	07-09 (3)	07-09 (1)
		20-22 (1)	09-10 (2)	04-05 (1)*
			10-13 (1)	05-06 (2)*
			13-15 (2)	06-07 (1)*
			15-19 (1)	
			19-22 (2)	
			22-03 (3)	
Caribbean, Central America & Northern Countries of South America	08-10 (1)	07-08 (1)	00-03 (1)	18-19 (1)
	10-12 (2)	08-11 (2)	03-06 (1)	19-20 (2)
	12-15 (3)	11-14 (2)	06-07 (2)	20-03 (3)
	15-16 (2)	14-15 (3)	07-09 (4)	03-05 (2)
	16-18 (1)	15-17 (4)	09-11 (3)	05-07 (1)
		17-19 (3)	11-15 (2)	19-21 (1)*
		19-20 (2)	15-17 (2)	21-02 (2)*
		20-21 (1)	17-22 (4)	02-06 (1)*
			22-00 (3)	
Peru, Bolivia, Paraguay, Brazil, Chile, Argentina & Uruguay	09-11 (1)	07-08 (1)	04-06 (1)	19-21 (1)
	11-13 (2)	08-10 (3)	06-08 (2)	21-03(2)
	13-15 (3)	10-15 (2)	08-15(1)	03-07 (1)
	15-16 (2)	15-17 (4)	15-16 (1)	21-06 (1)*
	16-18 (1)	17-18 (3)	16-17 (3)	
		18-19 (2)	17-19 (4)	
		19-20 (1)	19-01 (3)	
			01-04 (2)	
McMurdo Sound, Antarctica	11-13 (1)	08-10 (1)	04-07 (1)	23-05 (1)
	13-16 (2)	15-17 (1)	07-09 (2)	
	16-18 (1)	17-19 (2)	09-12 (1)	
		19-21 (1)	15-18 (1)	
			18-21 (1)	
			21-00 (3)	
			00-04 (2)	

MASTER DX PROPAGATION CHART
SOLAR PHASE: HIGH
SMOOTHED SUNSPOT RANGE: 60-90
SEASONS: SPRING & FALL
TIME ZONES: CST & MST (24-Hour Time)
CENTRAL USA TO:

Reception Area	10 Meters	15 Meters	20 Meters	40/80 Meters
Western & Central Europe & North Africa	09-12 (1)	07-08 (1) 08-09 (2) 09-12 (3) 12-14 (2) 14-15 (1)	05-07 (1) 07-09 (3) 09-11 (2) 11-14 (3) 14-17 (2) 17-20 (1)	17-19 (1) 19-22 (2) 22-02 (1) 20-21 (1)* 21-22 (2)* 22-00 (1)*
Northern & Eastern Europe	08-11 (1)	07-09 (1) 09-11 (2) 11-13 (1)	06-07 (1) 07-09 (2) 09-11 (1) 11-13 (2) 13-17 (1)	19-01 (1) 20-23 (1)*
Eastern Mediterranean & Middle East	09-12 (1)	07-09 (1) 09-12 (2) 12-14 (1)	23-02 (1) 07-12 (1) 12-17 (2) 17-22 (1)	19-23 (1) 20-22 (1)*
East Africa	10-15 (1)	07-10 (1) 10-15 (2) 15-17 (1)	06-12 (1) 12-17 (2) 17-20 (3) 20-21 (2) 21-23 (1)	19-21 (1) 20-22 (1)*
West & Central Africa	11-13 (1) 13-15 (2) 15-16 (1)	07-08 (1) 08-10 (2) 10-12 (3) 12-14 (4) 14-15 (3) 15-16 (2)	07-12 (1) 12-13 (2) 13-15 (3) 15-17 (4) 17-20 (2) 20-00 (1) 16-18 (1)	18-19 (1) 19-21 (2) 21-00 (1) 20-22 (1)*
Southern Africa	10-13 (1)	07-09 (1) 09-13 (2) 13-14 (3) 14-16 (2) 16-17 (1)	05-14 (1) 14-16 (2) 16-18 (3) 18-19 (2) 19-21 (1) 00-02 (1)	23-00 (1) 23-00 (1)*
Central & South Asia	17-19 (1)	07-10 (1) 18-20 (1)	06-07 (1) 07-09 (2) 09-11 (1) 19-22 (1)	06-08 (1) 19-21 (1)
Southeast Asia	09-11 (1) 16-19 (1)	08-11 (1) 16-17 (1) 17-19 (2) 19-20 (1)	06-07 (1) 07-09 (2) 09-12 (1) 17-18 (1) 18-20 (2) 20-22 (1)	06-08 (1) 17-19 (1)
Far East	15-18 (1)	07-09 (1) 14-16 (1) 16-19 (2) 19-21 (1)	07-09 (2) 09-11 (1) 17-20 (1) 20-00 (2) 00-07 (1)	02-05 (1) 05-07 (2) 07-09 (1) 05-07 (1)*
South Pacific & New Zealand	12-15 (1) 15-17 (2) 17-19 (1)	10-13 (1) 13-16 (2) 16-19 (3) 19-20 (2) 20-21 (1)	06-07 (2) 07-09 (3) 09-11 (2) 11-18 (1) 18-20 (1) 20-22 (3) 22-00 (2) 00-06 (1)	22-01 (1) 01-06 (3) 06-07 (2) 07-09 (1) 00-03 (1)* 03-06 (2)* 06-07 (1)*
Australasia	15-17 (1)	09-12 (1) 12-17 (2) 17-19 (3) 19-20 (2) 20-22 (1)	07-09 (2) 09-17 (1) 17-20 (2) 20-00 (1) 00-03 (2) 03-07 (1)*	02-04 (1) 04-07 (2) 07-09 (1) 04-05 (1)* 05-07 (2)* 07-09 (1)*
Caribbean, Central America & Northern Countries of South America	09-11 (1) 11-13 (2) 13-14 (3) 14-15 (2) 15-17 (1)	06-07 (1) 07-08 (2) 08-14 (3) 14-16 (4) 16-18 (3) 18-19 (2) 19-20 (1)	06-07 (2) 07-11 (3) 11-14 (2) 14-16 (3) 16-20 (4) 20-22 (3) 21-02 (2)* 02-06 (1)*	18-19 (1) 19-20 (2) 20-02 (3) 02-04 (2) 04-06 (1) 20-21 (1)* 21-02 (2)* 02-06 (1)*
Peru, Bolivia, Paraguay, Brazil, Chile, Argentina, & Uruguay	08-11 (1) 11-13 (2) 13-15 (3) 15-16 (2) 16-18 (1)	07-08 (1) 08-13 (2) 13-15 (3) 15-17 (4) 17-18 (3) 18-19 (2) 19-20 (1)	06-09 (2) 08-15 (1) 16-18 (4) 18-22 (3) 22-04 (2) 04-06 (1)	19-22 (1) 21-03 (2) 03-06 (1) 21-05 (1)*
McMurdo Sound, Antarctica	11-13 (1) 13-15 (2) 15-18 (3)	13-16 (1) 16-18 (2) 18-20 (1)	07-09 (2) 09-12 (1) 15-18 (1) 18-20 (2) 20-23 (3) 23-03 (2) 03-07 (1)	00-06 (1)

MASTER DX PROPAGATION CHART
SOLAR PHASE: HIGH
SMOOTHED SUNSPOT RANGE: 60-90
SEASONS: SPRING & FALL
TIME ZONE: PST (24-Hour Time)
WESTERN USA TO:

Reception Area	10 Meters	15 Meters	20 Meters	40/80 Meters
Western & Central Europe & North Africa	09-11 (1)	08-10 (1) 10-12 (1) 12-15 (1)	23-01 (1) 06-08 (1) 08-12 (1) 12-14 (3) 14-16 (2) 16-20 (1)	18-00 (1) 20-22 (1)*
Northern & Eastern Europe	Nil	08-12 (1)	23-01 (1) 06-07 (1) 07-09 (2) 09-13 (1)	19-23 (1) 20-22 (1)*
Eastern Mediterranean & East Africa	Nil	07-11 (1)	06-09 (1) 09-11 (2) 11-15 (1) 18-21 (1)	18-21 (1)
West & Central Africa	11-16 (1)	06-08 (1) 08-15 (2) 15-17 (3) 17-18 (2) 18-19 (1)	05-10 (1) 10-15 (2) 15-18 (3) 18-20 (2) 20-22 (1)	18-22 (1) 19-21 (1)*
Southern Africa	10-13 (1)	08-10 (1) 10-14 (2) 14-16 (1)	05-14 (1) 14-16 (2) 16-18 (3) 18-20 (2) 00-02 (1)	19-22 (1) 20-21 (1)*
Central & South Asia	17-19 (1)	07-09 (1) 16-17 (1) 17-19 (2) 19-21 (2)	06-07 (1) 07-09 (2) 09-11 (1) 17-19 (1) 19-20 (2) 20-22 (1)	05-08 (1)
Southeast Asia	16-19 (1) 09-11 (1)	08-09 (1) 09-10 (2) 10-14 (1) 14-17 (2) 17-18 (3) 18-19 (2) 19-21 (1)	07-08 (1) 08-10 (3) 10-11 (2) 11-21 (1) 21-00 (2) 00-02 (1)	00-02 (1) 02-06 (2) 06-08 (1) 02-06 (1)*
Far East	14-15 (1) 15-16 (2) 16-18 (1)	12-14 (1) 14-18 (2) 18-20 (1) 20-22 (1)	08-10 (2) 10-20 (1) 20-22 (2) 22-00 (1)	00-02 (1) 02-06 (2) 06-08 (1) 02-08 (1)*
South Pacific & New Zealand	12-15 (1) 15-17 (2) 17-19 (1)	08-12 (1) 12-16 (2) 16-17 (3) 17-18 (4) 18-20 (3) 20-21 (1)	09-10 (2) 10-12 (4) 12-16 (3) 16-19 (4) 19-20 (3) 20-00 (2) 00-09 (1)	19-20 (1) 20-22 (2) 22-06 (4) 06-08 (2) 08-09 (1) 21-23 (1)* 23-06 (2)* 06-07 (1)*
Australasia	11-15 (1) 15-17 (2) 17-18 (1)	10-12 (1) 12-17 (2) 17-19 (3) 19-20 (2) 20-21 (1)	07-08 (1) 08-10 (3) 10-12 (2) 12-17 (1) 17-18 (2) 18-20 (3) 20-22 (4) 22-00 (3) 00-02 (2) 02-04 (1)	00-03 (1) 03-05 (3) 05-07 (2) 07-08 (1) 02-03 (1) 03-05 (2) 05-07 (1)
Caribbean, Central America & Northern Countries of South America	10-12 (1) 12-14 (2) 14-16 (1)	06-07 (1) 07-08 (2) 08-14 (3) 14-16 (4) 16-17 (3) 17-18 (2) 18-19 (1)	06-07 (2) 07-09 (3) 09-10 (2) 10-14 (1) 14-16 (2) 16-18 (4) 18-22 (3) 22-00 (2) 00-06 (1)	18-20(1) 20-00 (3) 00-03 (2) 03-05 (1) 20-21 (1)* 21-01 (2)* 01-04 (1)*
Peru, Bolivia, Paraguay, Brazil, Chile, Argentina & Uruguay	08-12 (1) 12-13 (2) 13-15 (3) 15-16 (2) 16-18 (1)	00-02 (1) 07-11 (2) 11-13 (3) 13-15 (2) 15-16 (4) 16-17 (1) 17-18 (2) 18-19 (1)	20-05 (2) 05-15 (1) 15-16 (1) 16-18 (4) 18-20 (3)	18-19 (1) 19-23 (2) 23-03 (1) 20-02 (1)*
McMurdo Sound, Antarctica	11-13 (1) 13-15 (2) 15-17 (1)	12-15 (1) 15-18 (2) 18-20 (1)	05-06 (1) 06-08 (2) 08-11 (1) 16-19 (1) 19-20 (2) 20-23 (3) 23-02 (2) 02-05 (1)	00-06 (1)

MASTER SHORT-SKIP PROPAGATION CHART
SOLAR PHASE: HIGH
SMOOTHED SUNSPOT RANGE: 60-90
SEASON: SUMMER
TIME ZONES: LOCAL STANDARD AT PATH MID-POINT
(24 Hour Time)

Band (Meters)	50-250	Distance Between Stations (Miles) 250-750	650-1300	1300-2300
10	Nil	07-09 (0-1)* 09-13 (0-3)* 13-17 (0-1)* 17-21 (0-2)* 21-23 (0-1)*	07-09 (1)* 09-13 (3)* 13-17 (1-2)* 17-21 (2-3)* 21-07 (1)*	07-09 (1-0)* 09-13 (3-1)* 13-17 (2-1)* 17-21 (3-1)* 21-07 (1-0)*
15	Nil	07-09 (0-3)* 09-13 (0-3)* 13-17 (0-2)* 17-19 (0-3)* 19-21 (0-2)* 21-07 (0-1)*	07-09 (2)* 09-13 (3)* 13-17 (2)* 17-19 (2)* 19-21 (2)* 21-23 (1-2)* 23-07 (1)*	07-09 (2-1) 09-13 (3-2) 13-17 (2-3) 17-19 (3-4) 19-20 (2-3) 20-23 (2-1) 23-07 (1-0)
20	09-00 (0-1)	06-09 (0-2)* 09-15 (1-4)* 15-20 (1-3)* 20-00 (2-3)* 00-06(0-1)*	06-09 (2-3)* 09-16 (4)* 16-21 (3-4)* 21-00 (2)* 00-06 (1-2)*	06-09 (3-2) 09-15 (4-3) 15-16 (4-3) 16-21 (4) 21-23 (3) 23-00 (3-2) 00-06 (2-1)
40	07-11 (1-2)* 11-16 (2-4)* 16-20 (3-4) 20-22 (1-2) 22-07 (0-2)*	07-09 (2-4)* 09-11 (2) 11-16 (4-2) 16-17 (4-3) 17-20 (4) 20-22 (2-4) 22-04 (2-4) 04-07 (2-3)	07-09 (4-1) 09-11 (2-1) 16-17 (3-1) 17-20 (4-3) 20-04 (4) 04-05 (3-4) 05-07 (3)	07-17 (1-0) 17-20 (3-2) 20-05 (4) 05-07 (3-1)
80	06-11 (3-4) 11-15 (4-3) 15-21 (4) 21-04 (3-4) 04-06 (4)	07-09 (4-1) 09-11 (4-0) 11-15 (3-0) 15-17 (4-1) 17-19 (4-2) 19-21 (4-3) 21-04 (4) 21-06 (4) 06-07 (4-2)	07-09 (1-0) 09-15 (1-0) 15-17 (1-0) 17-19 (2-1) 19-21 (3-0) 21-04 (4-3) 04-06 (4-3) 06-07 (2-1)	07-17 (1) 19-21 (1-0) 21-03 (4-3) 03-04 (4-2) 04-05 (3-2) 05-07 (3-1) 06-07 (1)
160	17-18 (1-0) 18-19 (1) 19-21 (3-2) 21-23 (4-3) 23-05 (4) 05-07 (3-2) 07-08 (1) 08-09 (1-0)	18-19 (1-0) 19-20 (2-0) 20-21 (2-1) 21-23 (3-2) 23-03 (4-2) 03-05 (4-3) 05-07 (2-1) 07-08 (0-1)	20-21 (1) 21-00 (2-1) 00-03 (2) 03-05 (2) 05-06 (1) 06-07 (1-0)	20-22 (1-0) 22-00 (1) 00-05 (2-1) 05-06 (1-0)

MASTER SHORT-SKIP PROPAGATION CHART
SOLAR PHASE: HIGH
SMOOTHED SUNSPOT RANGE: 60-90
SEASON: WINTER
TIME ZONES: LOCAL STANDARD AT PATH MID-POINT
(24-Hour Time)

Band (Meters)	50-250	Distance Between Stations (Miles) 250-750	650-1300	1300-2300
10	Nil	Nil	09-11 (0-1) 11-15 (0-2) 15-17 (0-1)	08-09 (0-1) 09-11 (1-2) 11-15 (2) 15-17 (1-2) 17-19 (0-1)

Left chart (continued):

Band (Meters)	50-250	250-750	650-1300	1300-2300
15	Nil	09-18 (0-1)	07-09 (0-1) 09-11 (1-2) 11-16 (1-4) 16-18 (1-2) 18-20 (0-1)	07-09 (1) 09-11 (2-3) 11-16 (4) 16-18 (2-3) 18-20 (1-2) 20-22 (0-1)
20	11-15 (0-1) 09-11 (0-1) 11-13 (1-3) 13-15 (1-4) 15-17 (0-3) 17-19 (0-2) 19-21 (0-1)	15-09 (0-1) 07-09 (1-3) 09-11 (2-4) 11-13 (3-4) 13-15 (4) 15-17 (3-4) 17-19 (2-3) 19-21 (1-2) 21-23 (0-1)	05-07 (1) 07-09 (1-3) 09-11 (2-4) 15-17 (3-2) 17-19 (4) 19-21 (3-4) 19-21 (1-2) 21-23 (0-1)	07-09 (3-2) 09-15 (4-2) 15-17 (4) 17-19 (3-4) 19-21 (2-3) 21-23 (1-2) 23-04 (0-1)
40	07-09 (1-2) 09-17 (3-4) 17-19 (2-3) 19-21 (1)	07-09 (2-3) 09-15 (4-2) 15-17 (4-3) 17-19 (3-4) 19-21 (1-3) 21-03 (0-2) 03-07 (0-1)	07-09 (3-2) 09-15 (2-1) 15-17 (3-2) 17-19 (4) 19-21 (3-4) 21-03 (2-4) 03-07 (1-3)	07-09 (2-1) 09-15 (1-0) 15-17 (2-0) 17-19 (4-3) 19-03 (4) 03-07 (3)
80	08-21 (4) 21-01 (3-4) 01-04 (2-3) 04-7 (1-2) 07-08 (2-3)	08-09 (4-2) 09-16 (4-1) 16-18 (4-2) 18-01 (4) 01-04 (3-4) 04-07 (2-4) 07-08 (3)	08-09 (2-1) 09-16 (0) 16-18 (2) 18-06 (4) 06-07 (4-2) 07-08 (3-1)	08-09 (1-0) 09-16 (0) 16-18 (2-0) 18-20 (4-3) 20-04 (4) 04-06 (4-2) 06-07 (2-1) 07-08 (1)
160	09-17 (1-0) 17-19 (3-2) 19-07 (4) 07-09 (3-2)	17-19 (2-1) 19-07 (4) 07-09 (2-1)	17-19 (1-0) 19-21 (4-2) 21-04 (4) 04-06 (4-2) 06-07 (4-1) 07-09 (1-0)	19-21 (2-1) 21-04 (4-3) 04-06 (2-1) 06-07 (1-0)

MASTER SHORT-SKIP PROPAGATION CHART
SOLAR PHASE: HIGH
SMOOTHED SUNSPOT RANGE: 60-90
SEASONS: SPRING & FALL
TIME ZONES: LOCAL STANDARD AT PATH MID-POINT
(24-Hour Time)

Band (Meters)	Distance Between Stations (Miles) 50-250	250-750	650-1300	1300-2300
10	Nil	Nil	08-10 (0-1) 10-15 (1-2) 15-20 (0-1)	08-09 (1-0) 09-10 (1) 10-13 (2-1) 13-15 (2) 15-17 (1-2) 17-20 (1)
15	Nil	09-16 (0-1)	08-09 (0-1) 09-10 (1) 10-16 (1-3) 16-18 (0-3) 18-20 (0-1)	07-08 (0-1) 08-10 (1-2) 10-18 (3-4) 18-20 (1-3) 20-22 (0-1)
20	Nil	07-12 (0-2) 12-18 (0-3) 18-20 (0-2) 20-07 (0-1)	06-07 (0-2) 07-08 (2) 08-10 (2-3) 10-12 (2-4) 12-18 (3-4) 18-20 (2-3) 20-22 (1-2) 22-06 (1-2)	06-08 (2-1) 08-10 (3) 10-15 (4-3) 15-18 (4) 18-20 (3-4) 20-22 (2-3) 22-02 (1-2) 02-06 (1)
40	06-08 (1-2) 08-10 (2-4) 10-19 (3-4) 19-21 (2-3) 21-23 (1-2) 23-06 (0-1)	06-08 (3-2) 08-15 (4-3) 15-19 (4) 19-21 (3-4) 21-23 (2-3) 23-02 (1-2) 02-06 (1)	06-08 (3-2) 08-15 (3-1) 15-17 (4-2) 17-19 (4-3) 19-21 (4) 21-23 (3-4) 23-02 (2-3) 02-06 (1-2)	06-08 (2-1) 08-15 (1-0) 15-17 (2-0) 17-19 (3-2) 19-23 (4) 23-02 (3-4) 02-06 (2-3)
80	07-08 (3-4) 08-11 (4) 11-18 (4-3) 18-21 (4) 21-23 (3-4) 23-01 (2-3) 01-05 (1-2) 05-07 (2-3)	07-08 (4-2) 08-11 (4-1) 11-16 (3-0) 16-18 (4-2) 18-20 (4) 20-23 (4) 23-01 (3-4) 01-05 (2-3) 05-07 (3-2)	07*08 (2-1) 08-11 (1-0) 11-16 (1) 16-18 (2-1) 18-20 (3-2) 20-01 (4) 01-05 (3) 05-07 (2)	07-08 (1-0) 08-16 (0) 16-18 (1-0) 18-20 (2-1) 20-22 (4-2) 22-01 (4-3) 01-05 (3) 05-07 (2-1)
160	05-07 (4-2) 07-09 (3-1) 09-17 (2-0) 17-19 (3-1) 19-20 (4-2) 20-05 (4)	05-07 (2-1) 06.07 (2-0) 07-09 (1-0) 09-17 (1) 17-19 (1-0) 19-20 (2) 20-22 (4-3) 22-03 (4) 03-05 (4-3)	05-06 (1) 06-19 (0) 19-20 (2-1) 20-22 (3-2) 22-03 (4-3) 03-05 (3-2)	05-06 (1-0) 06-19 (0) 19-20 (1-0) 20-22 (2) 22-03 (3-2) 03-05 (2-1)

FOOTNOTES
Worldwide Charts:
• Predicted times of 80 meter openings. Openings on 160 meters are also likely to occur during those times when 80 meter openings are shown with a forecast rating of (2) or higher.

Shott Skip Charts:
• Predominantly sporadic-E openings.

Hemisphere from sundown, through the hours of darkness, until just after sunrise. During the daylight hours expect excellent short-skip openings between distances of 100 and 1,000 miles, and during the night, beyond 750 miles.

60 meters – Interpolate between 40 and 80 meters.

80 meters – **Summer:** Some DX should be possible to several areas of the world during the hours of darkness and the sunrise period, despite seasonally high static levels. Daytime skip will be limited to a range up to approximately 250 miles; nighttime skip should be possible between approximately 200 and 2,300 miles.

80 meters – **Winter:** Fairly good DX should be possible to most areas of the world during the hours of darkness and the sunrise period. Daytime short-skip openings should be possible up to about 500 miles, increasing to between approximately 500 and 2,300 miles at night.

80 meters – **Equinox:** Some fairly good worldwide DX should be possible from sunset, through the hours of darkness, until sunrise. Excellent short-skip openings should be possible during the day up to about 350 miles, increasing to between 500 and 2,300 miles at night.

160 meters – **Summer:** No daytime openings are expected on this band due to high ionospheric absorption. An occasional DX opening might be possible at night, but seasonally high static levels will severely limit openings on this band most of the time. Short-skip openings to distances of as much as 1,000 miles should be possible during the hours of darkness, with openings considerably beyond this range occasionally possible.

160 meters – **Winter:** No daylight openings are expected, but some fairly good DX should be possible to many areas of the world during the hours of darkness and the sunrise period. Signals from Europe and from the east and south should peak about midnight, while signals from the northwest and west should peak just before sunrise. Expect fairly good short-skip openings during the hours of darkness over ranges of as much as 1,500 miles and occasionally to 2,300 miles.

160 meters – **Equinox:** No daytime skip possible, but fairly good DX should be possible during the hours of darkness and the sunrise period to some areas of the world. Nighttime short-skip should be possible to distances of approximately 1,200 miles, and at times to 2,300 miles.

4.6 Master Propagation Charts – Very High Solar Phase Smoothed Sunspot Number Range: 90-120

Band-By-Band Summary

6 meters: During this phase, solar activity should

be high enough to permit occasional F2 layer DX openings on the amateur 6-meter band. The best time for such openings is during the afternoon in the spring and fall months toward South America and other areas in the Southern Hemisphere. An occasional opening may also be possible during the winter months toward Europe and the east before noon, toward the south during the early afternoon, and toward the northwest and west during the late afternoon. If the 6-meter band is going to open at all, it will do so at the same time that 10 meters is peaking in the same direction.

10 meters – Summer: Good daytime DX should be possible on this band during most of the daylight hours possible on north-south paths into South America, and to many parts of Africa and the South Pacific. Conditions should peak during the afternoon. Expect plenty of short-skip openings due to sporadic-E ionization over a range of between 500 and 1,300 miles, and considerably beyond this when sporadic-E ionization is intensive and widespread.

10 meters – Winter: Excellent worldwide DX should be possible from shortly after sunrise to well past sunset. Conditions should peak before noon for openings toward Europe, Africa, and the east; during the early afternoon for openings toward the south; and during the late afternoon for openings toward the northwest, west, and South Pacific areas. Often signals will be exceptionally strong, even when using very low power. Exceptionally good short-skip openings should be possible from just after sunrise to an hour or so after sunset over distances ranging from between approximately 1,000 and 2,300 miles.

10 meters – Equinox: Expect good DX openings to most areas of the world from just after sunrise until an hour or so after sunset. This should be the best season of the year for long openings into areas of the Southern Hemisphere. Expect the band to peak for DX during the afternoon hours. Short-skip should be possible most of the day over a range of between 1,000 and 2,300 miles.

12 meters – Interpolate between 10 and 15 meters.

15 meters – Summer: Good worldwide DX should be possible on this band during most of the daylight hours and into the early evening. Conditions should peak during the late afternoon. Short-skip openings should be possible during the hours of daylight and into the early evening over a range of 500 to 2,300 miles.

15 meters – Winter: Excellent DX is expected to all areas of the world. The band should open toward Europe and the east an hour or so after sunrise; peak toward the southwest and south during the noon and afternoon periods; and peak toward the South Pacific, Far East, and other areas in a westerly and northwesterly direction during the late afternoon and early evening. Regular short-skip should be possible beyond a range of approximately 750 miles during the daytime hours and into the early evening.

15 meters – Equinox: Excellent DX conditions are expected to all areas of the world, particularly for long openings into the Southern Hemisphere. The band should be open for DX from an hour or so after sunrise to well after sunset. Excellent short-skip openings should be possible during most of the daylight hours beyond a range of approximately 750 miles.

17 meters – Interpolate between 15 and 20 meters.

20 meters – Summer: Expect good DX conditions around the clock. The band should peak in all directions just after sunrise, and again toward the east and the south during the late afternoon and evening hours. Expect a peak toward the northwest, west, and toward the South Pacific area during the hours of darkness. Excellent short-skip openings should be possible during the daylight hours over distances as short as 350 miles and as long as 2,300 miles. During the hours of darkness, short-skip openings should range to distances of between 1,000 and 2,300 miles.

20 meters – Winter: Excellent worldwide DX should be possible from just after sunrise to well into the evening, with the band remaining open to some areas of the world around the clock. Peak conditions should occur for several hours after sunrise and again during the late afternoon and early evening. Expect short-skip openings during the hours of darkness at ranges from 1,000 to 2,300 miles.

20 meters – Equinox: Excellent worldwide DX conditions can be expected, particularly for openings into the Southern Hemisphere. The band should open for DX shortly after sunrise and remain open well into the evening hours, and around the clock to some areas. Peak conditions should occur for several hours after sunrise and again during the late afternoon and early evening. The short-skip range during the daylight hours should extend out to distances of between 500 and 2,300 miles, and to between 1,300 and 2,300 miles during the hours of darkness.

30 meters – Interpolate between 20 and 40 meters.

40 meters – **Summer:** Fairly good DX should be possible to most areas of the world from sunset, through the hours of darkness, to just after sunrise, despite seasonally high static levels. Excellent short-skip openings are expected during the hours of daylight up to a distance of approximately 750 miles, and again during the hours of darkness over distances of between 300 and 2,300 miles.

40 meters – **Winter:** Good worldwide DX should be possible to most areas of the world during the hours of darkness and the sunrise period. The band should open during the late afternoon toward Europe and the east, with signals peaking toward the east and

MASTER DX PROPAGATION CHART
SOLAR PHASE: VERY HIGH
SMOOTHED SUNSPOT RANGE: 90-120
SEASON: SUMMER
TIME ZONE: EST (24-Hour Time)
EASTERN USA TO:

Reception Area	10 Meters	15 Meters	20 Meters	40/80 Meters
Western & Central Europe & North Africa	Nil	07-08 (1) 08-11 (2) 11-14 (1) 14-17 (2) 17-19 (1)	08-13 (1) 13-14 (2) 14-16 (3) 16-22 (4) 22-00 (3) 00-04 (2) 04-06 (3) 06-08 (2)	19-21 (1) 21-22 (2) 22-00 (3) 00-01 (2) 01-02 (1) 21-23 (1)* 23-00 (2)* 00-01 (1)*
Northern & Eastern Europe	Nil	10-14 (1) 14-16 (2) 16-18 (1)	08-14 (1) 14-16 (2) 16-17 (3) 17-20 (4) 20-23 (3) 23-01 (2) 01-06 (1) 06-08 (2)	20-21 (1) 21-23 (2) 23-01 (1) 20-23 (1)*
Eastern Mediterranean & Middle East	Nil	10-12 (1) 12-16 (2) 16-17 (3) 17-18 (2) 18-19 (1)	11-13 (1) 13-15 (2) 15-18 (3) 18-22 (4) 22-01 (3) 01-02 (2) 02-05 (1) 05-07 (2) 07-09 (1)	19-21 (1) 21-23 (2) 23-00 (1) 21-23 (1)*
Western Africa	10-12 (1) 15-18 (1)	09-11 (1) 11-13 (2) 13-14 (3) 14-16 (4) 16-18 (3) 18-19 (2) 19-21 (1)	13-14 (1) 14-15 (2) 15-17 (3) 17-23 (4) 23-02 (3) 02-03 (2) 03-06 (1)	19-21 (1) 21-23 (2) 23-01 (1)
East & Central Africa	08-10 (1) 16-18 (1)	08-11 (1) 11-13 (2) 13-15 (3) 15-16 (4) 16-18 (3) 18-19 (2) 19-20 (1)	13-15 (1) 15-16 (2) 16-17 (3) 17-21 (4) 21-23 (3) 23-02 (2) 02-05 (1)	19-20 (1) 20-23 (2) 23-00 (1)
Southern Africa	09-12 (1)	00-02 (1) 07-09 (1) 09-10 (2) 10-12 (3) 12-13 (2) 13-14 (1)	23-00 (1) 00-02 (3) 02-04 (2) 04-07 (3) 13-14 (1) 14-16 (2) 16-18 (1)	19-20 (1) 20-22 (2) 22-01 (1) 22-00 (1)*
Central & South Asia	Nil	08-10 (1) 13-18 (1) 18-21 (2) 21-22 (1)	16-19 (1) 19-22 (2) 22-02 (1) 02-05 (2) 05-07 (1)	18-20 (1)
Southeast Asia	Nil	09-13 (1) 13-15 (2) 15-18 (1) 18-20 (1) 20-21 (1)	05-06 (1) 06-08 (2) 08-10 (1) 15-18 (1) 18-20 (2) 20-23 (1) 23-01 (2) 01-02 (1)	Nil
Far East	Nil	08-09 (1) 09-11 (2) 11-17 (1) 17-19 (2) 19-21 (1)	05-06 (1) 06-08 (3) 08-09 (2) 09-11 (1) 17-19 (1) 23-01 (1)	Nil
South Pacific & New Zealand	17-21 (1)	08-10 (1) 13-15 (1) 15-18 (2) 18-22 (3) 22-23 (3) 23-00 (1)	17-20 (1) 20-22 (2) 22-00 (3) 00-03 (4) 03-04 (3) 04-06 (2) 06-08 (3) 08-09 (2) 09-11 (1)	00-02 (1) 02-05 (2) 05-07 (1) 03-05 (1)*
Australasia	18-20 (1)	08-10 (1) 16-17 (1) 17-19 (2) 19-21 (3) 21-22 (2) 22-23 (1)	22-00 (1) 00-02 (2) 02-04 (3) 04-07 (2) 07-09 (3) 09-11 (2) 11-13 (1)	02-03 (1) 03-05 (2) 05-06 (1) 03-05 (1)*
Caribbean, Central America & Northern Countries of South America	10-13 (1) 13-16 (2) 16-18 (3) 18-19 (2) 19-20 (1)	07-08 (1) 08-10 (2) 10-15 (3) 15-19 (4) 19-21 (3) 21-23 (2) 23-00 (1)	05-06 (3) 06-08 (4) 08-10 (3) 10-15 (2) 15-17 (3) 17-00 (4) 00-03 (3) 03-05 (2)	18-19 (1) 19-22 (2) 22-03 (3) 03-04 (2) 04-05 (1) 19-21 (1) 21-03 (2) 03-04 (1)
Peru, Bolivia, Paraguay, Brazil, Chie, Argentina & Uruguay	10-13 (1) 13-15 (2) 15-17 (3) 17-18 (2)	06-07 (1) 07-10 (2) 10-14 (1) 14-15 (2) 18-19 (1) 17-20 (4) 20-23 (3) 23-01 (2) 01-02 (1)	15-16 (1) 16-18 (2) 18-19 (3) 19-01 (4) 15-17 (3) 03-04 (2) 04-06 (1) 06-08 (2) 08-10 (1)	20-23 (1) 23-04 (2) 04-06 (1) 00-06 (1) 01-03 (3)
McMurdo Sound, Antarctica	Nil	13-15 (1) 15-19 (2) 19-20 (1)	16-17 (1) 17-20 (2) 20-02 (3) 02-06 (2) 06-08 (1)	20-01 (1) 01-03 (2) 03-05 (1)

MASTER DX PROPAGATION CHART
SOLAR PHASE: VERY HIGH
SMOOTHED SUNSPOT RANGE: 90-120
SEASON: SUMMER
TIME ZONES: CST & MST (24-Hour Time)
CENTRAL USA TO:

Reception Area	10 Meters	15 Meters	20 Meters	40/80 Meters
Western & Central Europe & North Africa	Nil	10-15 (1) 15-17 (2) 17-19 (1) 22-00 (1)	00-04 (1) 04-06 (2) 06-15 (1) 15-16 (2) 16-18 (3) 18-20 (4) 20-22 (3) 22-00 (2)	19-22 (1) 22-00 (2) 00-01 (1) 21-23 (1)*
Northern & Eastern Europe	Nil	08-11 (1) 11-15 (2) 15-17 (1)	01-06 (1) 06-08 (2) 08-14 (1) 14-17 (2) 17-22 (3) 22-01 (2)	19-23 (1)
Eastern Mediterranean & Middle East	Nil	12-14 (1) 14-17 (2) 17-19 (1)	12-15 (1) 15-17 (2) 17-21 (3) 21-23 (2) 23-00 (1) 06-08 (1)	20-23 (1)
Western Africa	09-11 (1)	09-11 (1) 15-18 (1) 14-16 (3) 16-18 (2) 18-20 (1)	13-14 (1) 11-14 (2) 15-17 (3) 17-21 (4) 21-23 (3) 23-02 (2) 02-04 (1)	19-23 (1) 14-15 (2)
East & Central Africa	15-18 (1)	12-14 (1) 14-15 (2) 15-17 (3) 17-18 (2) 18-19 (1)	14-16 (1) 16-17 (2) 17-19 (3) 19-21 (4) 21-22 (3) 22-00 (2) 00-01 (1)	19-22 (1)
Southern Africa	08-11 (1)	23-01 (1) 07-09 (1) 09-11 (2) 11-12 (1)	22-23 (1) 23-01 (2) 01-04 (1) 10-12 (1) 12-14 (2) 14-16 (1)	20-22 (1) 22-23 (2) 23-00 (1)
Central & South Asia	Nil	14-17 (1) 17-20 (2) 20-22 (1) 08-10 (1)	16-18 (1) 18-21 (2) 21-05 (1) 05-07 (2) 07-09 (1)	Nil
Southeast Asia	Nil	09-10 (1) 10-13 (2) 13-18 (1) 18-21 (2) 21-23 (1)	02-06 (1) 06-09 (2) 09-10 (1) 21-22 (1) 22-00 (2) 00-01 (1)	Nil
Far East	Nil	08-10 (1) 12-14 (1) 17-19 (1) 19-22 (2) 22-00 (1)	00-03 (1) 03-05 (2) 05-09 (3) 09-10 (2) 10-12 (1)	03-04 (1) 04-05 (2) 06-08 (1)
South Pacific & New Zealand	15-21 (1)	12-15 (1) 15-17 (2) 17-19 (3) 19-21 (4) 21-22 (2) 22-23 (2) 23-00 (1)	16-18 (1) 18-22 (2) 22-01 (4) 01-04 (3) 04-06 (2) 06-08 (4) 08-10 (2) 10-12 (1)	22-00 (1) 00-02 (2) 02-04 (3) 04-06 (2) 06-07 (1) 00-06 (1)*
Australasia	16-20 (1)	13-14 (1) 14-16 (2) 16-18 (1) 18-19 (2) 19-21 (3) 21-22 (2) 22-23 (1)	21-23 (1) 23-00 (1) 00-02 (4) 02-04 (3) 04-06 (2) 06-08 (4) 08-10 (2) 10-11 (1)	00-02 (1) 02-06 (2) 06-07 (1) 03-06 (1)*
Caribbean, Central America, & Northern Countries of South America	10-12 (1) 12-14 (2) 14-16 (3) 16-17 (2) 17-18 (1)	07-08 (1) 08-10 (2) 10-15 (3) 15-18 (4) 18-19 (3) 19-20 (2) 20-22 (1)	02-04 (2) 04-06 (2) 06-08 (4) 08-10 (3) 10-15 (2) 15-17 (3) 17-22 (4) 22-02 (3)	19-20 (1) 20-22 (2) 22-03 (3) 03-04 (2) 04-05 (1) 21-00 (1)* 00-03 (2)* 03-04 (1)*
Peru, Bolivia, Paraguay, Brazil, Chile, Argentina & Uruguay	08-12 (1) 12-15 (2) 15-18 (3) 18-19 (2)	06-07 (1) 07-09 (2) 09-13 (1) 13-15 (2) 19-20 (1) 16-20 (4) 20-22 (2) 22-00 (2) 00-02 (1)	13-15 (1) 15-17 (2) 17-18 (3) 18-23 (4) 15-16 (3) 01-02 (2) 02-04 (1) 04-06 (2) 06-09 (1)	20-22 (1) 22-01 (2) 01-04 (3) 22-03 (1)* 23-01 (3)
McMurdo Sound, Antarctica	Nil	13-15 (1) 15-18 (2) 18-20 (1)	13-16 (1) 16-18 (2) 18-00 (3) 00-03 (2) 03-06 (1)	20-21 (1) 21-23 (2) 23-05 (1)

MASTER DX PROPAGATION CHART
SOLAR PHASE: VERY HIGH
SMOOTHED SUNSPOT RANGE: 90-120
SEASON: SUMMER
TIME ZONE: PST (24-Hour Time)
WESTERN USA TO:

Reception Area	10 Meters	15 Meters	20 Meters	40/80 Meters
Western Europe & North Africa	Nil	07-08 (1) 08-10 (2) 10-14 (1) 14-16 (2) 16-17 (1) 20-22 (1)	23-05 (1) 05-07 (2) 07-14 (1) 14-16 (2) 16-21 (3) 21-23 (2)	19-22 (1)
Northern, Central & Eastern Europe	Nil	06-08 (1) 13-16 (1) 20-22 (1)	13-15 (1) 15-20 (2) 20-23 (3) 23-00 (2) 00-07 (1)	19-21 (1)
Eastern Mediterranean & Middle East	Nil	06-08 (1) 12-19 (1) 19-21 (2) 21-22 (1)	12-15 (1) 15-19 (2) 19-21 (3) 21-23 (2) 23-00 (1) 05-07 (1)	Nil
West & Central Africa	07-10 (1)	06-10 (1) 10-12 (2) 12-16 (1) 16-18 (2) 18-19 (1)	12-14 (1) 14-17 (2) 17-19 (3) 19-21 (4) 21-23 (3) 23-03 (2) 03-07 (1)	20-23 (1)
East Africa	Nil	08-12 (1) 12-15 (2) 15-16 (1) 19-21 (1)	14-16 (1) 16-18 (2) 18-21 (3) 21-23 (2) 23-00 (1)	Nil
Southern Africa	Nil	07-09 (1) 09-11 (2) 11-12 (1) 22-00 (1)	14-16 (1) 21-22 (1) 22-00 (2) 00-06 (1) 06-08 (2) 08-10 (1)	19-22 (1)
Central & South Asia	Nil	07-09 (1) 09-11 (2) 11-13 (1)	22-04 (1) 04-08 (2) 08-11 (1) 17-19 (1) 19-21 (2) 21-22 (1)	Nil
Southeast Asia	Nil	07-08 (1) 08-10 (3) 10-12 (2) 12-15 (1) 18-20 (1) 20-22 (1) 22-00 (1)	22-00 (1) 00-02 (2) 02-04 (3) 04-06 (2) 06-08 (3) 08-10 (2) 10-13 (1)	02-06 (1)
Far East	13-15 (1)	08-09 (1) 09-11 (2) 11-13 (1) 13-14 (2) 14-16 (3) 16-18 (2) 18-21 (1)	18-20 (1) 20-22 (2) 22-00 (3) 00-02 (4) 02-04 (3) 04-06 (2) 06-09 (3) 09-11 (2) 11-14 (1)	01-02 (1) 02-05 (2) 05-06 (1) 02-04 (1)
South Pacific & New Zealand	11-13 (1) 13-18 (2) 18-19 (1)	08-10 (1) 10-11 (2) 11-13 (3) 13-15 (2) 15-17 (3) 17-20 (4) 20-21 (3)	16-18 (1) 18-20 (2) 20-01 (4) 01-05 (2) 05-07 (4) 07-10 (2) 10-12 (1) 21-22 (1) 22-00 (1)	21-22 (1) 22-00 (2) 00-05 (3) 05-06 (2) 06-07 (1) 23-01 (1)* 01-04 (2)* 04-06 (1)*
Australasia	13-16 (1) 16-19 (2) 19-20 (1)	06-08 (1) 12-14 (1) 14-17 (2) 17-19 (3) 19-21 (4) 21-22 (3) 22-00 (2) 00-02 (1)	19-21 (1) 21-23 (2) 23-04 (4) 04-06 (3) 06-08 (4) 08-09 (2) 09-12 (1)	23-01 (1) 01-03 (2) 03-05 (3) 05-06 (2) 06-07 (1) 01-06 (1).
Caribbean, Central America & Northern Countries of South America	08-10 (1) 10-12 (2) 12-14 (1) 14-16 (2) 16-17 (1)	07-08 (1) 08-12 (1) 12-14 (3) 14-17 (4) 17-18 (3) 18-20 (2) 20-22 (1)	08-10 (2) 10-13 (1) 13-15 (2) 15-17 (3) 17-23 (4) 23-02 (3) 02-05(2) 05-08 (3)	19-20 (1) 20-23 (2) 23-02 (3) 02-04 (2) 04-05 (1) 20-00 (1)* 00-02 (2)* 02-03 (1)*
Peru, Bolivia, Paraguay, Brazil, Chile, Argentina & Uruguay	08-12 (1) 12-14 (2) 14-16 (3) 16-18 (2)	05-06 (1) 06-08 (2) 08-12 (1) 12-14 (2) 18-20 (1) 16-20 (4) 20-22 (3) 22-23 (2) 23-00 (1)	13-15 (1) 15-17 (2) 17-18 (3) 18-23 (4) 14-16 (3) 00-02 (2) 02-04 (1) 04-06 (2) 06-09 (1)	20-22 (1) 22-01 (2) 01-04 (1) 21-02(1)* 23-00 (3)
McMurdo Sound, Antarctica	16-18 (1)	14-16 (1) 16-20 (2) 20-21 (1)	15-17 (1) 17-18 (2) 18-00 (3) 00-03 (2) 03-06 (1)	20-21 (1) 21-23 (2) 23-03 (1) 03-05 (2) 05-06 (1)

MASTER DX PROPAGATION CHART
SOLAR PHASE: VERY HIGH
SMOOTHED SUNSPOT RANGE: 90-120
SEASON: WINTER
TIME ZONE: EST (24-Hour Time)
EASTERN USA TO:

Reception Area	10 Meters	15 Meters	20 Meters	40/80 Meters
Western & Central Europe & North Africa	07-08 (1) 08-09 (2) 09-11 (4) 11-12 (3) 12-13 (2) 13-14 (1)	06-07 (1) 07-08 (2) 08-09 (3) 09-12 (4) 12-13 (3) 13-14 (2) 14-15 (1)	23-01 (2) 01-05 (1) 05-07 (2) 07-09 (3) 09-11 (2) 11-12 (3) 12-15 (4) 15-16 (3) 16-19 (2) 19-23 (1)	14-16 (1) 16-17 (2) 17-19 (3) 19-02 (4) 02-03 (3) 03-04 (2) 04-05 (1) 17-19 (1)* 19-20 (2)* 20-02 (3)* 02-03 (2)* 03-01 (1)*
Northern & Eastern Europe	07-08 (1) 08-10 (2) 10-12 (1)	06-07 (1) 07-08 (2) 08-10 (3) 10-12 (2) 12-13 (1)	23-02 (1) 02-04 (2) 04-06 (1) 06-07 (2) 07-11 (3) 11-13 (2) 13-14 (1)	16-19 (1) 19-23 (2) 23-03 (1) 19-02 (1)*
Eastern Mediterranean & Middle East	07-08(1) 08-10 (2) 10-12 (1)	07-08 (1) 08-09 (2) 09-11 (4) 11-12 (3) 12-13 (2) 13-14 (1)	06-08 (2) 10-13 (2) 13-16 (3) 16-21 (2) 21-23 (1) 23-02 (2) 02-06 (1)	18-20 (1) 20-22 (2) 22-00 (1) 20-23 (1)*
West & Central Africa	07-08 (1) 08-10 (2) 10-11 (3) 11-14 (4)	06-07 (1) 07-11 (2) 11-13 (3) 13-16 (4) 14-15 (1) 15-16 (2) 16-17 (1)	01-06 (1) 06-08 (2) 08-13 (1) 13-15 (2) 16-17 (3) 17-18 (2) 18-19 (1) 21-01 (2)	18-22 (1) 22-02 (2) 02-03 (1) 00-03 (1)* 15-16 (3) 16-18 (4) 18-21 (3)
East Africa	08-10 (1) 10-12 (2) 12-15 (3) 15-16 (2) 16-17 (1)	06-10 (1) 10-12 (2) 12-14 (3) 14-16 (4) 16-17 (1) 17-18 (2) 18-19 (1)	07-13 (1) 13-15 (2) 15-16 (3) 16-18 (4) 18-20 (2) 20-23 (2) 23-01 (1)	18-00 (1)
Southern Africa	07-08 (1) 08-10 (2) 10-12 (4) 12-15 (4) 13-14 (2) 14-15 (1)	07-09 (1) 09-11 (2) 11-12 (3) 12-15 (4) 15-17 (2) 17-18 (1)	12-14 (1) 14-15 (2) 15-18 (4) 18-20 (3) 20-01 (2) 01-03(1)	18-19 (1) 19-21 (2) 21-00 (1) 19-22 (1)'
Central & South Asia	08-10 (1) 17-19 (1)	07-08 (1) 08-10 (2) 10-11 (1) 17-19 (1)	06-07 (1) 07-09 (2) 09-12 (1) 18-20 (1) 20-23 (2) 23-01 (1)	06-08 (1) 20-22 (1)
Southeast Asia	00-10 (1) 10-11 (2) 11-13 (1) 18-20 (1) 18-20 (2) 20-21 (1)	09-10 (1) 10-12 (1) 12-14 (1) 17-18 (1) 19-22 (2) 22-03 (1)	06-07 (1) 10-12 (1) 12-14 (1) 17-19 (1)	05-07 (1) 07-09 (2) 09-11 (1) 17-19 (1)
Far East	17-18 (1) 18-19 (2) 19-20 (1)	16-17 (1) 17-18 (2) 18-20 (3) 20-21 (2) 21-22 (1)	16-18 (1) 18-20 (2) 20-22 (3) 22-00 (2) 00-02 (1) 02-04 (2) 04-07 (1) 07-09 (2) 09-11 (1)	05-08 (1) 05-07 (1)*
South Pacific & New Zealand	12-14(1) 14-17 (2) 17-19 (3) 19-20 (2) 20-21 (1)	08-10 (1) 10-13 (2) 13-16 (3) 16-18 (2) 18-20 (3) 20-21 (2) 21-22 (1)	12-19 (1) 19-22 (2) 22-00 (3) 00-02 (2) 02-04 (3) 04-06 (1) 06-07 (1) 07-09 (1) 09-12 (2)	01-02 (1) 02-04 (2) 04-07 (3) 07-08 (2) 08-09 (2) 04-05 (1)* 05-07 (2)* 07-08 (1)*
Australasia	09-10 (1) 10-11 (2) 11-12 (2) 15-17 (2) 17-19 (2) 19-20 (1)	08-10 (1) 10-12 (2) 12-16 (1) 16-18 (2) 18-20 (3) 20-21 (2) 21-22 (1)	07-09 (3) 10-12 (1) 12-15 (1) 15-17 (2) 17-20 (1) 20-22 (2) 22-02 (2) 02-04 (2) 04-07 (1)	03-05 (1) 05-07 (2) 07-09 (1) 05-08 (1)*
Caribbean, Central America & Northern Countries of South America	07-08 (1) 08-09 (3) 09-12 (4) 12-14 (3) 14-16 (4) 16-17 (3) 17-18 (2) 18-19 (1)	06-07 (1) 07-08 (3) 08-10 (4) 10-13 (3) 13-17 (4) 17-19 (3) 19-20 (2) 20-21 (1)	07-09 (4) 09-11 (3) 11-16 (2) 16-17 (3) 17-21 (4) 21-00 (3) 00-03 (2) 03-05 (1) 05-07 (2)	17-18 (1) 18-19 (2) 19-21 (3)* 21-04 (1) 04-05 (3) 05-06 (2)* 06-07 (1) 19-20 (1)* 20-22 (2)* 22-02 (3)* 02-04 (2)* 04-06 (1)*
Peru, Bolivia, Paraguay, Brazil, Chile, Argentina & Uruguay	07-08 (1) 08-11 (2) 11-14 (3) 14-16 (4) 16-17 (2) 17-19(1)	06-07 (1) 07-09 (2) 00-12(1) 12-14 (2) 14-16 (3) 16-18 (4) 18-19 (3) 19-20 (2) 20-21 (1)	13-14 (1) 14-15(2) 15-17 (3) 17-21 (4) 21-02 (3) 02-04 (2) 04-06 (1) 06-08 (2) 08-09 (1)	19-21 (1) 21-02 (2) 02-05 (1) 21-03 (1)*
McMurdo Sound, Antarctica	Nil	06-09 (1) 16-18 (1) 18-20 (2) 20-21 (1)	18-19 91) 19-20 (2) 20-00 (2) 00-02 (2) 02-04 (3) 04-06 (2) 06-08 (2) 08-09 (1)	00-05 (1)

MASTER DX PROPAGATION CHART
SOLAR PHASE: VERY HIGH
SMOOTHED SUNSPOT RANGE: 90-120
SEASON: WINTER
TIME ZONES: CST & MST (24-Hour Time)
CENTRAL USA TO:

Reception Area	10 Meters	15 Meters	20 Meters	40/80 Meters
Western Europe & North Africa	07-08 (1) 08-09 (2) 09-10 (3) 10-11 (4) 11-12 (1)	06-07 (1) 07-08 (2) 06-10 (3) 10-12 (4) 12-13 (3) 13-14 (2) 14-15 (1)	02-06 (1) 06-07 (2) 07-09 (3) 09-11 (2) 11-13 (3) 13-16 (2) 16-19 (1) 19-22 (2) 22-00 (1) 00-02 (2)	15-17 (1) 17-18 (2) 18-01 (3) 01-02 (2) 02-03 (1) 17-20 (1)* 20-01 (2)* 01-02 (1)*
Northern, Central & Eastern Europe	08-09 (1) 09-10 (2) 10-11 (1)	06-07 (1) 07-10 (2) 10-12 (1)	22-00 (1) 00-02 (2) 02-06 (1) 06-08 (2) 08-11 (3) 11-12 (2) 12-14 (1)	17-19 (1) 19-22 (2) 22-01 (1) 19-00 (1)*

Eastern Mediterranean & Middle East	08-09 (1) 09-10 (2) 10-11 (1)	07-08 (1) 08-11 (2) 11-12 (1)	04-06 (2) 06-10 (1) 10-12 (2) 12-14 (3) 14-18 (2) 18-22 (1) 22-02 (2) 02-04 (1)	18-20 (1) 20-22 (2) 22-23 (1) 20-22 (1)*
West & Central Africa	07-08 (1) 08-10 (2) 10-12 (3) 12-14 (4) 14-15 (3) 15-16 (2) 16-17 (1)	06-09 (1) 09-11 (2) 11-14 (3) 14-16 (4) 16-17 (3) 17-18 (2) 18-19 (1)	06-13 (1) 13-15 (2) 15-16 (3) 16-18 (4) 18-20 (3) 20-22 (2) 22-01 (1)	18-21 (1) 21-23 (2) 23-01 (1)
East Africa	08-09 (1) 09-12 (2) 12-14 (3) 14-15 (2) 15-16 (1)	08-10 (1) 10-13 (2) 13-15 (3) 15-17 (2) 17-18 (1)	11-14 (1) 14-16 (2) 16-19 (3) 19-22 (2) 22-00 (1)	19-00 (1)
Southern Africa	08-09 (1) 09-10 (2) 10-12 (3) 12-13 (2) 13-14 (1)	07-10 (1) 10-11 (2) 11-12 (3) 12-14 (4) 14-15 (3) 15-17 (2) 17-18 (1)	07-13 (1) 13-15 (2) 15-16 (3) 16-18 (4) 18-20 (3) 20-21 (2) 21-00 (1)	18-19 (1) 19-21 (1) 21-22 (1)
Central & South Asia	08-10 (1) 18-20 (1)	07-09 (1) 18-19 (1) 19-20 (2) 20-21 (1)	06-07 (1) 07-09 (2) 09-11 (1) 17-19 (1) 19-22 (2) 22-00 (1)	06-08 (1) 19-21 (1)
Southeast Asia	09-10 (1) 10-12 (2) 12-13(1) 16-17 (1) 17-19 (2) 19-20 (1)	09-10 (1) 10-12 (2) 12-14 (1) 16-18 (1) 18-20 (2) 20-21 (1)	07-08 (1) 08-09 (2) 09-11 (3) 11-13 (2) 13-18 (1) 18-20 (2) 20-21 (1)	04-07 (1)
Far East	16-17 (1) 17-19 (2) 19-20 (1)	15-16 (1) 16-17 (2) 17-19 (3) 19-20 (2) 20-21 (1)	15-17 (1) 17-18 (2) 18-20 (3) 20-23 (2) 23-01 (1) 01-03 (2) 03-07 (1) 07-09 (2) 09-11 (1)	02-08 (1) 04-07(1)*
South Pacific & New Zealand	10-14 (1) 14-16 (2) 16-18 (3) 18-19 (2) 19-20 (1)	08-09 (1) 09-11 (2) 11-13 (3) 13-14 (2) 14-16 (1) 16-17 (2) 17-19 (3) 19-20 (2) 20-21 (1)	06-07 (2) 07-09 (3) 09-12 (2) 12-18 (1) 18-20 (2) 20-00 (3) 00-03 (4) 03-04 (3) 04-05 (2) 05-06 (1)	23-01 (1) 01-02 (2) 02-06 (3) 06-07 (2) 07-08 (1) 03-07 (1)*
Australasia	08-09 (1) 09-11 (2) 11-12 (1) 15-17 (1) 17-19 (2) 19-20 (1)	08-09 (1) 09-10 (2) 10-12 (3) 12-14 (2) 14-15 (3) 15-17 (4) 17-19 (3) 19-20 (2) 20-21 (1)	05-07 (1) 07-08 (2) 08-10 (3) 10-12 (2) 12-15 (1) 15-17 (2) 17-20 (1) 20-22 (2) 22-03 (1) 03-05 (2)	02-04 (1) 04-07 (2) 07-09 (1) 03-06 (1)*
Caribbean, Central America & Northern Countries of South America	07-08 (1) 08-09 (3) 09-11 (4) 11-13 (3) 13-15 (4) 15-16 (2) 16-17 (1)	06-07 (1) 07-08 (2) 08-12 (3) 12-17 (4) 17-18 (3) 18-19 (2) 19-20 (1)	06-07 (2) 07-11 (3) 11-15 (2) 15-17 (3) 17-20 (4) 20-22 (3) 22-00 (2) 00-02 (3) 02-04 (2) 04-06 (1)	17-18 (1) 18-19 (2) 19-00 (3) 00-04 (4) 04-05 (3) 05-06 (2) 06-07 (1) 19-20 (1)* 20-22 (2)* 22-01 (3)* 01-02 (2)* 02-04(1)*
Peru, Bolivia, Paraguay, Brazil, Chile, Argentina & Uruguay	07-08 (1) 08-11 (2) 11-14 (3) 14-16 (4) 16-17 (2) 17-18 (1)	06-07 (1) 07-09 (2) 09-12 (1) 12-14 (2) 14-15 (3) 15-17 (4) 17-18 (3) 18-19 (2) 19-20 (1)	04-06 (1) 06-08 (2) 08-14 (1) 14-15 (2) 15-17 (3) 17-20 (4) 20-02 (3) 02-04 (2)	19-21 (1) 21-02 (2) 02-05 (1) 21-04 (1)*
McMurdo Sound Antarctica	Nil	07-09 (1) 16-18 (1) 18-20 (2) 20-21 (1)	17-19 (1) 19-22 (2) 22-00 (3) 00-02 (2) 02-04 (3) 04-05 (2) 05-06 (1)	22-05 (1)

MASTER DX PROPAGATION CHART
SOLAR PHASE: VERY HIGH
SMOOTHED SUNSPOT RANGE: 90-120
SEASON: WINTER
TIME ZONE: PST (24-Hour Time)
WESTERN USA TO:

Reception Area	*10 Meters*	*15 Meters*	*20 Meters*	*40/80 Meters*
Western Europe & North Africa	07-08 (1) 08-10 (2) 10-11 (1)	07-08 (1) 08-09 (2) 09-10 (3) 10-11 (2) 11-12 (1)	22.00 (1) 00-03 (2) 03-06 (1) 06-09 (2) 09-11 (3) 11-14 (2) 14-16 (1)	18-21 (1) 21.00 (2) 00-01 (1) 19-23 (1)*
Northern, Central & Eastern Europe	07-09 (1)	06-07 (1) 07-09 (2) 09-10 (1)	16-18 (1) 22-00 (1) 00-02 (2) 02-06 (1) 06-07 (2) 07-09 (3) 09-11 (2) 11-13 (1)	17-22 (1) 22-00 (2) 00-01 (1) 19-23 (1)*
Eastern Mediter-ranean & Middle East	07-09 (1)	07-08 (1) 08-10 (2) 10-11 (1)	22-00 (1) 00-03 (2) 03-07 (1) 07-10 (2) 10-14 (1) 14-16 (2) 16-18 (1)	18-21 (1)
West & Central Africa	08-00 (1) 09-11 (2) 11-14 (4) 14-15 (3) 15-16 (2) 16-17 (1)	06-08 (1) 08-11 (2) 11-12 (3) 12-15 (4) 15-16 (3) 16-17 (2) 17-18 (1)	05-10 (1) 10-13 (2) 13-15 (3) 15-17 (4) 17-18 (3) 18-19 (2) 19-21 (1) 00-03 (2)	18-22 (1)
East Africa	09-10 (1) 10-12 (2) 12-14 (1)	08-10 (1) 10-12 (2) 12-15 (3) 15-16 (2) 16-17 (1)	08-13 (1) 13-15 (2) 15-17 (3) 17-19 (2) 19-20 (1)	18-20 (1)
Southern Africa	08-10 (1) 10-12 (2) 12-14 (1)	07-09 (1) 09-12 (2) 12-15 (3) 15-16 (2) 16-17 (1)	07-12 (1) 12-14 (2) 14-15 (3) 15-17 (4) 17-19 (3) 19-20 (2) 20-21 (1) 00-02 (1)	18-20 (1)
Central & South Asia	17-19 (1)	07-10 (1) 16-17 (1) 17-19 (2) 19-20 (1)	06-07 (1) 07-09 (2) 09-11 (1) 16-18 (1) 18-20 (2) 20-22 (1)	05-07 (1) 17-20 (1)
Southeast Asia	09-11 (1) 14-15 (1) 15-17 (3) 17-18 (2) 18-19 (1)	08-09 (1) 09-11 (2) 11-13 (1) 13-15 (2) 15-18 (3) 18-19 (2) 19-21 (1)	07-08 (1) 08-09 (2) 09-11 (3) 11-13 (2) 13-14 (1) 18-19 (1) 19-21 (2) 21-22 (1)	03-08 (1) 04-06 (1)*
Far East	14-15 (1) 15-16 (2) 16-17 (4) 17-18 (3) 18-19 (2) 19-20 (1)	13-14 (1) 14-16 (3) 16-18 (4) 18-19 (3) 19-20 (2) 20-21 (1)	02-04 (1) 07-08 (1) 08-11 (2) 11-13 (1) 13-15 (2) 15-16 (3) 16-18 (4) 18-20 (3) 20-21 (2) 21-22 (1)	00-01 (1) 01-03 (2) 03-06 (3) 06-08 (2) 08-10 (1) 02-08 (1)*
South Pacific & New Zealand	10-12 (1) 12-14 (2) 14-16 (3) 16-17 (2) 17-19 (1)	07-08 (1) 08-09 (2) 09-11 (3) 11-15 (2) 15-17 (3) 17-19 (4) 19-20 (3) 20-21 (2) 21-22 (1)	02-06 (1) 06-07 (2) 07-09 (3) 09-11 (2) 11-17 (1) 17-18 (2) 18-20 (3) 20-23 (4) 23-00 (3) 00-02 (2)	22-00 (1) 00-03 (2) 03-06 (3) 06-07 (2) 07-08 (1) 00-06 (1)*
Australasia	10-13 (1) 13-15 (2) 15-17 (3) 17-19 (2) 19-20 (1)	08-09 (1) 09-12 (3) 12-15 (2) 15-17 (1) 17-18 (2) 18-20 (3) 20-21 (2) 21-22 (1)	18-20 (1) 20-22 (2) 22-02 (1) 02-05 (2) 05-06 (1) 06-08 (2) 08-10 (4) 10-12 (2) 12-14 (1)	01-03 (1) 03-06 (2) 06-08 (1) 01-03 (1)*
Caribbean, Central America & Northern Countries of South America	07-08 (1) 08-09 (2) 09-10 (3) 10-14 (4) 14-15 (3) 15-16 (2) 16-17 (1)	06-07 (1) 07-08 (2) 08-13 (3) 13-16 (4) 16-17 (3) 17-18 (2) 18-19 (1)	06-07 (2) 07-09 (4) 09-13 (2) 13-15 (3) 15-19 (4) 19-20 (3) 20-00 (2) 00-06 (1)	17-18 (1) 18-19 (2) 19-23 (3) 23-03 (4) 03-04 (2) 04-05 (1) 19-20 (1)* 20-22 (2)* 22-00 (3)* 00-02 (2)* 02-04 (1)*
Peru, Bolivia, Paraguay, Brazil, Chile	07-08 (1) 08-11 (2) 11-13 (3) 13-15 (4) 15-16 (3) 16-17 (2) 17-18 (1)	06-07 (1) 07-09 (2) 09-13 (3) 13-14 (2) 14-15 (3) 15-17 (4) 17-18 (3) 18-19 (2) 19-20 (1)	12-14 (1) 14-16 (2) 16-17 (3) 17-19 (4) 19-22 (3) 22-00 (2) 00-02 (3) 02-03 (2) 03-04 (1) 06-08 (1)	20-22 (1) 22-01 (2) 01-04 (1) 22-02 (1)*
McMurdo Sound, Antarctica	Nil	06-09 (1) 14-16 (1) 16-19 (2) 19-21 (1)	16-18 (1) 18-20 (2) 20-00 (3) 00-04 (2) 04-06 (1) 06-08 (2) 08-10 (1)	23-05 (1)

MASTER DX PROPAGATION CHART
SOLAR PHASE: VERY HIGH
SMOOTHED SUNSPOT RANGE: 90-120
SEASONS: SPRING & FALL
TIME ZONE: EST (24-Hour Time)
EASTERN USA TO:

Reception Area	*10 Meters*	*15 Meters*	*20 Meters*	*40/80 Meters*
Western & Central Europe & North Africa	08-09 (1) 09-10 (2) 10-12 (3) 12-13 (2) 13-15 (1)	06-07 (1) 07-08 (2) 08-11 (3) 11-14 (4) 14-15 (3) 15-16 (2) 16-17 (1)	03-06 (2) 06-09 (3) 09-12 (2) 12-13 (3) 13-16 (4) 16-19 (3) 19-22 (2) 22-03 (1)	17-18 (1) 18-19 (2) 19-01 (3) 00-03 (2) 03-04 (1) 19-21 (1)* 21-00 (2)* 00-02 (1)*
Northern & Eastern Europe	08-09 (1) 09-11 (2) 11-13 (1)	06-08 (1) 08-09 (2) 09-12 (3) 2-13 (2) 13-14 (1)	08-13 (1) 13-15 (2) 15-18 (3) 18-23 (2) 23-04 (3) 04-08 (2)	18-20 (1) 20-22 (2) 22-02 (1) 20-00 (1)*
Eastern Mediterranean & Middle East	08-09 (1) 09-12 (2) 12-13 (1)	07-09 (1) 09-10 (2) 10-11 (3) 11-13 (4) 13-15 (2) 15-16 (1)	05-07 (2) 07-14 (1) 14-18 (2) 18-20 (3) 20-22 (2) 22-00 (4) 00-02 (2) 02-05 (1)	19-20 (1) 20-22 (2) 22-23 (1) 20-22 (1)*
Western Africa	07-08 (1) 08-11 (3) 11-15 (4) 15-17 (3) 17-18 (2) 18-19 (1)	05-06 (1) 06-07 (2) 07-13 (3) 13-17 (4) 17-18 (3) 18-20 (2) 20-22 (1)	06-13 (1) 13-15 (2) 15-17 (3) 17-23 (4) 23-02 (3) 02-06 (2)	18-20 (1) 20-23 (2) 23-01 (3) 01-02 (2) 02-03 (1) 22-02 (1)*

Central USA (continued)

East & Central Africa

07-09 (1)	07-09 (1)	12-14 (1)	19-23 (1)
09-11 (2)	09-11 (2)	14-16 (2)	23-01 (2)
11-15 (3)	11-13 (3)	16-18 (3)	01-02 (1)
15-17 (2)	13-15 (4)	18-22 (4)	
17-19 (1)	15-17 (3)	22-01 (3)	
	17-18 (2)	01-03 (2)	
	18-19 (1)	03-05 (1)	

Southern Africa

07-09 (1)	06-10 (1)	12-15 (1)	18-19 (1)
09-11 (2)	10-13 (2)	15-17 (2)	19-21 (2)
11-12 (3)	13-15 (3)	17-18 (3)	21-22 (1)
12-14 (4)	15-17 (4)	16-20 (4)	19-21 (1)
14-15 (2)	17-18 (2)	20-23 (2)	
15-16 (1)	18-19 (1)	23-02 (3)	
		02-03 (2)	
		03-06 (1)	

Central & South Asia

08-10 (1)	07-08 (1)	06-09 (1)	05-07 (1)
17-19 (1)	08-10 (2)	17-19 (1)	19-21 (1)
	10-12 (1)	19-21 (2)	
	19-21 (1)	21-23 (1)	

Southeast Asia

08-09 (1)	07-08 (1)	04-06 (1)	05-07 (1)
09-11 (2)	08-10 (2)	06-07 (2)	
11-14 (1)	10-12 (1)	07-10 (1)	
18-21 (1)	15-17 (1)	14-16 (1)	
	17-19 (2)	21-23 (1)	
	19-21 (1)	23-01 (2)	
		01-02 (1)	

Far East

16-17 (1)	07-10 (1)	02-06 (1)	05-08 (1)
17-19 (1)	15-16 (1)	06-09 (1)	
19-20 (1)	16-17 (2)	09-11 (1)	
	17-19 (3)	19-21 (1)	
	19-20 (2)	21-22 (2)	
	20-21 (1)	22-00(3)	
		00-02 (2)	

South Pacific & New Zealand

11-12 (1)	08-09 (1)	18-20 (1)	01-02 (1)
12-14 (2)	09-12 (2)	20-22 (2)	02-03 (2)
14-16 (1)	12-16 (1)	22-00 (3)	03-05 (3)
16-17 (2)	16-18 (2)	00-02 (4)	05-07 (2)
17-19 (3)	18-21 (3)	02-05 (3)	07-08 (1)
19-20 (2)	21-22 (2)	05-07 (2)	02-03 (1)*
20-21 (1)	22-23 (1)	07-09 (4)	03-05 (2)*
		09-10 (2)	05-06 (1)*
		10-12 (1)	

Australasia

09-11 (1)	08-09 (1)	02-07 (2)	03-05 (1)
15-16 (1)	09-11 (2)	07-09 (3)	05-07 (2)
16-17 (2)	11-16 (1)	09-10 (2)	07-09 (1)
17-19 (3)	16-18 (2)	10-13 (1)	04-05 (1)*
19-20 (2)	18-20 (3)	13-15 (2)	05-06 (2)*
20-21 (1)	20-22 (2)	15-19 (1)	06-07 (1)*
	22-23 (1)	19-22 (2)	
		22-02 (3)	

Caribbean, Central America & Northern Countries of South America

07-08 (1)	06-07 (1)	06-08 (4)	18-19 (1)
08-09 (3)	07-08 (2)	08-10 (3)	19-20 (2)
09-11 (4)	08-10 (4)	10-15 (2)	20-03 (3)
11-13 (3)	10-15 (3)	15-18 (3)	03-05 (2)
13-16 (4)	15-18 (4)	18-00 (4)	05-07 (1)
16-17 (3)	18-20 (3)	00-03 (3)	19-21 (1)*
17-18 (2)	20-22 (2)	03-05 (2)	21-02(2)*
18-19 (1)	22-01 (1)	05-06 (3)	02-06 (1)*

Peru, Bolivia, Paraguay, Brazil, Chile, Argentina & Uruguay

07-08 (1)	06-07 (1)	15-16 (1)	19-21 (1)
08-10 (1)	07-10 (2)	16-17 (2)	21-03 (2)
10-14 (2)	10-14 (1)	17-18 (3)	03-06 (1)
14-15 (3)	14-15 (2)	00-02 (3)	21-05 (1)*
15-17 (4)	15-19 (4)	18-00 (4)	
17-18 (2)	19-21 (3)	02-04 (2)	
18-19 (1)	21-23 (2)	04-05 (1)	
	23-01 (1)	05-07 (2)	
		07-09 (1)	

McMurdo Sound, Antarctica

14-16 (1)	14-16 (1)	17-19 (1)	22-00 (1)
16-19 (2)	16-18 (2)	19-21 (2)	00-03 (2)
19-20 (1)	18-21 (3)	21-04 (3)	03-05 (1)
	21-22 (2)	04-06 (2)	
	22-23 (1)	06-08 (1)	

MASTER DX PROPAGATION CHART
SOLAR PHASE: VERY HIGH
SMOOTHED SUNSPOT RANGE: 90-120
SEASONS: SPRING & FALL
TIME ZONES: CST & MST (24-Hour Time)
CENTRAL USA TO:

Reception Area	10 Meters	15 Meters	20 Meters	40/80 Meters
Western & Central Europe & North Africa	08-10 (1)	07-08 (1)	23-06 (1)	17-19 (1)
	10-13 (2)	08-09 (2)	06-09 (2)	19-23 (2)
	13-14 (1)	09-13 (3)	09-11 (1)	23-02 (1)
		13-14 (2)	11-13 (2)	20-21 (1)*
		14-15 (1)	13-17 (3)	21-22 (2)*
			17-19 (2)	22-00 (1)*
			19-22 (1)	
			22-23 (2)	

Central USA (second group)

Northern & Eastern Europe

08-12 (1)	06-08 (1)	20-22 (1)	19-01 (1)
	08-12 (2)	22-00 (2)	20-23(1)*
	12-13 (1)	00-06 (1)	
		06-08 (2)	
		08-12 (1)	
		12-14 (2)	
		14-16 (3)	
		16-20 (2)	

Eastern Mediterranean & Middle East

08-12 (1)	07-08 (1)	06-13 (1)	19-22 (1)
	08-09 (2)	13-16 (2)	20-21 (1)*
	09-11 (3)	16-18 (3)	
	11-12 (2)	18-19 (2)	
	12-13 (1)	19-21 (1)	
		21-23 (2)	
		23-01 (1)	

West & Central Africa

08-09 (1)	07-10 (1)	10-12 (1)	18-19 (1)
09-11 (2)	10-12 (2)	12-15 (2)	19-21 (2)
11-13 (3)	12-14 (3)	15-17 (3)	21-00 (1)
13-16 (4)	14-17 (4)	17-20 (4)	20-22(1)*
16-17 (3)	17-18 (3)	20-22 (3)	
17-18 (2)	18-20 (2)	22-00 (2)	
18-19 (1)	19-21 (1)*	00-02(1)	

East Africa

08-10 (1)	07-10 (1)	10-14 (1)	19-21 (1)
10-14 (2)	10-12 (2)	14-16 (2)	20-22 (1)*
14-16 (1)	12-15 (3)	16-20 (3)	
	15-17 (2)	20-22 (2)	
	17-18 (1)	22-00 (1)	

Southern Africa

07-09 (1)	06-10 (1)	10-13 (1)	19-22 (1)
09-10 (2)	10-12 (2)	13-15 (2)	20-21 (1)*
10-13 (3)	12-13 (3)	15-16 (3)	
13-14 (2)	13-15 (4)	16-18 (4)	
14-15 (1)	15-16 (1)	18-20 (3)	
	16-17 (2)	20-22 (2)	
	17-18 (1)	22-00 (2)	
		00-02 (2)	
		02-04 (1)	

Central & South Asia

07-09 (1)	07-08 (1)	06-07 (1)	05-07 (1)
18-20 (1)	08-10 (2)	07-09 (2)	19-21 (1)
	10-11 (1)	09-11 (1)	
	18-19 (1)	17-19 (1)	
	19-20 (2)	19-21 (2)	
	20-21 (1)	21-22 (1)	

Southeast Asia

09-10 (1)	07-08 (1)	20-22 (1)	03-07 (1)
10-12 (2)	08-10 (2)	22-00 (2)	
12-14 (1)	10-12 (3)	00-06 (1)	
16-17 (1)	12-13 (2)	06-09 (2)	
17-19 (2)	13-17 (1)	09-11 (1)	
19-20 (1)	17-20 (2)	13-15 (1)	
	20-22 (1)		

Far East

15-16 (1)	08-11 (1)	03-06 (1)	03-08 (1)
16-17 (2)	15-16 (1)	06-09 (2)	05-07 (1)*
17-18 (2)	16-17 (2)	09-12 (1)	
18-19 (2)	17-20 (3)	19-21 (1)	
19-20 (1)	20-21 (2)	21-22 (2)	
	21-22 (1)	22-01 (1)	
		01-03 (2)	

South Pacific & New Zealand

10-11 (1)	08-09 (1)	18-20 (1)	22-00 (1)
11-13 (2)	09-12 (2)	20-22 (2)	00-01 (2)
13-15 (3)	12-17 (1)	22-00 (3)	01-06 (3)
15-17 (2)	17-18 (2)	00-03 (4)	06-07 (2)
17-19 (3)	18-22 (3)	03-05 (3)	07-08 (1)
19-20 (2)	22-00 (2)	05-07 (2)	00-02 (1)*
20-21 (1)	00-01 (1)	07-09 (3)	02-05 (2)*
		09-10 (2)	05-07 (1)*
		10-11(1)	

Australasia

08-11 (1)	07-08 (1)	05-07 (2)	02-04 (1)
13-14 (1)	08-11 (2)	07-09 (3)	04-06 (3)
14-15 (2)	11-13 (1)	09-12 (2)	06-07 (2)
15-18 (4)	13-14 (2)	12-14 (1)	07-08 (1)
18-19 (3)	14-16 (3)	14-16 (2)	04-05(1)*
19-20 (2)	16-18 (2)	16-20 (1)	05-06 (2)*
20-21 (1)	18-20 (3)	20-22 (2)	06-07 (1)*
		20-22 (4)	22-02 (3)
		22-00 (2)	02-04 (4)
		00-01 (1)	04-05 (3)

Caribbean, Central America & Northern Countries of South America

06-07 (1)	05-06 (1)	02-07 (2)	18-19 (1)
07-08 (3)	06-07 (2)	07-10 (3)	19-20 (2)
08-11 (4)	07-10 (4)	10-15 (2)	20-02 (3)
11-13 (3)	13-14 (2)	15-17 (3)	04-06 (1)
13-16 (4)	14-18 (4)	17-00 (4)	20-21 (1)"
16-17 (3)	18-20 (3)	00-02 (3)	21.02 (2)"
	17-18 (2)	20-22 (2)	02.05 (1)*
	18-20 (1)	22-01 (1)	

Western USA

Peru, Bolivia, Paraguay, Brazil, Chile, Argentina & Uruguay

06-08 (1)	06-07 (1)	13-15 (1)	19-20 (1)
08-09 (1)	07-10 (2)	15-16 (1)	20-02 (2)
09-13 (3)	10-13 (1)	16-18 (3)	02-05 (1)
13-14 (3)	13-14 (2)	18-00 (4)	21-03 (1)*
14-16 (4)	14-15 (3)	00-02 (3)	
16-17 (3)	15-19 (4)	02-06 (2)	
17-18 (2)	19-21 (3)	06-08 (1)	
18-19 (1)	21-23 (2)		
	23-01 (1)		

McMurdo Sound, Antarctica

11-14 (1)	13-16 (1)	16-19 (1)	22-01 (1)
14-18 (2)	16-18 (2)	19-20 (2)	01-04 (2)
18-20 (1)	18-21 (3)	20-03 (3)	04-06 (1)
	21-22 (2)	03-07 (2)	
	22-23(1)	07-10 (1)	

MASTER DX PROPAGATION CHART
SOLAR PHASE: VERY HIGH
SMOOTHED SUNSPOT RANGE: 90-120
SEASONS: SPRING & FALL
TIME ZONE: PST (24-Hour Time)
WESTERN USA TO:

Reception Area	10 Meters	15 Meters	20 Meters	40/80 Meters
Western Europe & North Africa	08-11 (1)	07-08 (1)	00-06 (1)	18-00 (1)
		08-09 (3)	06-08 (2)	20-22 (1)*
		09-11 (2)	08-11 (1)	
		11-12 (3)	11-13 (2)	
		12-13 (2)	13-15 (3)	
		13-14 (1)	15-19 (2)	
			19-22 (1)	
			22-00 (2)	
Northern, Central & Eastern Europe	08-10 (1)	07-08 (1)	20-22 (1)	19-23 (1)
		08-11 (1)	22-01 (2)	20-22 (1)
		11-13 (1)	01-06 (1)	
			06-08 (2)	
			08-10 (1)	
			10-12 (2)	
			12-14 (2)	
			14-16 (2)	
			16-18 (1)	
Eastern Mediterranean & Middle East	08-10 (1)	07-08 (1)	07-12 (1)	18-21 (1)
		08-10 (2)	12-15 (2)	
		10-12 (1)	15-18 (1)	
		19-21 (1)	18-22 (2)	
			22-02 (1)	
West & Central Africa	08-09 (1)	07-10 (1)	10-12 (1)	18-22 (1)
	09-12 (2)	10-12 (2)	12-14 (2)	
	12-14 (3)	12-14 (3)	14-16 (3)	
	14-16 (4)	14-17 (4)	16-20 (4)	
	16-17 (3)	17-18 (3)	20-22 (3)	
	17-18 (2)	18-19 (2)	22-23 (2)	
	18-19 (1)	19-20 (1)	23-00 (1)	
Southern Africa	08-09 (1)	06-10 (1)	06-13 (1)	19-22 (1)
	09-11 (3)	10-12 (2)	13-15 (2)	20-21 (1)*
	11-12 (1)	12-14 (3)	15-18 (3)	
		14-15 (2)	18-19 (2)	
		15-16 (1)	19-21 (1)	
			21-23 (3)	
			23-00 (2)	
			00-02 (1)	
Central & South Asia	17-19 (1)	07-08 (1)	05-07 (1)	05-07 (1)
		08-10 (2)	07-09 (2)	
		10-11 (1)	09-11 (1)	
		16-17 (1)	17-19 (1)	
		17-19 (2)	19-21 (2)	
		19-21 (1)	21-22 (1)	
Southeast Asia	08-10 (1)	07-08 (1)	22-00 (1)	02-07 (1)
	14-15 (1)	08-10 (1)	00-07 (2)	04-06 (1)*
	15-16 (2)	10-12 (2)	07-09 (2)	
	16-18 (3)	12-17 (1)	09-11 (2)	
	18-19 (2)	17-20 (2)	11-15 (2)	
	19-20 (1)	20-00 (1)		
Far East	13-14 (1)	07-12 (1)	11-21 (1)	00-02 (1)
	14-16 (2)	12-15 (2)	21-22 (2)	02-04 (2)
	16-17 (4)	15-17 (3)	22-03 (3)	04-08 (2)
	17-18 (3)	17-19 (4)	03-06 (2)	02-06 (1)
	18-19 (2)	19-20 (3)	06-08 (3)	
	19-20 (1)	20-21 (2)	08-11 (2)	
		21-22 (1)		

Region				
South Pacific & New Zealand	08-09 (1)	07-08 (1)	17-19 (1)	19-21 (1)
	09-11 (3)	08-11 (3)	19-21 (2)	21-23 (2)
	11-15 (2)	11-16 (2)	21-22 (3)	23-05 (4)
	15-16 (3)	16-18 (3)	22-00 (4)	05-06 (3)
	16-18 (4)	18-20 (4)	00-02 (3)	06-07 (2)
	18-20 (2)	20-21 (3)	02-04 (2)	07-08 (1)
	20-21 (1)	21-22 (2)	04-06 (1)	21-23 (1)*
		22-00 (1)	06-09 (2)	23-05 (2)*
			08-11 (1)	05-07 (1)*
Australasia	11-13 (1)	06-07 (1)	12-20 (1)	01-03 (1)
	13-16 (3)	07-09 (2)	20-22 (2)	03-05 (3)
	16-18 (4)	09-11 (1)	22-00 (3)	05-06 (2)
	18-20 (3)	11-13 (2)	00-03 (4)	06-08 (1)
	20-21 (2)	13-16 (1)	03-07 (2)	03-04 (1)*
	21-22 (1)	16-18 (2)	07-09 (3)	04-06 (21)*
		18-20 (4)	09-12 (1)	06-07 (1)*
		20-22 (3)		
		22-00 (2)		
		00-02 (1)		
Caribbean, Central America & Northern Countries of South America	06-07 (1)	05-06 (1)	06-08 (3)	18-20 (1)
	07-08 (3)	06-07 (2)	08-15 (2)	20-00 (3)
	08-10 (4)	07-09 (4)	15-17 (3)	00-03 (2)
	10-13 (3)	09-14 (3)	17-00 (4)	03-05 (1)
	13-16 (4)	14-18 (4)	00-02 (3)	20-21 (1)*
	16-17 (3)	18-20 (3)	02-06 (2)	21-01 (2)*
	17-18 (2)	20-22 (2)		01-04 (1)*
	18-20 (1)	22-00 (1)		
Peru, Bolivia, Paraguay, Brazil, Chile, Argentina & Uruguay	07-08 (1)	06-07 (1)	12-14 (1)	18-19 (1)
	08-09 (3)	07-09 (2)	14-16 (2)	19-01 (2)
	09-12 (2)	09-12 (1)	16-18 (3)	01-03 (1)
	12-14 (3)	12-14 (2)	18-23 (4)	20-02 (1)*
	14-16 (4)	14-15 (3)	23-02 (2)	
	16-17 (3)	15-19 (4)	02-06 (2)	
	17-18 (2)	19-20 (3)	06-08 (1)	
	18-19 (1)	20-22 (2)		
		22-02 (1)		
McMurdo Sound, Antarctica	11-15 (1)	14-16 (1)	16-19 (1)	22-02 (1)
	15-18 (2)	16-18 (2)	19-20 (2)	02-04 (2)
	18-19(1)	18-21 (3)	20-02 (3)	04-06 (1)
		21-23 (2)	02-04 (2)	
		23-00 (1)	04-06 (1)	
			06-08 (2)	
			08-10 (1)	

MASTER SHORT-SKIP PROPAGATION CHART
SOLAR PHASE: VERY HIGH
SMOOTHED SUNSPOT RANGE: 90-120
SEASON: SUMMER
TIME ZONES: LOCAL STANDARD AT PATH MID-POINT
(24-Hour Time)

Band (Meters)	50-250	Distance Between Stations (Miles) 250-750	650-1300	1300-2300
10	Nil	07-09 (0-1)*	07-09 (1)*	07-09 (1-0)*
		09-13 (0-2)*	09-13 (2-3)*	09-13 (3-1)*
		13-17 (0-1)*	13-17 (1-2)*	13-17 (2-1)*
		17-21 (0-2)*	17-21 (2-3)*	17-21 (3-1)*
		21-23 (0-1)*	21-07 (1)*	21-07 (1-0)*
15	Nil	07-09 (0-2)*	07-09 (2)*	07-09 (2)*
		08-13 (0-3)*	08-13 (3)*	09-13 (3)
		13-17 (0-2)*	13-17 (2)*	13-17 (2-3)
		17-19 (0-3)*	17-19 (3)*	17-19 (3-4)
		19-21 (0-2)*	19-21 (2)*	19-21 (2-3)
		21-07 (0-1)*	21-23 (1-2)*	21-23 (2)
			23-07 (1)*	23-07 (1)*
20	09-00 (0-1)*	06-09 (0-2)*	06-09 (2-4)	06-09 (4)
		08-15 (1-4)*	08-15 (4)	08-16 (4-3)
		15-20 (1-3)*	15-20 (3-4)	16-00 (4)
		20-00 (1-2)*	20-00 (2-4)*	00-02 (3)
		00-06 (0-1)*	00-02 (1-3)*	02-06 (2)
			02-06 (1-2)*	
40	07-11 (2-4)	07-09 (2-4)*	07-09 (4-2)	07-17 (1-0)
	11-20 (3-4)	09-11 (4-3)	08-11 (3-1)	17-18 (2-1)
	20-22 (2-3)	11-16 (4-2)	11-16 (2-1)	18-20 (3-2)
	22-00 (1-2)	16-18 (4-3)	16-17 (3-1)	20-05 (4)
	00-06 (0-2)*	18-20 (4)	17-18 (3-2)	05-06 (3-2)
	06-07 (1-2)	20-22 (3-4)	18-20 (4-3)	06-07 (3-1)
		22-04 (2-4)	20-04 (4)	
		04-07 (2-3)	04-05 (3-4)	
			05-07 (3)	

Band	50-250	250-750	650-1300	1300-2300
80	06-10 (4)	07-09 (4-1)	06-07 (2-1)	07-18 (1)
	10-18 (4-3)	09-10 (4-1)	07-09(1-0)	18-19 (1-0)
	18-00 (4)	10-16 (3-0)	09-16 (0)	19-20 (1)
	00-06 (3-4)	16-18 (3-1)	16-18 (1-0)	20-21 (2)
		18-19 (4-2)	18-19 (2-1)	21-03 (4-3)
		19-21 (4)	19-20 (3-1)	03-04 (4-2)
		21-06 (4)	20-21 (3-2)	04-05 (3-2)
		06-07 (4-2)	21-04 (4)	05-06 (3-1)
			04-06 (4-3)	06-07 (1)
160	17-18 (1-0)	18-19 (1-0)	21-21 (1)	20-22 (1-0)
	18-19 (1)	19-20 (2-0)	21-00 (2-1)	22-00 (1)
	19-21 (3-2)	20-21 (2-1)	00-03 (2)	00-05 (2-1)
	21-23(4-3)	21-23 (3-2)	03-05 (3-2)	05-06 (1-0)
	23-05 (4)	23-03 (4-2)	05-06 (1)	
	05-07 (3-2)	03-05 (4-3)	06-07 (1-0)	
	07-08(1)	05-07 (2-1)		
	08-09(1-0)	07-08 (0-1)		

MASTER SHORT-SKIP PROPAGATION CHART
SOLAR PHASE: VERY HIGH
SMOOTHED SUNSPOT RANGE: 90-120
SEASON: WINTER
TIME ZONES: LOCAL STANDARD AT PATH MID-POINT
(24-Hour-Time)

Band (Meters)	50-250	Distance Between Stations (Miles) 250-750	650-1300	1300-2300
10	Nil	Nil	07-09 (0-1)	07-09 (1)
			09-10 (0-3)	09-10 (3)
			10-15 (0-4)	10-15 (4)
			15-17 (0-3)	15-17 (3-4)
			17-19 (0-1)	17-18 (1-3)
				18-19 (1-2)
				19-20 (0-1)
15	Nil	08-17 (0-2)	06-08 (0-1)	06-07 (1)
			08-09 (2)	07-08 (1-2)
			09-11 (2-3)	08-09 (2-3)
			11-17 (2-4)	09-11 (3-4)
			17-18 (0-3)	11-17 (4)
			18-20 (0-2)	17-18 (3-4)
			20-22 (0-1)	18-20 (2-4)
				20-21 (1-2)
				21-22 (1)
20	09-11 (1-2)	08-09 (0-2)	07-08 (1-2)	07-08 (2-3)
	11-14 (1-3)	09-11 (2-4)	08-09 (2-3)	08-09 (3-4)
	14-15 (1-2)	11-14 (3-4)	09-17 (4)	09-10 (4)
	15-17 (0-1)	14-15 (2-4)	17-19 (3-4)	10-14 (4-3)
		15-17 (1-4)	19-20 (2-3)	14-19 (4)
		17-19 (1-4)	20-22 (1-3)	19-21 (3-4)
		19-20 (0-2)	22-00 (0-2)	21-22 (3)
		20-08 (0-1)	00-07 (1)	22-00 (2-3)
				00-03 (1-2)
				03-06 (1)
				06-07 (1-2)
40	07-08 (0-2)	07-08 (2)	07-08 (2)	07-08 (2-1)
	08-09(1-3)	08-09 (3)	08-11 (3-1)	08-15 (1-0)
	09-10 (2-4)	09-11 (4-3)	11-15(2-1)	15-17 (2-1)
	10-17 (4)	11-15 (4-2)	15-17 (4-2)	17-18 (3)
	17-18 (3-4)	15-18 (4)	17-18 (4-3)	18-04 (4)
	18-20 (2-3)	18-20 (3-4)	18-22 (4)	04-05 (4-3)
	20-22 (1-2)	20-22 (2-4)	22-02 (4-3)	05-07 (3-2)
	22-07 (0-1)	22-02(1-3)	02-05 (2-4)	
		02-07 (1-2)	05-07 (2-3)	
80	07-08 (2-3)	07-08 (3)	07-08 (3-1)	07-08 (1-0)
	08-10 (3-4)	08-09 (4-2)	08-09 (2-0)	08-16 (0)
	10-15 (4)	09-10 (4-1)	09-16 (1-0)	16-18 (1-0)
	15-21 (4)	10-15 (3-1)	16-18 (2-1)	18-20 (3-2)
	21-00 (3-4)	15-16 (4-1)	18-20 (4-3)	20-03 (4)
	00-04 (2-3)	16-18 (4)	20-04 (4)	03-04 (4-3)
	04-07 (1-2)	18-00 (4)	04-06 (3)	04-05 (3)
		00-04 (3-4)	06-07 (3-2)	05-06 (3-2)
		04-07 (2-3)		06-07 (2-1)
160	09-17 (1-0)	17-18 (2-1)	17-18 (1-0)	18-19(1-0)
	17-19 (3-2)	18-19 (2)	18-19 (2-1)	19-21 (2-1)
	19-05 (4)	19-21 (4-3)	19-21 (3-1)	21-03 (3)
	05-07 (3)	21-05 (4)	21-03 (4-3)	03-05 (4-2)
	07-09 (2-1)	05-06 (3)	03-05 (4)	05-06 (2-1)
		06-07 (3-1)	05-06 (3-2)	06-07(1-0)
		07-09 (1-0)	06-07 (1)	

MASTER SHORT-SKIP PROPAGATION CHART
SOLAR PHASE: VERY HIGH
SMOOTHED SUNSPOT RANGE: 90-120
SEASONS: SPRING & FALL
TIME ZONES: LOCAL STANDARD AT PATH MID-POINT
(24-Hour Time)

Band (Meters)	50-250	Distance Between Stations (Miles) 250-750	650-1300	1300-2300
10	Nil	09-13 (0-1)	07-09 (1)	07-08 (1)
			09-12 (1-2)	08-09 (1-2)
			12-13 (1-3)	00-12 (2-4)
			13-16 (0-3)	12-16 (3-4)
			16-18 (0-2)	16-18 (2-3)
			18-20 (0-1)	18-20 (1-2)
				20-21 (0-1)
15	Nil	07-09 (0-1)	07-08 (1)	07-08 (1)
		09-15 (0-2)	08-09 (1-2)	08-09 (1-3)
		15-19 (0-1)	09-15 (2-4)	09-15 (4)
			15-18 (1-3)	15-18 (3-4)
			18-19 (1-2)	18-19 (2-3)
			19-23 (0-1)	19-21 (1-3)
				21-23 (1-2)
				23-01 (0-1)
20	11-13 (0-1)	08-09 (0-3)	06-07 (1-2)	06-07 (2)
	13-16 (0-2)	09-11 (0-4)	07-08 (3)	07-08 (3)
	16-19 (0-1)	11-13 (1-4)	08-09 (3-4)	08-10 (4)
		13-16 (2-4)	09-18 (4)	10-15 (4-3)
		16-18 (1-4)	18-19 (3-4)	15-22 (4)
		18-19 (1-3)	19-22 (2-4)	22-23 (3-4)
		19-22 (0-2)	22-00 (1-3)	23-00 (3)
		22-08 (0-1)	00-02 (1-2)	00-02 (2)
			02-06 (1)	02-04 (1-2)
				04-06 (1)
40	06-07 (1-2)	06-07 (2-3)	06-07 (3-2)	06-08 (2-1)
	07-09 (2-3)	07-09 (3-4)	07-08 (4-2)	08-15 (1-0)
	09-18 (4)	09-11 (4-3)	08-09 (4-1)	15-16 (2-0)
	18-20 (3-4)	11-13 (4-2)	09-13 (2-1)	16-17 (2-1)
	20-22 (2-3)	13-15 (4-3)	13-15 (3-1)	17-19 (3-2)
	22-00 (1-2)	15-20 (4)	15-17 (4-2)	19-03 (4)
	00-06(1)	20-22 (3-4)	17-19 (4-3)	03-04 (3-4)
		22-00 (2-4)	19-00 (4)	04-06 (3)
		00-03 (1-3)	00-03 (3-4)	
		03-06 (1-2)	03-06 (2-3)	
80	07-11 (4)	07-08 (4-2)	07-08 (2-1)	07-08 (1-0)
	11-18 (4-3)	08-11 (4-1)	08-11 (1-0)	08-16 (0)
	18-22 (4)	11-16 (3-0)	11-16 (0)	16-18 (1-0)
	22-00 (3-4)	16-18 (3-2)	16-18 (2-1)	18-20 (2-1)
	00-07 (2-3)	18-20 (4-3)	18-20 (3-2)	20-22 (4-2)
		20-00 (4)	20-03 (4)	22-03 (4-3)
		00-05 (3-4)	03-05 (4-3)	03-05 (3-2)
		05-07 (3)	05-07 (3-2)	05-07 (2-1)
160	05-07 (4-2)	05-06 (2-1)	05-06 (1)	05-06 (1-0)
	07-09 (3-1)	06-07 (2-0)	06-19 (4)	06-19 (0)
	09-17 (2-0)	07-09 (1-0)	19-20 (3-2)	19-20 (2)
	17-19 (3-1)	09-17 (0)	20-22 (3-2)	20-22 (2)
	19-20 (4-2)	17-19 (1-0)	22-03 (4-3)	22·03 (3-2)
	20-05 (4)	19-20(2)	03-05(3-2)	03-05 (2-1)
		20-22 (4-3)		
		22-03 (4)		
		03-05 (4-3)		

FOOTNOTES

Worldwide Charts:
• Predicted times of 80 meter openings. Openings on 160 meters are also likely to occur during those times when 80 meter openings are shown with a forecast rating of (2) or higher.

Short Skip Charts:
• Predominantly sporadic-E openings.

the south between sunset and midnight. Signals from the northwest, west, and South Pacific should begin to build up about midnight, and reach a peak just before sunrise. Excellent short-skip openings should be possible during the daylight hours up to distances of approximately 1,000 miles, and between 750 and 2,300 miles during the hours of darkness.

40 meters – Equinox: Fairly good DX conditions are expected from just before sunset, through the hours of darkness, to an hour or so after sunrise to most parts of the world. Check particularly for openings into the Southern Hemisphere, which should peak between midnight and sunrise. During daylight hours, expect excellent short-skip openings up to a range of about 1,000 miles, and between 500 and 2,300 miles at night.

60 meters – Interpolate between 40 and 80 meters.

80 meters – Summer: DX openings to some areas of the world should be possible during the hours of darkness and the sunrise period, but be prepared for seasonally high static levels and generally weak signals. Daytime skip will be limited to a range of approximately 250 miles; nighttime skip should be possible to distances of between approximately 200 and 2,300 miles.

80 meters – Winter: Fairly good DX should be possible to many areas of the world during the hours of darkness and the sunrise period. The band should peak toward Europe and the east, and toward the south, from an hour or so after sundown to midnight, and toward the northwest, west, and southwest between midnight and dawn. Daytime short-skip openings should be possible up to a range of about 500 miles, increasing to between approximately 500 and 2,300 miles at night.

Solar Phase	Season	Time	10 meters	15 meters	20 meters	40 meters	80 meters	160 meters
Very High	Summer	Day	G	G	G	—	—	—
	Summer	Night	—	F	E	F	P	P
	Winter	Day	E	E	E	—	—	—
	Winter	Night	—	—	F	G	F	F
	Equinox	Day	E	E	E	—	—	—
	Equinox	Night	—	—	G	G	F	F
High	Summer	Day	F	G	G	—	—	—
	Summer	Night	—	—	G	G	F	P
	Winter	Day	E	E	E	—	—	—
	Winter	Night	—	—	F	E	G	F
	Equinox	Day	G	E	E	—	—	—
	Equinox	Night	—	—	F	E	G	F
Moderate	Summer	Day	P	F	G	—	—	—
	Summer	Night	—	—	G	G	F	P
	Winter	Day	F	E	E	—	—	—
	Winter	Night	—	—	P	E	G	F
	Equinox	Day	F	G	E	—	—	—
	Equinox	Night	—	—	F	G	G	F
Low	Summer	Day	P	F	G	—	—	—
	Summer	Night	—	—	F	G	F	P
	Winter	Day	P	F	E	—	—	—
	Winter	Night	—	—	P	G	G	F
	Equinox	Day	P	F	G	—	—	—
	Equinox	Night	—	—	F	G	G	F

Equinox = Spring & Fall

E = Excellent
G = Good

F = Fair
P = Poor

— = Not Likely

Table 4.10. Relative quality of DX propagation in each amateur HF band during day and night, for each season of the year, for each major phase of a solar cycle. See Tables 4.5 and 4.6 for applying this summary to the WARC and HF broadcasting bands, respectively. During periods of intense solar activity (smoothed sunspot numbers greater than 120, use data shown for Very high solar phase.

80 meters – Equinox: Some DX openings should be possible from sunset, through the hours of darkness, until sunrise. Check particularly for openings into the Southern Hemisphere between midnight and dawn. Excellent short-skip openings should be possible during the day to ranges as far as approximately 350 miles, increasing to 2,300 miles at night:

160 meters – Summer: No possibility for daytime skip due to high solar absorption and static levels. Nighttime openings to distances as far as about 1,000 miles should be possible on a regular basis, with occasional openings beyond this range possible from time to time.

160 meters – Winter: No daytime openings possible, but expect fair chances for DX openings during the hours of darkness and the sunrise period. Short-skip openings should be possible during the hours of darkness to ranges as far as approximately 1,500 miles on a regular basis, and less frequently for distances to 2,300 miles.

160 meters – Equinox: Do not expect any daytime skip, but look for DX openings to some parts of the world during the hours of dark and sunrise. Nighttime short-skip should be possible to ranges reaching to approximately 1,300 miles, and at times to 2,300 miles.

4.7 Summary of DX Band Conditions Throughout A Complete Solar Cycle

Table 4.10 summarizes the quality of DX propagation conditions that can be expected on each amateur HF band during day and night for each season of the year for each major phase of a sunspot cycle.

There is a direct relationship between the level of solar activity and DX capabilities on each of the HF bands. As the sunspot count increases, daytime DX conditions improve considerably on 10, 15 and 20 meters, while nighttime conditions improve on 20 meters but decline somewhat on 40, 80, and 160 meters. As a solar cycle declines, nighttime DX conditions on 40, 80, and 160 meters improve, while conditions on 20 meters deteriorate. Daytime DX conditions will deteriorate somewhat on 20 meters, and considerably on 10 and 15 meters.

4.8 References

1. Jacobs, G., W3ASK, "Propagation," published monthly in *CQ* magazine, Sayville, NY 11782 (now written by Hood, T., NW7US).

2. Updated smoothed sunspot numbers appear monthly in "Propagation," *CQ* magazine, Sayville, NY 11782. They also can be obtained at http://sidc.oma.be/silso/datafiles, as noted in the discussion of Figure 4.1.

Chapter 5

Ionospheric Forecasts and Space Weather

Relatively normal long-term variations in the ionosphere can be predicted well in advance and that's where the Master Propagation Charts in Chapter 4 are useful. Short-term variations also occur, but we do not have a full understanding of the causes for these yet. These short-term variations account for the day-to-day differences observed in the propagation of shortwave signals, and they explain why reception on a particular path may be good one day, fair on another day, and sometimes not possible at all. The short-term variations we observe are the reason for our propagation predictions having to be treated statistically over a month's time frame.

MUF Variation

It is important to note first that the MUF — the so-called Maximum Usable Frequency — is in fact *not* the actual maximum usable frequency for a given path. It is either a statistical product of the computations we perform in our propagation prediction programs or the measurements we make using a month's worth of data with ionosondes to characterize the F2 region of the ionosphere, the region responsible for most shortwave propagation worldwide, on a path. Specifically, the MUF is the frequency for a 3,000-km, single-hop refraction path that is expected to be open 50% of the time. In other words, it is the *median* frequency. You have a 50-50 chance of communicating at this frequency for the date and time specified on the path for which the MUF was computed.

The *classical* MUF is the *actual* maximum usable frequency on a given path for any given date and at any given time. Classical MUF values observed each day will be higher than the median 50% of the time, and the other 50% of the time they will be lower.

An example of the day-to-day variability of the F2 region of the ionosphere is plotted in Figure 5.1. The measured *classical* MUF (the actual maximum usable frequency) over the Wallops Island ionosonde at 1700 UTC (1 p.m. local) for each day of August 2009, is shown [reference 1].

This plot assumes the Wallops Island ionosonde is the midpoint of a 3,000-km path. The classical MUF at 1700 UTC varies from a low of about 11 MHz on Aug. 14, 2009 to a high of about 22 MHz on Aug. 16, 2009. There were no F2 region data for Aug. 10 because strong sporadic-E ionization blocked F2-region echoes. For some unknown reason, there were no data recorded on Aug. 17 after 0930 UTC.

With the classical MUF varying over a range of 2:1, we might think this variability was caused by day-to-day variations in the solar radiation at EUV wavelengths (about 10-100 nm, which is the region of the spectrum responsible for the F2 region). Figure 5.2 gives four space weather measurements for the month of August 2009.

The sunspot number for each day of August 2009, was zero. The 10.7 cm solar flux for each day varied between 67.8 and 70.2 sfu (solar flux units; 1 sfu equals 10^{-22} watts per square meter per second). That's a variation of +/- 1.4%. The 26-34 nm EUV (this wavelength band is responsible for about 60% of the F2 region) for each day varied between 8.92×10^9 and 9.32×10^9 photons per square cm per second. That's a variation of +/- 2.2%. Some basic ion production/ion loss calculations with the EUV flux indi-

Figure 5.1 Day-to-day variability of the MUF of the F2 region of the ionosphere over the Wallops Island ionosonde during August 2009.

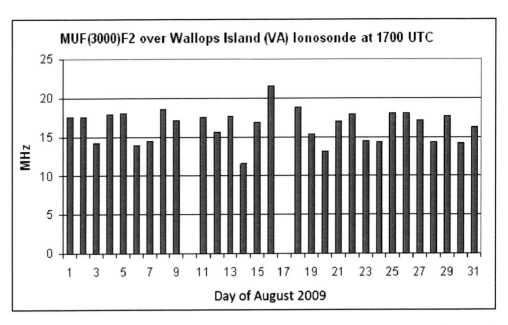

cate a variation of +/- 2.2% in EUV radiation would *not* cause a 2:1 change in the MUF, not by a long shot.

Could the 2:1 change in classical MUF be caused by the variability of the A index? On average the A index for August 2009, was just below 5, which corresponds to a K index of between 1 and 2 (we'll look at the relationship between the A index and the K index in more detail later in this chapter). Thus, the Earth's magnetic field was relatively quiet, and it was not the likely cause of the 2:1 variation in the MUF.

Signal Strength Variation

It's important to note the variation in the F2 region MUF is caused by a variation in the F2 region electron density. Some ionospheric absorption also occurs in the refraction process in the F2 region. It is called deviative absorption because it occurs when the electromagnetic ray is refracting. Thus, a variation in the F2 region electron density can cause the signal strength to vary.

Additionally, the variation of electron density is not just in the F2 region; it also occurs in the E region and the D region. The D region also affects signal strength through ionospheric absorption. It is called non-deviative absorption because the electromagnetic wave is not refracting in the D region. Figure 5.3 shows the signal strength of WWV in Boulder, Colorado in Fort Wayne, Indiana on 15 MHz during August, 2000, at 2300 UTC (7 p.m. local in Fort Wayne). August 2000 was four months after the first peak of Cycle 23.

The tabular data on the left side of Figure 5.3 is the 10.7 cm solar flux and the measured signal strength

data [the S-meter of the receiver that was used was calibrated in terms of power in dBm (dB referenced to 1 milliwatt) prior to acquiring the data]. The graph on the right side of Figure 5.3 is a scatter diagram showing the correlation between the daily signal strength and the daily 10.7 cm solar flux. The red dotted line is a linear trend line with $R^2 = 0.1714$. R^2 is the square of the correlation coefficient R between the daily signal strength on 15 MHz and the daily solar flux for August 2000. A correlation coefficient of 0.0 indicates no correlation; the data would scatter widely about the red dotted trend line. A correlation coefficient of 1.0 indicates perfect correlation; all the data points would fall on the red dotted trend line.

For these data, the correlation coefficient is 0.414 (which is the square root of 0.1714). It indicates there is some correlation but not enough to map signal strength to a unique value of 10.7 cm solar flux. Another way to look at this is to note at a solar flux of around 190, the signal strength could vary by 15 dB when the transmit power, transmit antenna and receive antenna are held constant [reference 2].

The MUF data of Figure 5.1 and the signal strength data of Figure 5.3 suggest another parameter besides solar radiation and geomagnetic field activity can cause the ionosphere to vary on a day-to-day basis. This third parameter is meteorological in nature – events at ground level and in the lower atmosphere that can couple to the ionosphere via gravity waves to cause traveling ionospheric disturbances (TIDs). A seminal research paper in 2001 by H. Rishbeth and M.

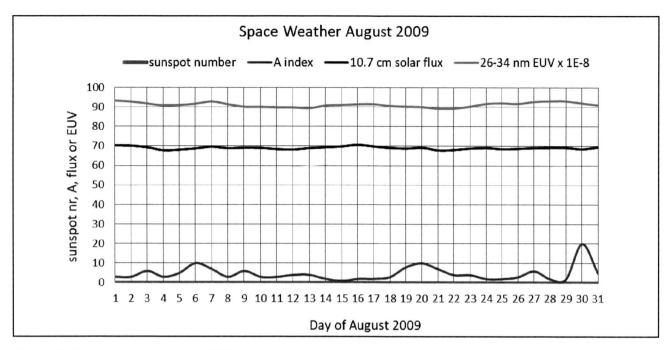

Figure 5.2 Space weather for August 2009.

Mendillo resulted in estimates of the contributions of each of the three parameters to the variation in the F2 region by analyzing 34 years of data (1957 – 1990) from 13 ionosondes. Their study concluded geomagnetic field activity and events at ground level and in the lower atmosphere were the major causes of the F2 region variability, with the contribution by solar radiation variation much less so. We'll review this paper in more detail in Chapter 6.

In light of the previous paragraph, correlating MUF and signal strength simply to solar radiation and not to the other two parameters cannot yield a com-

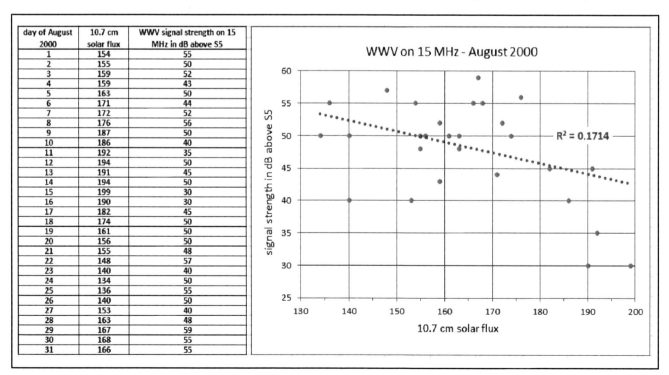

day of August 2000	10.7 cm solar flux	WWV signal strength on 15 MHz in dB above S5
1	154	55
2	155	50
3	159	52
4	159	43
5	163	50
6	171	44
7	172	52
8	176	56
9	187	50
10	186	40
11	192	35
12	194	50
13	191	45
14	194	50
15	199	30
16	190	30
17	182	45
18	174	50
19	161	50
20	156	50
21	155	48
22	148	57
23	140	40
24	134	50
25	136	55
26	140	50
27	153	40
28	163	48
29	167	59
30	168	55
31	166	55

Figure 5.3 Day-to-day variation of 15 MHz WWV in August 2000 at 2300 UTC in Fort Wayne, Indiana

plete answer. Correlating MUF and signal strength to solar radiation and geomagnetic field activity is a good step forward, and that is what will be reviewed in Section 5.1. Section 5.2 will look at WWV and other sources that provide space weather data. Section 5.3 will look at ways to assess the state of the ionosphere in real time. Section 5.4 will look at methods to assess propagation in real time. Section 5.5 will talk about space weather tools for teachers. Section 5.6 will summarize general WWV information.

5.1 Daily Forecasts for Ionospheric Propagation

Now that the Master DX Propagation Charts and the Master Short-Skip Propagation Charts in Chapter 4 have provided for long-term propagation predictions, the question to be answered is: "How can shortwave users tell if conditions are going to be good or bad on a particular day and on a specific path?" In this section we'll review a method developed by George Jacobs W3ASK, Theodore Cohen N4XX, and Robert Rose, K6GKU (SK). It will permit you to determine day-to-day conditions for up to 27 days in advance with reasonable accuracy.

Using the propagation indices shown next to the band openings in the charts in Chapter 4 and using the solar and geomagnetic field activity data available from WWV broadcasts and other sources, it is relatively easy to make your own daily forecasts. We'll go through a forecast and compare it to actual measured data to ascertain the accuracy of the method.

Although the words are often used interchangeably in the technical literature, we will apply the term "prediction" to *long-term* determinations of band openings that can be made for any phase of the solar cycle, months and even years in advance. The term "forecast" will apply to the *short-term* determinations of day-to-day variations in the quality of these band openings up to 27 days in advance, as is discussed in this section.

In Chapter 2 we talked about sunspots and 10.7 cm solar flux. We also looked at the correlation of sunspot numbers and 10.7 cm solar flux (Figures 2.12 and 2.13). For the daily forecast method, we'll use the daily 10.7 cm solar flux because it is more readily available and more objective to use than is the daily sunspot number. As well, we'll use the daily A index for the daily forecast method. Being an index from one

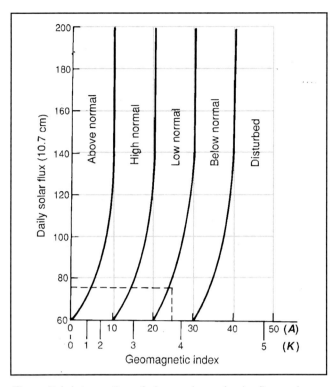

Figure 5.A Intersection of given values of solar flux and geomagnetic activity determine expected HF ionospheric propagation conditions. (Example: Solar flux is 75 and A-index is 25; expect Below Normal conditions.) Use this chart during a Low phase of solar activity (smoothed sunspot range: 0 to 30)

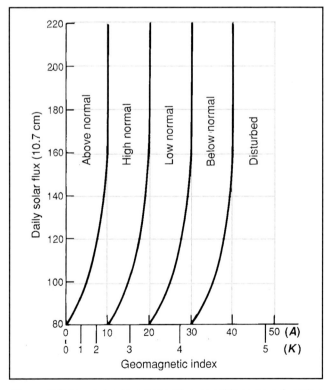

Figure 5.B Ionospheric propagation conditions as a function of solar flux and geomagnetic activity during a Moderate phase of solar activity (smoothed sunspot range: 30 to 60).

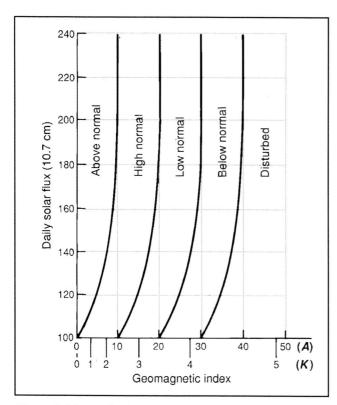

Figure 5.C Ionospheric propagation conditions as a function of solar flux and geomagnetic activity during a High phase of solar activity (smoothed sunspot range: 60 to 90).

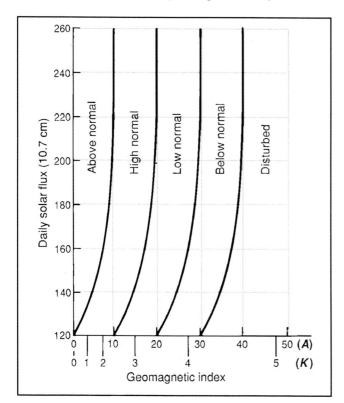

Figure 5.D Ionospheric propagation conditions as a function of solar flux and geomagnetic activity during a Very High phase of solar activity (smoothed sunspot range: 90 to 120).

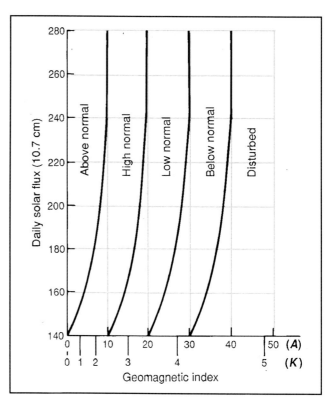

Figure 5.E Ionospheric propagation conditions as a function of solar flux and geomagnetic activity during an Intense phase of solar activity (smoothed sunspot range: greater than 120).

observatory, it can be slightly different than the daily planetary Ap index that comes out of many observatories. But the difference is minimal in the predictions that follow.

Mating the daily forecast method to a prediction from Chapter 4 is done with the five graphs shown in Figures 5.A, 5.B, 5.C, 5.D and 5.E.

Additionally, Tables 5.1 and 5.2 are needed.

Here are the steps to making a daily forecast.

Step 1 – Obtain the propagation index for the desired path opening from the appropriate Master DX Propagation Chart or the Master Short-Skip Propagation Chart in Chapter 4. Make sure you apply the station power and antenna gain to determine the proper propagation index per Section 4.1 in Chapter 4 under the Propagation Index discussion.

Step 2 – Obtain the latest 10.7 cm solar flux and the latest A index.

Step 3 – For the appropriate phase of solar activity, use the appropriate Figure 5.A, 5.B, 5.C, 5.D or 5.E and enter the 10.7 cm solar flux and A index to determine the expected conditions.

Step 4 – Use Table 5.1 to determine the expected signal quality from the expected conditions and the propagation index.

Step 5 – Use Table 5.2 to convert the expected signal quality into a subjective description of conditions and to obtain an expected signal-strength range.

Now let's go through a specific example. Let's forecast the signal strength of WWV on 15 MHz in Fort Wayne, Indiana during the month of August 2000.

For Step 1, we note that the path length from WWV to Fort Wayne is 1,051 miles (1691 km). We also note from Chapter 2 that the smoothed V1 sunspot number for August 2000, was 118.6. Based on the distance and the solar phase, we use the Master Short Skip Propagation Charts for Very High and summer to determine that the propagation index is (4), remembering that WWV runs 10 kW.

For Step 2, we'll forecast propagation for Aug. 22, 2000, a date we have chosen arbitrarily. The 10.7 cm solar flux was 148 and the A index was 2.

Using Figure 5.D and the 10.7 cm solar flux and A index, we determine that the expected conditions are Above Normal for Step 3.

For Step 4 using Table 5.1, the Above Normal expected conditions and the propagation index of (4) translates to an expected signal quality of A.

From Table 5.2, Step 5 says the expected signal-strength range is greater than S9 + 30 dB.

The measured signal strength on Aug. 22, 2000 was

S9 + 33 dB. Thus, the forecast was accurate. Using the 10.7 cm solar flux data and the A index data from Figure 5.3, we can forecast the signal strength for all the days of August 2000, and then compare them to the actual measured data (remembering the receiver S-meter was calibrated prior to the measurements) to see how accurate just using solar flux and geomagnetic field activity is in predicting propagation.

The results of this exercise showed that the signal strength was accurately predicted on 19 of the 31 days. That's an accuracy rate of 61%. This should not be surprising in light of the earlier discussion of the three parameters that cause the ionosphere to vary, and that these forecasts do not include one of the major contributors. Events at ground level and events in the lower atmosphere coupling up to the ionosphere were not evident when this forecast method was developed. At this moment in time, this is the best we can do until our understanding of those events can be assimilated into the forecasts.

A few comments on 10.7 cm solar flux and the A index are appropriate here since the daily forecasts are based on these two parameters. We will also comment about the sun's rotation period.

Solar Flux

The sun is a source of radio-frequency radiation. These emissions are caused by a variety of phenomena in the solar atmosphere, including the random collisions of electrons; the noise from the quiet sun is of the latter type. The flux, or energy level, of solar radio noise on Earth is monitored at a number of observatories, and daily values are published by various sources and broadcast on WWV at 18 minutes after each hour. These values are determined officially by the Dominion Radio Astrophysical Observatory, Penticton, British Columbia, Canada, and are issued daily at 2000 UTC.

	Propagation Index from Chapter 4			
Expected Conditions	(4)	(3)	(2)	(1)
Above Normal	A	A	B	C
High Normal	A	B	C	C-D
Low Normal	B	C	D	D-E
Below Normal	C	C-D	D-E	E
Disturbed	C	D	E	E

Table 5.1 Expected signal quality (A to E) as a function of the propagation index (1 to 4) and expected conditions. Example: a path opening with a predicted propagation index of (3) is expected to have a signal quality of C during Low Normal conditions.

Symbol	Signal Quality	Signal Strength
A	Excellent opening, exceptionally strong and steady signals	>S9 +30dB
B	Good opening, moderately strong signals a with little fading or noise	between S9 and S9 +30dB
C	Fair opening, signal between moderately strong and weak, with some fading and noise	between S3 and S9
D	Poor opening, signals weak with considerable fading and noise	between S1 and S3
E	No opening expected	- - - - -

Table 5.2 Signal quality (A to E) defined in terms of expected signal levels. Based on 1000 Watts ERP (for example, 100 Watts to an antenna with 10 dB gain – see Chapter 4). S9 = -73 dBm (50 µV) and 6 dB per S-unit.

Figure 5.4 The 'a' index versus the 'K' index.

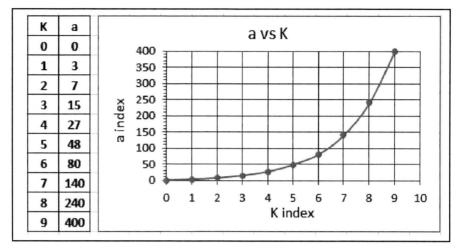

K	a
0	0
1	3
2	7
3	15
4	27
5	48
6	80
7	140
8	240
9	400

Magnetic Indices

Magnetic indices, also called geomagnetic indices or geomagnetic field activity, were discussed in Chapter 1. For the daily forecast method, we will use the daily A index (with a capital A), whether it be the daily A index from a specific observatory or the daily planetary Ap index computed using the data from several observatories. If you want to convert the three-hour K index to the equivalent three-hour a index, Figure 5.4 can be used. Averaging the eight daily three-hour a indices will give you the daily A index. Remember the small-case a refers to the three-hour linear equivalent of the logarithmic K index.

Solar Rotation Period

The sun makes one complete rotation on its axis in about 27 days. There is a very good chance if a group of sunspots or a coronal hole during the declining phase of a solar cycle is in a position to affect the earth's ionosphere today, it will be back in the same position about 27 days from now. Thus, one might expect ionospheric propagation conditions to recur every 27 days or so. Although the recurrence of similar ionospheric conditions every 27 days is not always observed — old sunspots can disappear and new ones form during one solar rotation — it does happen enough to be used for a longer-term forecast. Bear in mind too that a group of sunspots may also produce a coronal mass ejection that affects magnetic indices.

5.2   Sources of Space Weather Data

5.2.1 WWV

Before and during the early years of the space age,

WWV on 2.5, 5.0, 10.0, 15.0 and 20.0 MHz and WWVH on 2.5, 5.0, 10.0 and 15.0 MHz were the main sources of the two basic parameters that were thought to affect the ionosphere and shortwave propagation: 10.7 cm solar flux and the A index. Eventually these parameters became known as space weather data. Today, space weather data have expanded into many other parameters thanks to advances in science and satellites.

The WWV/WWVH broadcasts at 18 minutes (WWV) and 45 minutes (WWVH) after the hour contain the latest 10.7 cm solar flux and geomagnetic indices, a summary of recent significant activity, and a forecast of activity for the next 24 hours. These messages are updated every three hours (the updates are tied to the three-hour K index). Solar flares, proton events, geomagnetic activity, and stratospheric warming alerts also are broadcast, as necessary.

Here's a sample WWV/WWVH announcement:

Solar Terrestrial Indices for July 21 follow
Solar flux index is 70
Estimated planetary A index (Ap) is 4
Estimated planetary K index (Kp) at 1200 UTC is 1
No space weather storms in the last 24 hours
No space weather storms predicted in the next 24 hours

These basic parameters are posted on various websites and included in some amateur radio-related software. For example, VE7CC's PacketCluster network (software to enter and view the calls and frequency of stations heard or worked by others is available at http://www.bcdxc.org/ve7cc/) has a tab for these WWV reports. Other websites containing this information will be discussed shortly.

The complete listing of geophysical data, time, and audio services provided by WWV and WWVH, as well

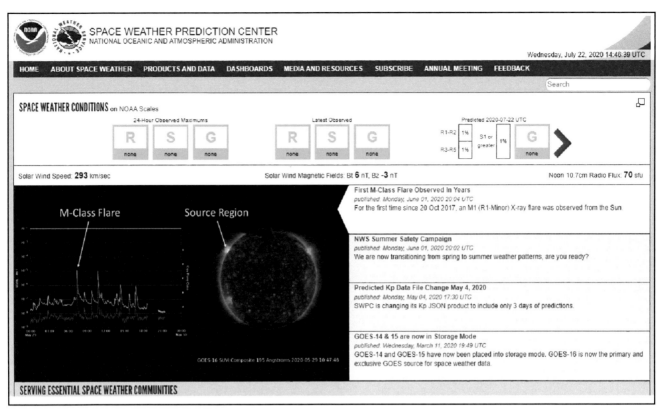

Figure 5.5 Opening information at the SWPC website.

5.2.2 The Internet

The internet has become a valuable asset for obtaining the entire gamut of space weather data. Many government agencies, professional scientists, amateur radio operators and makers of instruments that measure space weather maintain websites with space weather data and stories related to space weather. We'll look at several of these websites now. (It would be difficult to review every website that has space weather data, but those cited below will get you started.).

a) https://www.swpc.noaa.gov/

The Space Weather Prediction Center (SWPC) website contains a large amount of space weather data and related explanations to help you understand how the various measurements relate to the sun-earth environment. SWPC is a part of the National Oceanic and Atmospheric Administration, or NOAA.

Figure 5.5 is the first part of the SWPC home page. It includes the current space weather conditions in terms of the three disturbances to propagation (G = geomagnetic storms, S = solar radiation storms and R = radio blackouts) discussed in Chapter 1. Also included are four panels of current and relevant space weather topics.

Scrolling down the SWPC website gives Figure 5.6, which is six panels of current space weather data.

The top left image is the sun viewed at 19.5 nm wavelengths. The bright white areas are sources of EUV (extreme ultraviolet) radiation that mostly impact the F2 region of the ionosphere (there are not many bright white areas in the image since we're at solar minimum). The top center image monitors the sun for coronal mass ejections, or CMEs, which could disturb the F2 region of the ionosphere though a geomagnetic storm. The small dark blue circular area at the center is an occulting disk that blocks out the solar disk to allow us to see CMEs exploding from the sun. The top right image is the current forecast of the auroral oval, which could affect the entire high latitude ionosphere.

The bottom left image is the X-ray solar flux at the very short wavelengths of 0.1-0.8 nm (blue) and 0.5-4.0 nm (red). These wavelengths are much shorter than 10.7 cm, and give us an idea of the ionization in the D and E regions. The bottom center image is the proton flux. Red is for proton energies greater than 10 MeV (millions of electron volts), blue is for proton energies greater than 50 MeV and green is for proton energies greater than 100 MeV. An elevated proton flux indicates a big solar flare (M or X class) that could cause increased D region ionization in the polar cap, the area inside the auroral oval. The bottom right image is the last three days of the estimated planetary K index (Kp). The color code on the right is a visual aid to help determine the severity of the disturbances to the Earth's magnetic field.

Scrolling down even further is a long list of explanations of the various space weather parameters, an extensive list of SWPC products and data broken into eight categories: forecasts, reports, models, observations, summaries, alerts/watches/warnings, experimental and data access. There are dashboards for a quick view of space weather parameters related to specific areas, media/resources — including an education and outreach section — and a note about the annual Space Weather Workshop.

b) https://spaceweather.com/

This website is written daily by Tony Phillips. For many years he was a radio astronomer at the California Institute of Technology in Pasadena. Caltech is the institution that also manages and operates NASA's Jet Propulsion Laboratory. Phillips began writing spaceweather.com in 1998. Figure 5.7 is the landing page for the website.

This website is more story-oriented than the data-oriented SWPC website. Basic space weather data such as

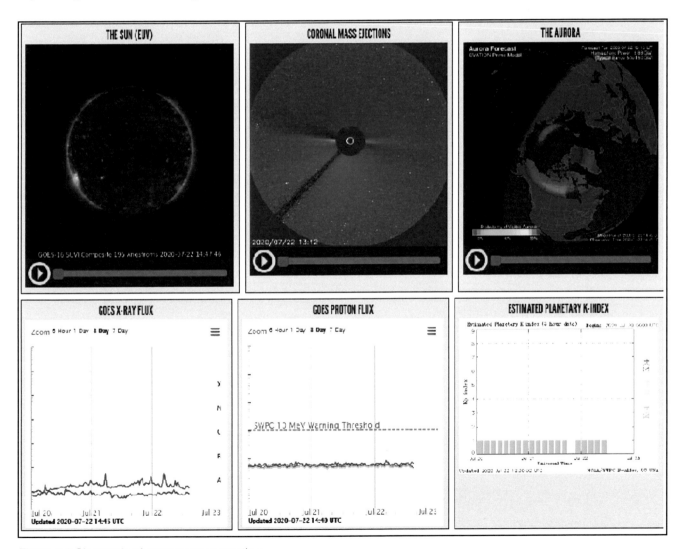

Figure 5.6 Six panels of current space weather.

sunspot number, spotless days, 10.7 cm solar flux, planetary K index, solar wind, and solar flares are included together with many stories about the various aspects of the sun-earth relationship. For solar observers, this website has much information about the current solar cycle. At the top right is a panel that allows you to read daily reports extending back to Jan. 1, 2001.

c) http://soi.stanford.edu/magnetic/index5.html

This website can be used in conjunction with any website reporting sunspots, especially when we are near solar minimum. It will allow you to determine to which solar cycle a sunspot likely belongs. Click on the "Latest" link at the top of the above-referenced page, and you'll be taken to the page as seen in Figure 5.8. The images in Figure 5.8 are from the Helioseismic and Magnetic Imager (HMI), which is one of three instruments on the Solar Dynamics Laboratory satellite. For

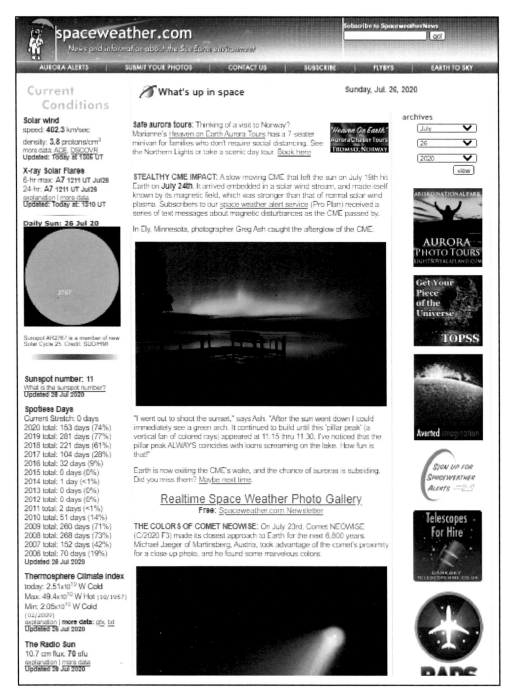

Figure 5.7 Initial view of the spaceweather.com website.

more information about the HMI instrument, visit http://hmi.stanford.edu/Description/hmi-overview/hmi-overview.html.

A magnetogram is an image showing the magnetic polarity of a sunspot region. Using either the color magnetogram, the first image on the left, or the black-and-white magnetogram, the second image from the left, note where the sunspot region is with respect to the solar equator, the line separating the northern solar hemisphere from the southern solar hemisphere. If the sunspot region is near the equator, it is from the old solar cycle. If it is at the higher solar latitudes, it is from the new solar cycle.

A second confirming clue as to which solar cycle a sunspot belongs is the polarity of the sunspot region. Note that the sunspot region has one color that leads the other color. For example, green leads yellow in the color magnetogram and white leads black in the black and white magnetogram. The two colors — either green-yellow or white-black — indicate the polarity of the sunspot region.

Sunspot regions in the same hemisphere from the old solar cycle and from the new solar cycle are of opposite polarity. Old sunspot regions in the northern solar hemisphere are of opposite polarity to old sunspot regions in the southern solar hemisphere. Likewise, new sunspot regions in the northern solar hemisphere are of opposite polarity to new sunspot regions in the southern solar hemisphere.

In the color magnetogram in Figure 5.8, old sunspots in the northern solar hemisphere from Cycle 24 are green leading yellow. Old sunspots in the southern solar hemisphere from Cycle 24 are yellow leading green. New sunspots in the northern solar hemisphere from Cycle 25 are yellow leading green. New sunspots in the southern solar hemisphere from Cycle 25 are green leading yellow. Thus, the sunspot region in the southern solar hemisphere in the color magnetogram, being at the higher solar latitudes and of opposite polarity to old sunspots in the southern solar hemisphere, confirms it is from Cycle 25.

d) http://sidc.oma.be/silso/datafiles

This website of the Royal Observatory of Belgium was referenced in Chapter 2 when the V2.0 sunspot numbers were discussed. It has the daily sunspot numbers, the monthly mean sunspot numbers, the smoothed sunspot numbers and the yearly mean sunspot numbers for the V2.0 sunspot values extending back to the beginning of recorded sunspot history. These data can be downloaded as a text file or as a csv file and plotted on the screen. You also can download hemispheric sunspot V2.0 values (southern and northern solar hemisphere) as daily values, monthly mean values and smoothed values from Jan. 1, 1992 onward. The monthly mean and smoothed hemispheric V2.0 values can be plotted on the screen.

For V1.0 sunspot values, similar data are available to those noted in the previous paragraph. You also

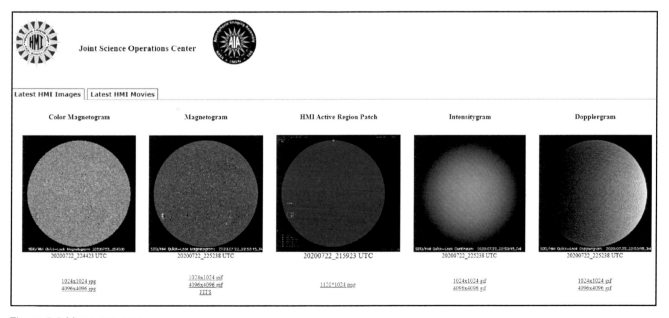

Figure 5.8 Magnetograms.

can download V1.0 and V2.0 Group Sunspot Numbers (GSNs).

This website should satisfy all of your needs in terms of sunspot numbers. With downloadable data files, you can plot and analyze sunspots to your heart's content.

e) Websites in the Amateur Radio community

Many amateur radio websites mirror the space weather data from the SWPC website, the spaceweather.com website, the HMI website, the Royal Observatory of Belgium website and other websites that focus on general and specific space weather parameters.

- The "Propagation" columnist in *CQ* magazine, Tomas Hood, NW7US, has an extensive solar and propagation website at http://www. hfradio.org/. Clicking on the link under "Shortwave Radio Propagation, Solar Cycle Information, and More?" will take you to the extensive data consisting of plots, movies, articles and discussions.

- Paul Herrman, NØNBH, maintains a very extensive website focusing on solar and propagation topics. You can visit his website at http://www.hamqsl.com/solar.html. The 14 links at the top of the home page take you to specific topics. NØNBH is the creator of the banner in Figure 5.9 (on the left side of the above referenced website). There are similar NØNBH banners to be found on various other websites. Here are several:

https://www.qrz.com/

https://www.fcarc.org/propagation.htm

https://www.on6zq.be/w/index.php/Propagation/NØNBH

https://ns6t.net/word/?page_id=88

Steve Saint Andrea, AG1YK, offers details about these banners in his article "Solar Banners – A Propagation Resource" on page 78 of the February 2014 issue of *QST*.

- Kevin Gibeau, VE3EN, has an extensive website focusing on solar issues. Visit his website at https://www.solarham.net/. If you're interested in sporadic-E openings on our 6-meter band, check out VE3EN's data for 2004-2014 during

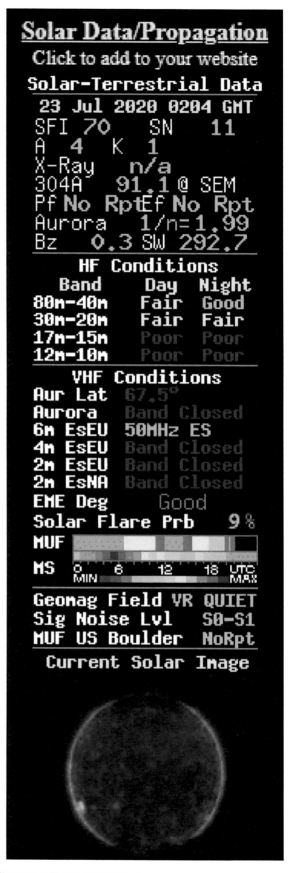

Figure 5.9 Typical NØNBH banner.

May, June, July and August for QSOs between North America and Europe at https://www.solarham.net/6m/data.htm.

- Tamitha Skov, best-known as the space weather woman, provides videos of solar conditions and propagation about every week. Visit her website at http://www.spaceweatherwoman.com/ for videos, audio podcasts, daily forecasts and other information.

5.2.3 Interpreting the Banner

The banner in Figure 5.9 or one of the other forms of it, is available on many websites. Let's briefly review the data and how that affects propagation.

Let's start by identifying an anchor point for HF propagation, that is, a starting point. That starting point is solar minimum, when the 10.7 cm solar flux has bottomed around 65 and the sunspot number is zero. We know there is still enough solar radiation at EUV wavelengths at solar minimum to allow our 160-through 30-meter bands to be open during the hours of darkness. Even our 20-meter band (and our 17-meter band to a lesser extent) can open worldwide at solar minimum during the day and early evening hours.

Three values in the banner will tell us how likely the higher bands will be open. Table 5.3 summarizes this data.

SN (V2.0) is the new sunspot number reported by the Royal Observatory of Belgium as of July 1, 2015. SFI is the 10.7 cm solar flux. 304A is 304 Angstroms, which translates to solar EUV radiation at 30.4 nm. The 304A value should be multiplied by 1E8 (1×10^8) to get the true number of photons per square centimeter per second.

For our 20-meter band (and lower frequencies) to be open, SN (V2.0) can be 0, SFI can be at minimum around 65 and 304A can be at minimum around 90.

For our 17-meter band, solar minimum is adequate for occasional openings. For more consistent open-

Band	SN (V2.0)	SFI	304A
20m and lower	0	65	90
17m	20	75	120
15m	35	85	145
10m	70	100	170
6m	145	150	250

Table 5.3 Rough estimates for minimum required values for band openings

ings, SN (V2.0) must be roughly 20 and above, SFI must be roughly 75 and above and 304A must be roughly 120 and above.

For our 15-meter band to be open, SN (V2.0) must be roughly 35 and above, SFI must be roughly 85 and above and 304A must be roughly 145 and above.

For our 10-meter band to be open, SN (V2.0) must be roughly 70 and above, SFI must be roughly 100 and above and 304A must be roughly 170 and above.

For our 6-meter band to be open, SN (V2.0) must be roughly 145 and above, SFI must be roughly 150 and above and 304A must be roughly 250 and above.

It's important to realize that the values in Table 5.3 must be somewhat consistent for more than just one day to affect propagation – at least a week is desired.

In general, we desire the K and A indices to be low, less than or equal to 3 for the K index and less than or equal to 15 for the A index. Higher values could result in decreased F2 region MUFs. Because the daily A index is an average of the eight three-hour K indices, a small, short-term spike in the K index — which may give us enhanced low- and mid-latitude propagation — may not show up much in the A index for reasons due to averaging.

B_z is the z-component of the Interplanetary Magnetic Field, or IMF, and SW is the speed of the solar wind. B_z and SW are correlated to the K and A indices – a moderately large negative B_z and a solar wind speed greater than roughly 500 km/second will likely indicate higher K and A indices. Aur Lat is the lowest latitude where visible aurora may be seen.

The parameter X-ray is the background X-ray flux. This comes from the lower left panel in Figure 5.6. At solar minimum this value will be around 1E-8 watts per square meter, and it will increase as a solar cycle ramps up. Large short-term spikes indicate possible increased D-region absorption.

P_f and E_f are the proton flux in the solar wind and the electron flux at geosynchronous altitudes, respectively. The P_f value will increase dramatically when a big solar flare emits relativistic protons that may funnel into the polar cap to cause increased D-region absorption on paths over the poles. The E_f value will increase dramatically when the Earth's magnetic field is disturbed from a coronal mass ejection or a coronal hole, indicating that trapped electrons are being accelerated and will precipitate into the auroral zone causing aurora displays.

Note there is no parameter directly tied to how strong our signals will be. Signal strength at HF is mostly determined by ionospheric absorption in the D region, and we don't have a consistent parameter to measure this.

All other words in the banner are mostly self-explanatory. Just remember we are trying to summarize some very complicated ionospheric processes into several parameters. Oversimplification can result in lost information.

5.3 Real-Time Assessment of the Ionosphere

Remembering that the maps in our propagation predictions give us a monthly median look at the ionosphere, are there ways to see what the ionosphere is doing in real-time? Yes, there are.

To see what the critical frequency of the F2 region (foF2) of the ionosphere is doing in real-time, visit https://sws.bom.gov.au/HF_Systems/6/5. This website is courtesy of the Space Weather Services in the Bureau of Meteorology of the Australian Government. Figure 5.10 is a sample image for July 23, 2020, at 1700 UTC.

The image was derived from worldwide foF2 ionosonde data and was updated every 15 minutes. Multiplying the foF2 values by 3 will give a good estimate of the MUF for a 3,000-km hop centered on the chosen location.

For foF2 at specific locations, visit https://www.ngdc.noaa.gov/stp/IONO/rt-iono/realtime/RealTime_foF2.html. Select the specific ionosonde and a map like Figure 5.11 will be displayed.

Seven days of data are given: today's data, yesterday's data and the past five days, but you can't tell which of the past five days are which. As a side note, sporadic-E critical frequency (foEs) data are available at https://www.ngdc.noaa.gov/stp/IONO/rt-iono/realtime/RealTime_foEs.html. Multiply foEs by 5 to determine the sporadic E MUF for a 2,000-km hop.

Worldwide F2 region MUF data are available at http://prop.kc2g.com/. Figure 5.12 is the image for July 23, 2020 at 1700 UTC (same date and time as used in Figure 5.10).

Note that the data contained in Figure 5.12 are approximately three times the data shown in Figure 5.10.

It's important to note the real-time ionosonde data take into account all the parameters that cause the ionosphere to vary in the short-term: solar radiation variation, geomagnetic field activity and events at ground level and in the lower atmosphere that couple to the ionosphere. In other words, our understanding of how the MUF varies in the short-term is very good

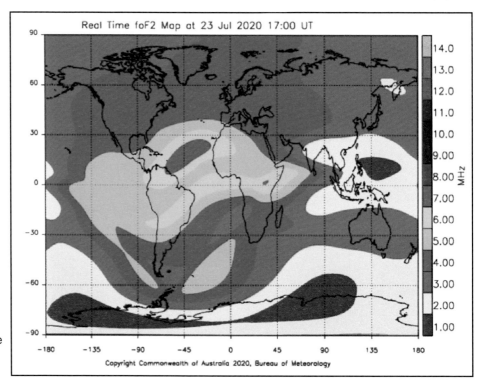

Figure 5.10 Worldwide real-time foF2 map.

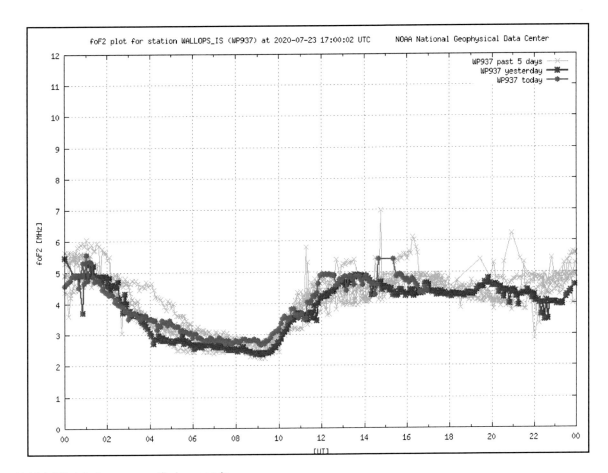

Figure 5.11 foF2 data from a specific ionosonde.

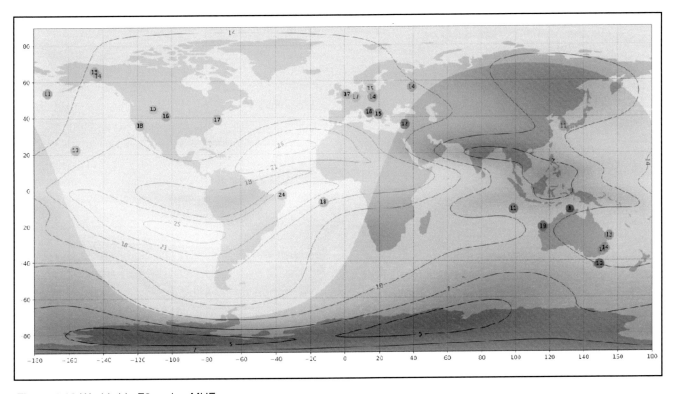

Figure 5.12 Worldwide F2 region MUF map.

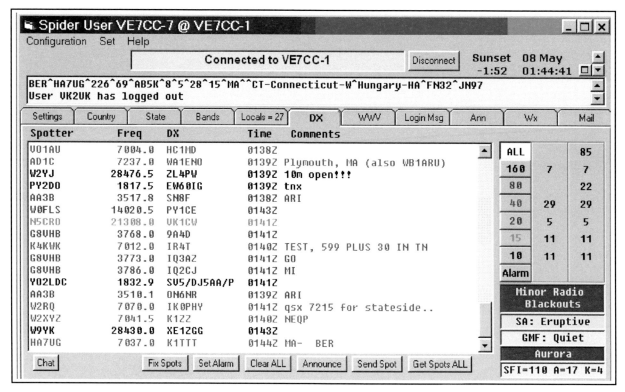

Figure 5.13 Typical PacketCluster screen shot.

using ionosonde data. Unfortunately, the data tell us little about the lower ionosphere, which ionosondes simply don't measure for reasons due to the small amplitude of the signals returned from the lower ionospheric layers. No D-region data are available and only daytime E-region data are available. Ionospheric absorption, which is determined from the electron density in the lower ionosphere, also are missing. Thus, we still need to know how to assess propagation in real time.

5.4 Real-Time Assessment of Propagation

5.4.1 PacketCluster

There are quite a few methods to assess real-time propagation. One method is to download and install PacketCluster software on your computer. Packet-Cluster software was mentioned earlier at the end of Section 5.2.1 in relation to accessing the current WWV data.

When someone using the PacketCluster network works or hears another station, they can notify everyone on the PacketCluster network. This is called "spotting" a station. A spot includes the call sign of

the spotter, the frequency, the station heard or worked by the spotting station, the time, and any comments. Figure 5.13, from http://www.bcdxc.org/ve7cc/, shows a typical screen.

Filters and options are available to only see spots from certain areas of the world — near your QTH, for example — and/or certain bands. You also can display spots for a specific station. Note that bands can be color-coded for easier viewing. There is much flexibility in the software, and the documentation at the referenced website will allow you to understand and use all the site's capabilities. It's easy to understand how an assessment of propagation can be determined by seeing what other people are working/hearing.

Similar to the data available on a PacketCluster is what can be found on the website http://www.dx summit.fi/#/ managed by the Radio Arcala group of Finland. This website is a listing of spots in real-time from around the world.

5.4.2 Putting Spots on a Map

Spots from PacketCluster networks can be plotted on a map of the world (or a map of a continent) to visualize who is working whom in near real-time. The following is one such website: https://www.dxmaps.

com/spots/mapg.php?Lan=E. Figure 5.14 shows a typical map from this website.

You have the option of choosing bands in two general categories: "LF – HF" or "VHF and up." You can view spots from the entire world or from a single continent. The color-coding of the great circle path tells what the likely propagation mode is. You also can add the gray line on the map, add time zones to the map and select from many other options.

5.4.3 Other "Spotting" Networks

Similar to the websites in Section 5.4.1 are two other spot-mapping applications. The first one is the Weak Signal Propagation Reporter Network (WSPRnet) at http://wsprnet.org/drupal/. This is a group of amateur radio operators using K1JT's MEPT_JT digital mode to probe radio frequency propagation conditions using very low power (QRP/QRPp) transmissions. There are many options to choose from on the home page. It is important to note that WSPR is not a QSO mode. It is

used to transmit a position, call sign and power level, and to see who hears and decodes it. Reports of these decodes are sent and tracked on the WSPRnet website.

The second website is the PSKReporter at https://pskreporter.info/. This application automatically gathers reception records of all digital mode activity and then makes those records available in near real-time to interested parties — typically the amateur who initiated the communication. They will be able to see where their signal was received. A total of 18 digital modes, including CW, can be monitored, with FT8 being the significantly dominant mode. The home page has a mapping link.

5.4.4 NCDXF/IARU Beacons

The NCDXF/IARU (Northern California DX Association/International Amateur Radio Union) International Beacon Project consists of 18 worldwide beacons that transmit on our 20-, 17-, 15-, 12- and 10-meter bands. Information is provided at https://www.

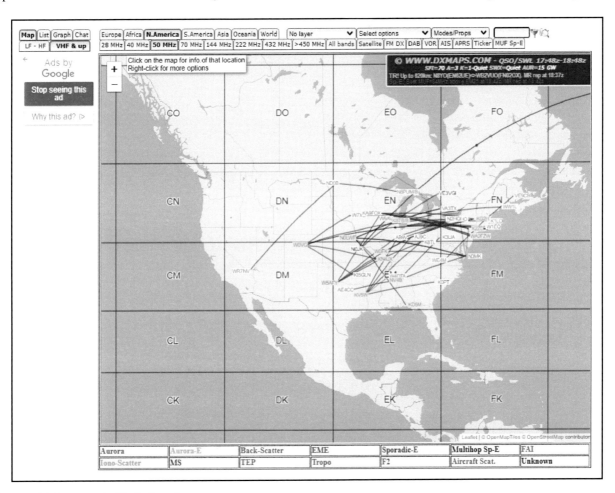

Figure 5.14 6m spots in North America.

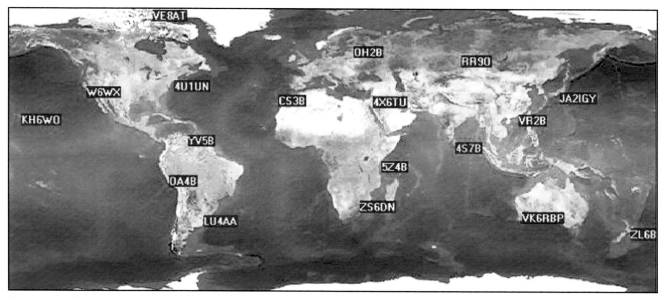

Figure 5.15 The worldwide NCDXF/IARU beacons.

ncdxf.org/pages/beacons.html. Each transmission by one of the 18 beacons on a given band lasts for 10 seconds. Thus, in three minutes, all 18 beacons transmit on a single band and give a picture of worldwide propagation. In 15 minutes, worldwide propagation on all five bands can be assessed. Figure 5.15 shows the 18 worldwide beacons.

A transmission consists of the call sign of the beacon sent at 22 words per minute followed by four one-second dashes. The call sign and the first dash are sent at 100 watts. The remaining dashes are sent at 10 watts, 1 watt and 100 milliwatts. When solar conditions are favorable (high number of sunspots/high 10.7 cm solar flux and a low K index), the beacons often can be heard at all four power levels. The time slot assignment for each beacon on each band can be found at the "Beacon Transmission Schedule and Status" link on the home page.

Alex Shovkoplyas, VE3NEA, (developer of the DX Atlas software) [reference 3] has written Faros, a sophisticated beacon program capable of monitoring all 18 beacons on all bands automatically with measurements of signal-to-noise, QSB, and propagation delay. Additionally, digital signal processing technology helps to accurately distinguish beacon signals from noise to avoid false reporting. Real time results are displayed and data are cumulated in graphic charts and logs suitable for analysis and web publishing.

Faros can be downloaded from http://www.dxatlas.com/Faros/. Install the latest Beacon.lst file (from https://www.ncdxf.org/beacon/beaconprograms.html) in the same folder as the "faros.exe" folder for proper operation. Figure 5.16 is a sample output from the Faros software.

With proper setup and calibration of your receiving system, the time delay through your receiver can be eliminated so propagation via short and long paths can be determined. Figure 5.16 shows the results of IK3XTV in Italy monitoring the OA4B beacon in Peru on 21 MHz on June 4, 2014.

From about 1500-2200 UTC, short path was available. From about 1400-1700 UTC, long path was available. What's intriguing are the two receptions around 1600 UTC; they appear between the short and long paths, suggesting a skewed path. A skewed path can occur if there is a sufficient horizontal electron density gradient to knock the electromagnetic wave off of one great circle path and onto another great circle path. All the details of this analysis are in [reference 4].

5.4.5 Other Beacons

Worldwide round-the-clock beacons abound in and very near our amateur radio bands. The IARU maintains an extensive worldwide list of HF beacons at https://iaruhfbeacons.wordpress.com/hf-beacons-2.

5.4.6 Reverse Beacon Network

Another tool to assess propagation in real-time is the Reverse Beacon Network (RBN). The RBN (the information is at http://www.reversebeacon.net/) is a network of automated stations monitoring the bands and reporting what stations they hear, when they hear the stations and how well they hear the stations. These receivers are known as skimmers.

You can call a quick CQ, and see which reverse beacons hear you, and how strong you are. You also can instantly determine what stations, from a given country or zone, have been heard, at what times and on what frequencies they were operating. These data will allow you to determine band openings in near real time on an animated map [reference 5].

At this writing, there are 140 worldwide skimmers on-line. An added bonus with the RBN is the ability to compare your signals to those of your friends and competitors, in near real time or historically so as to assess how well your station "gets out" as compared to others.

The RBN also is a powerful tool for the study of propagation. For example, Nathaniel Frissell, W2NAF, was among the authors of a peer-reviewed paper that used the RBN and WSPRNet to investigate the response of HF communications to solar activity [reference 6]. See Section 5.4.3 for more details.

5.5   Space Weather for Educators

In Section 5.2.2, we noted the Space Weather Prediction Center website had an education and outreach section. This is accessible at https://www.swpc.noaa.gov/content/education-and-outreach. Clicking on the "Outreach & Education Resources" link on the right side of the page lists many resources, including a curriculum for classroom activities for grades 7 through 12. This is a 106-page pdf document with four chapters of instruction and nine activities.

5.6   General WWV Information

Introduction

Precise time and frequency information is needed by electric power companies, radio and television stations, telephone companies, air traffic control systems, participants in space exploration, computer net-

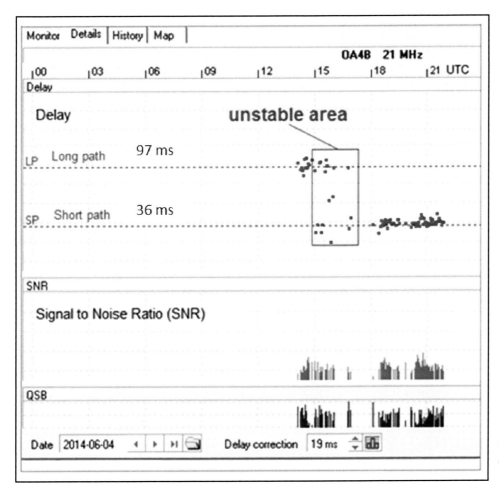

Figure 5.16 IK3XTV monitoring of the OA4B beacon.

works, scientists monitoring data of all kinds, and navigators of ships and planes. These users need to compare their own timing equipment to a reliable, internationally recognized standard. The National Institute of Standards and Technology (NIST), formerly the National Bureau of Standards, provides this for most users in the United States.

NIST began broadcasting time and frequency information from radio station WWV in 1923. Since then, NIST has expanded its time and frequency services to meet the needs of a growing number of users. NIST time and frequency services are convenient, accurate, and easy to use. They contribute greatly to the nation's space and defense programs, to manufacturers, and to transportation and communications. In addition, NIST services are widely used by the general public.

A detailed 80-page overview (2002 edition) of NIST time and frequency services and how to use them can be downloaded from https://tf.nist.gov/general/pdf/1383.pdf.

LF Services – WWVB

WWVB is a time-signal radio station near Fort Collins, Colorado on 60 kHz. No voice alerts are provided, but it can be used for propagation studies in the LF band (30-300 kHz).

Visit https://www.nist.gov/pml/time-and-frequency-division/radio-stations/wwvb for more information about WWVB.

Shortwave Services – WWV and WWVH

NIST operates two high-frequency radio stations, WWV and WWVH. WWV is in Fort Collins, Colorado, and WWVH is in Kauai, Hawaii. Both stations broadcast continuous time and frequency signals on 2.5, 5, 10, and 15 MHz. WWV also broadcasts on 20 MHz and, at this writing, transmits an experimental signal on 25 MHz as well. The broadcasts on all frequencies provide the same information. Although radio reception conditions in the high-frequency band vary greatly with factors such as location, time of year, time of day, the particular frequency being used, atmospheric and ionospheric propagation conditions and the type of receiving equipment used, at least one frequency should be usable at all times. As a general rule, frequencies above 10 MHz work best

in the daytime, and the lower frequencies work best at night.

Services provided by WWV and WWVH

WWV and WWVH provide time announcements, standard time intervals, standard frequencies, UT1 time corrections, BCD time code, geophysical alerts and announcements for the Military Auxiliary Radio System. Visit https://www.nist.gov/pml/time-and-frequency-division/radio-stations/wwv/wwv-and-wwvh-digital-time-code-and-broadcast for detailed information about WWV and WWVH.

Time announcements – These are made from WWV and WWVH once every minute. Since both stations can be heard in some locations, a man's voice is used on WWV, and a woman's voice is used on WWVH to reduce confusion. The WWVH time announcement occurs first, at about 15 seconds before the minute. The WWV time announcement follows at about 7.5 seconds before the minute.

Standard time intervals – The most frequent sounds heard on WWV and WWVH are the seconds pulses. According to the WWV website, these pulses are heard every second except on the 29th and 59th seconds of each minute. The first pulse of each hour is an 800 ms pulse of 1500 Hz. The first pulse of each minute is an 800 ms pulse of 1000 Hz at WWV and 1200 Hz at WWVH. The remaining seconds pulses are short audio bursts (5 ms pulses of 1000 Hz at WWV and 1200 Hz at WWVH) that sound like the ticking of a clock. When there is a voice announcement during a minute interval, only the ticks are transmitted.

Standard frequencies – Both WWV and WWVH broadcast standard frequency audio tones that alternate during most minutes of the hour. Most minutes feature a 500 or 600 Hz audio tone. However, a 440 Hz tone is broadcast once per hour, and some minutes do not include any audio tones at all. The schedule for the audio tones can be found at the website given three paragraphs above.

UT1 time corrections – UT1 is needed by some users who need time that is related to the rotation of the Earth, which is less stable than UTC. Applications such as celestial navigation, satellite observations of the Earth, and some types of surveying require time referenced to the rotational position of the Earth.

These users rely on the UT1 time scale. UT1 is derived by astronomers who monitor the speed of the Earth's rotation.

BCD time code – WWV and WWVH continuously broadcast a binary coded decimal (BCD) time code on a 100-Hz subcarrier. The time code presents UTC information in serial fashion at a rate of 1 pulse per second, carrying such information as the current minute, hour, and day of year. It also contains the 100-Hz frequency from the subcarrier. The 100-Hz frequency may be used as a standard with the same accuracy as the audio frequencies.

Geophysical alerts – The National Oceanic and Atmospheric Administration, or NOAA, uses WWV and WWVH to broadcast geophysical alert messages that provide information about solar terrestrial conditions. Geophysical alerts are broadcast from WWV at 18 minutes after the hour and from WWVH at 45 minutes after the hour. The messages are shorter than 45 seconds and are updated every three hours, typically starting at 0000 UTC. More frequent updates are made when necessary. The format for propagation disturbance is the G, S or R designation discussed in Chapter 1.

Military Auxiliary Radio System announcements – Radio Stations WWV and WWVH announce upcoming and current MARS and U.S. Department of Defense exercises. The WWV and WWVH announcements provide amateur radio participants with information that includes the purpose, dates, times and locations of the exercises. WWV airs MARS announcements on the 10th minute of each hour, and WWVH uses the 50th minute. Each announcement will air for about two weeks, prior to and during each exercise.

Accuracy and Stability

The time and frequency broadcasts are controlled by the NIST atomic frequency standards, which real-ize the internationally defined cesium resonance frequency with an accuracy of 1 part in 10^{13}. The frequencies transmitted by WWV and WWVH are held stable to better than ± 2 parts in 10^{11} at all times. Deviations at WWV are normally less than 1 part in 10^{12} from day to day. Incremental frequency adjustments not exceeding 1 part in 10^{12} are made at WWV and WWVH as necessary.

As a side note, due to the exceptional accuracy and stability of the WWV frequency, members of Ham Radio Science Citizen Investigation, or HamSCI, are using WWV transmissions on 5 MHz to study Doppler shift in the ionosphere at sunrise and during the North American solar eclipse of August 2017. The group's website is https://hamsci.org/

5.7   References

1. The tabular MUF data came from ftp://ftp.swpc.noaa.gov/pub/lists/iono_month/. This data could be imported into Excel and plotted. Unfortunately the data at this website only goes back to January 2014.

2. The receive antenna used for these measurements was a Tennadyne T6 log periodic dipole array at 60 feet. The T6 covers 14-30 MHz. The receiver used was a Yaesu FT-747GX (ham band transmit, general coverage receive). Measurements of WWV were also taken on 10 MHz at the same time.

3. DX Atlas is available at http://www.dxatlas.com/DxAtlas/. It is a map with prefixes, zones, grid squares, gray line, a choice of different map projections, the capability to plot a great circle route and more.

4. For an analysis of these two receptions, download the August 2017 and September 2017 Monthly Features at https://k9la.us.

5. At press time, the Google maps don't work. RBN personnel are working on a new approach using open-source maps.

6. Frissell, N.A., Vega, J.S., Markowitz, E, Gerrard, A.J., Engelke, W.D., Erickson, P.J., Miller, E.S., Luetzelschwab, R.C. and Bortnik, J; High-Frequency Communications Response to Solar Activity in September 2017 as Observed by Amateur Radio Networks; Space Weather, 17, https://doi.org/10.1029/2018SW002008.

Chapter 6

HF Propagation Prediction Programs

Awise old ham once said: "If you want to know what propagation conditions will be like tomorrow, check them today." That is called "now-casting," as contrasted with "forecasting." And while statistics have shown now-casting will be correct a fair amount of the time, we probably are better off using HF propagation prediction programs. This chapter will discuss what HF propagation prediction programs are, the evolution of these programs, the various types of programs available and a review of several prediction programs.

When we address propagation predictions in this chapter, we'll be talking about maximum usable frequencies – MUFs. But there are different MUFs, and an understanding of them is important. In this chapter, the following MUF definitions will be used.

1) Predicted monthly median MUF – This is a statistical value that comes out of our propagation predictions, and it defines the frequency that has a 50% probability of happening over a month's time frame for a given path at a given time. In this chapter, this version of MUF will be shortened to "predicted median MUF."
2) Observed monthly median MUF – This is also a statistical value, but it is derived from a month's worth of ionosonde data for a given path at a given time. It is what happened in the real-world over a month's time frame. This version of MUF will be shortened to "observed median MUF." Comparing the predicted median MUF to the observed median MUF will give you an indication of how accurate the prediction is for a given path at a given time.
3) The classical MUF (which is the name that will be used in this chapter) is the highest frequency propagated via ionospheric refraction alone for a given path at a given time. This value is not a median value. It is what is actually happening in the ionosphere at a specific time and date, and likely comes from ionosonde data. It can be above or below the observed median MUF (i.e., it is within the distribution about the observed median MUF). The classical MUF is also referred to as the basic MUF. As a side note, the operational MUF is the highest frequency that can be supported for a given path at a given time via refraction or via ionospheric and/or ground scatter. The operational MUF may be higher than the classical MUF.

6.1 HF Propagation Prediction Programs – What Are They?

HF propagation prediction programs make an assessment of what is **likely** to occur sometime in the future based on a collection of historical solar and ionospheric data.

Given the computer revolution of the 1980s and '90s, most ham shacks and SWL listening posts now sport a personal computer. Given this capability, it was inevitable that radio amateurs and other users of the HF spectrum would want to do their own propagation predictions, especially on those HF circuits they most use or in which they are most interested (for example, the path to that "rare one"). They also might want to determine the "gray line" times and coverage areas for their QTH as well as the reliability (the probability that a desired signal-to-noise ratio is achieved) they can expect on their "pet" paths, given current solar and geomagnetic conditions. Finally, amateurs and SWLs alike simply may want to know when propagation prob-

Figure 6.1 Correlation between the classical MUF and the daily sunspot number.

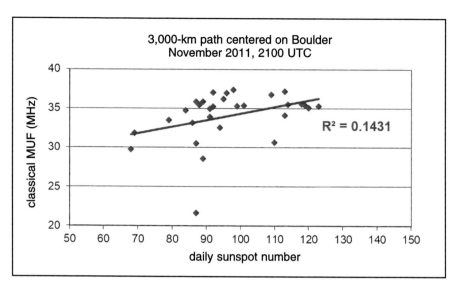

ably will *not* be possible, making it best just to leave the shack and do something else. Modern shortwave propagation prediction programs for the PC now can provide such information in the comfort of your home.

Given a specific set of geographical endpoints for a desired path, an HF propagation prediction program will: (1) determine the band of frequencies that should propagate over that path; and (2) provide information on the probable modes of propagation, expected signal strengths, signal-to-noise ratios, and/or path reliability. The program should be able to do this for any time of day, any month (season), any portion of the solar cycle, and between any two geographical endpoints in the world. Many programs do this, taking into account your transmitter's power and antenna's gain. Simply put, HF prediction programs indicate whether or not you can even expect to get your signal to that distant receiver, and if you can, whether or not it will be useful.

Most modern PC-based programs can do all of this quickly – in much less than a minute. That is quite a capability. Modern PC technology allows the radio amateur or the SWL to use prediction programs that originally required large mainframe computers. However, regardless of the level of complexity of the software, all of these programs carry one important caveat, one which often is overlooked but must be remembered if the predictions from any given program are to be interpreted properly: The numbers produced by shortwave prediction programs are "monthly median" values that were developed on a statistical basis. This means that 50% of the time (half the days of the month), the actual, observed value of whatever you are predicting will be higher

than the predicted value, and 50% of the time (the other half of the days of the month), the actual observed value will be lower than the predicted value. Unfortunately, it is very difficult to predict which *specific* days are the "good" days and which specific days are the "bad" days.

As an example, when a prediction program outputs a predicted median MUF of 30.0 MHz at a given time of day, what most likely would be observed on any given day at the given time is an actual *maximum usable frequency* somewhere between 26.2 and 33.8 MHz. The proper interpretation of this would be: 10 meters will be open on slightly more than half of the days of the month, 12 meters will be open on at least roughly 75% of the days of the month and 15 meters will be open on most of the days of the month. To reiterate, HF predictions are not absolutes, but rather, are statistical in nature over a month's time frame.

Finally, it must be recognized that all prediction models are based on data for times when the Earth's magnetic field is quiet. Some of the prediction programs allow the input of a single K-index, but this is not sufficient to produce valid results for periods characterized by solar/ionospheric disturbances. This topic will be discussed further in section 6.5.

6.2 Development of the Model of the Ionosphere for HF Prediction Programs

The discussion in this section is based on the work of Carl Luetzelschwab, K9LA [reference 1].

You might think deriving a model of the ionosphere for propagation prediction purposes should be a fairly simple endeavor. After all, scientists have long had data on the sun's activity (sunspot numbers) as well as data on ionospheric behavior (ionosonde data). However, simply correlating these two parameters on a daily basis yields poor results. Figure 6.1 shows the correlation of the daily sunspot number and the classical MUF for the F2 region for all days in November 2011 at 2100 UTC over the Boulder, Colorado ionosonde.

Note: the correlation of the classical MUF, not the critical frequency, foF2, is presented here. This is acceptable because the MUF is linearly related to foF2.

The correlation coefficient of 0.38 (the square root of 0.1431) is simply not adequate for use in making predictions with confidence. Some might think we should look at these data over a longer period of time. Or, perhaps, we should use the 3,000-km F2 classical MUF data for multiple stations worldwide over a month's period of time (or longer). But then, how do we account for the difference in geographic station locations? That is, how does the ionosphere above the tropics behave compared, say, to its behavior above a station located at higher Earth latitudes?

Clearly, there are no simple answers when we approach the problem of HF prediction in this way.

As shortwave radio emerged as a viable method of worldwide communications in the early years of the 20th century, predicting what frequency and time of day would support propagation from Point A to Point B quickly became an important issue. To make these predictions, a *reliable and accurate* model of the ionosphere was needed. And, to develop such a model, *reliable* data were needed. The piece of equipment responsible for taking reliable ionospheric data is the ionosonde.

The basic ionosonde technology was invented in 1925 by Gregory Breit and Merle Tuve, then of the Carnegie Institute for Science in Washington, D.C. By early 1930, the critical frequencies of the E, F1 and F2 regions were being measured manually once each week in the vicinity of Washington, D.C.; beginning in May 1933, automatic multi-frequency data were recorded at this site hourly. Weekly values of the noon F2 region critical frequency were averaged by month for September 1930, to December 1935.

To ensure the seasonal characteristics of the iono-

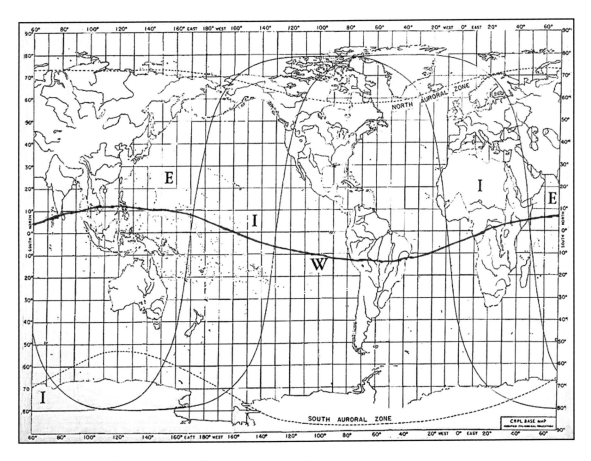

Figure 6.2 Map of ionospheric zones, auroral zones and magnetic equator.

Figure 6.3 Correlation between the observed median MUF and smoothed sunspot number.

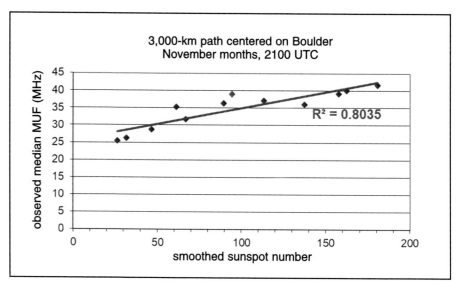

3,000-km path centered on Boulder
November months, 2100 UTC

$R^2 = 0.8035$

observed median MUF (MHz)

smoothed sunspot number

sphere were maintained, scientists began presenting data as monthly average critical frequencies. The characterization of the ionosphere was still local in nature, and the time zone used was that of the reporting station. Thus, the scientific community began to see the data accumulate upon which to build a statistical model for ionospheric parameters.

A decade would pass as more and more data were gathered. As well, the thrust moved from a local characterization of the ionosphere to global characterization. For reasons related to the globalization of ionosonde data, the ionosphere was divided into three zones: West, East and Intermediate as shown in Figure 6.2 (from one of the Central Radio Propagation Library's three-months-in-advance predictions).

The West zone was defined as where the magnetic equator (the red line in Figure 6.2) was south of the geographic equator; the East zone was defined to be where the magnetic equator was north of the geographic equator; and the two Intermediate zones were defined to be where the magnetic equator was transitioning between north and south of the geographic equator. The ionosphere was divided into these zones because scientists recognized that electrons, being charged particles, are affected by the earth's magnetic field. Characterizing the ionosphere with zones in this way was determined to be the optimal manner in which to categorize the increasingly voluminous quantity of worldwide data being acquired.

In 1947, scientists began discussing whether monthly average values or monthly median values of the critical frequency were preferred descriptors for prediction purposes. Thus, in September 1947, we began to see critical frequency data presented in terms of monthly median values. This likely occurred because a monthly median value was better for representing non-normal distributions of the critical frequency (an average value would be acceptable for representing a normal distribution).

There still appeared to be an issue with what format of the sunspot number to use: a monthly average value or a smoothed value? This issue was resolved in a 1948 paper (reference 2). This paper presented plots of the monthly median critical frequency of the F2 region at Washington, D.C., versus two representations of the sunspot cycle: (1) the monthly average sunspot number and (2) the monthly 12-month smoothed sunspot number. As shown in Figure 6.3, the plots developed using the smoothed sunspot numbers yielded highly correlated results.

With a correlation coefficient of 0.896 (square root of 0.8035), there now is much more confidence in any prediction made using these data. Compare this figure to Figure 6.1, noting how the data here are less scattered about the trend line.

That said, recall we still had defined three zones in the ionosphere. If the intention is to publish ionospheric maps of the world for the purpose of making worldwide HF predictions, it now would be necessary to shift the data format from one defined by "local" categories using bands of longitude and local times into "worldwide" categories in which the ionosphere is ordered about geomagnetic coordinates in universal time. The transition to worldwide data began in January 1963, and was described in a publication of ionospheric parameters [reference 3] from the now-defunct Central Radio Propagation Laboratory, or CRPL, in Boulder, Colorado. The new maps displayed worldwide ionosphere data versus longitude for every two hours of universal time. Figure 6.4 summarizes the timeline of the critical dates in the development of the current model of the ionosphere.

6.3 The Two Parts of Propagation Prediction Programs

Propagation prediction programs are composed of two parts: a propagation kernel and a man-machine interface.

(1) The Propagation Kernel. These are the programs that work together to describe the HF channel between two points with respect to the frequencies that will propagate and how strong the signal will be at the receiver. A simple propagation kernel would consist of models that predict:

(a) *Maximum Usable Frequency (MUF).* This is the *predicted median MUF* for a given path for both the E region and the F2 region. The MUF is a function of the time of day, season of the year, phase of the solar cycle and geographical location. It is generally believed that the MUF is a parameter that **cannot be influenced by transmit power and antenna gain.** That said, we'll talk about an interesting exception to this constraint involving *above-the-MUF* propagation later in this chapter when talking about one specific prediction program.

(b) *Lowest Usable Frequency (LUF).* This is the lower boundary of the band of frequencies that will support propagation between two points. The LUF is a signal-to-noise boundary created primarily by D-region absorption. It is not a clear, concise, limiting point due, in part, to the fact that noise, power and receiver sensitivities affect where this limit occurs. The LUF is a difficult parameter to model; many times, empirical models do a better job of estimating this parameter for day-to-day operations than do any other techniques.

(c) *Field Strength.* The field strength is a measure of the signal energy that appears at the receiver's antenna. This is in contrast to the signal energy that appears at the receiver's antenna terminal. For the latter, the voltage measured is a function of a number of factors, including the field strength at the antenna, gain of the antenna (at the angle of arrival) compared to an isotropic antenna, the impedance match between the receive antenna and the feedline, feedline losses, etc. Simply put, there is no easy way to develop a general-purpose computer program that allows for the input of a station's specific operational parameters for use in the calculation of signal energy at the receiver's antenna terminals. Most prediction programs allow you to enter files containing receive antenna characteristics for the prediction of signal strength.

(d) *Noise Model.* Most HF prediction programs include some form of man-made and galactic noise models. Values usually are developed from look-up tables or numerical maps, which are compiled and available from the International Telecommunication

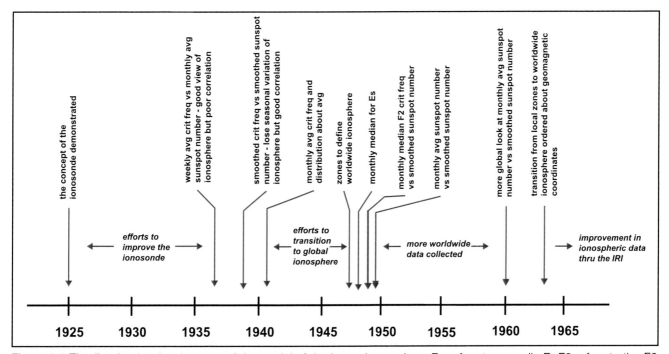

Figure 6.4 Timeline for the development of the model of the ionosphere, where Es refers to sporadic E, F2 refers to the F2 region of the ionosphere and the IRI is the International Reference Ionosphere that will be covered later in this chapter.

Union, Geneva, Switzerland [reference 4]. These data are used to determine signal-to-noise ratios, or whether or not there is sufficient received signal strength to overcome the ambient (background) noise.

(e) *Solar Zenith Angle as a function of Time of Day and Month.* This model determines the sun's location in the sky. Almost all methods of modeling require this information because most ionospheric parameters are defined in terms of the time of day and season of the year.

(f) *Path Length.* This is the great-circle distance between the transmitter and the receiver. This is used, in conjunction with predicted median MUFs and signal strengths, to determine the most favorable mode of propagation – single-hop, multi-hop, combined E and F modes, etc.

With a knowledge of the parameters listed above, the radio amateur can do a good job of determining the band of frequencies in which signals will propagate between two points and the relative signal levels to be expected. These parameters comprise a sufficient kernel for a simple propagation model. Most models today have much larger sets of models, and they provide significantly more detailed outputs, such a service probability, reliability, and free-space path loss, to name a few.

(2) The Man-Machine Interface (MMI). This is the part of the program that allows the user to interact with the propagation kernel. In the early days, when propagation programs were used only by scientists and engineers, the MMI was simple. The user knew the internal complexities of the program and developed ways of "coaxing" the answers out of the computer. The demand for easy-to-use HF propagation programs, however, led to a focus on the MMI.

The easier a program is to use, the more likely that it will be used by the radio amateur and shortwave listener. Thus, the operational differences in prediction programs are basically the user interface and the output format used to display the results. Program selection is, in general, a matter of personal preferences related to these two factors.

The existence of several different propagation kernels has led to the creation of different permutations of a program wherein the kernel is the same but the MMI is different. For example, *IONCAP* spawned *IONCAST*, *VOACAP*, *ICEPAC*, and *CAPMAN*. HF prediction program development over the past four to five decades has shown that a new or innovative prediction process will spawn new permutations,

with the major changes occurring in the MMI. Most often, the propagation kernel is left intact.

6.4   F2-Region Models

It should be no surprise that the F2 region is responsible for most long-distance propagation. With respect to propagation prediction programs, one thing should be understood: all current prediction programs use a monthly median model of the F2 region for reasons related to the short-term variability of this region not yet being fully understood.

Thankfully, the E region is far simpler in its make-up. For all intents and purposes, it is under direct solar control. All a prediction program needs is the solar zenith angle (how high the sun is in the sky at a given location and time) and the sunspot number to predict the E-region's critical frequency anywhere in the world.

Finally, given the characteristics of D region are difficult to measure on a consistent basis, its model is the least developed. The data we do have are from rocket flights, incoherent scatter radar measurements and theoretical chemical models, which are extremely complicated.

Several F2 region models have been developed over the last several decades. They fall into three broad categories: statistical, theoretical and empirical.

Statistical F2-region models

Statistical models use monthly median ionospheric data from ionosondes. These types of models are the most numerous, and their development began after World War II. It was at that time that ionosondes began to be installed around the world to take data on the F2 region of the ionosphere. (Daytime E region data were collected at the same time.) As these data accumulated, CRPL in 1962 developed a methodology by which to represent the complex properties of the ionosphere on a worldwide scale by numerical analysis of ionosphere data. The result was a set of well-defined mathematical expressions created by William Jones and Roger Gallet that could be programmed for use on large-scale digital computers [reference 5]. This capability also allowed graphical maps to be drawn for those who did not have access to such computers.

These graphical maps were published three months in advance of the targeted month by the CRPL, and the maps could be used to manually determine the F2 region predicted median MUF along any path, at any time in any month, and at a designated phase of a solar cycle. This was a tedious process, to be sure, but nevertheless, it was a step forward. In late 1971, these monthly graphical maps were replaced with a four-volume set of F2 region critical frequencies, F2 region predicted median MUFs for a 4,000-km path, and E-region MUFs for three levels of solar activity (smoothed sunspot numbers of 10, 110 and 160). The fourth volume consisted of instructions, charts and nomograms to be used with the three volumes of data.

For reasons related to the importance of HF communications after WWII, other countries also developed databases of their own of E- and F2-region ionospheric characteristics. In 1966, the International Radio Consultative Committee, or CCIR, published an atlas of ionospheric characteristics [reference 6] using ionosonde data from 1954, 1955, 1956, 1957, 1958 and 1964. The atlas also took advantage of the numerical mapping technique developed by Jones and Gallet.

Many F2 region models were developed out of the CCIR Atlas, usually with improvements. Some examples are the FTZ-MUF2 and MINIFTZ4 models from Deutsche Bundespost in Germany; Raymond Fricker's MICROMUF 2+ and MAXIMUF (he was a propagation engineer at the BBC) [reference 7]; the model in IONCAP (Ionospheric Communications and Analysis Prediction) which when first released around 1978, used oblique sounder data in its F2 region model; and one of the models in the Voice of America Coverage Analysis Program (VOACAP). These models are mentioned here because Robert R. Brown, NM7M, in 1997 [reference 8], made a comparison of some of these models which may be of interest for historical reasons.

Theoretical F2-region models

Theoretical models use a physics-based model of the ionosphere. As their input, they take solar data, geomagnetic data and atmospheric data to solve non-linear equations of momentum, energy and continuity for electron densities, among other parameters. These models are complicated and need large, mainframe computers to run. Google the name of the computer models below for more information.

1, SAMI3 (SAMI3 is Also a Model of the Ionosphere) by the Naval Research Laboratory
2. CTIPe (Coupled Thermosphere Ionosphere Plasmasphere Electrodynamics Model) by the Space Weather Prediction Center at NOAA
3. USU-GAIM (Utah State University Global

Assimilation of Ionospheric Measurements) by Utah State University
4. TIE-GCM (Thermosphere Ionosphere Electrodynamics General Circulation Model) by the National Center for Atmospheric Research
5. GITM (Global Ionosphere Thermosphere Model) by the University of Michigan

At the time of this writing, none are used in a propagation prediction program.

Empirical F2 region models

These models combine features of the statistical and theoretical models.

The International Reference Ionosphere (IRI) falls into this category. It uses monthly median data from the CCIR database and solves theoretical equations for electron temperature, ion composition, ion temperature, ion drift, and several other parameters. More on IRI can be found at http://irimodel.org/. Papers regarding the latest model can be found here as well.

IRI is a joint project of the Committee on Space Research (COSPAR) and the International Union of Radio Science (URSI). It began in 1968. In 1975, the IRI-75 model was released as a table of ionospheric parameters for equatorial, low- and middle-latitudes. The 1978 version, IRI-78, changed to the use of the CCIR database. In 1990, IRI-90 added the option for using the URSI database (which is claimed to have better over-ocean coverage). The IRI model is updated on a regular basis (roughly every five years); the current model is IRI-2016.

IRI-2016 includes two new model options: (1) the ability to compute height of the peak F2 region electron density in different ways, and (2) the ability to use the STORM model (more on STORM later in Section 6.6) for F2 electron density changes caused by geomagnetic field activity. Progress is also being made on a Real-Time IRI, in which real-time ionosonde measurements are assimilated into the model to provide timelier predictions. A final note: IRI-2016 internally applies a scaling factor to the inputted V2.0 sunspot numbers to maintain the original correlation between the V1.0 smoothed sunspot numbers and monthly median ionospheric parameters. Currently, this is the only propagation prediction program that corrects for the V2.0 sunspot record.

Finally, at the time this was written, PHaRLAP (a ray tracing program – more on it in Section 6.7) is the only propagation prediction program that uses the IRI-2016 model.

6.5 How Accurate Are HF Prediction Programs?

Solar, geomagnetic, and ionospheric conditions are controlled by nature. Computer propagation programs attempt to emulate or predict nature, but they cannot control it. For this reason, a propagation program model, no matter how complex, always will be imprecise. It is good to remember that propagation forecasting may be a highly developed art, but it is *not* a precise science!

Comparison of predicted and observed propagation parameters on a purely scientific basis would require a large database of observed measurements acquired over long periods of time, at the least, throughout a complete sunspot cycle. Such studies require international cooperation, and they can be extremely expensive and time consuming. For this reason, only a limited number of such studies have been conducted. Refer to reference 9 for details of one such study of the first propagation prediction program made available to amateur radio operators in 1982 for use with personal computers (more on this program is given in Section 6.7). This program's predicted data were verified against sounder data.

An important reminder: because the outputs of our propagation prediction programs are predicted median MUF and monthly median signal strength, or signal-to-noise ratio (SNR), we need a month's worth of data to properly validate a prediction. Using a contest weekend is not sufficient; it can't tell the entire story.

To demonstrate the effort required for a proper validation, Figure 6.5 shows a typical predicted median MUF value and a typical, predicted, median signal strength value. As seen here, for example, using the Predicted MUF chart, the classical (actual) MUF during the month will reach at least 15 MHz on (approximately) 25 days of the month.

Also included in Figure 6.5 are the distributions about the median values. The distributions should be validated as well, not just the median values. One way to validate the median value and the distribution about the median of the MUF prediction is, for example, to listen to WWV on multiple frequencies and note how many days of the month each frequency was received at your location. Likewise, the median value and the distribution about the median signal strength on a given frequency for each day of the month can be plotted to validate the signal strength prediction. To reiterate, a month's worth of data is needed to validate a prediction, even if you're just validating the median values and not the distributions themselves.

In short, the propagation models in the major HF prediction programs available today are judged for accuracy mainly by the user. A radio amateur will lose confidence in a program that often predicts band openings that do not occur. Conversely, a program that is observed to consistently predict openings with a high degree of accuracy will gain a high level of confidence among users. With this in mind, for the radio amateur or the SWL, the selection of an HF prediction program usually boils down to how "user-friendly" it is, how easy it is to set up, how easy it is to interpret the output, *and how accurate it is over time.*

6.6 What the Models Are Missing

Although the models of the ionosphere have become sophisticated over the past several decades,

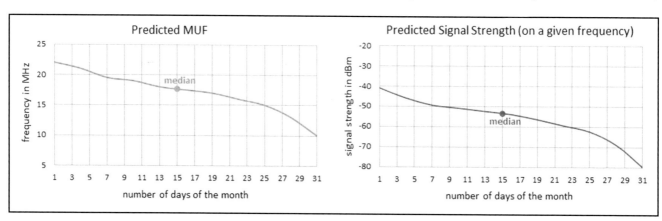

Figure 6.5 Predicted parameters that need validation.

Total daytime variability	Solar radiation contribution	Geomagnetic field activity contribution	Neutral atmosphere contribution
20%	3%	13%	15%

Table 6.1 Contributions by the three parameters that can cause the F2 region to vary.

there is one issue that none of them addresses and a couple issues that most do not address.

Neutral atmosphere contribution

The issue that none of them addresses originates from a paper by Henry Rishbeth and Michael Mendillo in 2001 [reference 10], as mentioned in Chapter 5.

The goal of the Rishbeth and Mendillo paper was to determine how much each of the solar radiation, geomagnetic field and neutral atmosphere activity parameters (events at ground level and in the lower atmosphere that couple to the ionosphere) contribute to the variation of the F2 region. The idea that events at ground level and in the lower atmosphere can

cause a variation in the ionosphere is not new. In a paper in 1968 by T.M. Georges [reference 11], the author wrote: "There is growing evidence that the periodicities of many, if not most, of the small-scale irregularities can be explained in terms of waves in the neutral atmosphere interacting with the ionized constituents of the upper atmosphere."

Rishbeth and Mendillo analyzed 34 years of day-time data (1957 – 1990) from 13 ionosondes. Their results are summarized in Table 6.1. These results are in terms of the standard deviation of the variation of the maximum F2 region electron density divided by the mean of the maximum F2 region electron density, and they are expressed as a percentage.

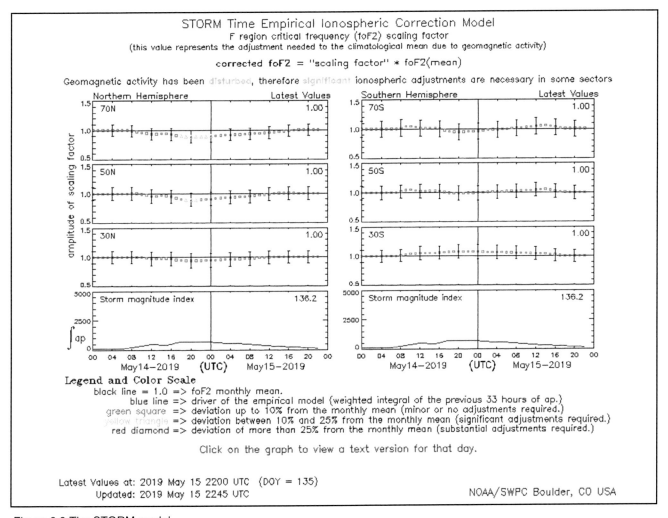

Figure 6.6 The STORM model.

As a check, because these values include standard deviations, $20\%^2$ should equal $3\%^2 + 13\%^2 + 15\%^2$. And it does.

What this tells us is that the variation in geomagnetic field activity and the variation in the neutral atmosphere contribute the most to the variation in the daytime F2 region. The variation in solar radiation comes in at a distant third.

We have parameters to measure solar radiation and geomagnetic field activity, but we don't yet have a parameter (or parameters) to measure what the neutral atmosphere is doing. It very well could be that any parameter (or parameters) for the neutral atmosphere will be tied to the period and amplitude of traveling ionospheric disturbances (TIDs).

A more recent study of the contribution of the three parameters to the variation of the F2 region maximum electron density was reported in 2018 [reference 12]. The conclusions published here are similar to those of Rishbeth and Mendillo.

STORM model

STORM is an empirical ionospheric correction model designed to capture the changes in the F2 region critical frequency (foF2) during geomagnetic storms. Data from 75 ionosonde stations and 43 geomagnetic storms were analyzed to design this model. The model is available at https://www.swpc.noaa.gov/products/storm-time-empirical-ionospheric-correction and is updated every three hours (in concert with the three-hour K index). Figure 6.6 is a sample output of this model.

The two hemispheres are broken out separately, and each is divided into three latitude bands. This is done for reasons related to the fact that geomagnetic storms can affect different parts of the world differently. The model uses the last 11 Kp values (these are converted to the equivalent ap values for actual use in the model). The results show the scaling factor to be applied to the monthly mean foF2.

Several of our propagation prediction programs allow for the input of a single K index to assess the impact of a geomagnetic storm on the F2 region of the ionosphere. Unfortunately, a single K index is *not* adequate. And, as mentioned earlier, the IRI-2016 model of the ionosphere is the only model at this time that includes the STORM model.

Above-the-MUF mode

Observations have shown that an operating frequency slightly above the classical (actual) MUF still will propagate. This is called an above-the-MUF mode, and it is thought that some form of scatter allows this condition to occur. Scatter implies loss, so there is additional loss incurred that many times can be tolerated — for example, along a path on one of our higher frequency bands that enjoys minimal ionospheric absorption.

At this time, VOACAP is the only propagation prediction program that has the above-the-MUF mode in its ionosphere model.

6.7   HF Propagation Prediction Programs

As mentioned throughout this book, the model of the ionosphere is a monthly median model, and it is correlated to a smoothed solar index, either the smoothed sunspot number or the smoothed 10.7 cm solar flux (given the smoothed values of both are highly correlated). But from where do we get the smoothed sunspot number or the smoothed 10.7 cm solar flux data?

For historic smoothed sunspot numbers up to and including November 2014, Chapter 2 gives V1.0 values in Appendix 1. You can use the V1.0 numbers as is.

For smoothed sunspot numbers for December 2014 and later, use the V2.0 numbers in Appendix 2 in Chapter 2, and multiply them by 0.7.

For future smoothed sunspot numbers and smoothed 10.7 cm solar flux, visit the Space Weather Prediction Center site at https://www.swpc.noaa.gov/products/predicted-sunspot-number-and-radio-flux. Use the "Sunspot Number Predicted" column (the data are presented in terms of the V2.0 record, so multiply those numbers by 0.7) or the "10.7 cm Radio Flux Predicted" column. Keep an eye on these data. They will change as Cycle 25 gets started and the predictions are updated.

An alternate option to using a smoothed solar index is to use what's called the effective sunspot number, which is abbreviated SSNe. The SSNe is the sunspot number that forces the model of the F2 region of the ionosphere to employ a "best fit" to the near real-time data from many ionosondes. In the words of Northwest Research Associates, Inc., the organization that produces the SSNe: "*The effective sunspot number index is defined as that SSN which will return a zero average-error between foF2 values generated from a model (to which the SSNe is input) and a set of foF2 observations. The SSNe is generated using mid-latitude foF2 observations from a single day as*

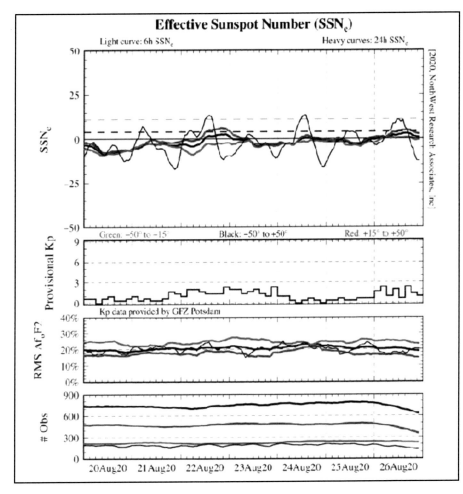

Figure 6.7 Sample SSNe and associated data.

input and is based on the URSI-88 model." Figure 6.7 is a sample plot of SSNe and associated data.

The SSNe will not yield a perfect fit to all the ionosonde data because worldwide ionospheric phenomena are not in lockstep. If the amount of ionization increases at Location A, it does not necessarily increase at Location B. In fact, ionization may increase at one location while it decreases at another location *at the same time.* The RMS error between SSNe and the observed foF2 is given in the third plot down, and typically runs 15-25%.

The heavy black curve of SSNe in the top plot (labeled 24h SSNe between -50° and +50° latitude) is probably the best one to use. Negative SSNe values need to be entered as 0 in your prediction program. For more information about SSNe, visit https://spawx.nwra.com/spawx/ssne24.html.

Now, below is a review of several propagation prediction programs of interest to the amateur and SWL communities.

MINIMUF-3.5

Because MINIMUF-3.5 was the first propagation prediction program available to amateur radio operators that ran on early home personal computers, some brief comments about this program are of interest.

In the December 1982, issue of *QST*, Robert Rose, K6GKU (SK) one of the co-authors of earlier editions of this book, introduced the MINIMUF-3.5 prediction program [reference 13]. Compared to today's standard, MINIMUF was crude. It was based on oblique sounder data instead of data from a worldwide net of vertical sounders. And, it only yielded MUF predictions; no signal strength predictions were computed.

Still, it could be considered the "father" of propagation predictions for the amateur radio community. Other prediction programs were spawned by MINIMUF. One such program was MUFplot by Base (2) Systems, which offered it for Apple, Commodore and IBM PC systems.

VOACAP

Voice of America Coverage Analysis Program, or VOACAP, was developed by Voice of America personnel from Ionospheric Communications Analysis and Prediction, or IONCAP. IONCAP was developed in the late 1970s by the Institute of Tele-communication Sciences (ITS), U.S. Department of Commerce, Boulder, Colorado, as a mainframe program. IONCAP became a standard by which other programs were judged.

VOACAP is an improved and corrected version of IONCAP, retaining all of the theory developed and used in the 1975-1985 timeframe. It is well-respected both as a propagation prediction program and as a propagation analysis program for reasons related to the variety of data it outputs. VOACAP has an added advantage that it is free.

To download VOACAP, follow the directions in Table 6.2.

```
go to http://greg-hand.com/versions/

download the executable file "itshfbc_180417a.exe"

run the executable file to install VOACAP
```

Table 6.2 Downloading VOACAP.

Assuming everything proceeds well during the installation, the user should have three generic propagation programs on their system: VOACAP, ICEPAC, and REC533. VOACAP is what we seek. ICEPAC (Ionospheric Communications Enhanced Profile Analysis and Circuit) is IONCAP with an improved model of the high-latitude ionosphere. REC533 is the International Telecommunication Union (ITU) HF planning model. We only will address VOACAP here, not ICEPAC nor REC533. Additionally, we only will address the VOACAP point-to-point version (predictions for Point A to Point B). We will not address any of the area coverage versions (i.e., predictions for a wide area of the world).

Now, let's get into running a propagation prediction using VOACAP. We'll run a prediction from Fort Wayne, Indiana, to the Cayman Islands (ZF) for January 2001 at 2300 UTC with V1.0 smoothed sunspot number of 109. Remember, our prediction program requires a smoothed solar index to output monthly median values, and if you're using the V2.0 smoothed sunspot numbers, be sure to multiply them by 0.7.

When you click on the VOACAP Point icon, the "VOACAP Point-to-Point data input" screen will appear. Here's where we set up all the parameters for the path we want.

For Method, let's go with Method 30, which is annotated as Short/Long smoothing (7-10,000 km) – Recommended. For the Year, select 2001. For Co-

efficients, go with CCIR (Oslo). The other coefficients (URSI) have not been validated as much as the CCIR coefficients. For Time, input 2300 UTC by selecting 2300 to 2300. For Groups, input 1.00 for monthly median results centered on the middle of the month. You can center the predictions on others days of the month by using, for example, 1.07 – this would center the predictions on Jan. 7. Input SSN = 109 (our assumed smoothed sunspot number for January 2001). For Transmitter, input latitude and longitude of 41.00 N and 85.00 W, respectively, and name it Fort Wayne. For Receiver, input 19.50 N and 80.80 W and name it ZF.

Next is Path. Toggle it to Short path. It shows the distances (kilometers, nautical miles, and statute miles) and the heading from the Transmitter to the Receiver. Toggle it to Long path to run a long-path prediction. For Frequencies, input 24.9 and 28.3 (these are in MHz).

Under System, select 150 for Noise (this is -150dBW at 3 MHz in a 1-Hz bandwidth – this is a rural noise environment). Select a 3.0 degree Min Angle (it's tough to put energy at lower elevation angles, especially on the lower frequency bands). Select the default 90% required Reliability. Select the default 3dB Multi Tol, and select the default 0.1 ms for Multi Del. For Req SNR (Required Signal-to-Noise Ratio), input 48 dB (which is in a 1-Hz bandwidth) as we're running the prediction for SSB. Select Normal for Absorp. Table 6.3 gives recommended required SNRs for various modes. VOACAP requires SNRs in a 1-Hz bandwidth.

For Fprob, use 1 for foE, foF1 and foF2. Use 0 for foEs. These are scaling factors used to vary the monthly median critical frequencies. For the summer months, you may want to try foEs = 0.7 (this comes from IONCAP).

For Tx Antenna, which is in Fort Wayne, select Sample.23 (horizontal dipole with 0.5 wavelength elements at 0.25 wavelengths above ground) in the

Mode	Required SNR in 1Hz bandwidth
AM (6 kHz)	51
SSB (3 kHz)	48
CW (500 Hz)	31
JT65 (2500 Hz)	9
FT8 (2500 Hz)	13
FT4 (2500 Hz)	16

Table 6.3 Required SNRs for various modes.

```
          CCIR Coefficients        ~METHOD 30   VOACAP 16.1207W   PAGE    1

    Jan    2001            SSN = 109.              Minimum Angle= 3.000 degrees
    Fort Wayne            ZF                     AZIMUTHS          N. MI.      KM
    41.00 N   85.00 W - 19.50 N   80.80 W   169.28  351.44   1308.6    2423.3
    XMTR  2-30 IONCAP #23[samples\SAMPLE.23   ] Az=169.3 OFFaz=360.0  0.100kW
    RCVR  2-30 IONCAP #23[samples\SAMPLE.23   ] Az=351.4 OFFaz=  0.0
    3 MHz NOISE = -150.0 dBW     REQ. REL = 90%    REQ. SNR = 48.0 dB
    MULTIPATH POWER TOLERANCE =  3.0 dB   MULTIPATH DELAY TOLERANCE =  0.100 ms


    23.0 25.9 24.9 28.3  0.0  0.0  0.0  0.0  0.0  0.0  0.0  0.0  0.0 FREQ
         1F2  1F2  1F2    -    -    -    -    -    -    -    -    -  MODE
         9.8  8.2 11.9    -    -    -    -    -    -    -    -    -  TANGLE
         8.6  8.5  8.7    -    -    -    -    -    -    -    -    -  DELAY
         341  303  392    -    -    -    -    -    -    -    -    -  V HITE
        0.50 0.66 0.14    -    -    -    -    -    -    -    -    -  MUFday
         131  132  153    -    -    -    -    -    -    -    -    -  LOSS
          20   20   -2    -    -    -    -    -    -    -    -    -  DBU
        -111 -112 -133    -    -    -    -    -    -    -    -    -  S DBW
        -176 -175 -177    -    -    -    -    -    -    -    -    -  N DBW
          65   63   44    -    -    -    -    -    -    -    -    -  SNR
           9    3   31    -    -    -    -    -    -    -    -    -  RPWRG
        0.80 0.86 0.42    -    -    -    -    -    -    -    -    -  REL
        0.00 0.00 0.00    -    -    -    -    -    -    -    -    -  MPROB
        0.37 0.44 0.18    -    -    -    -    -    -    -    -    -  S PRB
        23.6 15.2 25.0    -    -    -    -    -    -    -    -    -  SIG LW
         8.8  9.4 22.5    -    -    -    -    -    -    -    -    -  SIG UP
        25.4 17.9 26.8    -    -    -    -    -    -    -    -    -  SNR LW
        10.5 11.0 23.2    -    -    -    -    -    -    -    -    -  SNR UP
         4.1  2.8  5.5    -    -    -    -    -    -    -    -    -  TGAIN
         4.1  2.8  5.5    -    -    -    -    -    -    -    -    -  RGAIN
```

Figure 6.8 Sample VOACAP run.

TxAnt field. Input 7 in the Design field (this is 7 dBi, which is the typical gain of a horizontal dipole at the given height over average ground), and click "at Rx" to point it on the heading to the Cayman Islands identified in the Path parameters. Set the power to .1 kW (100w). Likewise, select Sample.23 for the Rx Antenna, which is in the Cayman Islands, input 7 in the Gain field, and click "at Tx" to point it toward Fort Wayne.

OK, everything is inputted. Now, click on "Run" and then "Circuit" to run the prediction from Fort Wayne to the Cayman Islands. The "Circuit" option gives tabular results for the hour range selected. The other option you may want to use is "Graph." It provides the results as plots. What you obtain with the "Circuit" option is a header with all the parameters you selected and the prediction. The actual prediction should appear similar to that shown in Figure 6.8. Note that future versions of VOACAP might have slightly different prediction values depending on what was responsible for pushing up the revision level.

The first column is the time. There's only one set of data as we're only looking at one time. The sec-

ond column is the predicted median MUF – 25.9 MHz for this path. Note that MUFday, which indicates the number of days in the month that the classical (actual) MUF should be at least 25.9 MHz, is 0.50 (as it should be, given 25.9 MHz is the monthly median value). The third and fourth columns are the desired frequencies. Let's focus on the 28.3 MHz prediction.

The MODE says it is one hop via the F2 region (1F2). The TANGLE says the elevation angle needed out of Fort Wayne for this mode is 11.9 degrees (our assumption of 3 degrees minimum is OK). The DELAY says it takes 8.7 milliseconds for the RF to get from Fort Wayne to the Cayman Islands via the 1F2 mode. The V HITE is the virtual height of the reflection point in the F2 region. The MUFday of 0.14 says 10 meters should be open on about four days (0.14 times 31) of this January month (unfortunately we don't know which specific days of the month these are) at 2300 UTC with a smoothed sunspot number of 109. The MUFday is lower than 0.50 because 28.3 MHz is higher than the 25.9 MHz predicted median MUF. Also note that the MUFday

Signal power in dBW	Signal power in dBm	S-units
-93	-63	10 dB over S9
-98	-68	5 dB over S9
-103	-73	S9
-109	-79	S8
-115	-85	S7
-121	-91	S6
-127	-97	S5
-133	-103	S4
-139	-109	S3
-145	-115	S2
-151	-121	S1

Table 6.4 Conversion between power and S-units.

for 24.9 MHz is 0.66 – it's higher than 0.50 because 24.9 MHz is lower than the predicted median MUF of 25.9 MHz.

The LOSS is the median total path loss in dB. The DBU is the predicted median field strength at the Cayman Islands in dB above 1 microvolt (μV) per meter. The S DBW is the median signal power at the Cayman Islands in dB above 1 watt. Likewise, N DBW is the median noise power at the Cayman Islands in dB above 1 watt. Table 6.4 converts dBW

to S-units (this assumes S9 = 50 μV and an S-unit is 6 dB – this is an old Collins Radio standard to which receivers of today may not adhere).

The SNR is the difference between S DBW and N DBW. At 28.3 MHz, the REL is the probability that the predicted monthly median SNR (-133 - (-177) = 44 dB) is exceeded by the REQ SNR (as seen, we inputted 48 dB). Thus, we'd expect the REL to be less than 0.50; indeed it is, and it tells us the required SNR is predicted to be met on only 13 days of the month (0.42 times 31). There are some additional parameters listed in Figure 6.8; they are explained in the program's manual, which can be downloaded.

As mentioned earlier, VOACAP also has graphs of the various output parameters, not just the tabular data as shown in Figure 6.8. Figure 6.9 is a sample plot from the preceding prediction that shows signal power in dBW (the colors), the predicted median MUF (black line, 50% probability) and the frequency of optimum traffic (FOT; blue line, 90% probability).

The desired frequencies, in our example, are shown by the thin horizontal black lines. It's easy to discern when the predicted median MUF is highest during the day and what to expect in terms of signal strength (using the conversion data in Table 6.4).

One final comment: if you're thinking about using ICEPAC, be aware this prediction program has *not*

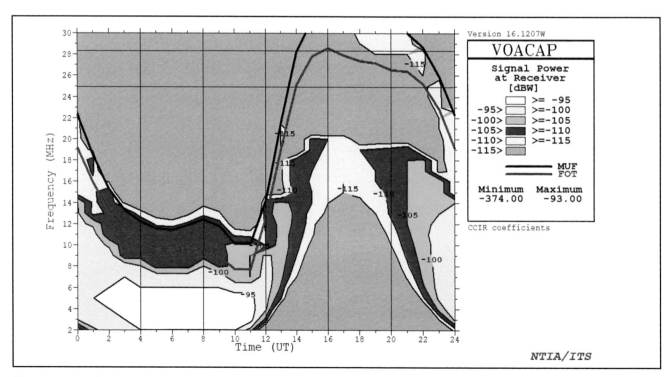

Figure 6.9 The SDBW graph.

been validated to the extent VOACAP has. So caution is the word.

VOACAP Derivatives

With VOACAP being so well-respected as both a propagation prediction and propagation analysis program, it's no wonder several derivatives of this program have been developed.

For example, there is an online VOACAP prediction application at https://www.voacap.com/hf/ by Jari Perkiömäki, OH6BG, James Watson, HZ1JW, and Juho Juopperi, OH8GLV. The operator is able to set the transmitter and receiver locations at the top. At the upper-right are four drop-down menus that allow for the setting of various parameters. A worldwide map with the selected path is displayed, with provisions available to change the date and the time to determine the location of the terminator (the line around earth separating daylight and darkness). The operator then can view propagation charts (plotted data) or a propagation wheel, as shown in Figure 6.10, that shows the path reliability for all bands and all times using color-codes.

An on-line propagation service based on VOACAP is available at https://www.k6tu.net/. Stuart Phillips, K6TU, developed this application with the goal of removing the learning curve behind VOACAP. At the same time, he sought to automate the generation of enough propagation predictions so as to enable their use as a planning and strategy tool for use in contesting and DXing. This website site is geared toward active contesters and DXers. There is a small yearly fee for the service.

VOAProp is another program that employs the VOACAP forecasting software. It was developed by Julian Moss, G4ILO, to satisfy the need for a program that would show what HF band propagation should be like on a particular day and on a particular band. Unfortunately G4ILO is a Silent Key (SK; that is, he has died), but the program is still available at this writing. It was the successor to G4ILO's HFProp prediction program. VOAProp provides a simplified graphical interface for VOACAP so that you can obtain an overall idea of how propagation should be at a given time and date without getting bogged down in details. Steve Nichols, G0KYA, chairman of the Propagation Studies Committee of the Radio Society of Great Britain, notes that VOAProp will never be updated but "it is a solid little program that is easy to use." VOAProp is available at http://www.g4ilo.com/voaprop.html.

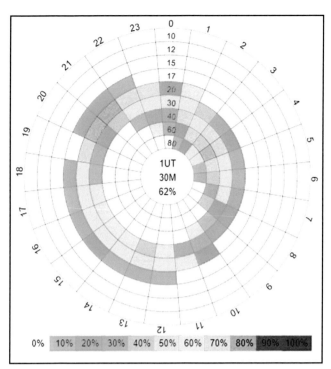

Figure 6.10 Propagation wheel.

HamCAP is another program that uses the VOACAP forecasting software but with its own "front end." It was developed by Alex Shovkoplyas, VE3NEA. VE3NEA also developed DX Atlas and the FAROS software to monitor the NCDXF/IARU beacons (see Chapter 5, Section 5.4.4 and Reference 3 of Chapter 5). HamCAP can work in conjunction with DX Atlas, yielding a worldwide map in three different projections with the ability to add one of several ionospheric parameters to the map, or the auroral ovals or the gray line. HamCAP is available at http://www.dxatlas.com/HamCap/.

ACE-HF (Animation Communication Effectiveness - High Frequency) uses both the IONCAP and VOACAP ionospheric models to provide propagation movies. Information about ACE-HF can be found at http://www.longwaveinc.com/software_solutions/. A review of ACE-HF was done by Tomas Hood, NW7US, *CQ* Magazine's current Propagation column editor; the review can be found at http://www.hfradio.org/ace-hf/.

W6ELProp

W6ELProp is the Windows version of the popular MINIPROP (1985-1989) and MINIPROP PLUS (1992-1996) DOS versions. W6ELProp was released in early 2001, and it underwent a number of revisions before reaching the final Version 2.70 in 2002.

W6ELProp was written for Windows 95, Windows 98, Windows ME, Windows XP, Windows 2000 and Windows NT. Unfortunately, author Sheldon Shallon, W6EL, became a Silent Key in April 2015, and it is believed that the source code was never released. Problems have been discovered using W6ELProp with Windows Vista and Windows 7, 8 and 10. Installing the program in the administrator mode and other such tactics seem to help.

W6ELProp is very user-friendly. It's free and can be downloaded at www.qsl.net/w6elprop. After it's installed and started, click on the Options menu. In the Default Terminal folder, enter your call and your latitude and longitude (from www.qrz.com, for example).

Next go to the Frequencies and Constants folder. For the frequencies, enter the frequencies for which you'd like predictions. Note W6ELProp only allows frequencies down to 3.0 MHz. That is, the software does not perform predictions for 160 meters.

For Additive Signal Level Constants, input your station-specifics in dB referenced to 100 watts and a dipole. For example, if you have an older 1000-watt amp that does 80-10 meters but excludes the WARC bands (30, 17 and 12 meters), you'd add 10 dB [10 log (1000 W/100 W)] to all but the WARC frequencies. If you have a tri-bander for the 20-, 15-, and 10-meter bands, then add an additional 6 dB on those frequencies (that's roughly the gain of a small tri-bander over a dipole). Table 6.5 shows the frequencies and additive signal-level constants for the above scenario.

In the Prediction Parameters folder, go with Minimum Radiation Angle = 1.0 degree (we're a little optimistic here), Noise Bandwidth = 3000 Hz for SSB (use 500 Hz for CW), Signal Level Suppression Threshold = 0 dB, Man-Made Noise Environment as dictated by your QTH, and put a check in the Suppress Zero-Availability Predictions box.

In the User Preferences folder, go with Sunspot Number for the Primary Solar Index, Signal Levels for the Primary Signal Display, UTC for Time Display, 3 minutes for map Auto Upgrade Interval, and Low for Frequency Map Resolution.

Now click on the Save My Settings and Exit button. Don't forget to do this! You should now be back at the main screen.

Click on the Predictions menu. Then select On-Screen. Hit "enter" and the default call, latitude, and longitude that you entered earlier should show up on the left side of the window as Terminal A. For this example, the author's default data will be used.

Frequencies (MHz)	Additive Signal Level Constants (dB)
3.7	10.0
7.1	10.0
10.1	0.0
14.2	16.0
18.1	0.0
21.2	16.0
24.9	0.0
28.3	16.0

Table 6.5 Additive Signal Level Constants.

Let's run a prediction from Fort Wayne, Indiana to Argentina. If you don't know the prefix for Argentina, click on Select from Atlas and select Search by Name. Scroll down until you see Argentina. Highlight it, and then click OK. The prefix, the latitude, the longitude, and the name should show up as Terminal B. For a Date, let's select Dec. 15, 2003, which is typed using the format MM/DD/YY.

For Solar Index, earlier we selected Sunspot Number as the Primary Solar Index. The smoothed sunspot number should be entered here. For December 2003, we'll enter 47. For the K Index, enter -1, which indicates the predictions will be for an average K index (recall the earlier comment about using a single K index to determine the effect of a geomagnetic storm).

Now click on OK. After a couple of seconds, data should appear specific to the chosen path: the latitude and longitude of both terminals, sunrise and sunset for both terminals, the bearings, and the short- and long-path lengths. Click on Show Predictions, and a screen should appear as shown in Figure 6.11.

One of the most obvious features here is the difference observed between the data for the lower frequencies (80, 40, and 30 meters) and the higher frequencies (17, 15, 12, and 10 meters). They're essentially 180 degrees out of phase. This is because ionospheric absorption drives propagation on the lower bands, so they're best only during the night, whereas the amount of ionization (which is linked to the MUF) drives propagation on the higher bands, so they're best during the day.

The first column in the figure is the time in UTC. The second column is the predicted median MUF. At 1700 UTC, the classical, or actual, MUF on half the days of the month (the median) will be at least 29.7 MHz. On the other half of the days of the month, actual MUF will be lower than 29.7 MHz. To reiterate from the VOACAP predictions, we don't know which days are best.

The letters A, B, C, and D in each operating frequency column refer to the probability (in terms of the number of days of the month) that the desired frequency is below the predicted monthly median MUF. This probability is called Availability, and is the equivalent to MUFday in VOACAP. W6ELProp puts Availability into four categories, and the definitions of the limits for each category are at the bottom of the prediction page. For example, the 28.3 MHz column at 1530 UTC shows a C. This means 10 meters should be open on 8 to 16 days of the month (25% to 50%). From 1600 to 1900 UTC the probability increases to 16 to 24 days of the month (B = 50% to 75%).

Each frequency column also has a number. The number is the predicted monthly median signal strength in dB above 0.5 μV. Assuming S9 is 50 μV and an S-unit is 6 dB (as was the case in the VOACAP prediction), the dB values in W6ELProp translate to S-units, as follows in Table 6.6.

For 28.3 MHz from 1600 UTC to 1900 UTC, the monthly median signal level is predicted to be about S8 (36 dB ref 0.5 μV). Being a median value, on 50% of the days of the month, the signal strength could be somewhat above that level, and on the other 50% of the days, it will be below the predicted value. Again, we can't know which days will be best.

One last comment about W6ELProp: check out the Rectangular Map feature under the Map menu.

```
                    W6ELProp Short-Path Prediction for 12/15/2003

       TERMINAL A: 41.00 N  85.40 W  K9LA        Sunrise/Set: 1302/2212 UTC  Bearing to B: 160.3 deg
       TERMINAL B: 36.50 S  61.00 W  Argentina   Sunrise/Set: 0847/2311 UTC  Bearing to A: 341.6 deg
       SSN:  47.0  Flux: 103.2  K: Average                                   Path Length:  8970 km

                                    SIGNAL LEVELS IN dB ABOVE 0.5 μV
   UTC   MUF    3.7 MHz   7.1 MHz  10.1 MHz  14.2 MHz  18.1 MHz  21.2 MHz  24.9 MHz  28.3 MHz
   0000  12.3    51 A     48 A     45 A      48 D
   0030  11.1    51 A     48 A     45 B      48 D
   0100  10.8    40 A     48 A     45 B      48 D
   0130  10.5    53 A     48 A     45 B      48 D
   0200  10.4    53 A     48 A     45 B      48 D
   0230  10.4    53 A     48 A     45 B      48 D
   0300  10.5    53 A     48 A     45 B      48 D
   0330  10.6    53 A     48 A     45 B      48 D
   0400  10.8    53 A     48 A     45 B      48 D
   0430  10.4    53 A     48 A     45 B      48 D
   0500  10.7    53 A     48 A     45 B      48 D
   0530  11.0    53 A     48 A     45 B      48 D
   0600  11.0    53 A     48 A     45 B      48 D
   0630  11.1    53 A     48 A     45 A      48 D
   0700  11.3    53 A     48 A     45 A      48 D
   0730  11.5    53 A     48 A     45 A      48 D
   0800  11.6    53 A     48 A     45 A      48 D
   0830  11.8    57 A     47 A     45 A      48 D
   0900  11.1    50 A     46 A     44 B      48 D
   0930  10.6    29 A     47 A     43 B      47 D
   1000  10.6    24 A     30 A     45 B      46 D
   1030  11.4     5 A      7 D     27 C      44 D
   1100  12.0             21 A     24 B      43 D
   1130  13.1                      26 A
   1200  14.2                       6 D
   1230  16.4                       2 C      33 A
   1300  17.3                       1 A      20 C     31 D
   1330  20.2                                18 A     30 A     37 C      28 D
   1400  22.6                                16 A     29 A     36 B      27 D
   1430  24.7                                15 B     28 A     36 A      27 C      37 D
   1500  26.5                                14 A     25 A     35 B      26 B      37 D
   1530  27.9                                13 A     12 A     35 A      26 A      36 C
   1600  28.9                                12 A     12 A     35 A      26 A      36 B
   1630  29.5                                12 A     12 A     34 A      26 A      36 B
   1700  29.7                                12 A     12 A     34 A      26 A      36 B
   1730  29.7                                12 A     12 A     35 A      26 A      36 B
   1800  29.5                                13 A     27 A     35 A      26 A      36 B
   1830  29.0                                14 A     28 A     35 A      26 A      37 B
   1900  28.4                                15 A     28 A     36 A      27 A      37 B
   1930  27.5                                18 A     29 A     37 A      27 A      37 C
   2000  26.2                                20 A     30 A     37 A      28 B      38 D
   2030  24.7                       1 A      20 A     31 A     38 A      28 C      38 D
   2100  23.0                       7 A      22 A     33 A     39 A      29 D      39 D
   2130  21.0                      14 A      39 A     34 A     40 C      30 D
   2200  19.5             6 A      18 A      41 A     35 A     41 D
   2230  17.5            20 A      22 A      43 A     37 C     42 D
   2300  16.0    19 A    34 A      41 A      46 A     38 D
   2330  14.2    44 A    32 A      44 A      48 B     40 D

   Availabilities  A: 75 - 100%   B: 50 - 75%   C: 25 - 50%   D: 1 - 25%
   Signal levels suppressed if below 0 dB relative to 0.5 μV or if predicted availability is zero
```

Figure 6.11 W6ELProp prediction.

Signal level in dB ref 0.5 uV	Signal power in dBm	S-units
50	-63	10 dB over S9
45	-68	5 dB over S9
40	-73	S9
34	-79	S8
28	-85	S7
22	-91	S6
16	-97	S5
10	-103	S4
4	-110	S3
-2	-116	S2
-8	-121	S1

Table 6.6 Translating W6ELProp signal levels to dBm and S-units.

Figure 6.12 is this map at 0100 UTC for the prediction described here.

This map is great for visualizing openings on the lower bands, where the dark ionosphere provides the best nighttime propagation. For example, at 0100 UTC, the path from Fort Wayne to Argentina should be open on the lower bands. Earlier it was mentioned that W6ELProp only supports analyses at frequencies down to 3.0 MHz. This mapping feature will bridge this gap for wavelengths down to 160 meters. As

well, it's not bad for contemplating operations on 80, 60, 40 and 30 meters, either!

W6ELProp also provides plots of various parameters, not just tabular data as in Figure 6.11.

Non-VOACAP Prediction Programs

Advanced Stand Alone Prediction System, or ASAPS, provides the prediction of skywave communication system performance in the MF and HF radio spectrum (1-30 MHz) and basic surface wave performance in the medium frequency (300 kHz - 3 MHz) and low HF (3-5 MHz) ranges. It is based on an ionospheric model developed by Space Weather Services and ITU-R/CCIR models. It uses a T-index (named for its developer, Jack Turner) for input, which is derived from observed values of maximum ionospheric frequencies. The T-index can be best regarded as an "effective sunspot number." It's akin to the SSNe parameter that was discussed earlier. ASAPS is offered for sale by Space Weather Services, Bureau of Meteorology, Australian Government. Information can be found at https://www. sws.bom.gov.au/Products_and_Services/1/2.

Predtest is offered by Gwyn Williams, G4FKH. It can be found at http://www.predtest.uk/. The prediction engine used, which is ITURHFProp (also known as REC533 as mentioned earlier), is the latest offering from the ITU (International Telecommunication Union). Worldwide predictions only are run from the

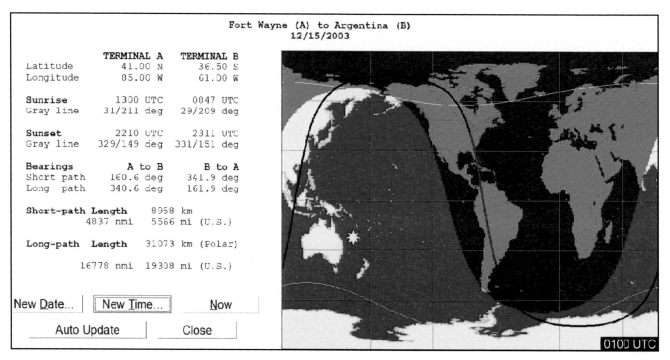

Figure 6.12 W6ELProp mapping feature.

central United Kingdom. Thus, this program is applicable only for those in that area. The predictions are used in the RSGB magazine *Radio Communications*, also known as *RadCom*.

Ray Tracing Programs

There are two ray tracing programs available for amateur radio community use. These programs, which can trace an electromagnetic ray through the ionospheric, incorporate provisions that take into account:

1) the effect of the Earth's magnetic field, and
2) collisions between electrons and neutral atmospheric constituents for ionospheric absorption calculations.

Although these programs could be used for propagation predictions, ray traces generally take a long time to run; as such, these programs are best considered as propagation analysis tools.

Proplab Pro V3 is a Windows® program offered for sale by Solar Terrestrial Dispatch in the province of Alberta, Canada. This program is the more user-friendly of the two. There are many parameters to properly input for an accurate ray trace, and this is another reason why it is more of a propagation analysis tool than a propagation prediction tool. Proplab Pro V3 uses the IRI-2007 model of the ionosphere. Figure 6.13 is a sample ray trace.

This sample ray trace shows the lower frequencies don't travel as high into the ionosphere and so, take shorter hops. Eventually, as transmit frequency is increased, the ray goes through the ionosphere (10.65 MHz). This is the point where the ionization is insufficient to refract the signal back to Earth at the given elevation angle of 5 degrees.

Two options are available for ray tracing: 2D ray-tracing (two-dimensional; only straight paths) and 3D ray tracing (three dimensional; skewed paths). Visit http://shop.spacew.com/ for prices and ordering instructions.

PHaRLAP (Provision of High-Frequency Raytracing Laboratory for Propagation studies) is a Matlab toolbox (Matlab is a numerical computing environment) for the study and modeling of the propagation of radio waves in the earth's ionosphere). PHaRLAP provides 2D and fully magneto-ionic 3D numerical ray-tracing engines. PHaRLAP can use the IRI-2016 model of the ionosphere or a user-specified model (applicable in solar eclipse studies, for example). Visit https://www.dst.defence.gov.au/opportunity/pharlap-

provision-high-frequency-raytracing-laboratory-propagation-studies for more information.

Just remember that both of these programs use a monthly median model of the F2 region.

Don't Want to Mess Around with Computers for Predictions?

If you don't want to bother with setting up the various input parameters on your computer to run predictions, there are two options available for non-computer users.

The first option is to use the Master DX Propagation Charts and the Master Short-Skip Propagation Charts in Chapter 4 of this book. The short-skip predictions also are very useful for sporadic-E propagation in the summer months, an area in which the ionospheric models are somewhat lacking.

The second option is the propagation predictions compiled by Dean Straw, N6BV, found in the ARRL Antenna Book CD. The predictions included are applicable to more than 240 different worldwide locations. The data are presented in tabular format.

6.8   Future of HF Prediction Programs

Looking to the future, efforts are underway to better understand the day-to-day variability of the F2 region. Solar radiation indeed instigates ionization, but geomagnetic field activity and events at ground level and in the lower atmosphere that couple to the ionosphere also contribute to the amount of ionization at any given point on Earth.

As research into those events at ground level and in the lower atmosphere that couple to the ionosphere continues, parameters to define these events and the effects on the ionosphere of these events will be developed. Once understood, relevant data then can be an inputted to our prediction programs. Eventually we may have daily propagation predictions incorporating such phenomena.

Until this effort reaches a more advanced state, assimilative models of the ionosphere will be further developed. Assimilative, as mentioned at the end of Section 6.4, means real-time ionosonde measurements are taken into the model. Real-time ionosonde data or real-time total electron content (TEC) data will be used to develop techniques that can be used for real-time ionospheric predictions.

Experimental and theoretical research into the lower atmosphere and lower ionosphere will bring a better understanding of the D region. Then, our

Figure 6.13 Proplab ray trace at night.

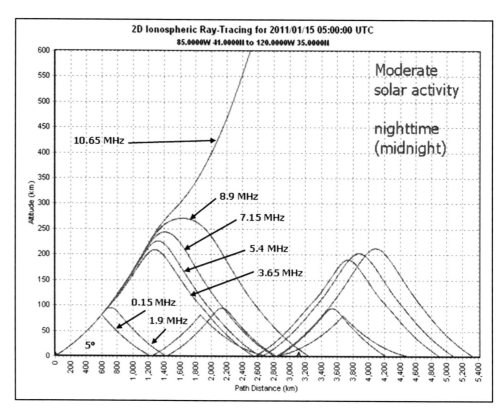

model of the D region for ionospheric absorption calculations will be improved.

Perhaps, one day, our understanding of how sporadic-E clouds form will be completed. This data then will be a part of our ionospheric prediction models. We'll be able to accurately predict on what day, at what time and to where sporadic-E is available. Who knows? Sporadic-E may then not be known as "sporadic" anymore!

Finally, propagation prediction programs likely will find their way into our radios as part of the front panel menu. When we turn the radio on, the space weather parameters will be downloaded and propagation on the selected band will be displayed. It may even be possible that propagation to specific or "needed" countries, having already been identified in your radio because of your DX chasing activities, will be displayed, giving you a leg up on the competition. There are lots of possibilities here.

As they say, "The best is yet to come!"

6.9   Summary

We have reviewed many HF propagation prediction programs, some in great detail. Did we compare their outputs with a common scenario? No, that would be meaningless, as has been noted earlier. For the detailed reviews, we used the examples provided because we are comfortable with them.

The best way to find the "right" program for you is to acquire an HF prediction program, either one of the free ones or one in your price range. Exercise it, and compare the results with your "on-the-air" observations. You will find cases where the predictions will be "right-on." Then again, there will be cases where the predictions are "dead-wrong."

Compare notes with friends, especially those using other programs. The program that does the best job on your HF circuits probably will be the one you finally select. But only *you* can decide which is best for you.

Lastly, there are many other prediction programs that have come and gone in the past several decades. For example, some old DOS programs on 3.5-inch disks and 5¼-inch floppy disks still can be found that have unique (and useful!) information and unique formats the newer programs don't have. Examples are DXAID by Oldfield, and GCPATHS and IONPARA by Brown, NM7M (SK). Every once in a while, even these programs can come in handy!

6.10   References

1. https://k9la.us/Feb16_Development_of_the_Model_of_the_Ionosphere_with_Feb_2017_Update.pdf.

2. Ionospheric Radio Propagation, National Bureau of Standards Circular 462, U.S. Department of Commerce, June 25, 1948.

3. *Ionospheric Predictions for April 1963*, Central Radio Propagation Laboratory, U.S. Department of Commerce, Jan. 25, 1963.

4. Radio Noise, Recommendation ITU-R P.372-13, *P Series Radiowave Propagation*, International Telecommunication Union, 07/2015.

5. Jones, William B., and Gallet, Roger M., Representation of Diurnal and Geographic Variations of Ionospheric Data by Numerical Methods, *Journal of Research of the National Bureau of Standards-D, Radio Propagation*, Vol. 66D, No. 4, July-August 1962.

6. Report 340, CCIR Atlas of Ionospheric Parameters, International Radio Consultative Committee (CCIR), Geneva, 1983.

7. Fricker, R., A Microcomputer Program for the Critical Frequency and Height of the F layer of the Ionosphere, 4th International Conference on Antennas and Propagation (ICAP 85), 16-19 April 1985, pp. 546-550.

8. Brown, Robert R., NM7M (SK), *Validation of an F-Layer Algorithm for the Ionosphere*, Communications Quarterly, Spring 1997.

9. Rose, R. B., J. N. Martin (NOSC), and P.H. Levine (Megatek Corp), "MINIMUF-3: A Simplified HF MUF Prediction," Naval Oceans Systems Center Technical Report TR186, San Diego, California, Feb. 1, 1978.

10. Rishbeth, H. and Mendillo, M., Patterns of F2-layer Variability, *Journal of Atmospheric and Solar-Terrestrial Physics*, 63 (2001), 1661-1680.

11. Georges, T.M., Effects of Ionospheric Motions and Irregularities on HF Radio Propagation, pages 137-151, in Low-Frequency Waves and Irregularities in the Ionosphere, edited by N. D'Angelo, Astrophysics and Space Science Library, 1968.

12. Fang, Tzu-Wei, Fuller-Rowell, T., Yudin, V., Matsuo, T., Viereck, R., Quantifying the Sources of Ionosphere Day-to-day Variability, *Journal of Geophysical Research: Space Physics*, Oct. 17, 2018.

13. Rose, R. B., MINIMUF: A Simplified MUF Prediction Program for Microcomputers, *QST*, December 1982, pp. 36-38.

Chapter 7

Uncommon HF and VHF Ionospheric Propagation

Uncommon (but extremely rewarding, at times) ionospheric conditions can affect radio signals at frequencies well up into the VHF band (30 to 300 MHz), although at HF (3 to 30 MHz), many uncommon (or unusual) effects are masked by conventional propagation modes. In the VHF band, however, unusual ionospheric effects appear more pronounced because signal propagation in this band usually involves line-of-sight paths over relatively short distances.

In this chapter we review some uncommon conditions under which ionospheric propagation may be possible on the 50 and 144 MHz amateur bands and the characteristics of such openings, which may result from regular F_2-layer reflection, sporadic-E (Es), aurora, meteor ionization, transequatorial propagation (TEP) and ionospheric scatter. We also will review some unusual propagation phenomena observed on the HF bands, including auroral-E (Eau), gray line propagation and propagation over paths that extend more than halfway around the world (long-path openings).

7.1 VHF Propagation By Regular F_2-layer Ionization

During most of any solar cycle, regular F_2-layer ionospheric openings generally occur at frequencies as high as about 30 MHz. However, F2-layer ionospheric openings may be possible on frequencies as high as, or higher than, 50 MHz during years of extremely high solar activity. In fact, transcontinental openings on the 50 MHz band took place for many hours at a time during the maximum periods of solar activity for Cycles 18 through 22. Openings on 50 MHz were observed as well between the United States and all other continents during these cycles' maxima. In particular, the maximum of Cycle 22 (1988-1992: smoothed V1.0 sunspot numbers in the range of 94-158) was characterized by a sustained period of high solar activity that resulted in many 50 MHz DX openings. Even Cycles 23 and 24, which were, relatively speaking, smaller cycles, provided short periods of 50 MHz F2 propagation during the winter months around their solar maxima.

For smoothed V1.0 sunspot numbers greater than about 120, and for stations in the United States, F2-layer openings on the 50 MHz band, if they do occur, peak during the winter months to Europe and the Far East and during the spring and fall months to Africa, South America, Australasia, and other areas in the more-or-less southerly direction. Signal levels often are exceptionally strong during these openings, and communications over great distances may be possible with relatively low power levels.

During periods of high solar activity, regular F2 layer openings on 50 MHz are a daytime phenomenon, with the band opening to Europe during the hours before noon, to Africa during the noontime period, to South America during the afternoon and, sometimes, extending into the early evening hours, and to the Far East and Australasia during the late afternoon and early evening hours, local standard time in the United States.

Propagation conditions in the 28 MHz band often provide indications of 50 MHz openings during the fall, winter, and spring months. When F2-layer openings are observed on 28 MHz over distances of 1,200 miles or less, the classical MUF is rising rapidly, and 50 MHz also may be open in the same general direction, but over a considerably greater distance.

There is little likelihood of any F2 layer, 50 MHz openings taking place during periods of low solar activity.

The regular F2 layer of the ionosphere is never sufficiently ionized to propagate signals on the 144 MHz band. This would require an F2-layer critical frequency of greater than 48 MHz. However, during Cycle 22, especially in the winters of 1988-1989 and 1989-1990, F2 values in the southwest and on the West Coast of the United States regularly approached 16 MHz, which is the lower limit where F2-layer propagation will support 50 MHz communications.

Chapter 8 will address the advantage in using the FT8 and the other digital modes when propagation is marginal and signal-to-noise conditions are challenging.

7.2 Sporadic-E (Es) Ionization

Clouds or patches of abnormally intense ionization, which are capable of reflecting radio waves of frequencies much higher than those reflected by the regular E or F layers, frequently form immediately beneath the normal E layer. These clouds usually cover a rather small geographical area, being approximately 50 to 100 miles in diameter. They occur more or less at random and are relatively short lived, usually dissipating within a few hours. Because this sporadic ionization generally occurs at about the same height as does the regular E layer, it is called sporadic-E, or Es.

As a result of an intensely ionized sporadic-E cloud, it is possible, at times, to communicate over relatively long distances on the 50 MHz band, as shown in Figure 7.1.

On some occasions, sporadic-E can occur on 144 MHz as well. Further, the effects of sporadic-E often are observed on the HF bands (most often on 10, 12 and 15 meters). Sporadic-E also could occur on the lower bands, but at these lower frequencies, the normal E region may mask sporadic-E. If sporadic-E does occur on the lower frequencies, it would likely be at night when the normal E region and the F2 region have a low amount of ionization.

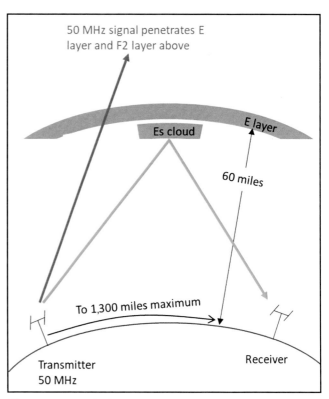

Figure 7.1 50 MHz short-skip propagation is possible by means of sporadic-E (Es) reflection.

The height at which the sporadic-E cloud occurs limits one-hop propagation to a maximum distance of approximately 1,300 miles (approximately 2,000 km). For this reason, band openings due to Es, whether on HF or VHF, are generally referred to as "short-skip" openings. During periods of geographically widespread sporadic-E ionization, which often happens during the summer months, multi-hop propagation is possible. Transatlantic sporadic-E openings on 10 and 15 meters, consisting of at least three hops, have been completed, as have 50 MHz openings with multiple-hops from North America to Europe, Japan, the Mideast and Africa.

Whether long-distance QSOs at the higher latitudes are truly the result of multiple hops or other mechanisms is still up in the air — literally. Han Higasa, JE1BMJ, wrote an article "SSSP: Short-path Summer Solstice Propagation" [reference 1]. It was translated to English by Chris Gare, G3WOS, and ran in the UK Six Metre Group (UKSMG) quarterly magazine *Six News*. The major highlight of JE1BMJ's hypothesis (see Figure 7.2) is his postulation of a chordal hop using Polar Mesosphere Summer Echoes, or PMSE. PMSE occur in the Northern Hemisphere summer months, and there appears to be enough ionization to refract grazing-angle RF at 50 MHz.

James R. Kennedy, K6MIO, reviewed mechanisms of extreme distance sporadic-E propagation in his paper "An Overview of Extreme Es Propagation" [reference 2]. Figure 7.3 gives examples of the possible different mechanisms examined.

We'll probably never know which mechanism actually occurs in any given instance.

Reflection from sporadic-E clouds takes place with very little signal loss. Further, the amount of ionospheric absorption incurred in the D region is inversely proportional to the square of the frequency; the higher the frequency, the less the absorption. Thus, use of Es propagation results in exceptionally strong signal levels during most openings, even when very low power levels are used. Note that *reflection*, not

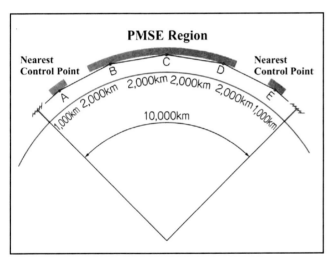

Figure 7.2 JE1BMJ's SSSP hypothesis.

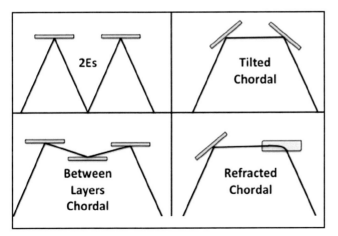

Figure 7.3 Various K6MIO hypotheses.

refraction, is believed to occur with sporadic-E, as the sporadic-E cloud is so thin (a couple to several km thick) that there isn't enough vertical extent for refraction, or gradual bending, to occur. Also, quite often it is possible to maintain communications considerably off the great circle path between two stations by means of back- and side-scatter from sporadic-E clouds. For example, a station in eastern New York State may be able work another station in the central part of the state if both stations point their antennas toward the same Es cloud that is located, for example, over Georgia.

The ionized clouds that produce sporadic-E behave erratically. For example, they are known to drift in a westerly or northwesterly direction at approximately 150 to 250 miles per hour. The drift appears to be due to winds that exist in the lower ionosphere. Because of this drift, skip zones change rapidly, and it is not uncommon for signal levels during sporadic-E openings to fade out completely from an S-9-plus level, often within a matter of minutes.

Sporadic-E ionization has long been the object of scientific investigation by amateur operators and research scientists. Studies have shown, for example, that in the mid-latitudes (United States, Europe, etc.), the diurnal variations in sporadic-E occurrence have a tendency to peak during the late morning hours and again around sunset, although, as seen in Figure 7.4, Es can occur at any time.

The green shading highlights times and months of the maximum probabilities. Note that the data are from 1957 and 1958. Although dated, these data are still valid; they have been confirmed with on-the-air results and other studies such as occultation data from GPS studies [reference 3].

More specifically, during the summer months, peaks in sporadic-E activity are observed between 10 a.m. and noon, local time at the midpoint of the path, and again from about 6 to 8 p.m. Thus, sporadic-E propagation is primarily a daytime phenomenon during the summer, decreasing rapidly in occurrence after local sundown. During the winter, sporadic-E mostly occurs in the early evening.

With respect to seasonal variations in the occurrence of mid-latitude Es propagation, a summer maximum with a secondary winter peak is clearly observed in on-the-air activity and in Figure 7.4. In fact, nearly 80%

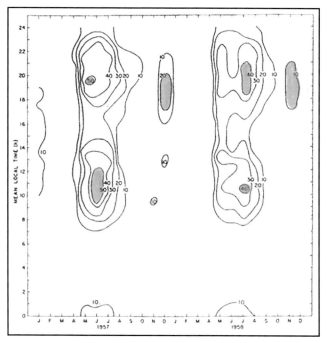

Figure 7.4 Sporadic-E probabilities on 6 meters versus hour of the day and month.

from 2004 through 2013 for May, June, July and August [reference 4].

The data show the number of contacts (QSOs) on 6 meters from the eastern half of North America to east and west mainland Europe from DX Cluster Spots for each day during the indicated months for the 10 years of the study. To count as an opening, five or more contacts between multiple stations must have been completed. Eastern North America consists of the USA's 1/2/3/4/8/9 call areas and the Canadian VO1, VE1, VE2, VE3, VE9, VY2 call areas.

Up to now, we have discussed sporadic-E in the mid-latitudes (also known as temperate latitudes – that is, the geographic latitudes between 35 and 50 degrees north and south). Sporadic-E also occurs in the auroral zone and in the equatorial zone (Eeq). In fact, sporadic-E occurs most frequently, and with the greatest intensity, in these areas. Figure 7.6 shows the patterns of sporadic-E at all latitudes. [reference 5].

The image at the top of Figure 7.6 is representative of the auroral zone region (also referred to as the high latitudes or the polar region), and the data were obtained from observations/measurements in Greenland. In this region, sporadic-E, similar to mid-latitude sporadic-E, is a nighttime phenomenon, with little seasonal variation. In the late evening and early morning hours, a high-latitude cousin of sporadic-E called auroral-E occurs in the auroral oval (specifically, it occurs in the ring or belt, itself, that encircles the geomagnetic pole, not within the "empty" oval) when the K index is elevated. Auroral-E will be further discussed in Section 7.3.

The center image of Figure 7.6 is representative of the high temperate zone (mid-latitudes), and has been

of all Es propagation observed in North America and Europe takes place from May through August, with a maximum of openings occurring in June. A secondary maximum is evident in the month of December, with a definite minimum occurring in March.

At mid-latitudes in the Southern Hemisphere, similar patterns have been observed: late morning and early evening openings in their summer months of November to February and early evening openings in their winter month of June.

A more detailed look at openings during the Northern Hemisphere summer can be seen in Figure 7.5, which shows data acquired by Kevin Gibeau, VE3EN,

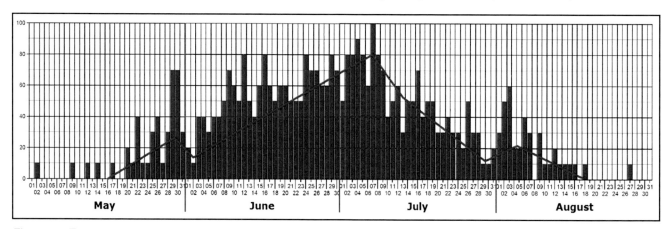

Figure 7.5 Ten Years of summer Es openings from Eastern U.S. and Canada to Western Europe.

discussed in the previous text together with Figures 7.4 and 7.5. These data were obtained from observations/measurements in Washington, D.C.

The image at the bottom of Figure 7.6 is representative of the equatorial zone (also referred to as the low latitudes), and the data were obtained from observations/measurements in the South American country of Peru. In equatorial regions, sporadic-E is essentially a daytime phenomenon, with little seasonal variation. Note that Eeq occurs roughly 90% of the time. In Southeast Asia, it appears almost daily.

Attempts have been made to determine the relationship between Es occurrence and solar cycles. Morgan

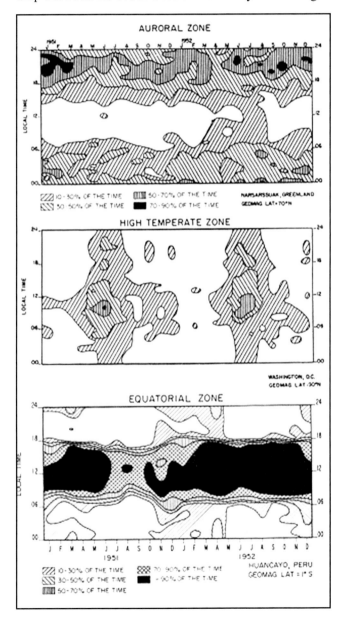

Figure 7.6 Patterns of worldwide sporadic-E

C. Monroe K7ALE and Dorothy B. Monroe K7ALF [reference 6], for example, found in the declining years of Cycle 19, F2 propagation effects diminished as anticipated, but there persisted a marked *inverse* relationship between sunspot activity and available DX communication time in the 50-54 MHz range via Es propagation. As sunspot numbers and F2-supported DX declined steadily, 50 MHz Es-supported DX time increased steadily.

Patrick Dyer, WA5IYX [reference 7], found a similar relationship from his studies. He observed Es occurrence was very high during 1965, a time when solar activity was very low (V1.0 smoothed sunspot numbers on the order of 15). On the other hand, Es occurrence was very low in 1969, when solar activity was at a peak (V1.0 smoothed sunspot number on the order of 110). Dyer, however, also found a high level of Es to have occurred during 1968, when solar activity was near maximum. Cycle 22 did nothing to resolve this controversy. For all of the volatility in solar activity that occurred in 1989, sporadic-E openings were somewhat above average in number but about the same as the number observed in the previous two years.

Work by Emil Pocock, W3EP, and Dyer [reference 8] reported Es was observed on 85 days in 1989, with openings lasting a total of 7,750 minutes. This number can be compared to 89 days in 1987, and 80 days in 1988, with the average for the period between 1980 and 1989 being 74.2 days. Roughly 81% of the openings in 1989·occurred in May, June, July, and August, while 13% occurred during November and December.

More recent data shown in Figure 7.7 from the previously referenced work published on the website of Kevin Gibeau, VE3EN, also show there isn't a strong relationship between solar activity and sporadic-E.

We thus are led to conclude at this time there is no definitive relationship between Es and the solar cycle.

Although we can't predict exactly when Es will occur, we can use Es openings on the 21 and 28 MHz bands to get a good idea if 50 MHz Es will occur. The geometry of propagation is such that as the skip distance *decreases* on the 21 and 28 MHz bands, the highest frequency that will be reflected by a sporadic-E cloud *increases*. By observing the *minimum* skip distance heard on 21 and 28 MHz during an Es opening,

Figure 7.7 VE3EN data for Es over 10 years.

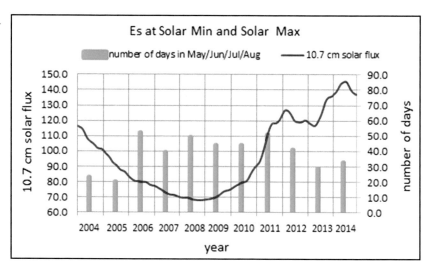

and by using the chart shown in Figure 7.8, it should be possible to tell whether or not 50 MHz is "open," and if it is open, what the skip distance might be.

To demonstrate how this technique works, consider the following example. Suppose the minimum skip distance observed on 28 MHz in a southwesterly direction is 400 miles. It is the distance to the nearest skip station heard that is important. From Figure 7.8, the intersection between 400 miles and the 28 MHz curve corresponds to an equivalent Classical MUF of 60 MHz. This means that 50 MHz short-skip openings in a southwesterly direction are very likely to occur. The minimum skip distance expected on 50 MHz can now be found from Figure 7.8 by locating the intersection between 60 MHz on the vertical scale and the 50 MHz curve. The resulting distance on the horizontal scale is found to be 900 miles. A useful rule of thumb to remember is that when skip stations less than 500 miles away are heard on 28 MHz, or less than 250 miles away on 21 MHz, chances are very good that 50 MHz will open in the same direction.

From most locations in the continental United States, 1,300-mile Es openings should extend into both Canada and Mexico. From the southern third of the country, it also should be possible to work a rather large number of countries in Central America and in the West Indies during 15, 10, and 6-meter sporadic-E openings. At times long-distance (DX) FM radio (88-108 MHz) reception also improves considerably during the summer months as a result of sporadic-E ionization. Signals that normally cannot be received at distances of more than 75 or 100 miles suddenly are propagated as far as 1,300 miles, often with very strong signal levels.

The full theory of sporadic-E ionization is not yet known. Some theories suggest meteor debris is the source of electrons, which are assembled into thin sheets by shearing forces associated with rapid wind movements in the ionosphere. Sporadic-E cannot be modeled theoretically, but it can be described statistically in terms of the likelihood of its occurrence as a function of the time of day, season, and geographical location (see Figure 7.4). Because sporadic-E supports signal propagation so well, statistical measures related to its occurrence should be enough to exploit it.

7.3 Propagation at High Latitudes

There are many different modes of high-latitude HF and VHF propagation. The most common modes will be reviewed here; they all depend on auroral ionization. The cause of auroral ionization does not have a simple answer – it is the result of very complicated processes, and misconceptions can creep in when trying to simplify the explanation (this is true of other "simple" explanations with respect to propagation). Here's an explanation of auroral ionization from Philip Erickson, W1PJE, who is an ionospheric physicist at the MIT Haystack Observatory in Massachusetts [reference 9]:

"The sun's continuously expanding outer atmosphere, or solar wind, is electrically charged and consists of low energy electrons and protons. It also has a magnetic field from embedded currents as it travels away from the sun into the space between planets. When the sun has a dynamic

increase in energy output, either from coronal mass ejections (CMEs) or coronal interaction regions (CIRs), this creates a change in solar wind properties such as speed and magnetic field strength. This new energy couples into the Earth's magnetosphere through both increased particle pressure (which is proportional to the particle density times the square of the solar wind speed) and through magnetic interactions from the solar wind's magnetic field, which pushes on the front of the magnetosphere.

"Some of this storm-time action is also electrodynamic, as the charged solar wind blows across the magnetic field at the north and south poles much like a generator. From all this increased energy input, electric potential (voltage) drops are created which can act on particles in the magnetosphere, which is filled with low to high energy hydrogen, helium, and oxygen ions from many sources, including ionospheric outflow and solar wind ions. These voltage drops, from hundreds to thousands of volts and beyond, can accelerate trapped electrons in the magnetosphere, causing them to precipitate into the polar regions of the Earth via the high latitude magnetic field lines. The result can be a nighttime auroral display."

Of all natural phenomena, auroras are probably the most breathtaking and spectacular. They arc across the night sky as yellowish-green dancing ribbons and violently throbbing rays, or as great draperies folding and unfolding. Some of the rarer displays also may

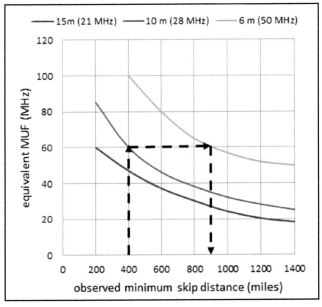

Figure 7.8 Chart describing the correlation between Es openings on 10 and 15 meters and posssible 6-meter openings at the same times.

contain shades of red and purple. They occur at low F layer heights in the ionosphere and can be seen obliquely from the ground for distances up to about 600 miles from the zenith point. For those who have never seen an aurora, use your browser and search for "video of auroral display."

Observations made over the past 100 years, and intensified during the past decade with investigations using high-flying airplanes and satellites, have defined areas of the world where auroras occur most frequently. The zone of maximum occurrence in the Northern Hemisphere, where they are seen on approximately 250 nights a year, arcs across northern Alaska, central Canada, the southern tip of Greenland and Iceland, the northern tip of Norway, and the northern coasts of Russia and Siberia.

The shape of the oval is skewed and it is centered on the geomagnetic pole (where the magnetic field lines are near-vertical), with the widest bulge occurring in the midnight sector and the narrowest portion facing towards the sun in the noon sector. The Earth rotates under the auroral oval. As geomagnetic activity increases (elevated K index), the equatorward edge of the oval starts to migrate southward. The distance of this migration is proportional to the size of the disturbance. During quiet times, auroras may be seen 10 to 40 nights a year in the northern areas of the U.S. mainland. In the southern states, several years may pass before one is seen. The DOS program DXAID Version 4.5 (1994) by Oldfield (no longer available) allowed the user to plot the auroral oval on a great circle map versus date, time and K index. Figure 7.9 shows the auroral oval at Midwest longitudes for Dec. 15 at 0700 UTC (around local midnight) at K indices of 1, 5 and 9.

At K=1, the equatorward edge of the northern auroral oval is at the southern tip of Hudson Bay. At K=5, the equatorward edge of the northern auroral oval is over Lake Michigan. At K=9, the equatorward edge of the northern auroral oval is over Tennessee. Note that the southern auroral oval doesn't look like an oval – that's because the maps in Figure 7.9 are great circle maps (also known as azimuth equidistant projection maps). These maps become distorted as distances increase from the center.

Auroras play havoc with shortwave communications. The excessive ionization that causes auroras

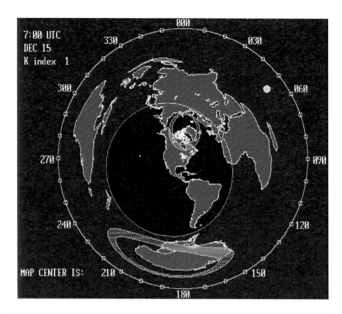

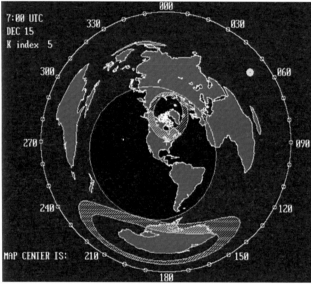

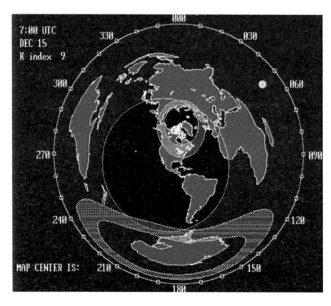

Figure 7.9 Auroral oval versus K index. The yellow dot is the overhead sun in the daylight area of the Earth. The darker area is nighttime. Great circle paths from the center of the map are straight lines. The distance from the center of the map to the outer perimeter is 20,000 km (12,500 miles), which is halfway around the world. These images come from DXAID Version 4.5 as mentioned in the text.

also causes severe signal absorption. Like the luminous aurora itself, auroral zone absorption is strictly a high-latitude phenomenon. This absorption is caused by energetic electrons arriving in the ionosphere during geomagnetic disturbances. It can occur around-the-clock, with its major peak occurring in the mid-morning. The occurrence of this type of absorption is most pronounced around the statistical center of the auroral zone band ("ring"), with a latitudinal spread of about 8 degrees. It produces a sporadic interruption of usable signals caused by increased absorption in the D region. Its effects are quite short lived (typically, tens of minutes). In Chapter 8 we'll take a more detailed look at what the ovals mean in terms of actual ionization levels.

Absorption caused by an active (disturbed) auroral zone acts like a conducting screen, preventing shortwave transmissions from passing through the region. For this reason, transpolar communications to and from the United States are extremely difficult and often unreliable during periods of auroral absorption. The presence of auroral effects on propagation frequently can be detected by a unique fading component that consists of a low-frequency "flutter" (ranging from 100 to 1,000 Hz) that the aurora superimposes on a signal. During periods of intense auroral activity, this fading component often is strong enough to render a voice signal unintelligible.

So-called "auroral flutter," or Doppler, is caused by the turbulence in the ionosphere that, in turn, is caused by huge, electric ionospheric currents that exist at auroral and polar latitudes. The auroral and polar ionospheres, at F-layer altitudes, consist of a "patch-work quilt" of electron clouds, all being propelled along the high-latitude current system. When this system is bombarded with additional particle radiation, the current becomes turbulent, causing vast differences in the electron densities of the F-layer "patches." At times, the F-region may appear enhanced; oftentimes it will disappear. Simply put, the ionosphere above 55 degrees north and south latitudes is not a simple refracting layer, as it is usually modeled. Signals do not propagate through the polar region as they do at mid-latitudes.

Because they are caused by the same phenomenon, a geomagnetic storm, there is a close relationship between ionospheric storms and the occurrence of auroras. The first effects of the geomagnetic storm are felt at high latitudes; then, these effects migrate southward as the storm intensifies. As the severity of the storm increases, the affected area spreads farther south. During the intense ionospheric storms of March 1989, auroras were observed *overhead* in Dallas, Texas.

7.3.1 VHF propagation via Aurora

While auroral displays can seriously disrupt communications on the amateur HF bands, propagation on 50 and 144 MHz often improves during these periods. Stated another way, the HF operator's famine often is the VHF operator's feast! This is good enough reason for the amateur interested in VHF propagation to check the WWV broadcasts at 18 minutes after each hour, and to make use of Figures 5.A through 5.E in Chapter 5 of this book. When a combination of solar flux and current geomagnetic activity (the Boulder *K* index) falls into the Below Normal or Disturbed regions of Figures 5.A through 5.E, it's time to check 50 and 144 MHz for auroral reflection. Look, too, for sporadic-E openings.

Ionization associated with auroras often is sufficiently intense to reflect or scatter 50 and 144 MHz signals over distances of up to about 1,200 miles when propagation over such paths by other modes may not be possible. Further, auroral ionization varies rapidly in intensity and height. This is what causes multi-path distortion on VHF signals reflected from an aurora. Voice modulation often is unintelligible on 50 MHz and is nearly always unusable on 144 MHz. Thus, while voice communications may be possible using SSB, experience has shown that CW is the most effective way to communicate.

Geographically, the more northerly the latitude, the greater the number of VHF auroral openings. In the U.S., the northern tier of states experiences fairly good openings between 50 and 75 days a year. In the central states, openings may occur between 10 and 35

days a year while considerably fewer openings occur in the southern tier of states. During prolonged geomagnetic storms, auroral openings may occur and re-occur several times throughout the day for several days in a row.

Because auroras occur in the northern areas of the Northern Hemisphere, north is the optimum antenna bearing to establish communications by auroral propagation modes. Once communications are established, antennas should be rotated slowly to maximize propagation.

Most auroras are produced either by coronal mass ejections (most prevalent around solar maximum) or by coronal holes (most prevalent during the declining phase of a solar cycle). If they are Earth-directed, look for higher K indices and propagation via auroral. Lastly, propagation via the aurora also may occur on 10 meters.

7.3.2 Auroral-E propagation at HF

To distinguish it from common sporadic-E, another E region propagation mode is called auroral-E (Eau). During high-latitude studies conducted from August 1991 to August 1992 on a 960 km east-west path in Alaska (from Cape Wales to Fairbanks) on 25.545 MHz [reference 10], a total of 1,446 observations demonstrated auroral-E is predominantly a nighttime phenomenon. Figure 7.10 shows the auroral-E scenario for this 960 km path for Oct. 15, 1991

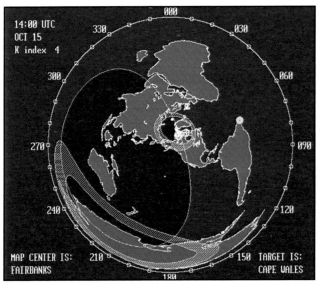

Figure 7.10 The 960-km short path (red line) from Cape Wales to Fairbanks.

at 1400 UTC when the K index is 4. Readily visible is the auroral oval (or ring, or belt) in both hemispheres. Again, the projection used distorts the ring around the southern pole.

In general, when the K-index is sufficiently high as to place the ring of the auroral oval over the propagation path, the overall likelihood of auroral-E propagation is at least 50%. Auroral-E occurrence centers around mid-path local midnight time, and occurs for several hours before and several hours after local midnight.

The average duration for such openings is 10-20 minutes, although a few will last in excess of an hour. On average, auroral-E occurs on 61% of the days during the spring and fall months, about 70% of the days during the summer months, and only 51% of the time during the winter months. The ionization is sufficient to elevate signals 20 to 30 dB above the noise.

In summary, auroral-E propagation is restricted to paths where the reflection/refraction points lie in the auroral zone. During disturbed times, as the oval expands equatorward, the number of propagation opportunities increases.

A good example of auroral-E propagation on our ham bands is QSOs from the U.S. Midwest to the Scandinavian countries (Norway, Sweden, Finland and Denmark) on the 15-meter and 10-meter bands in the late afternoon in the Midwest. The first hop is usually via the F2 layer, with the last hop into the Scandinavian countries being via auroral-E.

7.3.3 HF propagation via patches of F2 ionization drifting across the polar cap

In his "Propagation" column in the September 1993 issue of *Worldradio*, Robert Brown, NM7M (SK), discussed his observations on hearing the RS-12 satellite's 10-meter signals in the winter when it was still below the horizon to the north. This meant 28 MHz was propagating across the dark polar cap to NM7M's location (QTH). Based on the usual (i.e., mid-latitude) model for the ionosphere, this shouldn't happen, as the critical frequencies and the resulting (medium) maximum usable frequencies across the dark polar cap wouldn't be sufficiently high as to support 28 MHz propagation.

After some detective work, NM7M found that the scientific community had observed patches of F2

region ionization drifting across the dark polar cap. This was the likely mechanism that had supported the propagation of RS-12's 28-MHz signal to NM7M's QTH. From a paper by D.J. McEwen and D.P. Harris [reference 11], we can understand some of the characteristics of this propagation mode.

The authors made observations during the winter months (November through February) of 1990/1991, 1991/1992, 1992/1993, and 1993/1994. The instrument used for the observations was a photometer. Emissions at 630 nm (the wavelength of the airglow from excited oxygen atoms at F-region heights) were monitored. The unit of measurement is the rayleigh (R), which is a special unit of measurement adopted in airglow and auroral photometry. One R equals 10^6 photons per square cm per second.

Because this is an optical measurement, the authors needed clear moonless nights to make observations. There were 77 such nights during the four-year period. Enhanced 630 nm emissions were observed on 76 of these nights. On average, there were seven drifting patches seen on each of the 76 nights. The average emission measured was about 150 R above background levels, with a trend toward more enhanced emissions during the higher sunspot-number winters. This indicates the electron density in the enhanced 630 nm airglow regions was a few times higher than was the electron density outside the enhanced regions.

Figure 7.11 shows an actual QSO between a station in the U.S. state of Georgia (the plus sign at the cen-

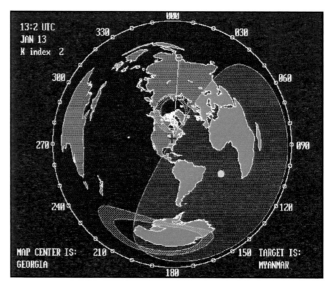

Figure 7.11 QSO aided by drifting patches of F2 region ionization across the dark polar cap.

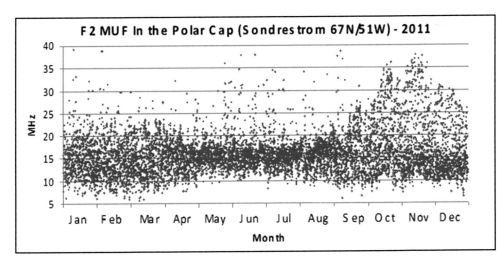

Figure 7.12 Seasonal pattern of drifting patches pf F2 region ionization in the polar cap.

ter of the map) and a station in Myanmar (the plus sign with a circle around it) on 10 meters on Jan. 13, 2000 at 1302 UTC, with a K index of 2, that is believed to have been aided by these drifting patches. The map is centered on Georgia, and the path to Myanmar is the straight white line headed north out of Georgia. The diameter of the polar cap is approximately 5000 km, so an F2 hop is very likely needed to get across the polar cap.

From Reference 10, the source of the drifting patches appears to be near the dayside auroral oval, which would be around the southern tip of Greenland for the time of this actual QSO. The patches drift across the central polar region in an anti-sunward direction. The average cross-sectional dimension of a patch was 500-600 km.

Figure 7.12 shows measured F2 region maximum usable frequencies, or classical MUFs, from an ionosonde in the polar cap for the year 2011. The winter months are favored.

There have been other reported QSOs that are believed to be aided by these F2 region patches that drift across the polar cap. Examples are the 20 meter QSOs between Finland and the Pacific Northwest of North America during winter when the polar cap is in darkness.

7.3.4 Sun-Aligned Arc (Theta Aurora) on 50 MHz

On June 21, 2006, a historic 6-meter opening took place between Alaska (KL7) and Europe. The band opened up between 1130 and 1230 UTC with seven EU QSOs in the log of Kevin Forster, NL7Z (now KL7KY). Raymond Vrolijk, PA4PA, was first to

work NL7Z, and other contacts followed with Sweden (SM), Denmark (OZ) and Germany (DL). An important observation was that PA4PA confirmed his six-element Yagi (on a 20-foot boom at a height of 40 feet) was pointed along the great circle path to Alaska for maximum signal strength. Figure 7.13 shows this 7,000-km short path (the white line from the center of the map heading north-northeast) between Alaska and the Netherlands (the plus sign with a circle around it).

The path goes across the polar cap in daylight and encounters the auroral oval twice. Going across the polar cap suggests drifting patches of F2 region ionization. Although the drifting patches are more abundant in the dark polar cap in winter and not in daylight in summer, Figure 7.12 still indicates a low probability for daylight in summer.

With respect to sporadic-E in the polar cap, a look at the Qaanaaq, Greenland ionosonde (in the center of the polar cap but not directly under the great circle path from Alaska to the Netherlands) for June 2005, and June 2006, showed the sporadic-E critical frequency foEs greater than 10 MHz (which is what would be needed for a maximum usable frequency of 50 MHz) to have occurred only 14 times out of the 5760 data points (0.24%). Although this is a very low probability, we can't rule it out (just like we can't rule out drifting patches of F2 region ionization) as these QSOs obviously have a very low probability of occurring.

Did auroral-E help? On the Netherlands end of the path, the auroral oval is roughly 2,000 km distant from the Netherlands. Thus, it is unlikely that a refraction from the auroral oval occurred – the auroral oval would have had to have been about 1,000 km away. On the Alaska end of the path, an auroral-E hop could be possible, but other modes would then have to be involved.

A lesser-known mode could be a sun-aligned auroral arc. This is also known as a trans-polar arc, and even a theta aurora due to the similarity to the Greek letter theta. Figure 7.14 is an example of this mechanism. The image is from the southern auroral oval, and it shows a sun-aligned auroral arc transiting the entire polar cap.

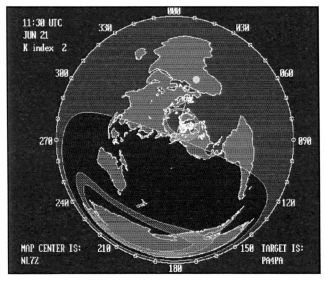

Figure 7.13 Alaska to Europe on 6 meters on June 21, 2006.

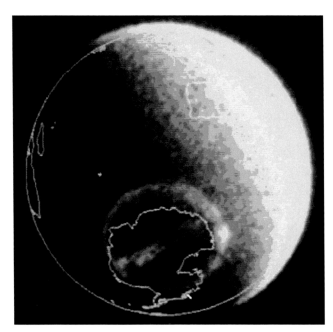

Figure 7.14 A representative sun-aligned arc across the southern auroral oval.

The statistical pattern of sun-aligned arcs is as follows [reference 12]:

a. They generally extend along a line from the noon portion (on the left in Figure 7.14) to the midnight portion (on the right in Figure 7.14) of the auroral oval, which fits the scenarios of the QSOs

b. They can extend across the entire polar cap as seen in Figure 7.14

c. They occur during quiet geomagnetic field conditions, which fits the scenarios of the QSOs

d. The luminosity (and hence electron density) is brighter in the summer months and weaker in the winter months, which fits the scenarios of the QSOs

e. The luminosity along the arc is usually less intense than the average luminosity elsewhere along the auroral oval, which may be a negative point for this mechanism

f. Another negative is that none of the research papers found gave any statistics on how prevalent sun-aligned arcs/theta aurora is during the summer

Many times, without sufficient evidence such as ionosonde data or TEC (total electron content) data, an explanation must be based solely on the best match between the statistical pattern of the propagation mode and the characteristics of the observed QSOs. These 6-meter QSOs are a good example of this, and it could be that drifting patches of F2 region ionization, or sporadic-E in the polar cap, or sun-aligned arcs/theta aurora together with aurora-E contributed to the enabling of these QSOs.

7.4 VHF Propagation via Meteor Ionization

Meteors, or "shooting stars" as they often are called, are particles of mineral and metallic matter that continually enter the Earth's atmosphere from outer space. It has been computed that hundreds of millions of meteors, most of them microscopic, enter the Earth's atmosphere every 24 hours. Their number increases significantly during certain times of the year when meteor showers occur.

As large meteors enter the Earth's atmosphere at velocities of up to 50 miles per second, the intense heat generated by friction due to the upper air causes the meteors to leave an ionized trail behind as they burn 30 to 100 miles (55 to 185 km) above the Earth. This ionization often is intense enough to reflect or scatter VHF signals over distances of several hundred miles. Signals reflected by meteor ionization can be identified by the very short, sudden burst in signal strength that takes place when the radio signal intersects the ionized trail. The signal level increase, on the order of 20 to 40 dB, is sharp and sudden; it may last from a few seconds to half a minute before fading into the background noise level. A Doppler shift also may be noticed on signals reflecting from a meteor trail. This is caused by the rapid motion of the reflecting point. In some cases, the shift may amount to as much as 2 kHz, and it can last for several seconds.

For the radio amateur, meteor-reflected signal bursts are of little communication value unless they occur frequently enough or are of sufficient duration to permit the transmission of information. A 50 MHz signal may appear as a few readable words while on 144 MHz, the burst is shorter by almost a factor of 10, often being nothing more than a ping. At this rate, even during major meteor showers, it requires a great deal of time and patience to transmit information between stations. For this reason, high keying speeds are preferable to voice transmissions, although the exchange of voice information may at times be possible on 50 MHz, especially when using voice controlled (VOX) SSB.

The above notwithstanding, in general, conventional communication techniques cannot be used for meteor-burst communications. Stations should arrange schedules and alternate transmit-receive times. For example, a station could transmit for 15 seconds and then listen for 15 seconds. This is not to preclude random contacts by transmitting and listening in the "blind." Further, given today's personal computer technology, amateurs can generate complex, high-data-rate signals. A great example of this is suite of meteor scatter waveforms developed for meteor scatter by Joseph Taylor, K1JT, and Steven Franke, K9AN [reference 13].

During a typical 24-hour period, between 300 and 500 meteor-reflected signal bursts lasting 5 seconds or longer can be counted on 50 MHz. Approximately 25% of these signal bursts will last from between 10 and 30 seconds, and occasionally, one may last considerably longer. A great number of bursts will be heard on 28 MHz and the lower frequency bands while considerably fewer will be heard on 144 MHz and higher frequencies.

While meteors may appear at any time, most of them enter the Earth's atmosphere between midnight and dawn, peaking between 5 and 7 a.m., local time. Because the optimum ionization altitude of meteor trails is between 45 and 65 miles (80 to 120 km), the optimum communication range is approximately 800 miles, with a maximum range of about 1,200 miles. Seasonally, considerably more meteors enter the Earth's atmosphere during June and July than at any other time, with a minimum number observed during January and February.

Shower Name	Date of Peak Intensity	Shower Duration (Days)	Number of Meteors per Hour
Quadrantids	January 3	1	35-40
Lyrids	April 21	2	12-15
Eta Aquarids	May 5	7	12-20
Delta Aquarids	July 29	10	20-30
Perseids	August 12	5	50
Orionids	October 21	3	20-25
Taurids	November 5 & 12	20	12-15
Leonids	November 17	4	20-25
Geminids	December 13	5	40-50
Ursids	December 22	2	15

Table 7.1 A list of major meteor showers. The date of peak intensity may vary by a day, and the intensity of the various showers may vary from year to year. About 20 other showers of less intensity also occur during the year - 7 between January and June, and 13 between July and December.

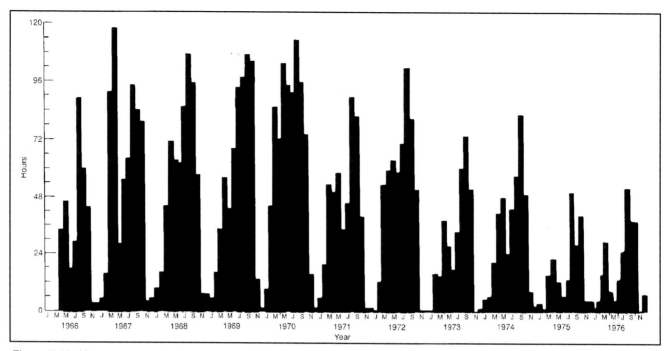

Figure 7.15 Hours-per-month of VHF transequatorial propagation (from Stuart Kingan, Reference 15). (Note: Horizontal axis designators are every other month-January, March, May, July, etc.)

From time to time, but on a regular basis, the Earth moves through areas in space in which there are very large swarms of meteors. During such periods, called meteor showers, meteors enter the Earth's atmosphere with more than average frequency. During many showers, meteors will appear at the rate of one or two a minute, and during certain very large showers, many thousands may be observed during a single night. The possibility of 50 and 144 MHz communications by means of ionized meteor trails increases considerably during meteor showers.

Table 7.1 lists the major showers, the approximate dates on which they occur, and the average number of meteors that probably will enter the Earth's atmosphere each hour during these periods. While meteor-burst communication can be quite difficult, and can require a great deal of patience and time to move a small amount of information, it does provide a means of intermittent ionospheric communication on VHF bands over distances of between approximately 800 and 1,200 miles.

7.5 Trans-Equatorial Propagation (TEP) on 28, 50 and 144 MHz

Strong 50 MHz band openings, and even moderately strong 144 MHz band openings, can occur, partic-ularly during periods of moderate to high solar activity. These openings, which occur at times when the expected Classical MUF in the path is considerably lower than 50 MHz, are called transequatorial (TE) or TEP openings.

Transequatorial propagation was first observed by radio amateurs during the solar maximum of Cycle 18, which took place during 1947. It resulted in XE1KE in Mexico working Argentine stations on 50 MHz. Amateurs also pioneered the use of this mode of propagation during subsequent solar cycles.

In the early 1960s, Stanford Research Institute (SRI) scientists probed the ionospheric path that tran-sited the magnetic equator between Hawaii and Rarotonga in the Cook Islands during the American High Altitude Nuclear tests. They found a mode of propagation that not only would support signals at frequencies greater than 64 MHz, but also, that occurred practically every evening [reference 14, reference 15]. This mode of propagation was first observed in 1958, at the peak of Cycle 19, when a portable TV receiver taken to Rarotonga could rou-tinely receive Hawaiian TV signals in the early evening. This phenomenon was first thought to be caused by exceptionally high critical frequencies due to the very intense solar maximum. However, the oblique sounder work of SRI in 1962 showed it to be a unique mode of propagation now known to be TEP.

In 1966, a group of radio amateurs, led by Stuart Kingan, ZK1AA, started what turned out to be an 11-year measurement project focusing on TE propagation over the path between Hawaii and Rarotonga. *This path is unique because the magnetic and geographic equator almost coincide and because it is within one degree of being purely a north-south path.* The project involved monitoring VHF signals from north of the equator (mostly TV signals) on a scanning receiver in Rarotonga. This project, which was conducted entirely by radio amateurs without any outside assistance, produced a very detailed look at TE propagation.

The nighttime mode of transequatorial propagation occurs across the magnetic equator. Propagation paths as short as 2,500 km and as long as 5,000 km can occur. This phenomenon never occurs before sunset, and it lasts until local midnight. Once conditions in the F region favor the onset of TE propagation on any particular longitude in the area affected, the strength and upper frequency limit all tend to increase up to 2200 local time, at which time TE propagation starts to wane. The conditions causing the phenomenon move from west to east at approximately 300 km per hour. Transequatorial propagation is very sensitive to solar activity. At solar maximum,

TE openings occur between 24 and 30 days a month (or about 96-120 hours a month), with the peak months of occurrence being July through October. In early November, the mode abruptly disappears. At solar minimum, the occurrence rate drops off to 18-20 days a month (36-48 hours a month), with September being the single peak month. These characteristics can be seen in Figure 7.15, originally hand-drawn by Kingan [reference 16].

In the Western Hemisphere, the magnetic equator lies approximately 20 degrees south of the geographical equator, and it roughly follows an arc that extends from Lima, Peru, to Recife, Brazil, and that passes through La Paz, Bolivia. The optimum distances for TE openings range between 1,500 miles (2,400 km) and 2,500 miles (4,000 km) above and below the equator. Thus, for example, *typical TE paths exist between Puerto Rico and Argentina, from southern Europe to southern Africa and from Japan to northern Australia.* Figure 7.16 [reference 17] shows these three typical TE paths (of course there are transequatorial paths at every longitude, but these three paths have a sizeable number of amateur radio operators on each end).

Figure 7.17 shows the mechanism of TE propagation – two areas of higher electron density (plasma frequencies are proportional to electron density) on either side of the magnetic equator that enable a long

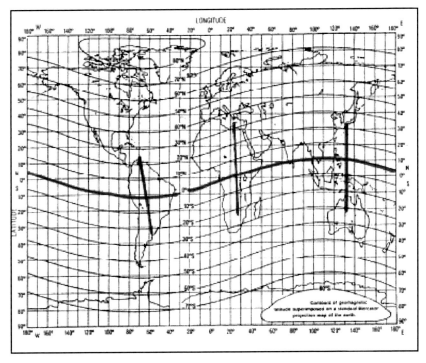

Figure 7.16 Three typical transequatorial paths. The red line is the magnetic equator. The blue lines are the three paths orthogonal to the magnetic equator.

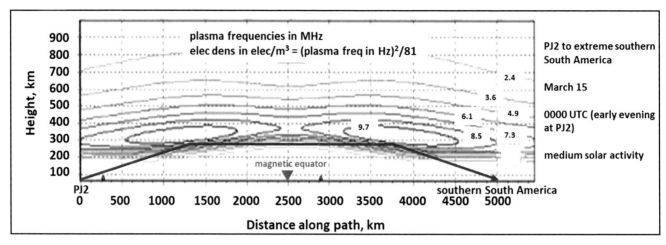

Figure 7.17 The mechanism of trans-equatorial propagation.

chordal hop across the magnetic equator without a ground reflection and only transiting through the absorbing D region twice. Without these areas of higher electron density, two hops would be required. The two areas of higher electron density on either side of the magnetic equator are the signature of trans-equatorial propagation.

In the Western Hemisphere, and for smoothed sunspot numbers greater than 75, 50 MHz TE openings occur almost every night during the spring and summer, when the sun is "over" the equator, over an area extending from Mexico City in the north to southern Chile and Argentina in the south. Within this area there is little variation in signal level from night to night, and circuit reliability is high. Less frequent openings extend into the southern and central area of the United States (perhaps with help from normal F2 propagation or sporadic E), with openings falling off rapidly at greater distances to the north.

Signal characteristics vary with path length, with serious flutter fading observed on short paths. Solid, voice-quality signals often are observed on the longer paths.

While we primarily have discussed 50 MHz TE skip and the spectacular openings that may result, TE openings also occur on the 10-, 12-, 15-, 17-, and 20-meter bands. Occurring during the evening hours (8 to 11 PM local time at the path midpoint), TE openings on these bands, particularly on 20 meters, can take place during periods of low solar activity. This is why openings between the western U.S., and Australia and New Zealand, are commonplace, even at solar minimum.

Remember, signals must cross the magnetic equator roughly in a north-south direction or transequatorial openings generally will not be possible. A right-angle crossing is optimal, but TE contacts have been reported between stations as much as 20 degrees off a right-angle crossing.

The transequatorial Classical MUF is approximately 1.5 times greater than the daylight Classical MUF observed on the same path. Thus, 50 MHz TE openings may be expected during the evening hours when a Classical MUF of 34 MHz is observed during the daytime. Note, too, that TE openings often may occur on 50 MHz when propagation is not possible on lower frequency bands, on the same path, and at the same time.

In sum, transequatorial openings occur most often during periods of moderate and high solar activity with the probability of occurrence dropping sharping during solar minimum. Although they may occur during any season, openings will occur most often in August and September; very seldom do they occur in November and December. Transequatorial propagation is a nighttime phenomenon, with most openings occurring between 8 and 11 p.m. local time, at the path midpoint.

7.6 Ionospheric Scatter on the Higher HF Bands and 50 MHz

When a signal is at a frequency equal to or below the Classical MUF, ionospheric propagation takes place by refraction from the ionized layers existing in the Earth's atmosphere. In this case, signals strike the ionosphere obliquely and are normally refracted in a forward direction, with a very small amount of energy scattered back towards the Earth in more or less random directions. When the frequency is above the Classical MUF, the signal will penetrate the ionosphere, but some energy may also be scattered in all directions. We'll have more about this in Chapter 8. Scatter may take place from any of the ionosphere's layers, including the D layer.

Until the post-war introduction of super-sensitive receivers, advanced modulation techniques, and improved antenna designs, scatter signals were of little communication value. Today, with a good receiver, high-gain antennas, and high transmitter power, scatter openings often are observed, particularly on the 21, 24, 28, and 50 MHz bands, when these frequencies are considerably above the Classical MUF. However, only a small part of a signal's energy is returned to Earth by scatter; such signals are generally, although not always, weak and fluttery.

Scatter appears to occur most often from ionospheric regions in the vicinity of the magnetic equator. In northern and temperate regions, ionospheric scattering increases considerably with increases in magnetic activity and during ionospheric storms. While 50 MHz scatter openings can occur at any time, they seem to peak during the evening hours of the spring and fall, and during periods of high and moderate solar activity.

To communicate by means of forward-scattered signals, it is usual for both stations to direct their antennas at each other along the great circle path. To communicate by means of back- or side-scattered signals, it is often best to orient both antennas at the apparent point of scatter, which may be considerably off the great-circle path. This point often can be determined by slowly rotating antennas until signal strength is maximized.

Signals scattered in a forward direction from the E layer may permit 50 MHz openings over distances of between approximately 600 and 1200 miles while openings over considerably greater distances may be possible with signals scattered by the F layers. Back or side-scattered signals often may permit ionospheric communications between stations separated by relatively small distances, although the signals themselves may have traversed considerable distances.

Side-scattered signals often can be used to establish communications on paths that deviate from a great

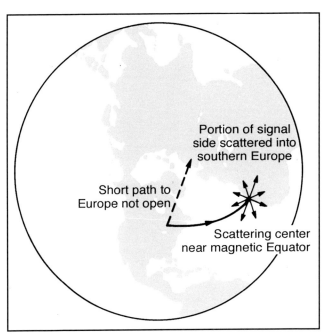

Figure 7.18 It is possible to use side-scatter propagation for communication between the U.S. and Europe on 21, 24 and 28 MHz.

circle. On the HF bands, and on the 10-, 12-, and 15-meter bands in particular, such off-path scatter reflections frequently produce unexpected band openings. Figure 7.18 is an example of long-distance side scatter propagation.

Here, insufficient ionization in the atmosphere, or a high level of absorption (due, for example, to auroral activity), prevents communication on great-circle paths between the United States and Europe on the 10-, 12- and 15-meter amateur bands. However, when amateurs in the U.S. point their antennas into central Africa, towards the magnetic equator, the higher level of ionization found there often causes signals to be scattered, with a portion of the energy being side-scattered into Europe. European operators, whose antennas should be pointed roughly south to southwest, should now be able to communicate with operators in the U.S., since a portion of their signals will be side-scattered to the west.

In using side scatter to communicate between the U.S. and western Europe, the path is optimized, roughly, between 1200 and 1500 UTC (or early afternoon in western Europe). During this period, the combination of east-west propagation between the U.S. and Africa, and of north-south propagation between Africa and western Europe, is favorable for

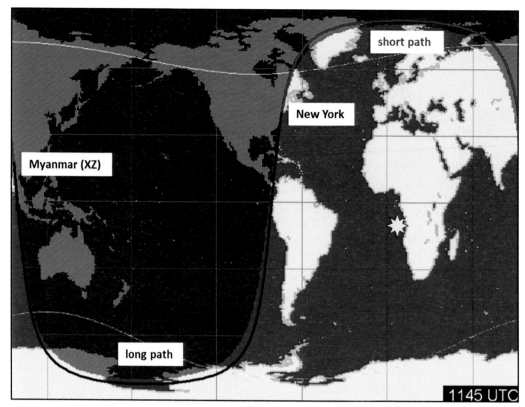

Figure 7.19 The gray line morning long path between New York and Myanmar (XZ) on Feb. 22 at 1145 UTC.

the propagation of side-scattered signals on this path. Another similar path is from the U.S. Midwest to Japan on the 10-, 12- and 15-meter bands. Stations in the Midwest point their antennas to the southwest (the true great circle path to Japan is to the northwest).

The technique described above often is very useful during DX contests, especially during periods of low solar activity.

In passing, it should be noted that scattering centers for radio signals are not always located in the ionosphere. At times, signals that have been reflected from the ionosphere are scattered in all directions when they strike the ground. A portion of the ground scattered energy is then returned to the vicinity of the signal source via the same ionospheric path, and in this way, communications can be established between stations whose separation prevents the use of surface waves or more conventional means of ionospheric propagation.

Finally, it is not possible to determine whether a signal has been scattered from the ionosphere or from the ground by listening to the quality of the scattered signal.

7.7   Gray Line Propagation

The gray line, or the "twilight zone," as it is sometimes called, is that band around the Earth that sepa-

rates the areas of daylight and darkness. In astronomical terms, the gray line is called the "terminator," and it is a somewhat fuzzy region because of the Earth's atmosphere.

When the long great circle path between two locations is aligned with (or very near to) the terminator, it is called gray line propagation. Figure 7.19 (from the mapping feature in W6ELProp by W6EL with additional annotations) provides an example of a gray line propagation path in the morning for a U.S. East Coast station.

Beginning with observations in 1975 on the 80-meter long path from California to Europe around sunrise and sunset [reference 18], propagation along the gray line was determined to be extremely efficient. The major argument for this was: the D layer, which absorbs high-frequency signals, is absent from the gray line zone. Examining the physics of propagation along the terminator, however, raised issues that didn't support this conclusion. These issues will be reviewed in Chapter 8, and an alternate explanation for gray line propagation efficiency will be offered. Regardless of the true explanation, knowing how to use gray line propagation is important for today's communicator.

For U.S. East Coast paths in the morning (for example, Figure 7.19), you want to point your antenna (if you have a directional antenna) to the southwest. For U.S. East Coast paths in the evening (see Figure 7.20), you want to point your antenna to the southeast.

Before the internet and personal computers, identifying gray line paths was accomplished using either manual homebrew aids (for example, a piece of cardboard and a globe) or a Geochron clock (https://www.geochron.com/). In 1982, the company Xantek offered a mechanical gray line calculator called the DX Edge. It used a rectangular projection of the world along with 12 transparent slides (one for the 15th day of each month of the year) that fit over the world map. Sliding the appropriate transparency over the world map showed the terminator separating the daylight and nighttime portions of the Earth, which thusly displayed the gray line path. Moving the transparency in time showed how the gray line path moved across the Earth, toward, and away from, one's location. The DX Edge was a boon to operators who "worked" the gray line, especially amateurs who stalked DX on the 160-meter band (Top Band) in the hours just before their local dawn in hopes of working an elusive "new country."

With the introduction of personal computers, determining gray line paths became easy using software with mapping features. Software programs offering mapping features include W6ELProp (the propagation prediction software reviewed in Chapter 6) and DX Atlas (http://www.dxatlas.com/). There are gray line maps that can be found with your browser, such as https://dx.qsl.net/propagation/greyline.html, https://www.smeter.net/propagation/views/current-gray-line.php, https://w3wvg.com/_mgxroot/page_10735.html and others. Just type "gray line maps" into your favorite browser and do a search.

Figures 7.19 and 7.20 are examples of the long (and short) great circle path aligned with (or very near to) the terminator – classical gray line propagation. There are other documented paths when the long great circle path is farther from the terminator. Figure 7.21 shows this scenario for an evening 160 meter CW QSO between Maine in the U.S. and Japan on Jan. 2, 2015 at 2127 UTC [reference 19].

Along the southern extreme of the path over Antarctica, the great circle path is in much daylight, where absorption would be prohibitive, especially on 160 meters. This path is usually called a "crooked" path, as hams are aware that the true great circle long path is likely not available. This concept of a "crooked" path is the basis of an alternative explanation for gray line propagation that will be discussed in Chapter 8.

Using the gray line methods outlined here, you will be able to determine those days when the sunrise and

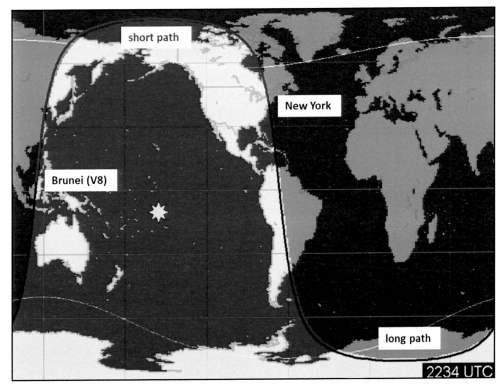

Figure 7.20 Gray line evening long path between New York (W2) and Brunei (V8) on Feb. 22 at 2234 UTC.

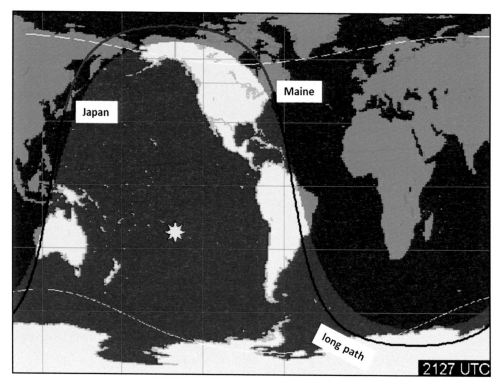

Figure 7.21 Evening gray line path from Maine to Japan on 160 meters in January 2015 at 2127 UTC.

sunset "windows" are open for you to work into certain areas. It is even possible to set up schedules months in advance, because the gray line will optimize your chances of communicating with, or hearing, stations in those elusive countries around the world.

7.8 Long Path Propagation

Except for the antipodal point (a point exactly on the opposite side of the world), any two points on Earth are linked by both a short and a long great circle path. The great circle bearing along the short path is the reciprocal of the long-path bearing; that is, they differ by 180 degrees. The distance along the short path is always less than 20,000 kilometers, while the distance along the long path is equal to about 40,000 kilometers minus the short path distance. The Earth is not a perfect sphere; it is an oblate sphere (slightly flattened at the poles), thus the short path and long path distances depend somewhat on the headings.

For example, the short great circle bearing from a station in the U.S. in northeast Indiana to a station in Japan is found to be 327 degrees, and the distance is approximately 10,540 kilometers; the long-path bearing is 147 degrees, and the distance is approximately 29,490 kilometers. Figure 7.22 (from DX Atlas by VE3NEA with additional annotations) shows these paths.

Determining which path, short or long, should be best comes down to the frequency being used, the amount of ionospheric absorption (which determines signal strength) and the amount of ionization (which determines the classical MUF). On the lower HF bands (160 meters through 40 meters), the amount of ionization is usually high enough on both paths and

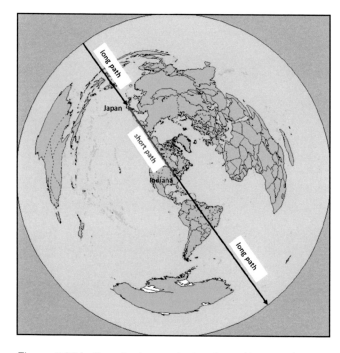

Figure 7.22 Indiana to Japan-short path and long path

Month	Smoothed V2.0 sunspot number 30 (low phase)	Smoothed V2.0 sunspot number 115 (high phase)	Smoothed V2.0 sunspot number 215 (intense phase)
January	20 meters	20 meters	20 meters
February	20 meters	20 meters	20 meters
March	20 meters	20 meters	17 meters
April	20 meters	17 meters	17 meters
May	20 meters	17 meters	17 meters
June	20 meters	17 meters	17 and 15 meters (tied)
July	20 meters	17 meters	15 meters
August	20 meters	17 meters	17 meters
September	20 meters	20 meters	20 meters
October	20 meters	20 meters	17 meters
November	20 meters	20 meters	20 meters
December	20 meters	20 meters	20 meters

Table 7.2 Best band for long path from Seattle to South Africa.

thus which path prevails is the path that has the least amount of ionospheric absorption. On the higher HF bands (15 meters through 10 meters), ionospheric absorption is usually minimal (because the amount of absorption is inversely proportional to the square of the frequency) on both paths and so, which path prevails is the path that has the necessary amount of ionization to refract signals back to Earth.

The short and long paths on the middle bands (30, 20 and 17 meters) do not depend solely on ionospher-

ic absorption as do the lower HF bands; nor do they depend solely on the amount of ionization as do the higher HF bands. The short and long paths on these bands can tolerate some increased ionospheric absorption and don't need a high amount of ionization. The result of this is that these three middle bands should offer the best probability of long path.

Propagation predictions using W6ELProp confirm this conclusion. On a representative long path from Seattle, Washington, to South Africa on the 15th of

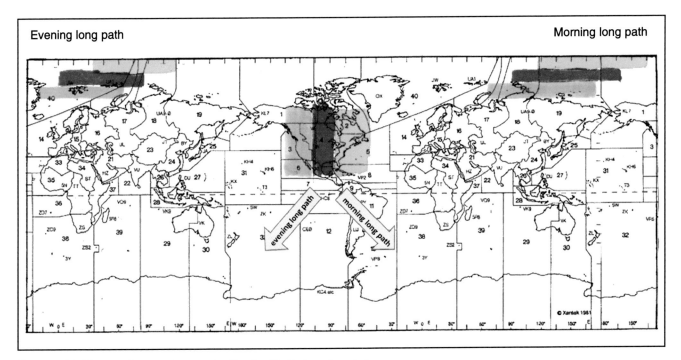

Figure 7.23 10-meter long path opportunities for North America stations.

Mode	VHF Bands (MHz)	Latitude Peak	Time of Day Peak	Seasonal Peak	Optimum Sunspot Period	Approximate Distance (miles)	Band Opening Period	Signal Characteristics
Normal F-layer refraction	50	Temperate	Daytime	Winter	High	E-W paths 1888-5000 N-S paths 1800-6000	Several minutes to an hour or more	Exceptionally strong
Normal F-layer refraction	50	Low and equatorial	Afternoon to late evening	Spring & Fall	High	E-W paths 1888-5000 N-S paths 1800-6000	Several minutes to an hour or more	Exceptionally strong
Sporadic-E	50 & 144	High, Polar	Night	Spring & Fall	High & Moderate	300-1300	Several minutes to an hour or more	Weak to strong with flutter fading
Sporadic-E	50 & 144	Temperate	Before noon & early evening	Late Spring & Summer	All	800-2400 on 50 MHz 1100-1300 on 144 MHz	Several minutes to an hour or more	Exceptionally strong
Sporadic-E	50 & 144	Equatorial	All day	All seasons	All	800-2400 on 50 MHz 1100-1300 on 144 MHz	Several hours to all day	Strong with flutter fading
Normal Aurora	50 & 144	High & Temperate	Late afternoon & early evening	Spring & Fall	High & Moderate (under elevated K indices)	300-1200	Several minutes to an hour or more	Weak to strong with flutter fading, voice distorted, CW recommended
Sun-Aligned Arcs	50	High	Day	Summer	Low (under quiet magnetic conditions)	400-1200	Half an hour around noon local time	Strong
Meteor	50 & 144	All	Night & early morning	June & July, shower periods	All	800-1200	Several seconds to a half minute per burst	Strong bursts, Hi-speed CW & meteor scatter waveforms (per Reference 13) recommended
Trans-equatorial	50 & 144	Low & Temperate	Evening thru midnight	Spring & Fall	High & Moderate	2400-5400	From one to several hours	Weak to moderately strong, flutter fading
Ionospheric Scatter	50	Low & High	Evening through Midnight	Spring & Fall	High & Moderate	600-2400	A few minutes to several hours	Weak, fluttery signals

Table 7.3 Summary of Uncommon Propagation at VHF.

every month at V2.0 smoothed sunspot numbers of 30 (low phase of a solar cycle), 115 (high phase) and 215 (intense phase), Table 7.2 identifies the best band for long path over all the times of the day.

The definition of "best band" is the band that has the highest predicted monthly median signal strength concurrent with the highest predicted monthly median MUF. Note that 20 meters dominates on this long path during a low phase of a solar cycle. During a high phase, 20 and 17 meters share the honor. During an intense phase, 20 and 17 meters give up two months to 15 meters.

Long path propagation predictions were also run from the U.S. Midwest to Reunion Island in the Indian Ocean, and from the U.S. East Coast to Australia, to confirm that 20 meters and 17 meters also are the best bands on other paths.

Remember: Table 7.2 only indicates the best bands for long path over all months and all phases of a solar cycle. There may be long path openings on the other bands too, but they will occur at lower signal strengths and on fewer days of the month. In general, long path openings will occur most often on the lower bands around solar minimum while on the higher bands, they will occur most often around solar maximum.

With Cycle 25 in its ascent, let's look at long path opportunities on 10 meters. Around Cycle 25 solar maximum (expected in the 2023-2025 time frame), there will likely be 10-meter long path openings regardless of the fact that Cycle 25 may be a small cycle. Figure 7.23 (from the 1982 DX Edge operating aid by Xantek with additional annotations) shows possible 10-meter long path openings from the U.S. West Coast, Midwest and East Coast to various areas of the world.

Figure 7.23 is applicable for a smoothed V2.0 sunspot number greater than 100 (smoothed 10.7 cm solar flux greater than 120) and for March through September. If you're on the U.S. East Coast, in the morning point your antenna to the southeast and look for stations at longitudes indicated by the light blue horizontal bar under the "morning long path" annotation. In the evening, point your antenna to the southwest and look for stations at longitudes indicated by the light blue bar under the "evening long path" annotation. The opportunity for both morning and evening long paths from a given location are very dependent on amateur radio operation populations. The evening long path from the U.S. East Coast may not be very productive for this reason.

The evening 10-meter long path from the U.S. West Coast to Europe, the Mideast and the Indian Ocean can be very productive, but the morning long path to Asia can be tough because there are not many hams on the other end [reference 20].

The 10-meter long path from the U.S. Midwest can be very productive for both the evening path (to Europe and the Mideast) and the morning path (to Japan and Southeast Asia). Historical logbook data from stations in Texas confirm this dual opportunity.

Sometimes both long path and short path can be open at the same time. If you don't have a directional antenna to attenuate one of these paths, it may be very difficult to copy either path due to the interference. In spite of this relatively rare occurrence, long path has a mystique that warms your heart when a QSO is made via this mode.

A final comment for VHF enthusiasts is that there have been documented long path contacts on 6 meters. These have been few and far between, but they are possible at solar maximum of a big solar cycle.

7.9 Summary of Uncommon Propagation at VHF

Table 7.3 summarizes the various uncommon propagation modes and their signal characteristics that are most noticeable on VHF frequencies. While propagation at any given time may be associated with a particular mode, there are times when several modes may be involved. All in all, propagation due to phenomena in the ionosphere takes place often enough at the very high frequencies to add an extra dimension of interest to operators using the 50 and 144 MHz bands.

7.10 References

1. Higasa, JE1BMJ, "SSSP: Short-path Summer Solstice Propagation," CQ Ham Radio (Japan), September 2006.

2. Kennedy, KH6/K6MIO, "An Overview of Extreme Es Propagation," Proc. 46th Conference of the Central States VHF Society, pp 63-74, ARRL, 2012.

3. Wu, D.L., C.O. Ao, G. A. Hajj, M. Juarez, "Sporadic E morphology from GPS-CHAMP radio occultation," Journal of Geophysical Research, Vol. 100, A01306, doi:10.1029// 2004JA010701, 2005.

4. https://www.solarham.net/6m/data.htm

5. Davies, K., Ionospheric Radio, page 145, Peter Peregrinus Ltd, 1990

6. Monroe, M., K7ALE, (SK) and D. Monroe, K7ALF (SK), "50 MHz Propagation Effects," CQ, November 1964.

7. Dyer, Pat ,WA5IYX, "A Seven Year Study of 50 MHz Sporadic-E Propagation," CQ, August 1972.

8. Pocock, E., W3EP, and P. J. Dyer, WA5IYX, "The Sporadic-E Season of 1989 in Review," QEX, October 1990, pp. 17-19.

9. https://www.haystack.mit.edu/.

10. Rose, R.B., and R.D. Hunsucker, "Auroral-E Observations: the First Year's Data," NRaD Technical Document 2449, Naval Command, Control and Ocean Surveillance Center, RDT&E Div., San Diego, California, February 1993.

11. McEwen, D.J. and D.P. Harris, "Occurrence patterns of F layer patches over the north magnetic pole," Radio Science, Volume 31, Number 3, pages 619-628, May-June 1996.

12, Cumnock, J.A., "High-latitude aurora during steady northward interplanetary magnetic field and changing IMF B_y," Journal of Geophysical Research, Vol. 110, A02304, doi:10.1029/2004JA010867, 2005.

13. https://physics.princeton.edu/pulsar/K1JT/doc/wsjt/

14. Nielson, D.L., "Oblique Soundings of a Trans-equatorial Path," Stanford Research Institute, 1964.

15. Nielson, D.L., "Long Range VHF Propagation Across the Geomagnetic Equator," Stanford Research Institute, 1969.

16. Kingan, S. G., "A Study of the Behavior and Geographical Distribution of Nighttime V.H.F. Trans equatorial Propagation in the Central Pacific," TEN ERP, Conf. Proceedings, June 22-24, 1993, Naval Postgraduate School, Monterey, California.

17. https://k9la.us/Trans-Equatorial_Propagation.pdf.

18. Hoppe, D., K6UA, P. Dalton,W6NLZ, and F. Capossela, K6SSS, "The Gray Line Method of DXing," CQ, September 1975.

19. https://k9la.us/Aug15_K1FK_to_JA_Via_160m_via_Long_Path_revised.pdf.

20. Hagen, J., N6AV, "10-Meter Long Path," The DX Magazine, January 1988

Additional Notes and Comments

The previous chapters provided a fundamental understanding of solar phenomena and propagation issues. By now you should be comfortable with how the ionosphere affects propagation. You also should have a good understanding of sunspots and the sunspot cycle and of the many methods scientists use to predict sunspot cycles. The background provided also should have given you the ability to use the CQ Master Propagation and Short-Skip Propagation Charts in ways that will allow you to make the best use of your time on the bands. Together with an understanding of ionospheric forecasts in relation to space weather, the material in this handbook should have given you a good grasp of how propagation predictions are developed, how they work, and the knowledge to run your own predictions with two currently popular prediction programs. Finally, the material here is intended to give you an appreciation for the fact the ionosphere is highly dynamic in the short term, giving you many uncommon propagation opportunities.

This final chapter discusses several additional phenomena that will provide you with an even deeper understanding of propagation on a number of topics.

8.1 Polarization

Polarization was discussed briefly in Chapter 1. This section offers more details.

When we send an electromagnetic wave toward the ionosphere from our transmit antenna, the polarization is constant and determined by the construction (geometry) and orientation of the transmit antenna until it enters the ionosphere at D-region altitudes. In the ionosphere, two characteristic waves propagate: the ordinary wave (o-wave; this is the wave that propagates as if the magnetic field is not present) and the extraordinary wave (x-wave; this is the wave affected by the Earth's magnetic field). Figure 8.1 shows this general concept.

How much energy from our transmit antenna (e.g., a Yagi-Uda in Figure 8.1) couples into each characteristic wave depends on the type and placement of the

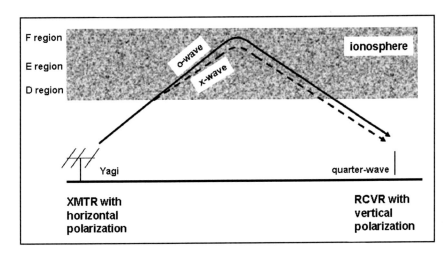

Figure 8.1 The ordinary and extraordinary waves in the ionosphere.

transmit antenna, which, in this case, is a 3-element Yagi-Uda array mounted horizontal to the ground.

We have no control over the polarization of the two characteristic waves as they propagate through the ionosphere. The polarization of each characteristic wave in the ionosphere depends only upon the direction of propagation with respect to the Earth's magnetic field at every point along the path (measured in three dimensions).

When the two characteristic waves exit the D region at the other end of the path, the characteristic wave that couples the most energy into the receive antenna (in Figure 8.1, a quarter-wave vertical) will give rise to the strongest signal, assuming each characteristic wave propagates over the same path with the same amount of ionospheric absorption.

That last assumption is usually true for propagation on our higher HF bands – say, 40 through 6 meters. On frequencies lower than 7 MHz, the path through the ionosphere and the amount of ionospheric absorption each characteristic wave incurs can be significantly different depending on how close the operating frequency is to the electron gyrofrequency, the rate at which electrons spiral about Earth's magnetic field lines. The gyrofrequency will range from about 700 kHz to 1.7 MHz, depending on where you are in the world. For example, on 160 meters (~1.8 MHz), the extraordinary wave is refracted more, and so, it takes shorter hops. Additionally, the absorption for the extraordinary wave is significantly greater. Thus, both characteristic waves may be available on 10 meters, while only one is available on 160 meters (the ordinary wave, because the extraordinary wave is absorbed).

The Earth's magnetic field plays an important role in signal propagation on our low bands (80 and 160 meters). For reasons related to the Earth's magnetic field, there is more impact on our signals in these bands because of signal polarization than we generally acknowledge.

8.2   Ray Tracing

Chapter 6 discussed several HF prediction programs, including two ray tracing programs: (PHaRLAP and Proplab Pro V3). Although ray tracing programs could be used for propagation predictions, they generally are used more as analysis tools than as prediction tools because of the time required to perform the calculations to trace the rays.

Ray tracing is one of many tools used to better understand what happens to signal propagation

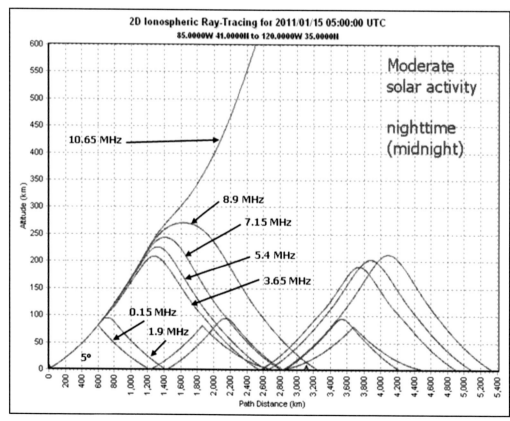

Figure 8.2 (reproduction of Figure 6.13) Proplab Pro V3 ray trace at night.

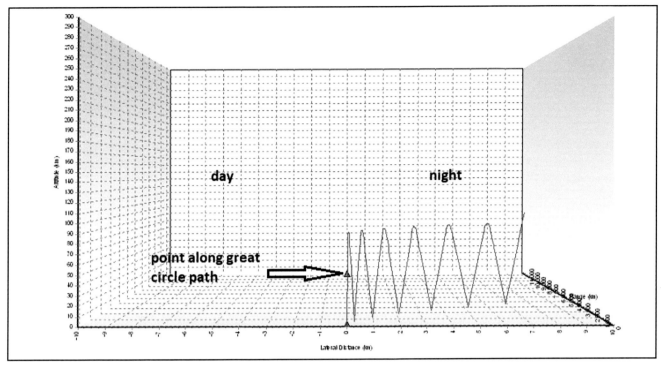

Figure 8.3 Ray trace (ordinary wave) looking south along the long path from 41°N, 85°W (northeast Indiana) to India (VU) on February 15 at 1239 UTC on 1.82 MHz at solar minimum.

through the ionosphere. It is a valuable visual aid that translates much data into a concise picture. Figure 6.13 in Chapter 6 is an excellent example of this concept. Figure 6.13 is reproduced here as Figure 8.2.

As noted early in Chapter 1, the amount of refraction incurred by an electromagnetic wave propagating through a medium of given electron density is inversely proportional to the square of the signal frequency. The amount of bending (refracting) increases as we move down in frequency, with the result that hops are shorter, as seen in Figure 8.2.

It would be possible to perform a great number of predictions using VOACAP or W6ELProp (or your favorite program) to generate tabular data that confirm this observation. But there can be no question that simply viewing ray traces really drives home the point.

In Sections 8.3, 8.4 and 8.5 of this chapter, ray tracing will be used to provide further analyses of three important issues in propagation.

8.3 An Alternate Explanation for Gray Line Propagation

The Gray Line Propagation section in Chapter 7 (Section 7.7) reiterated the accepted perception that propagation along the gray line is extremely efficient

for reasons thought to be related singularly to the absence of the D layer (which absorbs signals) along the gray line path. However, when one examines the physics pertaining to gray line propagation with the aid of ray tracing, three issues arise with this explanation.

First, there are D-layer electron density data from incoherent scatter radar [reference 1] that indicate D-layer ionization still exists at and around sunrise and sunset. This might explain why gray line propagation isn't something that occurs every day. The days such propagation *does* occur, then, might indicate periods of reduced D-layer ionization along the terminator, the region separating day from night.

Second, Figure 8.3 is a ray trace from Proplab Pro V3 along the great-circle long-path from northeast Indiana to India (VU) when the great-circle path is aligned with the terminator, which is the definition of gray line propagation. This scenario is similar to Figure 7.21 in Chapter 7.

The important takeaway from this ray trace is that here, the RF at 160 meters refracts to the right. Because we're looking south from northeast Indiana along the long path at sunrise, the night ionosphere is on the right and the day ionosphere is on the left. An electromagnetic wave will refract away from the

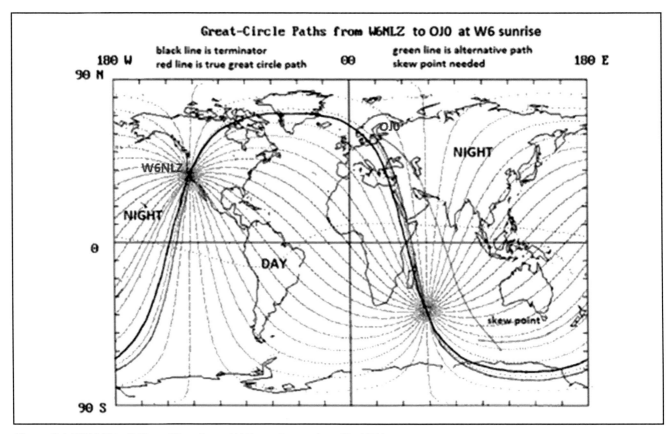

Great-Circle Paths from W6NLZ to OJ0 at W6 sunrise

Figure 8.4 W6NLZ to OJ0 on 80 meters at W6 sunrise on Jan. 28, 1974.

higher electron density in the day ionosphere into the night ionosphere. Thus, 160-meter RF has a difficult time following a gray line path. Put another way, it will be bent toward the nighttime portion of the sky.

Not shown on the ray trace is the fact that ionospheric *absorption* of the ordinary wave has already reached 150 dB, having only propagated roughly 4,000 km toward India on the long path; this is a prohibitive amount of absorption and is the result of residual D-region electrons being present in the ionosphere. The extraordinary wave also refracts to the right, and so, it has significantly more ionospheric absorption than the ordinary wave because 1.82 MHz is near the electron gyrofrequency. Performing a ray trace on 80 meters (3.52 MHz) yields a similar result, with the wave refracting to the right and a prohibitive amount of absorption, although less than on 160 meters.

Third, gray line propagation appears to be mostly reported on the long path; it rarely is reported on the short path. That said, however, Steve Nichols, G0KYA, did perform a study [reference 2] of short-path gray line propagation between his location in the United Kingdom (G) and the Falkland Islands (VP8)

around his sunrise in November 2002. He did observe small enhancements in signal level at times on 40 meters and 80 meters. No other studies of this type, however, are known.

Based on these three issues, some observers have proposed an alternative explanation for gray line propagation: the electromagnetic wave is taking a shortcut across the dark ionosphere (where absorption is minimal, and where the physics of RF propagation drives it, as seen in Figure 8.3). This requires a refraction of the wave from one great circle path to another great circle path by virtue of the existence of a skew point (i.e., a sufficiently high gradient in the horizontal electron density). Figure 8.4 shows this alternative explanation for a gray line path between W6 and OJ0 (Market Reef) at W6 sunrise (1457 UTC) on Jan. 28, 1974 [from reference 18 in Chapter 7].

The green lines are the alternative explanation; each wave from each end of the path is a great circle route, and they propagate into the dark ionosphere, where absorption is minimal. The skew point, where the two green great circle paths intersect, is annotated southwest of Australia, and it would likely be the result of ionization at the equatorward edge of the southern auroral oval. For a more detailed analysis of this alternate explanation, see Edgar Callaway, N4II [reference 3].

This alternate explanation is not new. Measurements of azimuth angles of arrival of signals around 10 MHz in 1931 [reference 4] indicated the RF "preferred" to take a shortcut across the dark ionosphere. Regardless of which explanation is correct (true gray line propagation or signal propagation via a shortcut across the dark ionosphere), it would be difficult to determine a preference for either without more D-layer data and/or time of flight measurements and angle of arrival measurements. Unfortunately, studies involving the D layer are few and far between today.

A final comment: you may see reference to different "twilights" in relation to gray line propagation.

a) Civil twilight – the sun is between 0 and 6 degrees below the horizon

b) Nautical twilight – the sun is between 6 and 12 degrees below the horizon

c) Astronomical twilight – the sun is between 12 and 18 degrees below the horizon

Remember: these twilights are defined in terms of visible light, which has nothing to do with ionospheric ionization because photons at visible light wavelengths do not have enough energy to ionize atmospheric constituents.

8.4   Notes on 160-meter (Topband) Propagation

Much has been said about 160-meter propagation (topband) in the previous chapters. Two articles in *CQ* magazine are highly recommended for reading. The first is by Cary Oler and Theodore Cohen, N4XX [reference 5] and the second is a follow-up article by Carl Luetzelschwab, K9LA [reference 6]. These two articles provide an in-depth understanding of what makes 160 meters tick.

Both articles examine and provide examples of ducting on 160 meters in the electron density valley that occurs above the E-region peak in the nighttime ionosphere (Figure 5 in Oler and Cohen, and Figure 2 in Luetzelschwab), including discussions of how a signal enters and leaves this duct.

At mid- to high latitudes, magneto-ionic theory (the theory of an electromagnetic wave propagating in a

Frequency	Characteristic wave	Absorption in dB
137 kHz	Ordinary	16
137 kHz	Extraordinary	34
475 kHz	Ordinary	29
475 kHz	Extraordinary	48
1.82 MHz	Ordinary	28
1.82 MHz	Extraordinary	142

Table 8.1 Absorption data for a 2900-km path on 2200, 630 and 160 meters.

plasma in the presence a magnetic field) indicates that the polarization of the ordinary wave on 160 meters is a thin ellipse with its major axis parallel to the Earth's magnetic field. At mid- to high latitudes, the magnetic field is approaching vertical; thus, a vertical antenna on 160 meters at these latitudes is considered optimal. The latter notwithstanding, remember: the ionosphere is dynamic, and sometimes, horizontal polarization at these latitudes might be best for certain applications. Consider: at times, high-angle rays (such as those exiting a duct) may be better received on antennas employing horizontal polarization.

8.5   Propagation on 2200 meters (137 kHz) and 630 meters (475 kHz)

2200 meters

Referring to Figure 8.2 above, we see an electromagnetic wave on 150 kHz does not propagate high into the ionosphere. The trajectory of an electromagnetic wave on 137 kHz (2200 meters) would behave similarly. The reason for this is, there are still sufficient D-region electrons low in the ionosphere (even at night) to refract these very low frequencies. The result of this is that at 137 kHz, RF propagates via very short hops, and the hops are refracted between the D region and earth.

An interesting phenomenon is observed regarding ionospheric absorption on 2200 meters. Because RF radiation doesn't propagate high into the ionosphere, radiation does not incur as much absorption as it does on 630 and 160 meters. Table 8.1 shows absorption data for a 2,900-km east-west path in North America at night during solar minimum in January.

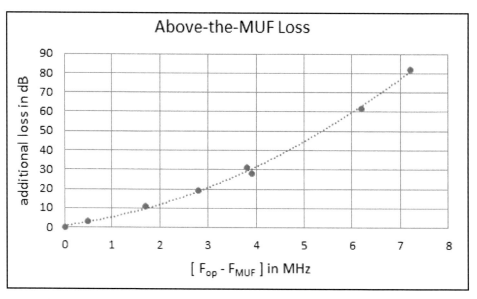

Figure 8.5 Additional loss resulting from excursions of the operating frequency (F_{op}) above the classical MUF (F_{MUF}).

For all three bands, 2200 meters (137 kHz) has the least absorption on this path. And, on all frequencies for this path, the extraordinary wave has more absorption. The reduced absorption of the ordinary wave at low frequencies also explains why Loran-C was a worldwide navigation system at 100 kHz.

The greatest problems with propagation on 2200 meters are the 1-watt EIRP (effective isotropic radiated power) limit, the very low efficiency of transmit antennas, which requires significant transmit power to reach the EIRP limit, and man-made noise. Still, amateur operator ingenuity always has prevailed, and resulted in some interesting long-distance QSOs over challenging paths.

630 meters

Table 8.1 shows absorption on 630 meters (475 kHz) and on 160 meters (1.82 MHz) for this 2,900-km path is similar. This suggests propagation on 630 meters should be similar to propagation on 160 meters. However, the issues cited above for 2200 meters carry forward to 630 meters, but to a lesser degree. The EIRP limit on 630 meters is 5 watts (except in parts of Alaska, where it is 1 watt), so on 630 meters, the limit it is 7 dB higher than on 2200 meters. Also on the plus side for 630 meters are higher transmit antenna efficiencies that can be obtained and the lower man-made noises encountered (by tens of dB).

Again, amateur operator ingenuity will prevail. Some very impressive worldwide QSOs have been made on 630 meters with digital modes. Using the data from these contacts, we will increasingly learn more over time about propagation on 630 meters.

8.6 Above-the-MUF Propagation

As mentioned in Chapter 6, observations have shown an operating frequency slightly above the actual MUF (the so-called classical MUF) still can provide a useful signal. This is called an above-the-MUF mode, and it is thought some form of scatter allows this condition to occur. Scatter implies loss, so there is additional loss incurred that many times can be tolerated (for example, on a path on one of our higher frequency bands that has minimal ionospheric absorption). VOACAP is the only propagation prediction program that has the above-the-MUF mode capability embedded in its ionosphere model.

By performing propagation predictions with VOACAP at varying smoothed sunspot numbers, we can extract the additional above-the-MUF loss versus how high the operating frequency is above the predicted median MUF. Figure 8.5 shows these data on a one-hop 2,900-km path on 21.1, 24.9 and 28.3 MHz.

Let's work through an example using Figure 8.5 to show the impact of the above-the-MUF mode.

If we do a prediction from northeast Indiana to California at a smoothed V1.0 sunspot number of 100 in October at 1700 UTC, the predicted median MUF is 28.7 MHz and the predicted signal strength on 28.3 MHz is -72 dBm using small Yagi-Uda antennas on each end of the path. For this scenario, the operating frequency is *slightly* below the predicted MUF, and gives very close to an S9 signal. Again, remember: the predicted medium MUF is the *monthly median*; half of the days of the month the actual MUF will be below this frequency and half of the days of the month, the actual MUF it will be above this frequency.

Now, let's assume the classical MUF (what the actual MUF is right now) is 24.4 MHz (within the distribution about the predicted median MUF). Figure 8.5 indicates for the operating frequency to be 3.9 MHz above a possible value for an excursion below the predicted median MUF (28.3 MHz – 24.4 MHz), the additional loss would be around 30 dB (5 S-units). Five S-units below S9 would be S4 – still a workable signal.

If there is room for additional loss (generally on the higher bands and 6 meters, where ionospheric absorption is minimal), the operating frequency can be several MHz above the classical MUF. A caveat is in order: the above-the-MUF mode is based on observational data, and there may be more variability than Figure 8.5 indicates.

For more reading on above-the-MUF, read McNamara [reference 7].

8.7   The Digital Mode Advantage

Amateur activity during the recent solar minimum between Solar Cycles 24 and 25 has been the most active in history on our higher bands (15 meters, 12 meters, 10 meters and even 6 meters) for reasons related the advantage that the digital modes offer.

From the WSJT-X documentation (WSJT stands for **W**eak **S**ignal Communication by K1**JT**) available

at reference 13 in Chapter 7, Table 8.2 shows the detection capabilities of three digital modes in terms of the S/N (signal-to-noise) ratio in a 2500-Hz bandwidth, together with the advantage of the indicated digital mode over the CW mode.

Typically, a CW operator can copy a signal with a 0 dB S/N ratio in a 250-Hz bandwidth. This translates to a -10 dB S/N limit in a 2500-Hz bandwidth. This translation was necessary to make the CW bandwidth equivalent to the same bandwidth as the digital modes.

Presenting the data in terms of an assumed noise level in a 2500-Hz bandwidth yields Figure 8.6.

The below-the-noise advantages over CW using the three digital modes cited above are shown in Figure 8.6. Note from Table 8.2 that the "sensitivity" is tied to the amount of time it takes to complete a QSO. JT65, the slowest digital mode of the three listed, offers the largest advantage over CW. FT4, the fastest digital mode of the three listed, still offers a decent advantage over CW.

Section 8.6 discussed the above-the-MUF mode. The digital modes, with their ability to "hear" signals

Mode	Time to make a contest QSO	S/N limit in 2500 Hz	Advantage over ability to copy CW
JT65	~4 minutes	-25dB	15 dB
FT8	~1 minute	-21 dB	11 dB
FT4	~20 seconds	-16 dB	6 dB
CW	~15 seconds	-10 dB	------

Table 8.2 S/N limits for three digital modes and CW in a 2500 Hz bandwidth.

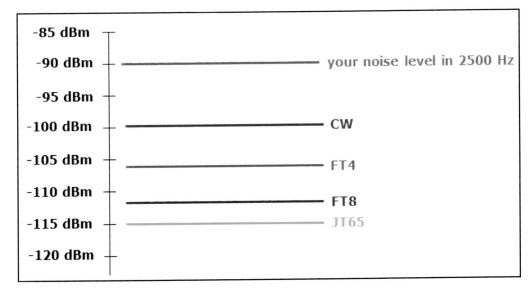

Figure 8.6 Below-the-noise advantage of three digital modes compared to CW

Figure 8.7 Prediction of visible aurora on Sept. 8, 2017 at 0110 UTC.

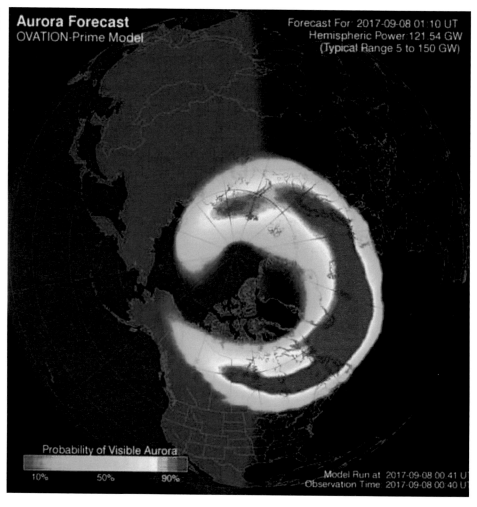

Aurora Forecast
OVATION-Prime Model

Forecast For: 2017-09-08 01:10 UT
Hemispheric Power: 121.54 GW
(Typical Range 5 to 150 GW)

Probability of Visible Aurora

10%   50%   90%

Model Run at 2017-09-08 00:41 UT
Observation Time: 2017-09-08 00:40 UT

further embedded in noise, will provide even more advantage under conditions when the classical MUF is below the operating frequency. Use the digital modes at solar minimum, even on the higher bands. You may be pleasantly surprised.

8.8   A Look Inside the Auroral Oval

Chapter 5 briefly mentioned the Ovation-Prime model on the Space Weather Prediction Center website, a model that predicts where visible aurora is likely to occur. Figure 8.7 shows the output using this model for Sept. 8, 2017 at 0110 UTC.

Per the legend, visible aurora is predicted to occur with very high certainty in the nighttime portion of the oval. Does this mean the orange/red portion of the auroral oval is full of detrimental ionization?

To answer this question, back up in time to when the prediction of visible aurora was performed using data from the Polar Operational Environmental Satellites (POES). These predictions were called

PMAPs (the initial "P" stood for power), and they were the forerunner to the Ovation-Prime maps.

An example of a PMAP is Figure 8.8a; it is for the northern auroral oval on Dec. 23, 2000 at 0238 UTC. The orange/red coloring indicates a high probability of visible aurora in the oval. Again, the question is: "does this mean the orange/red portion of the auroral oval is full of detrimental ionization?"

Figure 8.8b is from the Defense Meteorological Satellite Program (DMSP) for Dec. 23, 2000, at 0156 UTC (about 20 minutes later than the PMAP). The DMSP image shows where visible aurora occurred – this is indicated by the many intense but long thin arcs. There is some diffuse aurora equatorward of the intense arcs, mostly at the southern tip of Hudson Bay. This was a nice cloudless night, as evidenced by the numerous city lights showing up.

Thus, the oval was not full of detrimental ionization. Remember, the PMAP (and the Ovation-Prime image) is a prediction of where visible aurora **could**

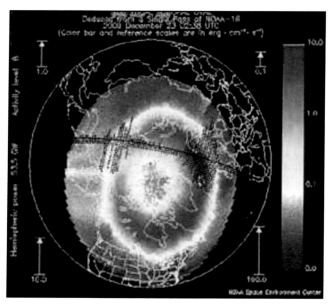

Figure 8.8a PMAP 12/23/2000 0238 UTC

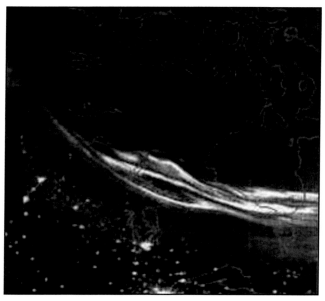

Figure 8.8b DMSP 12/23/2000 0256 UTC

occur. So, don't shy away from elevated K indices; generally they suggest not-too-good propagation, but interesting things can still happen.

More PMAPs and DMSP images, and significantly more information about the auroral oval, are available from Carl Luetzelschwab, K9LA [reference 8].

8.9   Antipodal Focusing

The Earth is a sphere, so your location on the surface has a point located exactly on the opposite side of the globe. A line drawn through your location to this location on the opposite side of the Earth goes straight through the center of the Earth, and the other point is your antipode.

The antipode has two interesting physical features. First, all great circle routes from your location go through your antipode. So you can point your directional antenna to any heading and that heading will go through your antipode. Figure 8.9 is from an old DOS program by Bob Brown, NM7M (SK). It is an example of great circle routes from a location in Colorado, with the antipode at Amsterdam Island in the Indian Ocean. An important note: with the surface of our planet being about 71% water, many antipodes from populated areas are in the oceans, where there aren't any hams to observe antipodal propagation!

Second, your antipode is 20,000 km — half the circumference of the Earth — away from you as the crow flies on the great circle route. Thus, each great circle route isn't really a short path (less than 20,000 km) or a long path (greater than 20,000 km).

The first of these two features leads to an interesting hypothesis about propagation to the antipode. Because all paths arrive at the antipode, they could all arrive in-phase and provide a significant signal enhancement; this is called antipodal focusing.

However, this hypothesis assumes a homogeneous worldwide ionosphere over a perfect sphere that is perfectly conducting. In the real world, the Earth isn't a perfect sphere; it's an oblate spheroid, a sphere that is squashed at the poles and swollen at the equator. The ionosphere isn't homogeneous throughout the world; there's day and night, for example. And the ionosphere certainly isn't perfectly conducting.

What the real world does is blunt the "significant signal enhancement" hypothesis to some degree. There have been experiments with antipodal propagation that show some focusing. They also show this focusing isn't limited to just the antipode. These results are reviewed by Carl Luetzelschwab, K9LA [reference 9].

8.10   Non-Reciprocal Communications

The laws of reciprocity require that propagation of a radio signal from point A to point B should be via the same path that signals propagate from point B to point A. At times, however, this does not appear to be the case, and radio amateurs often refer to this condition as "one-way skip." In fact, non-reciprocal

Figure 8.9 Great circle routes (dotted lines) from Colorado in 10° increments. The dotted line about the geographic equator is the magnetic equator.

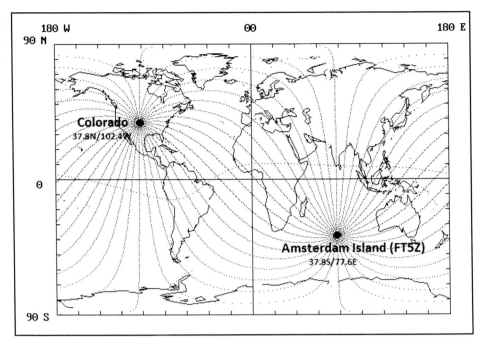

communications almost always can be shown to result from differences in the signal-to-noise ratios of the signals received at each end of an HF circuit. Put another way, even if two operators use identical stations, the signal-to-noise ratios of the received signals can differ, and they can do so by significant amounts!

To see this, consider the fact that atmospheric noise levels throughout the world vary as a function of frequency, geographic location, time of day, and season of the year. Add to this the interference caused by other stations, together with manmade noise generated by appliances, power lines, and so forth, and it's not hard to imagine that the noise levels measured at any two stations could differ by 20 dB or more. Such situations often are encountered on the bands below 20 MHz, where atmospheric noise dominates.

For example, summertime noise levels in the Northern Hemisphere as a result of thunderstorm activity significantly degrade the signal-to-noise ratios of all signals received. However, everything else being equal, operators in the Southern Hemisphere, who are experiencing winter conditions, should receive signals with considerably higher signal-to-noise ratios than will their counterparts in the Northern Hemisphere.

Under these conditions, and if you are in the Northern Hemisphere, operators in the Southern Hemisphere should be able to hear and understand you better than you are able to hear them. This may

leave you both frustrated as they continue to answer your repeated CQs while, at the same time, you are unable to hear their responses to you above the noise. Of course, for this example, the situation is reversed when it is winter in the Northern Hemisphere and summer in the Southern Hemisphere. Regardless of the situation, what appears to be "one-way skip" could simply be the result of nothing more than a high noise level at one end of a path.

Other possible explanations for one-way skip could be different transmitter power levels, different receiver sensitivities, separate transmit and receive antennas (transmitting on a vertical so you're heard in every direction, but listening on a directional receive antenna not pointed at the station answering you) and QRM (for example, when North American operators can't work European operators just as a band is opening because of all the strong signals the Europeans are hearing from other Europeans). Another explanation that needs further study is polarization mismatch on both ends of a path, as mentioned in Section 8.1.

Finally, one example of apparent non-reciprocal communications with which topband operators may be familiar occurs just before sunrise in January on the U.S. East Coast when signals from Japanese (JA) stations literally can be heard being "dumped" out of the E-region valley (duct) onto a small region on the Earth. This is the so-called "spotlight" propagation.

The signal levels under these conditions will, at times, be unbelievably high. And yet, with the exception of a few East Coast operators whose stations *just* happen to be located in the spotlight, none will be able to inject enough energy into the duct to produce a readable signal at the western end of the link, in Japan.

8.11 Fading

Some degree of fading, or fluctuation in a signal's level, occurs on all signals refracted by the ionosphere. Fading may be rapid or slow, deep or shallow. Slow fading causes a signal to change in level over periods of a few minutes or more; rapid fading causes fluctuations over a period of a few seconds, or less. In practice, both slow and rapid fading can occur at the same time.

Slow fading is caused by variations in absorption in the D layer and, to a lesser extent, in the E layer. It also is caused by slow, random movement or motion within the ionosphere itself, particularly in the vertical plane.

Rapid fading is caused by irregularities and instabilities that exist in the ionosphere, particularly in the equatorial region and in the auroral zones, and during periods of radio storminess. As we have seen, these irregularities cause a signal to separate along a number of similar but closely related paths and to arrive at the receiver as a group of independent signals, with random phase relationships. These differences in phase, caused by multi-path propagation, produce a corresponding variation in signal strength. At one extreme, when the arriving signal components are in phase, the signal level will be at a maximum. On the other hand, when they are completely out of phase, the signal will disappear. At times, a fading cycle caused by multi-path propagation can be so rapid (e.g., auroral flutter) it will render a signal unintelligible.

8.12 Spread-F

The existence of spread-F has been known for as long as there have been ionospheric measurements. Spread-F gets its name from the fact that vertical sounder measurements no longer show a nice, clear trace for the F2 region (as was seen in Photo 1.A in Chapter 1), but rather, exhibit a fuzzy, diffuse trace that results from spreading of the returned time delayed signals. Figure 8.10 is an example of spread-F.

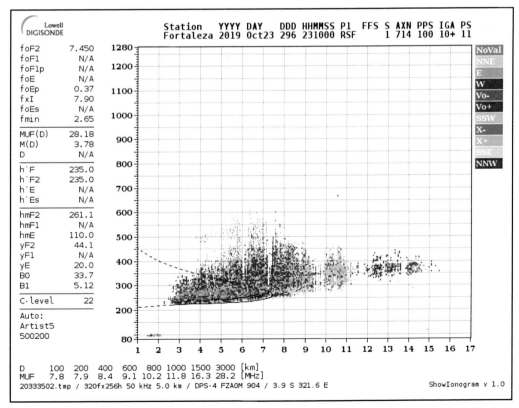

Figure 8.10 Low-latitude ionogram from Fortaleza, Brazil (3.9°S/38.4°W) on Oct. 23, 2019, at 2310 UTC showing spread-F.

The question that immediately comes to mind is: "What does spread-F do to an HF signal?" To answer this question, consider the following. During periods when spread-F occurs, the ionosphere's F region no longer is a uniform, refracting layer; instead, it is characterized better as a turbulent medium comprised of "blobs" (or patches), each having different electron densities.

As the signal ray enters the patchy ionosphere, it is split into many smaller, and weaker, signal rays. Each ray follows a more or less independent route, moving from one patch to another. Because each ray is in the ionosphere a different amount of time, the signal that finally emerges has been stretched in time. The effect on the "spread" HF signal, then, is lower overall signal strength, signal stretching (distortion), and signal flutter.

A second question is: "How often is this phenomenon a problem?" Studies conducted in 1992 and 1993 indicate spread-F occurs more than is generally believed. When it occurs, spread-F produces a hollow, auroral warble with which many of us are familiar.

Historically, spread-F was thought to occur in the band that is bounded by plus or minus 20 degrees centered around the geomagnetic equator, and above 40 degrees geomagnetic latitude. It rarely occurs between 20 and 40 degrees geomagnetic latitudes. The entire United States is above 40 degrees geomagnetic latitude, and so, it would be expected that spread-F should be relatively common.

During tests conducted by the U.S. Navy in October 1992, between Monterey and San Diego, California, the first observations of mid-latitude spread-F were observed on 5.6 MHz. Spread-F observed over this path was not as intense as that found when the measurement system was moved to higher latitudes (specifically, to Alaska).

Tests at high latitudes showed the F-layer in the auroral and polar regions is comprised of diffuse, turbulent media, with spreading being more the norm than the exception. Modern HF prediction models have no capability to simulate the irregular, patchy F-layer. This is one reason why these models fail to accurately predict propagation conditions over high-latitude paths.

At geographical mid-latitudes, spread-F is a night-time phenomenon. At high latitudes, in the winter, it

occurs almost 100% of the time while in the summer, it occurs almost 100% of the time at night and 50-60% of the time during the day.

Spread-F is more a detriment to propagation than a propagation mode. Read more about spread-F with Chunhua Jiang, et al [reference 10].

8.13 Summary

If you'd like more information about propagation than what is in this book, read the many references given at the end of all the chapters.

You also can subscribe to the many organizations that have peer-reviewed technical papers such as the American Geophysical Union (with the *Journal of Geophysical Research: Space Physics*, for example), the European Geosciences Union (with *Annales Geophysicae*, for example), ScienceDirect (with the *Journal of Atmospheric and Solar-Terrestrial Physics*, and *Advances in Space Research*, for example) and others.

Lastly, you can search the internet for specific topics related to propagation issues that weren't discussed in this book. Some suggestions are:

a) Single-day dayside F2 region enhancements
b) Weddell Sea Anomaly
c) Mid-latitude F2 region enhancement at night at solar minimum
d) F region trough
e) South Atlantic Anomaly
f) F2 region saturation

These suggested topics all are concerned with the F2 region. This supports the fact that the F2 region is *not* under direct solar control (as is the E region), with factors other than sunspot number and solar zenith angle influencing the F2 region.

8.14 References

1. Trost, Thomas F., "Electron Concentrations in the E and Upper D Region at Arecibo," *Journal of Geophysical Research*, Vol. 84, No. A6, June 1, 1979.

2. Nichols, Steve, G0KYA, "The twilight zone revisited – recent grey-line research," *RadCom*, May 2006 (the monthly publication of the Radio Society of Great Britain).

3. Callaway, Ed, N4II, "Gray Line Propagation, or Florida to Cocos (Keeling) on 80m," *QEX*, November/December 2016.

4. Namba, Shogo, Eiji Iso, and Shigetoshi Ueno, "Polarization of High-Frequency Waves and Their Direction Finding," *Proceedings of the Institute of Radio Engineers*, Volume 19, Number 11, November 1931.

5. Oler, Cary and Dr. Theodore J. Cohen, N4XX, "The 160-Meter Band: An Enigma Shrouded in Mystery," *CQ* Magazine, March and April 1998.

6. Luetzelschwab, Carl, K9LA, "Ducting and Spotlight Propagation on 160 Meters," *CQ* Magazine, December 2006.

7. McNamara, Leo F., Terence W. Bullett, Evgenii Mishin and Yuri M. Yampolski, "Nighttime above-the-MUF HF propagation on a midlatitude circuit," *Radio Science*, Volume 43, Issue 2, April 2008. This paper is free access and available at https://agupubs.onlinelibrary.wiley.com/doi/full/10.1029/2007RS003742

8. https://k9la.us/A_Look_Inside_the_Auroral_Zone.PDF

9. https://k9la.us/A_Review_of_Antipodal_Propagation_-_K9LA_RSGB_Convention_2017.pdf

10. Jiang, Chunhua, Guobin Yang, Jing Liu, Tatsuhiro Yokoyama, Tharadol Komolmis, Huan Song, Ting Lan, Chen Zhou, Yuannong Zhang and Zhengyu Zhao, "Ionosonde observations of daytime spread F at low latitudes," *JGR Space Physics*, Nov. 17, 2016. This paper is free access and is available at https://agupubs.onlinelibrary.wiley.com/doi/full/10.1002/2016JA023123

Index